TRANSPORTATION ISSUES, POLICIES AND R&D

HIGHWAY SAFETY

BACKGROUND, PROGRAMS AND VEHICLE SAFETY

TRANSPORTATION ISSUES, POLICIES AND R&D

Additional books and e-books in this series can be found
on Nova's website under the Series tab.

TRANSPORTATION ISSUES, POLICIES AND R&D

HIGHWAY SAFETY

BACKGROUND, PROGRAMS AND VEHICLE SAFETY

BERTHA G. BALDWIN
EDITOR

Copyright © 2020 by Nova Science Publishers, Inc.

All rights reserved. No part of this book may be reproduced, stored in a retrieval system or transmitted in any form or by any means: electronic, electrostatic, magnetic, tape, mechanical photocopying, recording or otherwise without the written permission of the Publisher.

We have partnered with Copyright Clearance Center to make it easy for you to obtain permissions to reuse content from this publication. Simply navigate to this publication's page on Nova's website and locate the "Get Permission" button below the title description. This button is linked directly to the title's permission page on copyright.com. Alternatively, you can visit copyright.com and search by title, ISBN, or ISSN.

For further questions about using the service on copyright.com, please contact:
Copyright Clearance Center
Phone: +1-(978) 750-8400　　Fax: +1-(978) 750-4470　　E-mail: info@copyright.com.

NOTICE TO THE READER

The Publisher has taken reasonable care in the preparation of this book, but makes no expressed or implied warranty of any kind and assumes no responsibility for any errors or omissions. No liability is assumed for incidental or consequential damages in connection with or arising out of information contained in this book. The Publisher shall not be liable for any special, consequential, or exemplary damages resulting, in whole or in part, from the readers' use of, or reliance upon, this material. Any parts of this book based on government reports are so indicated and copyright is claimed for those parts to the extent applicable to compilations of such works.

Independent verification should be sought for any data, advice or recommendations contained in this book. In addition, no responsibility is assumed by the Publisher for any injury and/or damage to persons or property arising from any methods, products, instructions, ideas or otherwise contained in this publication.

This publication is designed to provide accurate and authoritative information with regard to the subject matter covered herein. It is sold with the clear understanding that the Publisher is not engaged in rendering legal or any other professional services. If legal or any other expert assistance is required, the services of a competent person should be sought. FROM A DECLARATION OF PARTICIPANTS JOINTLY ADOPTED BY A COMMITTEE OF THE AMERICAN BAR ASSOCIATION AND A COMMITTEE OF PUBLISHERS.

Additional color graphics may be available in the e-book version of this book.

Library of Congress Cataloging-in-Publication Data

ISBN: 978-1-53617-176-1

Published by Nova Science Publishers, Inc. † New York

CONTENTS

Preface vii

Chapter 1 Every Life Counts: Improving the Safety
of Our Nation's Roadways 1
Subcommittee on Highways and Transit

Chapter 2 Traffic Safety: Improved Reporting Could Clarify States'
Achievement of Fatality and Injury Targets 179
United States Government Accountability Office

Chapter 3 Federal Traffic Safety Programs: In Brief (Updated) 209
David Randall Peterman

Chapter 4 Federal Highway Traffic Safety Policies:
Impacts and Opportunities 221
David Randall Peterman

Chapter 5 Issues with Federal Motor Vehicle Safety Standards 259
Bill Canis

Chapter 6 Commercial Truck Safety: Overview 285
David Randall Peterman

Chapter 7 Smart Cars and Trucks: Spectrum Use for Vehicle Safety 305
Bill Canis and Jill C. Gallagher

Index 311

PREFACE

According to the National Highway Traffic Safety Administration (NHTSA), 37,133 people lost their lives in accidents on U.S. roadways in 2017 1. That means an average of 101 people died each day in motor vehicle crashes, equating to roughly one fatality every 15 minutes. The FAST Act has funded programs to ensure safety on our Nation's roads. These include grants to improve physical roadway infrastructure; grant programs to reduce crashes, injuries, and fatalities involving large trucks and buses; grant programs to incentivize States to adopt laws and regulations to improve highway safety; and grants to assist State enforcement of vehicle and driver safety measures. This book discusses traffic safety issues.

Chapter 1 - This is an edited, reformatted and augmented version of Hearing before the Subcommittee on Highways and Transit of the Committee on Transportation and Infrastructure, House of Representatives, One Hundred Sixteenth Congress, First Session, dated April 9, 2019.

Chapter 2 - Over 37,000 people were killed in traffic crashes on the nation's highways in 2017. Within the U.S. Department of Transportation (DOT), two agencies— NHTSA for behavioral factors and FHWA for highway infrastructure—provide about $3 billion annually to states for programs to improve traffic safety. To ensure that states are held accountable for these funds, NHTSA and FHWA developed performance management frameworks that require states to use performance measures and targets in tracking traffic fatalities and serious injuries. GAO was asked to review NHTSA's and FHWA's traffic safety performance management frameworks. This report examines the extent to which: (1) states have met fatality and serious injury targets, and NHTSA's and FHWA's approaches to assessing states' achievements, and (2) states have used performance measures and targets to make traffic safety funding decisions. GAO analyzed state-reported targets and NHTSA data from 2014 through 2017—the most recent data available— for all 50 states, the District of Columbia, and Puerto Rico; surveyed these states on the use of performance measures and targets; reviewed requirements in NHTSA's and FHWA's frameworks; and interviewed officials from NHTSA, FHWA, and 10 states, selected to obtain a mix of population sizes, geographic locations, and other factors.

Chapter 3 - Driving is one of the riskiest activities the average American engages in. Deaths and serious injuries resulting from motor vehicle crashes are one of the leading causes of preventable deaths. In 2017, 37,133 people were killed in police-reported motor vehicle crashes in the United States, and in 2016 an estimated 3.14 million people were injured. Many of the people who die in traffic crashes are relatively young and otherwise healthy (motor vehicle crashes are the leading cause of death for people between the ages of 17 and 23). As a result, while traffic crashes are now the 13th leading cause of death overall, they rank seventh among causes of years of life lost (i.e., the difference between the age at death and life expectancy). In addition to the emotional toll exacted by these deaths and injuries, traffic crashes impose a significant economic toll. The Department of Transportation (DOT) estimated that the annual cost of motor vehicle crashes in 2010 was $242 billion in direct costs and $836 billion when the impact on quality of life of those killed and injured was included. About one-third of the direct cost came from the lost productivity of those killed and injured; about one-third from property damage; 10% from present and future medical costs; 12% from time lost due to congestion caused by crashes; and the remainder from the costs of insurance administration, legal services, workplace costs, and emergency services.

Chapter 4 - In 2017, 37,133 Americans were killed in crashes involving motor vehicles. Motor vehicle crashes are a leading cause of death for Americans overall, and the number one cause of death for teenagers. Millions of people are injured in crashes annually, and motor vehicle crashes are estimated to have cost some $242 billion in 2010 in lost productivity, medical costs, legal costs, property damage, and time lost in congestion caused by crashes. As measured by the number of deaths per mile people are driving, the rate at which people are killed in traffic crashes declined significantly from 1929, when records began to be kept, until 2014, but has risen by almost 10% between 2014 and 2016. Congress has played a role in improving highway safety. Making road travel safer was one of the responsibilities Congress gave to the federal Department of Transportation (DOT) when it created the department in 1966. Congress has directed DOT to improve the safety of automobile design and of road design, as well as to support programs to improve driver behavior. An oft-cited statistic in traffic safety is that as many as 90% of road deaths are due at least in part to driver error or misbehavior (such as driving too fast for conditions or driving while drunk or distracted). Driver behavior is a state, not federal, matter; in an effort to address it, Congress has enacted programs that encourage states to pass laws to promote safer driving. The role of driver behavior versus road design and traffic management is a subject of debate. Some analysts note that road designs and traffic management arrangements often allow, or even encourage, driver error and misbehavior, and so play a larger role in crashes than is often recognized. One of the core highway capital improvement programs authorized by Congress is intended to fund safety improvements to highway infrastructure. A federal study estimated that half of the improvement in highway fatality rates between 1960 and 2012 was attributable to improvements in vehicle safety technologies, with social and demographic changes, driver behavior interventions, and improvements in road design playing smaller roles. Most of the vehicle safety technologies analyzed in the study increased the likelihood that vehicle occupants would survive a crash. More recently, technological improvement has focused on preventing crashes. While some crash-prevention technologies, such as automatic braking and lane departure warnings, are available now, others, such as vehicle-to-vehicle communication and vehicles that can operate without human intervention, are not yet on the market. Even when these become commercially available, given that most vehicles remain in use for well over a decade, it may be many years before the majority of cars on the road incorporate these technologies. While U.S. crash and injury rates are no longer declining, and even rising, several other nations have significantly improved their highway safety rates in the past few years, surpassing the U.S. rates. The International Transport Forum's Road Safety Annual Report 2018 found that between 2010 and 2016, 26 of the 32 nations tracked in the report had reduced their number of traffic deaths, some by over 30%; during the same period, the number of U.S. deaths increased by 14%. Policy options that might further reduce traffic crashes, injuries, and fatalities include encouraging states to adopt stronger laws regarding use of seat belts and motorcycle helmets and encouraging the use of automated traffic enforcement to reduce speeding and failure to stop at red lights and stop signs. While a majority of the population supports mandatory motorcycle helmet laws and automated traffic enforcement, and these measures are demonstrably effective in reducing deaths, these measures provoke opposition from a smaller but vociferous portion of the population.

Chapter 5 - Federal motor vehicle safety regulation was established more than 50 years ago by the National Traffic and Motor Vehicle Safety Act (P.L. 89-563) to address the rising number of motor vehicle fatalities and injuries. The National Highway Traffic Safety Administration (NHTSA) administers vehicle safety laws and has issued dozens of safety standards, including regulations affecting windshield wipers, hood and door latches, tires, and airbags. NHTSA has estimated that between 1960 and 2012, federal motor vehicle safety standards saved more than 600,000 lives, and the risk of a fatality declined by 56%. Although dozens of technologies were made subject to federal standards in the decades after federal regulation began, a NHTSA study reported that more than half of the lives saved—329,000—were from use of seat belts. While the federal standard was helpful in reducing fatalities, the study found that the passage of state laws allowing police to issue tickets if a driver or passengers are not wearing seat belts caused the number of lives saved to climb from 800 per year to 6,000 per year. In addition to promulgating and enforcing vehicle safety standards, NHTSA investigates vehicle defects that affect safety and issues vehicle or parts recalls if safety defects are discovered. In recent years, the number of vehicle and parts recalls has risen significantly, from 16.3 million vehicles and parts in 2013 to 87.5 million in 2015. The rising number of recalls is due to stricter laws and reporting requirements, larger fines, delayed detection of vehicle problems by NHTSA, and several high-visibility cases, including General Motors' faulty ignition switch and Takata airbags. Recalls rarely obtain 100% completion rates, leaving many defective vehicles on the road long after a recall is initiated. A recent study by J.D. Power, a market research company, showed that between 2013 and 2015, recalls of fewer than 10,000 vehicles had a 67% completion rate, while recalls of more than a million vehicles had a completion rate of only 49%. The larger recalls are thought to result in fewer repaired vehicles because of the difficulty in finding and notifying larger numbers of owners, a lengthened repair period due to lack of an adequate supply of replacement parts, and the ability of manufacturers to use more personalized communications, such as telephone calls, in smaller recalls. Many emerging technologies, such as automatic emergency braking and lane departure warning, are expected to reduce vehicle injuries and deaths in the future. Over time, these separate technologies will be combined as vehicles are built with higher levels of automation. To deal with these rapid changes, NHTSA has broadened the agency's approach beyond the traditional rulemaking to include new means of interacting with manufacturers and other vehicle safety stakeholders, such as voluntary agreements to accelerate use of life-saving technologies. The 2015 Fixing America's Surface Transportation (FAST) Act included significant vehicle safety provisions, including a new requirement that rental car fleets be covered by recalls, new methods for notifying consumers about recalls, larger penalties for violations, and a longer period for consumers to obtain remedies for defects. Congress remains interested in motor vehicle safety; proposed legislation calls for used vehicles to be subject to recalls, NHTSA to provide more public access to safety information, civil penalties to be increased, regional recalls to be terminated, and federal standards to be issued to secure electronic motor vehicle data from hackers.

Chapter 6 - More than 11 million large trucks travel U.S. roads, and almost 4 million people hold commercial driver's licenses. In 2015, large trucks were involved in more than 400,000 motor vehicle crashes serious enough to be registered by police, with nearly 100,000 of those crashes causing injuries and around 3,600 resulting in fatalities. To address this situation, Congress has assigned the U.S. Department of Transportation (DOT)—primarily the Federal Motor Carrier Safety Administration (FMCSA)—responsibility for regulating the safety practices of commercial motor carriers and drivers. In addition, the National Highway Traffic Safety Administration (NHTSA) in DOT is responsible for the safety of the vehicles themselves through its role in setting vehicle safety standards. Truck crash, injury, and fatality rates have generally been rising since 2009 after declining over many years. This increase may be due in part to marginally skilled or inexperienced drivers entering the industry, or to higher levels of work and stress among veteran drivers, or to other factors. Two FMCSA proposals concerning driver safety have proven particularly contentious.

- In March 2017, FMCSA abandoned its attempt to require drivers to take a 34-hour rest period, including two consecutive early morning periods, at least once a week. The proposed "restart rule" encountered strong objections from drivers as well as motor carriers, and an FMCSA study could not confirm that the rule would lead to sufficient improvement in safety to satisfy Congress.
- In March 2016 FMCSA began a joint rulemaking with the Federal Railroad Administration to require that commercial drivers (or train operators) who exhibit certain risk factors be screened for obstructive sleep apnea, which interferes with sound sleep and thus increases the risk of crashes. In the past, efforts to address sleep apnea among drivers met resistance from drivers who feared they might be prohibited from driving commercial vehicles, and Congress prohibited FMCSA from addressing sleep apnea among drivers except through a formal rulemaking.

FMCSA has introduced stricter training standards for new drivers, and has instituted a database intended to help prevent drivers barred from commercial driving due to convictions for driving under the influence of drugs or alcohol from bypassing the prohibition and continuing to drive. FMCSA has also barred drivers from using handheld phones or texting in order to reduce driver distraction. Motor carriers have frequently sought to increase driver productivity and reduce costs by pushing for standards allowing longer or heavier trucks. Although efforts to permit longer trucks were rejected by Congress in 2015, Congress did approve a number of exceptions and waivers to federal weight limits. FMCSA and NHTSA have jointly proposed to require that all large trucks be equipped with speed limiters, a proposal over which the trucking industry is divided. Congress also has taken an interest in FMCSA's Compliance, Safety, and Accountability Program, which is intended to allow it to focus resources on carriers most in need of supervision from a safety standpoint. Legislation in 2015 required FMCSA to obtain external review of the system it proposes to use to measure carrier safety.

Chapter 7 - Increasing the autonomy of cars and trucks is seen as an effective way to reduce the 94% of vehicle-related accidents that are caused by human error. While some semiautonomous safety technologies, such as automatic braking and adaptive cruise control, are in use today, autonomous safety technologies under development would require cars and trucks to communicate with each other (vehicle-to-vehicle, or V2V) and with their surroundings (vehicle-to-infrastructure, or V2I). V2V communication is expected to reduce the number of accidents by improving detection of oncoming vehicles and providing driver warnings. V2I communication is expected to help highway operators monitor and manage traffic and provide drivers with information such as weather and traffic conditions. These technologies are part of a congressional mandate to invest in and advance a broader set of intelligent transportation systems to improve traffic flow and safety. For vehicles to communicate wirelessly, they need access to radio waves, or radio frequencies. In the United States, the Federal Communications Commission (FCC) manages commercial use of the radio frequency spectrum, and allocates spectrum for specific uses. In 1999, the FCC allocated the 5.9 gigahertz (GHz) band to Dedicated Short- Range Communications (DSRC) uses. DSRC technologies, installed in cars and trucks and on roadways, enable V2V and V2I communications. Integrating DSRC technologies in vehicles and on roadways is in its early stages. Meanwhile, the proliferation of cell phones and other devices has increased demand for spectrum, and a competing technology, Cellular Vehicle-to- Everything (C-V2X), has emerged as an alternative to DSRC for vehicular communications. In May 2019, the FCC announced it would consider whether the 5.9 GHz band should (1) remain dedicated to DSRC technologies, (2) be allocated to C-V2X, (3) be allocated to automotive communications technologies generally, or (4) be shared with wireless devices. The FCC's decision has important competitive implications for the automotive, electronics, and telecommunications industries, and may affect the availability of safety technologies and the path toward vehicle automation.

In: Highway Safety
Editor: Bertha G. Baldwin

ISBN: 978-1-53617-176-1
© 2020 Nova Science Publishers, Inc.

Chapter 1

EVERY LIFE COUNTS: IMPROVING THE SAFETY OF OUR NATION'S ROADWAYS[*]

Subcommittee on Highways and Transit

PURPOSE

The Subcommittee on Highways and Transit will meet on Tuesday, April 9, 2019, at 10:00 a.m. in HVC 210, Capitol Visitor Center, to receive testimony related to "Every Life Counts: Improving the Safety of our Nation's Roadways." The purpose of this hearing is to assess the safety of our Nation's roads and learn what can be done to lower the number of traffic-related fatalities and injuries. The Subcommittee will hear from a National Transportation Safety Board (NTSB) Member, the Vice Mayor of Neptune, Florida, the City of Alexandria's Chief of Police, the League of American Bicyclists, the National Safety Council, and the American Traffic Safety Services Association.

BACKGROUND

According to the National Highway Traffic Safety Administration (NHTSA), 37,133 people lost their lives in accidents on U.S. roadways in 2017[1]. That means an average of 101 people died each day in motor vehicle crashes, equating to roughly one fatality every

---

[*] This is an edited, reformatted and augmented version of Hearing before the Subcommittee on Highways and Transit of the Committee on Transportation and Infrastructure, House of Representatives, One Hundred Sixteenth Congress, First Session, dated April 9, 2019.
[1] "Fatality Analysis Reporting System (FARS) Encyclopedia." National Highway Traffic Safety Administration, https://wwwfars.nhtsa.dot.gov/Main/index.aspx.

15 minutes. There were a total of 5,977 pedestrian fatalities in 2017, and preliminary reports indicate that number increased in 2018, leading to the highest rate of pedestrian fatalities since 1990[2]. There were 783 cyclist deaths in 2017 and 852 cyclist deaths in 2016. And, the 5,172 motorcyclist fatalities in 2017 is more than twice what it was two decades ago. According to the National Safety Council, injuries from motor vehicle incidents totaled more than 4.6 million in 2017.

According to the Centers for Disease Control (CDC), unintentional injury is now the third leading cause of death for Americans. Motor vehicle accidents are the leading cause of unintentional injury deaths, second only to opioid overdoses. Roadway injuries are the eighth leading cause of death globally, according to the World Health Organization (WHO), and are the number one cause of death for children ages 5–14 and youth ages 15–29.

The FAST Act (P.L 114–94), enacted on December 4, 2015, reauthorized Federal surface transportation programs through September 30, 2020. This legislation built on the foundation established by the Intermodal Surface Transportation Efficiency Act of 1991 (ISTEA) (P.L. 102-240), the Transportation Equity Act for the 21st Century (TEA–21) (P.L 105–178) enacted in 1998, the Safe, Accountable, Flexible, Efficient Transportation Equity Act: A Legacy for Users (SAFETEA–LU) (P.L. 109–59) enacted in 2005, and the Moving Ahead for Progress in the 21st Century Act (MAP– 21) (P.L. 112–141) enacted in 2012.

As part of each of these multi-year authorization bills, Congress has directed guaranteed Federal funding toward programs to ensure safety on our Nation's roads. These include grants to improve physical roadway infrastructure; grant programs to reduce crashes, injuries, and fatalities involving large trucks and buses; grant programs to incentivize States to adopt laws and regulations to improve highway safety; and grants to assist State enforcement of vehicle and driver safety measures. Congress has also mandated that U.S. Department of Transportation (DOT) agencies undertake numerous rulemakings in each of these areas to address outstanding safety concerns, many of which are discussed below.

In 2016, FHWA, FMCSA, and NHTSA announced, in partnership with the National Safety Council, the launch of the "Road to Zero" coalition. The goal of the coalition is to end fatalities on the Nation's roads within the next 30 years. The DOT committed $3 million in grants over three years to organizations working on life-saving programs. The Road to Zero Coalition focuses on promoting strategies proven to save lives, such as seat belt use, traffic safety enforcement, and education campaigns. The coalition also focuses on developing new evidence-based strategies to addressing changes in driver behavior.

---

[2] "New Projection: 2018 Pedestrian Fatalities Highest Since 1990." Governors Highway Safety Association, 28 Feb. 2019, https://www.ghsa.org/resources/news-releases/pedestrians19.

National Transportation Safety Board

The NTSB was created by Congress on April 1, 1967, as an independent Federal agency charged with investigating all civil aviation accidents and significant accidents in other modes of transportation. The NTSB determines the probable cause of the accidents and issues safety recommendations aimed at preventing future accidents. Since its inception 50 years ago, the NTSB has investigated thousands of accidents and made more than 14,500 recommendations to improve transportation safety, including over 2,400 highway safety recommendations. Over 80 percent of NTSB safety recommendations have been acted upon favorably, saving lives. Specific information on NTSB recommendations is included below.

Federal-Aid Highways

The Highway Safety Improvement Program (HSIP) is a Federal-aid program, funded out of the Highway Trust Fund, which provides funding to projects that will achieve a significant reduction in traffic fatalities and serious injuries on public roads, including local roads and roads on tribal land. In order to use HSIP funding, a State must have an approved comprehensive, data-driven strategic highway safety plan (SHSP) that defines State safety goals and describes a program of strategies to improve safety. Funding provided under HSIP is apportioned to States to implement highway safety improvement projects, which are included in a State's SHSP, to correct or improve hazardous road locations and features, or to address highway safety problems.

The FAST Act increased funding for the HSIP program, providing a total of $11.6 billion to States and tribes over five years. The FAST Act also increased funding for the rail-highway grade crossing program, funded out of HSIP. The set-aside increases from $225 million in FY 2016 to $245 million in FY 2020. The FAST Act amended eligible uses of HSIP funds to include only those listed in statute, most of which are related to physical infrastructure improvements to enhance safety, and specifically added the following eligible uses: installation of vehicle-to-infrastructure communication equipment; pedestrian hybrid beacons; and roadway improvements that provide separation between pedestrians and motor vehicles.

The FAST Act also included "complete streets" language, which encourages States to adopt standards to provide for the safe and adequate accommodation of all surface transportation users, including pedestrians, bicyclists, motorists and transit riders of all ages and abilities. Comparable Senate language to require States and Metropolitan Planning Organizations (MPOs) to adopt such policies was not retained in the final Conference Report. The FAST Act also promotes the use of alternate design guides in order to right size projects and accommodate all users, which contributes to more livable communities and expands safe transportation options.

Policies such as complete streets help reduce accidents and fatalities for all road users by addressing a wide range of elements unique to each community, such as pedestrian accessibility, street crossings, and bus and bike lanes. In November 2018, the NTSB released a special investigative report to address pedestrian safety[3]. Their recommendations included calling on FHWA to expand its support of state and local safety projects in order to develop a broad network of safety improvements, as well as establishing a national metric of pedestrian safety activity to improve local planning.

National Highway Traffic Safety Administration

NHTSA's mission is to save lives, prevent injuries, and reduce economic costs due to traffic accidents on the Nation's roadways through education, research, and by promulgating and enforcing safety standards. The FAST Act reauthorized NHTSA's behavioral highway safety programs. Section 402 of title 23, United States Code, requires States to have safety plans approved by the Secretary and designed to reduce fatalities, injuries, and property damage resulting from traffic accidents. Funding is distributed to States with approved plans through a formula based on population and public road mileage. The FAST Act increased funding to carry out state highway safety plans and reduced administrative requirements for States.

The majority of motor vehicle deaths are linked to human behavior. Of the 37,133 traffic related fatalities which occurred in 2017:

- 10,874 (29 percent) were crashes where at least one driver was alcohol-impaired;
- 9,717 (26 percent) were in crashes where at least one driver was speeding, and;
- 3,166 (9 percent) were in crashes involving distracted driving.

Traffic fatality data for each state can be found here: https:// crashstats. nhtsa.dot.gov/Api/Public/ViewPublication/812581.

NHTSA has also analyzed the economic costs of motor vehicle crashes and found that traffic-related accidents cost the U.S. $242 billion in 2010[4]. Of that, $43 billion was attributed to alcohol-impaired crashes, and $52 billion was attributed to speed-related crashes. Seat belt use prevented 12,500 fatalities, 308,000 serious injuries, and $50 billion in injury related costs in 2010. However, the failure of a substantial portion of the

---

[3] "Special Investigation Report: Pedestrian Safety." National Transportation Safety Board, 25 Sept. 2018, https://www.ntsb.gov/safety/safety-studies/Documents/SIR1803.pdf.

[4] "The Economic and Societal Impact of Motor Vehicle Crashes, 2010 (Revised)." National Highway Traffic Safety Administration, May 2015, https://crashstats.nhtsa.dot.gov/Api/Public/ ViewPublication/812013.

driving population to buckle up caused 3,350 unnecessary fatalities, 54,300 serious injuries, and cost society $10 billion in easily preventable injury related expenses. In 2017, motor vehicle injuries are estimated to have cost the U.S. economy $433.8 billion, including medical expenses, lost wages and productivity, property damage, and other similar expenses, according to the National Safety Council.

States can use their Section 402 funding on activities to carry out their States safety plans, including activities to improve enforcement of traffic safety laws. In their campaign Save LIVES, which aims to significantly lower traffic fatalities and injuries by 2050, the WHO included investment in traffic safety enforcement as one of its top six priorities.

The CDC also recommends greater enforcement of seat belt laws to help lower the number of traffic-related fatalities caused by not using a restraint[5]. The majority of Americans recognize the importance of wearing a seat belt, with the national use rate at almost 90 percent. However, of the passengers killed in motor vehicle accidents in 2017, 47 percent were not using a restraint. Despite a continued steady rate of fatalities due to alcohol impairment in recent years, traffic safety enforcement is steadily declining. According to data from the FBI, the number of drunk driving arrests decreased 24 percent from 2005 to 2017[6].

State Safety Grants

In order to assist and incentivize States to improve safety in areas known to contribute to fatalities, Congress authorized the National Priority Safety Program (Section 405 of title 23, U.S.C.). Through this program, NHTSA makes grant funding available to States that adopt or implement programs or laws to: increase the use of occupant protection devices; reduce the number of alcohol impaired driving fatalities; encourage the adoption of laws which prohibit distracted driving; improve motorcyclist safety; improve the timeliness, accuracy, completeness, uniformity, integration, and accessibility of state safety data; and encourage the adoption of state graduated driver licensing laws. The FAST Act also added two new grants under Section 405, the 24–7 Sobriety Program and the Non-Motorized Safety program, which makes States with combined pedestrian and bicycle fatalities that exceed 15 percent of total crash fatalities in that State eligible to receive funding to reduce such fatalities. Each State must meet specific criteria in each national priority program to qualify for funding. The FAST Act provided grant funding ($1.4 billion over five years) for this program. In 2019, the Non-

---

[5] "What Works: Strategies to Increase Restraint Use." Centers for Disease Control and Preven- tion, 21 Jan. 2015, https://www.cdc.gov/motorvehiclesafety/seatbelts/strategies.html.
[6] "2017 Crime in the United States." Federal Bureau of Investigation, https://ucr.fbi.gov/crime- in-the-u.s/2017/crime-in-the-u.s.-2017/tables/table-69/table-69.xls.

Motorized Safety Grants program was fully utilized with each of the 25 states eligible for the grant receiving it.

The FAST Act also made limited changes to the Alcohol-Ignition Interlock Law, Distracted Driving, and Graduated Driver Licensing Incentive grants in order to increase the number of States eligible for those grants. To learn which States met the criteria for each grant program see: https://www.nhtsa.gov/sites/nhtsa.dot.gov/files/documents/fy19/grantdeterminations/and/deficiencies/in/stateapplications.pdf Despite the changes made to these safety grants under the FAST Act, states have not adapted their programs to qualify, leaving the program underutilized. The table below shows the number of states who were unsuccessful in meeting the programs' criteria in 2019. Additionally, in each program, fewer States applied for grants in 2019 than in 2018. For example, seventeen states applied for Graduated Driver Licensing Law grants last year, compared to only four states applying in 2019.

Program	Ignition Interlocks (405d)	Comprehensive Distracted Driving (405e)	Graduated Driver Licensing Law (405g)
Applied	13	17	4
Awarded	5	4	0
Not Awarded	8	13	4
Did Not Apply	43	39	52
Not Eligible	0	0	0

The NTSB's FY 2019–2020 Most Wanted List includes recommendations to eliminate distractions, including a nationwide ban on the use of personal electronic devices by all drivers, and increased high-visibility enforcement for speeding and drug and alcohol impaired driving. The full list of recommendations can be found here: https://www.ntsb.gov/safety/mwl/Documents/2019-20/2019-20-MWL-SafetyRecs.pdf.

Drugged Driving

An emerging area of safety concern is drugged driving. NHTSA's most recent Roadside Survey of Alcohol and Drug Use by Drivers found that 20 percent of drivers tested positive for at least one drug that could affect safety[7]. However, this figure does not represent or confirm how many drivers were impaired since a positive marijuana test can detect marijuana use in the past week. A 2016 AAA Foundation for Traffic Safety report found that an estimated 4.9 percent of drivers drove within an hour of using marijuana[8]. In 2016, NHTSA conducted a study in Virginia called the Drug and Alcohol

---

[7] "2013–2014 National Roadside Study of Alcohol and Drug Use by Drivers." National High-way Traffic Safety Administration, May 2017, https://www.nhtsa.gov/sites/nhtsa.dot.gov/files/documents/13013-nrs/drug/092917/v6/tag.pdf.

[8] "2016 Traffic Safety Culture Index." AAA Foundation, Feb. 2017, https://aaafoundation.org/ 2016-traffic-safety-culture-index/.

Crash Risk: A Case-Controlled Study, the largest of its kind ever conducted, which assessed whether marijuana use by drivers is associated with greater risk of crashes[9]. The survey found that marijuana users are more likely to be involved in accidents, but that the increased risk may be due in part because marijuana users are more likely to be in groups at higher risk of crashes, particularly young men.

Unlike the current 0.08 percent Blood Alcohol Content impairment standard, there is currently no impairment standard for marijuana. Marijuana has a larger variation in how it affects people than alcohol, making it more difficult to establish a uniform impairment standard. The FAST Act required NHTSA to report to Congress on several outstanding challenges of marijuana-impaired driving, including methods to detect marijuana-impaired driving, impairment standard feasibility, methods to differentiate the cause of a driving impairment between alcohol and marijuana, and the role and extent of marijuana impairment in motor vehicle accidents. That report was issued in July 2017 and provided three recommendations to address marijuana-impaired driving:

- Increase training and resources for law enforcement officers using the most efficient and effective techniques to detect and recognize impairment in drivers;
- Continue research to enable development of an impairment standard for driving under the influence of marijuana, and;
- Encourage States to collect data regarding the prevalence of marijuana use by drivers and among those arrested for impaired driving[10].

NTSB recommendations for drugged driving include more research to get better data to understand the scope of the problem and the effectiveness of countermeasures[11]. NTSB also recommends States should increase the collection, documentation, and reporting of driver breath and blood test results for alcohol and drugs following crashes. This is most readily done through NHTSA's National Roadside Survey (NRS).

In recent years, Congress has blocked NHTSA's ability to continue this survey through an appropriations rider. In March 2018, the U.S. Government Accountability Office issued a report to Senate and House Appropriations Committees which found that NHTSA had improved NRS methodology to address previous concerns leading to its prohibition[12]. Their audit found there are key differences in how the NRS is conducted as compared to a traditional law enforcement checkpoint. As a result, participation in the

---

[9] "Drug and Alcohol Crash Risk: A Case-Control Study." National Highway Traffic Safety Ad- ministration, Dec. 2016, https://www.nhtsa.gov/sites/nhtsa.dot.gov/files/documents/ 812355/drugalcoholcrashrisk.pdf.

[10] "Marijuana-Impaired Driving a Report to Congress." National Highway Traffic Safety Ad- ministration, July 2017, https://www.nhtsa.gov/sites/nhtsa.dot.gov/files/documents/812440-mari- juana-impaired-driving-report-to-congress.pdf.

[11] "End Alcohol and Other Drug Impairment—Highway." National Transportation Safety Board, https://www.ntsb.gov/safety/mwl/Pages/mwlfs-19-20/mwl5-fsh.aspx.

[12] "National Roadside Survey: NHTSA Changed Methodology to Address Driver Concerns." U.S. Government Accountability Office, 12 March 2018, https://www.gao.gov/assets/700/ 690593.pdf.

NRS is entirely voluntary and has never resulted in an arrest, unlike law enforcement checkpoints. In response to these findings, the FY 2019 Transportation, Housing, and Urban Development Appropriations Act did not include the prohibition.

Autonomous Vehicles

Autonomous vehicles offer many safety improvements over human drivers, but they too have limitations. Within the jurisdiction of the Committee on Transportation and Infrastructure safety issues such as safely navigating road construction zones, pulling aside for emergency vehicles, understanding police controlled intersections are all unique challenges for autonomous vehicles. Roadway infrastructure needs to compliment autonomous vehicles include road striping and smart traffic lights. Finally, educating human drivers to anticipate and react accordingly to the driving style of autonomous vehicles will also need to be part of the process.

WITNESSES

- The Honorable Jennifer Homendy, Member, National Transportation Safety Board
- The Honorable Fred Jones, Vice Mayor, City of Neptune Beach, Florida, on behalf of Transportation for America
- Mr. Michael L. Brown, Chief of Police, City of Alexandria
- Mr. Jay Bruemmer, Vice President, K & G Striping, Inc., on behalf of the American Traffic Safety Services Association
- Mr. Mike Sewell, Active Transportation Service Line Leader, Gresham Smith, on behalf of The League of American Bicyclists
- Mr. Nicholas Smith, Interim President and Chief Executive Officer, The National Safety Council

EVERY LIFE COUNTS: IMPROVING THE SAFETY OF OUR NATION'S ROADWAYS

Tuesday, April 9, 2019
House of Representatives,
Subcommittee on Highways and Transit,
Committee on Transportation and Infrastructure,
Washington, DC.

The subcommittee met, pursuant to notice, at 10 a.m., in room HVC–210, Capitol Visitor Center, Hon. Eleanor Holmes Norton (Chairwoman of the subcommittee) presiding:

Ms. NORTON. The subcommittee will come to order. I want to welcome us all to today's hearing.

It is a priority for me and I hope for the members of this committee. It is certainly equally important to the other issues we are going to be considering as we move toward reauthorization.

I do not see how we can reauthorize another transportation surface bill without considering not only how to build it, but how to make it safe for those who use it. I am going to ask Members to check on your district the way I did mine, and I wonder if your experience is like mine.

In 2015, the District of Columbia pledged to end roadway fatalities by the year 2024. That must have been a year that was given to us by the Department of Transportation or somebody.

Yet, every year since that pledge there has been an increase in fatalities. In the last 2 years of available data, traffic-related deaths in my own district spiked by 35 percent. That is why I am asking Members to look at their districts because I do not believe, unfortunately, that I am alone.

Nationwide, in 2017, 37,133 people lost their lives in motor vehicle related crashes. Now, I spell that number out. Usually I round off the numbers, but I purposely did not do it for the purposes of this hearing because each number represents a life lost.

Every day we lose more than 100 lives in traffic-related accidents. Some of those may be people walking in the streets or in the roads, and we have had an increase in those fatalities in my own district as well. Some of them may be people riding in automobiles or trucks.

In 2016, the Department of Transportation announced the so-called Road to Zero. It was a coalition with a goal of completely eliminating roadway deaths within 30 years. Well, all I can say is we are off to a poor start.

That is why pedestrian and traffic safety is a priority for me as chair of this subcommittee. I am anxious to learn from today's witnesses, representing an increasingly diverse array of populations who use our roadways, including pedestrians and bicyclists, and now people riding scooters, and law enforcement on what we can do about this trend.

I would very much like this reauthorization to transform our approach to roadway safety to help us get anywhere close to zero deaths. That is an admirable goal. It is a goal we ought to set.

We need to improve how we design our transportation networks. We need to improve how we educate the users of those networks, and we need to understand how to enforce the proven strategies that we already claim will save lives and apparently have not done so.

Some in Congress may still live in the 20th century of transportation in wanting to eliminate the very small amount of funding that is used for transportation alternatives, but I think the people have already moved ahead of Congress and are already on the roads using alternative modes of transportation.

All of these modes of transportation must be treated equally, not cars over scooters, not bicycles over walking. All must be treated as equally valid choices that people have chosen to move people. The options belong not to Congress but to the State and local communities who must be able to pursue the smartest and most efficient and right-sized projects to meet their own mobility needs of their own citizens.

I am a big proponent of technology as holding promise to save lives, but human error and human choice today are very real problems, and we do not have the technology in place and will not have it in place for some time to save lives.

So we cannot wait to remove humans from the equation before making the real progress we have promised to make.

The three leading causes of motor vehicle deaths remain linked to the same human factors: alcohol impairment, speeding, and distracted driving. I am particularly interested in hearing from our witnesses on why we have not been able to curb this longstanding issue, road safety, and what we can do to stop these fatalities.

I look forward to today's discussion and thank each of our witnesses for sharing their insights, your much needed insights, with us.

I would like to ask the ranking member, Mr. Spano, who is here for our ranking member, for his comments at this time.

Mr. SPANO. Thank you, Chairwoman Norton.

I want to welcome everybody to the hearing today.

The current Federal surface transportation law, the FAST Act, expires on September 30th, 2020. Last month this subcommittee held a hearing to kick off its process to reauthorize Federal surface transportation programs.

Today's hearing builds on that and is focused on how Congress can improve the safety of our Nation's roads. In 2017, as the Chair noted, 37,133 fatalities occurred on our Nation's highways according to the National Highway Traffic Safety Administration.

While this is a 1.8 percent decrease from 2016, more can and should be done to further reduce highway fatalities. The Federal Surface Transportation Safety Programs are administered by different modal administrations within the Department of Transportation. These programs provide nonFederal partners with resources to improve the safety of the Nation's surface transportation system.

Today's hearing focuses on the safety programs administered by the Federal Highway Administration and the National Highway Traffic Safety Administration. These programs require States to have a data-driven, performance-based approach to address their unique highway safety challenges.

As we continue with our reauthorization process, it is important that we gather feedback on how well these programs are working and what other policy and programmatic change this committee should consider.

With that I want to thank our witnesses for being with us this morning, and I look forward to hearing their testimony on this very important topic.

Madam Chair.

[Mr. Spano's prepared statement follows:]

Prepared Statement of Hon. Ross Spano, a Representative in Congress from the State of Florida

Thank you, Chairwoman Norton. I want to welcome everyone to today's hearing. The current Federal surface transportation law, the FAST Act, expires on September 30, 2020. Last month, this subcommittee held a hearing to kick off its process to reauthorize Federal surface transportation programs. Today's hearing builds on that and is focused on how Congress can improve the safety of the Nation's roads.

In 2017, 37,133 fatalities occurred on our Nation's highways, according to the National Highway Traffic Safety Administration. While this is a 1.8 percent decrease from 2016, more can be done to further reduce highway fatalities.

The Federal surface transportation safety programs are administered by different modal administrations within the Department of Transportation. These programs provide non-Federal partners with resources to improve the safety of the Nation's surface transportation system.

Today's hearing focuses on the safety programs administered by the Federal Highway Administration and the National Highway Traffic Safety Administration. These programs require states to have a data-driven, performance-based approach to address their unique highway safety challenges.

As we continue with our reauthorization process, it is important that we gather feedback on how well these programs are working and what other policy and programmatic changes the committee should consider.

With that, I want to thank our witnesses for being with us this morning, and I look forward to hearing their testimony on this very important topic.

Ms. NORTON. Thank you.

And we will hear now from the chairman of the full committee, Mr. DeFazio.

Mr. DEFAZIO. Thank you, Madam Chair.

Somehow we seem to have become sort of inured to the fact that 100 people a day die in motor vehicle accidents. Yes, there is hortatory like, "Oh, we are going to move to zero," but it is not being followed up with decisive action out of the Department of Transportation or in many State DOTs.

So I am hopeful that as we move toward reauthorization of the FAST Act that we can put new direction and new emphasis on how to deal with this horrible toll.

You know, obviously drunk driving is a big problem. That goes to enforcement issues. Speeding, enforcement issues. Distractions, I think a lot of States have yet to adopt laws regarding distractions, and there are new technologies that are potentially going to build distractions into the automobiles or after-market distractions like heads-up displays where you can read your email on the windshield while you are driving.

We have to deal with all of these evolving problems and then deal with the more traditional problems we have had.

There has been also an alarming increase in pedestrian deaths, which the Chair mentioned, and cycling and pedestrian, and some of that can be dealt with as we rebuild this crumbling system, and when we look to Complete Streets or other ways to better segregate traffic, pedestrians and bicycles, that can help prevent some of those deaths.

In some cities, they are putting in bike boxes at the front because the right turn is the most common cause of a vehicular collision with a cyclist, and you know, there are other things we can do that are pretty simple, not that expensive, but have not really been exploited to their potential.

So I am looking forward to creative and innovative ideas. I look forward to the witnesses giving us some of those ideas.

And with that I would yield back the balance of my time. [Mr. DeFazio's prepared statement follows:]

Prepared Statement of Hon. Peter A. DeFazio, a Representative in Congress from the State of Oregon, and Chair, Committee on Transportation and Infrastructure

Thank you, Chair Norton and Ranking Member Davis, for holding this hearing. I am pleased that the subcommittee is prioritizing roadway safety—a topic that has not received the level of attention it deserves.

We can and must do more to save lives and prevent injuries on our roads. Currently, more than 100 people a day die in motor vehicle accidents—that's one life lost every fifteen minutes. Pedestrian deaths have also risen sharply in the last decade—an increase of 45 percent since 2009—and now account for 16 percent of all roadway fatalities. Somehow this has become tolerable.

A total of 37,133 people were killed on our roadways in 2017. Let me put this in context—this is the equivalent of about 218 fully loaded airplanes falling out of the sky each year and yet somehow this has not spurred Americans to demand that enough is enough. If that weren't bad enough, when you consider that the top causes of motor vehicle deaths are drunk driving, speeding, and distractions, you realize these deaths are entirely preventable.

At a time when transportation is changing rapidly thanks to innovation, data sharing, and automation, it's shocking we still aren't making big strides in safety. We should be holding ourselves to a higher standard, because when it comes to roadway safety every single life counts. While we invest billions of dollars in research for cancer and other diseases and allocate new resources to combatting the opioid crisis, we have failed to seriously invest in lowering deaths on our Nation's roadways.

So what can we do? Making substantial progress towards saving lives requires a clear sense of—and strong commitment to—the goal of safety as the highest priority. Two decades ago, Sweden launched an effort called Vision Zero which set forth a road safety approach with a simple aim: "No loss of life is acceptable." This model has been replicated in several countries around the world, and it guides the mission of the U.S. Department of Transportation and the Road to Zero Coalition. And, many U.S. cities have independently adopted policies to work towards zero deaths in roadway accidents. Congress needs to demonstrate its commitment to making Vision Zero a reality as well.

Unfortunately, highway safety has not been a high priority in transportation talks in Congress in recent years. In the development of both the FAST Act and MAP–21, there was a stark shift in the discourse over safety in Congress. Instead of developing solutions to promote safety, we sparred over proposals to ease state requirements on safety funding and exempt industry after industry from safety regulations. As Congress develops a bill to build 21st-century infrastructure, ensuring safety of the users of that infrastructure must be a top priority of this committee. Given that two-thirds of fatalities are tied to drunk driving and excessive speed, I want to double down on Federal actions that we know work—education and enforcement. And we need to look at safety from all angles—not just promoting more responsible behavior by road users, but by ensuring that roadway design takes into account all users through smart policies, such as complete streets. Addressing the unique elements of each community, such as pedestrian accessibility, street crossings, and bus and bike lanes, rather than a cookie-cutter approach can have a profound impact on reducing traffic accidents and fatalities.

I look forward to today's discussion and learning what Congress can do to raise the bar on safety.

Ms. NORTON. Thank you, Mr. Chairman.

Before I introduce today's panel, I want to note that we had many more stakeholder groups who were interested in speaking about safety than we could accommodate at today's hearing, and that is really very encouraging to me that so many wanted to come forward to speak to this issue.

It does speak to the rising consciousness and the pressure, I think, Congress needs to find ways, along with those in the States, to move this issue.

I, therefore, ask unanimous consent to enter into the hearing record written statements from ITS America, Advocates for Highway and Auto Safety, and the American Road and Transportation Builders Association.

Without objection, so ordered.

[The information is on pages 121–129.]

Ms. NORTON. We want to move now to our witnesses:

The Honorable Jennifer Homendy, Member of the National Transportation Safety Board; The Honorable Fred Jones, vice mayor, city of Neptune Beach, Florida, on behalf of Transportation for America;

Mr. Michael L. Brown, chief of police, city of Alexandria, Virginia;

Mr. Jay Bruemmer, vice president, K&G Striping Inc., on behalf of the American Traffic Safety Services Association;

Mr. Mike Sewell, transportation service line leader, Gresham Smith, on behalf of the League of American Bicyclists;

Mr. Nicholas Smith, interim president and chief executive officer of the National Safety Council.

Thank you for being here. I look forward to your testimony.

Without objection, our witnesses' full statements will be included in the record.

You may proceed, Ms. Homendy.

TESTIMONY OF HON. JENNIFER HOMENDY, MEMBER, NATIONAL TRANSPORTATION SAFETY BOARD; HON. FRED JONES, VICE MAYOR, CITY OF NEPTUNE BEACH, FLORIDA, ON BEHALF OF TRANSPORTATION FOR AMERICA; MICHAEL L. BROWN, CHIEF OF POLICE, ALEXANDRIA (VIRGINIA) POLICE DEPARTMENT; JAY BRUEMMER, VICE PRESIDENT, K&G STRIPING, INC., ON BEHALF OF THE AMERICAN TRAFFIC SAFETY SERVICES ASSOCIATION; MIKE SEWELL, ACTIVE TRANSPORTATION SERVICE LINE LEADER, GRESHAM SMITH, ON BEHALF OF THE LEAGUE OF AMERICAN BICYCLISTS; AND NICHOLAS J. SMITH, INTERIM PRESIDENT AND CHIEF EXECUTIVE OFFICER, THE NATIONAL SAFETY COUNCIL

Ms. HOMENDY. Good morning, Chairwoman Norton, Congressman Spano, Chairman DeFazio, and members of the subcommittee. Thank you for inviting the NTSB to testify today.

The NTSB is an independent Federal agency charged by Congress with investigating major transportation disasters. We determine the probable cause of crashes and issue safety recommendations to Federal, State, and local agencies, and organizations to prevent future tragedies and injuries and save lives.

We are not a regulatory agency in the conventional sense. We do not adopt or enforce safety standards. Since 1967, the NTSB has issued nearly 15,000 safety recommendations, about 2,500 of which are aimed at improving highway safety.

Overall, more than 80 percent of those have been adopted, including recommendations that ensure airbags are safer, child restraint fitting stations are available nationwide, and the design and construction of schoolbuses are improved.

Every 2 years, we release a "most wanted list" of transportation safety improvements to highlight issues that we believe are the greatest risk to safety.

Our most recent list identifies 10 priorities, 7 of which affect highway safety. Today I want to focus on speeding, impaired driving, and pedestrian safety.

Speeding is one of the most common factors in motor vehicle crashes. In 2016, more than 10,000 people were killed in speeding related crashes, about the same number of people killed in alcohol impaired driving crashes. Yet our attitude toward speeding is much different. It is seen as more socially acceptable.

Together we need to change that mindset. In July 2017, we issued a study focused on reducing speeding related crashes. We found that, one, we need to change how we set speed limits in this country. Federal guidance to States is leading to ever-increasing speed limits, and as a result, deaths on our Nation's roadways.

From 2012 to 2016, we went from 32 States with maximum speed limits at or above 70 to 41. Seven of those States are at or above 80.

We need to increase enforcement through the use of technologies, like automated speed enforcement and point-to-point enforcement. We need in-vehicle technologies to address speeding like speed limiters, and we need NHTSA to issue performance standards for such technologies.

We need national leadership to address speeding, which should include a campaign like Click It or Ticket, to change driver behavior and incentive grants to States to encourage them to implement programs to combat speeding.

We also need to better address impairment in transportation. Twenty-nine die on our Nation's roads daily due to alcohol-impaired driving crashes. That is one every 48 minutes.

We recommend reducing the BAC limit to .05 or lower, and that NHTSA provide incentive grants to States to do so.

We recommend requiring ignition interlocks for all convicted DWI offenders, and we want NHTSA to accelerate widespread implementation of technology to enable vehicles to detect driver impairment.

Finally, pedestrian safety. Over the last 10 years, pedestrian fatalities have increased by 27 percent, while overall highway fatalities have decreased by 12 percent.

In 2016, the NTSB began investigating a series of highway crashes and issued a study that included 11 recommendations to DOT focused on improving pedestrian safety.

We recommend strengthening Federal standards on vehicle head- lights; improving vehicle designs to reduce pedestrian fatalities and injuries; and ensuring collision avoidance technologies like pedestrian detection systems and automatic emergency braking are standard on all vehicles.

We need better street designs. Traditional planning is geared towards motor vehicle traffic. So we recommend that States and MPOs implement a pedestrian safety action plan and that FHWA provide more resources for State and local pedestrian safety projects.

Finally, we need better data to support the decisionmaking process. For example, in 2015, Portland, Oregon, identified 30 high crash streets and intersections that accounted for 57 percent of deadly crashes.

By analyzing injury and crash data, Portland was able to determine where best to invest resources.

In closing, let me emphasize that more than 100 people die on our highways every single day. In our view, one death is too many. We must change a culture that is willing to accept those losses, and we need your help to implement proven solutions.

Thank you again for the opportunity to testify today, and I am happy to answer any questions.

[Ms. Homendy's prepared statement follows:]

Prepared Statement of Hon. Jennifer Homendy, Member, National Transportation Safety Board

Good morning Chairwoman Norton, Ranking Member Davis, Chairman DeFazio, and Ranking Member Graves, and the Members of the Subcommittee. And, let me offer my congratulations to Vice Chair Finkenauer on her selection as Vice Chair of the Subcommittee. Thank you for inviting the National Transportation Safety Board (NTSB) to testify before you today.

In 1967, Congress established the NTSB as an independent agency within the United States Department of Transportation (USDOT) with a clearly defined mission to promote a higher level of safety in the transportation system. In 1974, Congress reestablished the NTSB as a separate entity outside of the USDOT, reasoning that "no federal agency can properly perform such (investigatory) functions unless it is totally separate and independent from any other . . . agency of the United States."[13] Because the USDOT has broad operational and regulatory responsibilities that affect the safety, adequacy, and efficiency of the transportation system, and transportation accidents may suggest deficiencies in that system, the NTSB's independence was deemed necessary for proper oversight.

The NTSB is charged by Congress with investigating every civil aviation accident in the United States and significant accidents in other modes of transportation— highway, rail, marine, and pipeline. We determine the probable cause of the accidents we investigate, and we issue recommendations to federal, state, and local agencies, and other entities, aimed at improving safety, preventing future accidents and injuries, and saving lives. The NTSB is not a regulatory agency in the conventional sense—it does not promulgate operating standards and does not certificate organizations and individuals. The goal of our work is to foster safety improvements, through formal and informal safety recommendations, for the traveling public.

On call 24 hours a day, 365 days a year, our investigators travel throughout the country and to every corner of the world in response to transportation disasters. In addition, we conduct special transportation safety studies and coordinate the resources of the federal government and other organizations to assist victims and their family members who have been impacted by major transportation disasters. Since our inception, we have investigated more than 146,000 aviation accidents and thousands of surface transportation accidents. We have issued more than 14,650 safety recommendations to more than 2,400 recipients in all transportation modes, over 82 percent of which have been implemented.

In the case of highway accidents, current law grants the NTSB jurisdiction to investigate those "highway accident[s], including a railroad grade crossing accident, the Board selects in cooperation with a State."[14] The NTSB has a distinguished record of contributing to highway safety for decades. For example, as a result of the NTSB's investigative work and safety recommendations, automobile airbags for all citizens are safer, child restraint fitting stations are available nationwide, and graduated driver licensing programs for teenagers have been implemented by many states. Additional examples of safety improvements inspired by or resulting from investigations or recommendations of the NTSB include improvements in the design and construction of school buses, highway barrier improvements, and center highmounted rear brake lights on automobiles. Although there is no way to quantify the accidents that did not happen or the lives that were not lost because of the efforts of the NTSB, the tangible safety improvements that can be directly associated with the work of the NTSB have saved countless lives and avoided millions and perhaps billions of dollars in injuries and property damage.

---

[13] Independent Safety Board Act of 1974 § 302, Pub. L. 93-633, 88 Stat. 2166-2173 (1975).
[14] 49 U.S.C. § 1131(b).

Our goal is zero deaths and injuries on our nation's roadways; to eliminate the more than 37,000 people killed in crashes on US highways in 2017.[15]

On February 4, 2019, we announced our Most Wanted List of Transportation Safety Improvements (MWL) for 2019-2020.[16] First issued in 1990, the MWL serves as the agency's primary advocacy tool to help save lives, prevent injuries, and reduce property damage resulting from transportation accidents. The NTSB created the program to increase industry, Congressional, and public awareness of the transportation safety issues identified in our accident investigations and safety studies. Safety issues highlighted on the MWL receive increased emphasis and become the primary focus of our advocacy activities.

The issues selected for the MWL are chosen from our safety recommendations and emerging areas. Selections are based on the magnitude of risk, potential safety benefits, timeliness, and probability of advocacy efforts to bring about change. Issues selected have been thoroughly validated by our investigations. They are issues we identify as having received insufficient or inadequate action. They are issues that could create a high safety risk if not addressed.

Our 2019-2020 list includes seven areas that affect highway safety:

- Implement a Comprehensive Strategy to Reduce Speeding-Related Crashes
- End Alcohol and Other Drug Impairment
- Eliminate Distractions
- Strengthen Occupant Protection
- Increase Implementation of Collision Avoidance Systems in All New Highway Vehicles
- Reduce Fatigue-Related Accidents
- Require Medical Fitness—Screen for and Treat Obstructive Sleep Apnea

My testimony today will focus on those areas most closely related to pedestrian and passenger vehicle safety.

Most Wanted List of Transportation Safety Improvements

Implement a Comprehensive Strategy to Reduce Speeding-Related Crashes

Speeding—either exceeding the speed limit or driving too fast for conditions—is one of the most common factors in motor vehicle crashes in the United States. National Highway Traffic Safety Administration (NHTSA) data show that in 2016, 10,291 people

---

[15] National Highway Traffic Safety Administration, *2017 Motor Vehicle Crashes: Overview* (Washington, DC: NHTSA, 2018).
[16] National Transportation Safety Board, *2019-2020 Most Wanted List* (Washington, DC: NTSB, 2019).

were killed in crashes in which at least one driver was speeding. This represents 27 percent of the traffic fatalities that year, and a 5.6-percent increase from 2015. Speeding increases the likelihood of being involved in a crash, and it increases the severity of injuries sustained by all road users in a crash.

On July 25, 2017, we adopted a safety study, *Reducing Speeding-Related Crashes Involving Passenger Vehicles*, which examined the causes and trends in speeding-related crashes and countermeasures to prevent them.[17] The study focused on five safety issues:

- speed limits
- data-driven approaches for speed enforcement
- automated speed enforcement
- intelligent speed adaptation
- national leadership

Speed limits are a critical component of speed management, but Federal Highway Administration (FHWA) guidance through the Manual of Uniform Traffic Control Devices (MUTCD) emphasizes that states and localities set speed limits within 5 miles per hour (mph) of which 85% of vehicles are traveling. The focus on the 85th percentile has led to increasing speed limits across the United States. For example, in 2012, 35 states had maximum speed limits at or above 70 mph; that increased to 41 states by 2016, with 7 of those states at or above 80 mph. The NTSB recommends deemphasizing the 85th percentile approach; requiring consideration of factors which are currently only optional, such as crash history, roadway characteristics, and roadway conditions; and incorporating a safe systems approach for urban roads (evaluating pedestrian and bicycle traffic).

Speed limits must also be enforced to be effective. Successful enforcement is achieved through law enforcement commitment to data-driven, high-visibility enforcement. However, law enforcement reporting of speeding-related crashes is inconsistent, which leads to underreporting of speeding-related crashes. This underreporting leads stakeholders and the public to underestimate the overall scope of speeding as a traffic safety issue nationally and hinders the effective implementation of data-driven speed enforcement programs.

Automated speed enforcement (ASE) is also widely acknowledged as an effective countermeasure to reduce speeding-related crashes, fatalities, and injuries. However, only 14 states and the District of Columbia use it. Many states have laws that prohibit or place operational restrictions on ASE, and federal guidelines for ASE are outdated and not well known among ASE program administrators. Point-to-point enforcement, which is based on the average speed of a vehicle between two points, can be used on roadway segments

---

[17] National Transportation Safety Board, *Reducing Speeding-Related Crashes Involving Passenger Vehicles*, (Washington, DC: NTSB, 2018).

many miles long. This type of ASE has had recent success in other countries, but it is not currently used in the United States. We recommend that state and local agencies use ASE and that the FHWA work with NHTSA to assess the effectiveness of point-to-point enforcement in the United States.

In addition to enforcement efforts to address speeding, there needs to be increased leadership and attention for this at the national level. Current federal-aid programs do not ensure that states fund speed management activities at a level commensurate with the national impact of speeding on fatalities and injuries. Also, unlike other traffic safety issues with a similar impact (such as alcohol-impaired driving) there are no nationwide programs to increase public awareness of the risks of speeding. Although the USDOT has established a multi-agency team to coordinate speeding-related work throughout the department, this team's work plan does not include means to ensure that the planned actions are completed in a timely manner.

National, state, and local traffic safety stakeholders have repeatedly highlighted that—unlike other crash factors such as alcohol impairment or unbelted occupants—speeding has few negative social consequences associated with it. Surveys show drivers generally disapprove of speeding. However, most are complacent about the risks involved and speeding is a common behavior. Safety stakeholders told NTSB that because the dangers of speeding are not well-publicized, drivers underappreciate the risks of speeding in terms of crash causation. Stakeholders also expressed the belief that, to change public perceptions of speeding, a coordinated effort among safety advocacy groups, with strong leadership from the federal government, is needed. The lack of a national traffic safety campaign was cited as a key issue hindering the effective implementation of speeding prevention programs.

NHTSA, through its Traffic Safety Marketing (TSM) group, provides marketing materials and advice for states to use in developing traffic safety campaigns It also coordinates national traffic safety events. Our study found that none of the traffic safety events that NHTSA sponsored in 2016 addressed speeding. TSM does make available marketing materials that state and local agencies can use in their own campaigns. However, in the absence of a national speeding campaign, there is incomplete participation among states and little consistency among the individual state campaigns.

We concluded that traffic safety campaigns that include highly publicized, increased enforcement can be an effective speeding countermeasure. This led us to recommend that NHTSA collaborate with other traffic safety stakeholders to develop and implement an ongoing program to increase public awareness of speeding as a national traffic safety issue. The program should include, but not be limited to, initiating an annual enforcement mobilization directed at speeding drivers.

Another way to increase public awareness of speeding as a traffic safety issue is by providing states with financial incentives to be more engaged in addressing speeding. Highway Safety Program grants are allocated based on the population and road miles in each state, and these funds can be spent on any of 10 different focus areas (which includes speeding) according to a state's Highway Safety Plan. In contrast, National Priority Safety Programs funds are directed toward seven different priority areas, with the funding level for each priority area (rather than the overall total) established by Congress. Each priority area has specific eligibility requirements that incentivize states to conduct particular traffic safety activities. Speeding is not one of the seven priority areas.

The Highway Safety Program allows states significant leeway to spend funds according to their particular traffic safety priorities, including speeding; but it does not provide a means to encourage states to focus on national priorities. In contrast, National Priority Safety Program grants are specifically designed to encourage states to focus additional traffic safety efforts in areas of national importance. However, these funds currently cannot be used for speed management. Thus, we concluded that current federal-aid programs do not require or incentivize states to fund speed management activities at a level commensurate with the national impact of speeding on fatalities and injuries and recommended that NHTSA establish a program to incentivize state and local speed management activities.

In the study, we also recommended completion of all actions in the USDOT 2014 Speed Management Program Plan, FHWA assess of the effectiveness of point-to-point speed enforcement in the U.S., incentivizing passenger vehicle manufacturers and consumers to adopt intelligent speed adaptation systems, including speed limiters, and increasing the adoption of speeding-related Model Minimum Uniform Crash Criteria Guideline data elements and improving consistency in law enforcement reporting of speeding-related crashes.

End Alcohol and Other Drug Impairment in Transportation

The issue area of alcohol and other drug impairment in transportation has been on every Most Wanted List we have published since 1990, and we have made hundreds of recommendations to address this issue. Impairment in transportation continues to be a public health concern, with more than 10,000 highway fatalities each year in the United States involving alcohol-impaired drivers. Impairment by over the counter medications, prescription drugs, synthetic drugs, and illicit substances is also a rising concern.

We have recommended a comprehensive approach to address substance-impaired driving to prevent crashes, reduce injuries, and save lives. When it comes to alcohol use, research shows that impairment begins before a person's blood alcohol concentration (BAC) level reaches 0.08 percent, the current illegal per se limit in every state except Utah, which was the first state to enact 0.05 BAC law in 2017. In fact, by the time BAC reaches 0.08, the risk of a fatal crash has more than doubled.[18]

---

[18] Compton, R.P., R.D. Blomberg, H. Moskowitz, M. Burns, R.C. Peck, and D. Fiorentino. 2002. "Crash Risk of Alcohol-Impaired Driving." *Alcohol, Drugs and Traffic Safety—T2002. Proceedings of the 16th International Conference on Alcohol, Drugs and Traffic Safety (August 4–9, 2002)*. Montreal, Canada:

We have recommended that states lower the per se BAC threshold to 0.05 percent or lower. Further, we have recommended that NHTSA seek legislative authority to award incentive grants for states to establish a per se BAC limit of 0.05 or lower for all drivers not already required to adhere to lower BAC limits.[19] To further deter impaired driving, we have also recommended high-visibility enforcement of impaired driving laws using passive alcohol-sensing technology, as well as encouraged the development of technology that will enable vehicles to detect driver impairment, like the Driver Alcohol Detection System for Safety[20]. We have also made recommendations to reduce recidivism by driving while intoxicated (DWI) offenders. Recommended strategies include requiring ignition interlocks for all convicted DWI offenders and making special efforts to target repeat offenders.[21]

In the United States, ignition interlocks have historically been viewed as a sanction for repeat or high-BAC offenders; however, in recent years, the movement has been toward mandating ignition interlocks for all DWI offenders, including first-time offenders. Currently 32 states plus the District of Columbia have all-offender ignition interlock laws.

Research evaluation of ignition interlock programs over the last two decades has found that ignition interlock devices are effective in reducing recidivism among DWI offenders, sometimes by as much as 62 to 75 percent. One study examined the effectiveness of laws that require alcohol interlock installations for first-time offenders as well as repeat or high-BAC offenders; it found an additional benefit in reducing repeat DWI offenses.[22] Another study estimated 1,100 deaths could have been prevented in 1 year had interlock devices been required for drivers with recent DUI convictions.[23]

Based on the lack of significant progress in reducing alcohol-impaired driving fatalities over the last two decades, it is clear that more can be done to prevent these tragedies. The evidence shows that ignition interlock technology can—and should— be embraced in this battle.

Drugs other than, or in combination with, alcohol also pose an ongoing, increasing threat to highway safety. On March 29, 2017, near Concan, Texas, a pickup truck crossed into the opposite travel lane and collided with a mediumsize bus, killing the bus driver and 12 passengers. We determined that the probable cause of the crash was the failure of the pickup truck driver to control his vehicle due to impairment stemming from his use of

---

International Council on Alcohol, Drugs and Traffic Safety. Blomberg, Richard D., Raymond C. Peck, Herbert Moskowitz, Marcelline Burns, and Dary Fiorentino. 2005. *Crash Risk of Alcohol Involved Driving: A Case-Control Study*. Stamford, CT: Dunlap and Associates, Inc.

[19] National Transportation Safety Board, Safety Recommendation H-13-001.
[20] National Transportation Safety Board, Safety Recommendation H-12-048.
[21] National Transportation Safety Board, *Reaching Zero: Actions to Eliminate Alcohol-Impaired Driving*, Rpt. No. SR-13/01 (Washington, DC: NTSB, 2013).
[22] A. T. McCartt and others, Washington State's Alcohol Ignition Interlock Law: Effects on Re- cidivism Among First DUI Offenders, (Arlington, VA: Insurance Institute for Highway Safety, 2012).
[23] A. K. Lund and others, "Contribution of Alcohol-Impaired Driving to Motor Vehicle Crash Deaths in 2005," *8th Ignition Interlock Symposium, Seattle, Washington* (2007).

marijuana in combination with misuse of a prescribed medication.[24] As part of this investigation, we found that law enforcement officers need advanced training to identify the signs and symptoms of impairment as well as additional tools, such as roadside drug screening devices, in order to better detect drivers operating under the influence of drugs. Oral fluid drug screening devices can improve the ability of law enforcement officers to detect drug-impaired drivers. We recommended that NHTSA develop and disseminate best practices, identify model specifications, and create a conforming products list for oral fluid drug screening devices. We also urged NHTSA to evaluate best practices and countermeasures found to be the most effective in reducing fatalities, injuries, and crashes involving drug-impaired drivers and provide additional guidance to the states on drug-impaired driving.[25]

Eliminate Distractions

Drivers and operators in all modes of transportation must keep their hands, eyes, and minds focused on operating their vehicles. According to NHTSA, distraction was reported to be involved in almost 3,200 highway fatalities, or 8.6 percent of all fatalities in 2017.[26]

On August 5, 2010, in an active work zone in Gray Summit, Missouri, a truck-tractor was struck in the rear by a pickup truck, which was then struck in the rear by a school bus carrying 23 passengers. The school bus was then struck by another school bus carrying 31 passengers. The driver of the pickup and one passenger seated in the rear of the lead school bus were killed. A total of 35 passengers from both buses, the two bus drivers, and the driver of the truck-tractor sustained injuries ranging from minor to serious. We determined that the probable cause of the initial collision was the pickup driver's distraction, likely due to his ongoing text messaging conversation. As a result of this investigation, we recommended that the 50 states and the District of Columbia ban the nonemergency use of portable electronic devices (other than those designed to support the driving task) for all drivers, and to use high-visibility enforcement and targeted communication campaigns.[27] Currently, 16 states ban hand-held use and new laws are being considered in many other states this year. In the seven years since we made these recommendations, we continue to encounter crashes where use of personal electronic devices played a part. Real change will require a three-pronged approach that includes strict laws, proper education, and effective enforcement.

---

[24] National Transportation Safety Board, *Pickup Truck Centerline Crossover Collision with Me- dium-Size Bus on US Highway 83, Concan, Texas, March 29, 2017*, Rpt. No. HAR-18/02 (Washington, DC: NTSB, 2018).
[25] National Transportation Safety Board, Safety Recommendation H-18-056 and H-18-057.
[26] National Highway Traffic Safety Administration, *Traffic Safety Facts, 2017 Fatal Motor Vehicle Crashes: Overview* (Washington, DC: US Department of Transportation, NHTSA, 2017). DOT HS 812 603, p. 5.
[27] National Transportation Safety Board, *Multivehicle Collision, Interstate 44 Eastbound, Gray Summit, Missouri, August 5, 2010*, Rpt. No. HAR-11/03 (Washington, DC: NTSB, 2011).

Strengthen Occupant Protection

We have investigated many crashes in which improved occupant protection systems, such as seat belts, child restraints, and other vehicle design features, could have reduced injuries and saved lives. Recent investigations have highlighted the importance of proper use of the safety equipment, effective design, and readily accessible and identifiable evacuation routes on larger passenger vehicles, such as limousines, school buses, motor coaches, and other commercial vehicles.

Seat belts are the best defense against motor vehicle injuries and fatalities because they protect vehicle occupants from the extreme forces experienced during crashes. Unbelted vehicle occupants frequently injure other occupants, and unbelted drivers are less likely than belted drivers to be able to control their vehicles. In addition, seat belts prevent occupant ejections. In 2016, only 1 percent of vehicle occupants using seat belts were ejected, while 29 percent of unbelted vehicle occupants were ejected. Among those occupants completely ejected from their passenger vehicles, 81 percent were killed. NHTSA estimates that seat belts saved the lives of nearly 15,000 motor vehicle occupants age 5 and older in 2016, nationwide. Further, had all passenger vehicle occupants age 5 and older used seat belts in 2016 an additional 2,456 lives could have been saved. From 1975 through 2015, seat belts saved more than 344,000 lives nationwide.

Since 1995, we have recommended that states enact legislation providing for the primary enforcement of seat belt laws, which would allow law enforcement officers to stop a vehicle solely because occupants are not wearing seat belts. Currently, 34 states and the District of Columbia authorize primary enforcement of their seat belt laws, but only 29 states apply the law to all passenger seating positions. In 2015, we recommended that states enact legislation for primary enforcement of a mandatory seat belt use law for all vehicle seating positions equipped with a passenger restraint system.[28] This recommendation covers all motor vehicles, including buses. Primary enforcement of mandatory seat belt use laws remains the best way to raise and maintain high seat belt use rates. States that have enacted primary enforcement seat belt laws have historically experienced increases in seat belt use rates between 5 and 18 percentage points. The increased use is based on the realization by drivers that they may be stopped for violating the seat belt law.[29]

We have a long history of investigating school bus crashes. We have found compartmentalization to be effective in frontal collisions, but have also identified the limitations of passenger seats with no belts or lap belt only restraints. Modern school bus seat technology has overcome previous capacity issues, and the installation and proper use of passenger seat belts, particularly lap/shoulder belts, has made school buses safer in severe side impacts and rollovers. On November 21, 2016, six students died, and more

---

[28] National Transportation Safety Board, Safety Recommendation H-15-042.
[29]. Centers for Disease Control and Prevention, *Primary Enforcement of Seat Belt Laws*, https://www.cdc.gov/motorvehiclesafety/calculator/factsheet/seatbelt.html

than 20 others were injured in Chattanooga, Tennessee, when a Hamilton County Department of Education school bus struck a utility pole, rolled onto its right side, and collided with a tree. Contributing to the severity of the crash was the lack of passenger lap/shoulder belts on the bus.[30] In a special investigation report we developed following this crash, we recommended that jurisdictions which do not yet require passenger belts in large school buses enact legislation to require that all new large school buses be equipped with passenger lap/shoulder belts for all passenger seating positions.[31] The report also focused on the benefits of electronic stability control (ESC) and automatic emergency braking (AEB) in improving driver and vehicle safety.[32]

We have also made recommendations to NHTSA regarding front, side, and rear underride protections for tractor-trailer and single unit trucks to reduce underride and injuries to passenger vehicle occupants. Specifically, as a result of our safety investigations, we have recommended that NHTSA establish performance standards for front, side, and underride protection systems for single-unit trucks with gross vehicle weight ratings over 10,000 pounds, and to require such systems on all such newly manufactured trucks.[33] Each of these recommendations are currently classified "Open-Unacceptable Response." We have also recommended that NHTSA require side and rear underride systems for newly manufactured trailers with gross vehicle weight ratings over 10,000 pounds.[34] Each of these recommendations is currently classified "Open-Acceptable Response."

Increase Implementation of Collision Avoidance Technologies

More than 90 percent of crashes on United States roadways can be attributed to driver error.[35] For more than two decades, we have been advocating implementation of various technologies to help reduce driver error. Vehicle-based collision avoidance technologies, such as forward collision warning (FCW) and autonomous emergency braking (AEB) systems, are important for avoiding or mitigating the impact of rear end crashes, which represent nearly half of all two-vehicle crashes. Other driver-assist and collision avoidance technologies, such as adaptive cruise control, advance lighting, blind spot detection, and lane departure warning systems can aid drivers and help reduce the occurrence of other types of crashes. These technologies improve visibility, help maintain safe distance between vehicles, alert drivers to impending hazards and potential crashes, or automatically brake to mitigate the consequence of a crash.

---

[30]. National Transportation Safety Board, Selective Issues in School Bus Transportation Safety: Crashes in Baltimore, Maryland, and Chattanooga, Tennessee, Rpt. No. SIR-18/02 (Washington, DC: NTSB, 2018).

[31] National Transportation Safety Board, Safety Recommendations H-18-009 and H-18-010

[32]. The report concluded that the technology could have assisted the driver in maintaining ve- hicle control and mitigated the severity of the crash by reducing the speed of the vehicle.

[33]. National Transportation Safety Board, Safety Recommendations H-10-012, H-10-013, H-13- 013, H-13-014, H-13-015, and H-13-016.

[34]. National Transportation Safety Board, Safety Recommendations H-14-002 and H-14-004.

[35]. National Highway Traffic Safety Administration, Critical Reasons for Crashes Investigated in the National Motor Vehicle Crash Causation Survey. February 2015, (DOT HS 812 115).

In 2015, we issued a special investigation report regarding the use of forward collision avoidance systems to prevent and mitigate rear-end crashes. The report was based on the examination of current research into the effectiveness of collision avoidance systems and investigations of nine crashes—that resulted in 28 fatalities and injuries to 90 vehicle occupants—involving passenger or commercial vehicles striking the rear of another vehicle. As part of this report, we recommended that passenger and commercial vehicle manufacturers install FCW and AEB as standard equipment, and, in order to incentivize manufacturers, that NHTSA expand the New Car Assessment Program (NCAP) to include ratings for various collision avoidance technologies.[36] Most recently, on the night of January 19, 2016, a motorcoach occupied by a driver and 21 passengers collided with an unmarked crash attenuator and concrete barrier on a highway in San Jose, California, during low visibility conditions. Two passengers were ejected and died, and the driver and 13 passengers were injured. Upon later testing, we determined that had the bus been equipped with a collision avoidance system, the system could have detected the crash attenuator and alerted the driver to the hazard to mitigate or prevent the crash.[37]

Reduce Fatigue-Related Accidents

On March 20, 2016, a passenger car, driven by an 18-year-old and carrying three passengers ranging in age from 17 to 19, crossed a median and collided with a truck-tractor in combination with a semitrailer in Robstown, Texas. The three teenage passengers were killed. We determined the probable cause of this crash was the car driver's loss of control due to fatigue-induced inattention.[38]

NHTSA reported that, in 2015, more than 72,000 police-reported crashes involved drowsy driving, and those crashes resulted in 41,000 injuries and 846 deaths. However, NHTSA has acknowledged that these numbers likely are underestimated.[39] Other research conducted by the AAA Foundation for Traffic Safety estimated that more than 6,000 people are killed in drowsy-driving related crashes each year.[40]

We have issued more than 200 safety recommendations addressing fatigue-related problems across all modes of transportation. Tackling the problem of fatigue in highway transportation requires a comprehensive approach focused on research, education, training, technology, sleep disorder treatment, regulations, and on- and off- duty scheduling policies and practices. Some of our earliest recommendations called for research to better understand the problem of fatigue in transportation, and over the past

---

[36] National Transportation Safety Board, *The Use of Forward Collision Avoidance Systems to Prevent and Mitigate Rear-End Crashes*, Rpt. No. SIR-15/01 (Washington, DC: NTSB, 2015).
[37]. National Transportation Safety Board, *Motorcoach Collision With Crash Attenuator in Gore Area, US Highway 101*, Rpt. No. HAR-17/01 (Washington, DC: NTSB, 2017).
[38] National Transportation Safety Board, *Passenger Vehicle Median Crossover Crash, US Highway 77, Robstown, Texas, March 20, 2016*, Rpt. No. HAB-16/09 (Washington, DC: NTSB, 2016).
[39] National Highway Traffic Safety Administration, Asleep at the Wheel: A National Compen- dium of Efforts to Eliminate Drowsy Driving. March 2017, DOT HS 812 352.
[40] AAA Foundation for Traffic Safety, *Prevalence of Motor Vehicle Crashes Involving Drowsy Drivers*, United States, 2009-2013, November 2014.

three decades, several studies have been done. But research only goes so far; we must now implement what we have learned.

Other Highway Safety Issues

Pedestrian Safety

Until 2010, the number of pedestrians killed in highway crashes decreased for 35 years, but then reversed course. In 2017, the number of pedestrians who died in traffic crashes was 5,977, an increase of more than 45 percent since 2009.[41] Pedestrian deaths in recent years account for 16 percent (or almost one in six) of all highway fatalities.

In May 2016, we hosted a pedestrian safety forum, bringing together federal and state officials and experts to discuss key aspects of the issue.[42] Additionally, between April and November 2016, we worked with local law enforcement partners to initiate 15 investigations into fatal pedestrian crashes. The investigative work on these crashes illustrated a variety of pedestrian safety issues. This work culminated in the adoption last September of our Special Investigation Report: Pedestrian Safety that included the completed investigations, a review of the literature, and information about promising countermeasures.[43]

The report found that vehicle-based countermeasures, such as improved headlights, vehicle designs that reduce injuries to pedestrians, and collision avoidance systems would improve pedestrian safety. We recommended that NHTSA revise Federal Motor Vehicle Safety Standard 108 to improve vehicle lighting, develop performance test criteria for manufacturers to use in evaluating the extent to which automated pedestrian safety systems will mitigate pedestrian injuries, and incorporate those systems into the New Car Assessment Program.

It also found that effective street designs for pedestrian safety are highly context-dependent and best managed by local interests. However, local officials would benefit from having improved resources, tools and funding support to develop and implement those plans. We recommended that FHWA expand its support of state and local safety projects beyond its current focus cities.

Additionally, the study addressed limitations in the data available to decision makers who are working to reduce pedestrian crashes. Planners need localized pedestrian data to support the decision-making process. However, the most complete set of pedestrian crash data is more than two decades old. Thus, we recommended that NHTSA and the Centers for Disease Control work together to develop a detailed pedestrian crash data set

---

[41] National Highway Traffic Safety Administration, Traffic Safety Facts: Pedestrians. March 2019. (DOT HS 812 681).

[42] National Transportation Safety Board, *Forum: Pedestrian Safety*, (Washington, DC: National Transportation Safety Board, 2016).

[43] National Transportation Safety Board, *Pedestrian Safety*, SIR-18/03 (Washington, DC: 2018).

combining highway crash data and injury health data with the goal of producing a national database of pedestrian injuries and fatalities. Further, we urged NHTSA to develop a detailed pedestrian crash data set that represents the current, complete range of crash types and that can be used for local and state analysis. Finally, we recommended that FHWA develop definitions and methods for collecting pedestrian exposure data.

Motorcycle Safety

We are concerned about the growing number of motorcyclists killed or injured in motorcycle crashes. In 2016, more than 5,000 motorcyclists were killed nationwide, or about 14 motorcyclists per day. The number of motorcycle crash fatalities has more than doubled over the last two decades. According to NHTSA, motorcycles are the most dangerous form of motor vehicle transportation. Motorcycles represent only 3 percent of the vehicles on our roads, but motorcyclists accounted for 14 percent of all traffic fatalities.[44]

These concerns led us to complete a safety report in October 2018, which assessed select risk factors associated with the causes of motorcycle crashes in the United States and made recommendations for improving motorcycle crash prevention.[45] The data analyzed in this report was provided by FHWA, from its 2016 Motorcycle Crash Causation Study (MCCS). The MCCS represents the most recent data available for studying motorcycle crashes in the United States since the USDOT published its comprehensive Motorcycle Accident Cause Factors and Identification of Countermeasures report in 1981.

We concluded many high-risk traffic situations between motorcycles and other motor vehicles could be prevented if vehicle drivers were better able to detect and anticipate the presence of a motorcycle when entering or crossing a road, making a turn or changing lanes. We also determined stability control systems on motorcycles could reduce single-vehicle crashes involving loss of control which would reduce the prevalence of motorcyclists killed or injured by impacts with fixed roadside objects.

There is a need for enhanced braking and stability control systems on motorcycles. More than a third of the crashes analyzed involved a loss of control that contributed to crash causation. More widespread availability of enhanced braking and stability control systems on motorcycles could improve safety by enhancing the effectiveness of braking, collision avoidance performance, and stability control for both novice and experienced riders.

In 2007, following a 2-day public forum on motorcycle safety at which it heard from a group of panelists representative of all important aspects of motorcycle safety, NTSB

---

[44] National Highway Traffic Safety Administration, Traffic Safety Facts: Motorcycles, 2016 Data, February 2018, DOT HS 812 492.

[45] National Transportation Safety Board, *Select Risk Factors Associated with Causes of Motor- cycle Crashes*, SR-18/01 (Washington, DC: 2018).

recommended that states require all motorcycle riders to wear a helmet compliant with U.S. Federal Motor Vehicle Safety Standard (FMVSS) 218.[46] The use of a compliant safety helmet is the single critical factor in the prevention and reduction of head injury. The effectiveness of appropriately designed motorcycle helmets in preventing and mitigating head injury is unequivocal. NHTSA estimates that helmets are 37 percent effective in preventing fatal injuries to motorcycle riders and 41 percent effective for motorcycle passengers.

Universal helmet laws do increase helmet use. Numerous state studies have shown that helmet law repeals led to reduced usage and increased fatalities. Likewise, enactment of a universal helmet law leads to increased usage and reduced motorcycle deaths. Currently, 19 states, plus the District of Columbia, have a universal helmet law. The remarkable effectiveness of universal helmet laws in preventing death and disability among motorcyclists is a powerful argument for the adoption of such laws, especially in light of the more than 5,200 motorcyclists who were killed on our highways in 2016. For more than 70 years, research has shown that helmets protect motorcyclists and passengers from death and serious injury.

Bicycle Safety

In 2017, almost 800 bicyclists were killed in the United States, representing 2 percent of all traffic deaths. As bicycling becomes more popular as a form of active transportation, especially in urban areas, it is timely and important to ensure and improve roadway safety for bicyclists. We have begun a safety study to identify proven countermeasures that can improve bicyclist safety. In this study, we are exploring improved bicycle infrastructure, advanced vehicle-based technologies, and approaches to increase bicycle helmet use. We anticipate that the study will be published late this year.

Automated Vehicles

The use of automated vehicle (AV) controls and systems is accelerating rapidly in all modes of transportation. We have monitored AV development and we have a long history of calling for systems to assist the operator by providing an increased margin of safety, such as automatic emergency braking. AVs that incorporate systems proven to enhance safety hold enormous potential benefits for safety.

In 2018, the USDOT updated a federal AV policy focused on highly automated vehicles. Late last year, in response to a call for comments, we commented that NHTSA's proposed AV policies are notable for the voluntary approach to manufacturers' safety selfassessments, testing and validation of system safety, and AV reporting requirements. We applauded NHTSA's efforts to work with industry. However, its general and voluntary guidance of emerging and evolutionary technological

---

[46] National Transportation Safety Board, Safety Recommendations H-07-37, H-07-38, and H- 07-39.

advancements shows a willingness to let manufacturers and operational entities define safety. The most recent AV guidance (AV 3.0) is only focused on SAE Level 3 and above while not providing guidance for Level 2 vehicles.

The USDOT has an important responsibility to ensure the safe development and deployment of AV technologies at all levels of automation, and this safety should not be voluntary. However, the policy thus far has carried an overarching message of promoting AV development, but a clear connection to minimum safety requirements has not yet been crafted. NHTSA can and should provide this required safety leadership. We urge NHTSA to lead with detailed guidance and specific standards and requirements.

Conclusion

Thank you for the opportunity to testify before you today. While my testimony has discussed many safety concerns, these are only some of the safety improvements we have identified as needed to prevent crashes, reduce injuries, and save lives. A list of safety recommendations we have made for highway safety that are reflected in our MWL is included with this testimony. I look forward to responding to your questions.

APPENDIX: 2019–2020 MOST WANTED LIST RECOMMENDATIONS FOR HIGHWAY SAFETY

Implement A Comprehensive Strategy To Reduce Speeding-Related Crashes		
Recommendation #	Overall Status	Subject
H-05-020	Open— Acceptable Response	TO THE TEXAS DEPARTMENT OF TRANSPORTATION: Install variable speed limit signs or implement alternate countermeasures at locations where wet weather can produce stopping distances that exceed the available sight distance.
H-12-020	Open— Unacceptable Response	TO THE NATIONAL HIGHWAY TRAFFIC SAFETY ADMINISTRATION: Develop performance standards for advanced speed-limiting technology, such as variable speed limiters and intelligent speed adaptation devices, for heavy vehicles, including trucks, buses, and motorcoaches.
H-12-021	Open— Unacceptable Response	TO THE NATIONAL HIGHWAY TRAFFIC SAFETY ADMINISTRATION: After establishing performance standards for advanced speed- limiting technology for heavy commercial vehicles, require that all newly manufactured heavy vehicles be equipped with such devices.
H-17-018	Open— Acceptable Response	TO THE UNITED STATES DEPARTMENT OF TRANSPORTATION: Complete the actions called for in your 2014 Speed Management Program Plan, and periodically publish status reports on the progress you have made.

Implement A Comprehensive Strategy To Reduce Speeding-Related Crashes		
Recommendation #	Overall Status	Subject
H-17-019	Open— Acceptable Response	TO THE NATIONAL HIGHWAY TRAFFIC SAFETY ADMINISTRATION: Identify speeding-related performance measures to be used by local law enforcement agencies, including, but not limited to, the numbers and locations of speeding- related crashes of different injury severity levels, speeding citations, and warnings, and establish a consistent method for evaluating data-driven, high-visibility enforcement programs to reduce speeding. Disseminate the performance measures and evaluation method to local law enforcement agencies.
H-17-020	Open— Acceptable Response	TO THE NATIONAL HIGHWAY TRAFFIC SAFETY ADMINISTRATION: Identify best practices for communicating with law enforcement officers and the public about the effectiveness of data-driven, high-visibility enforcement programs to reduce speeding, and disseminate the best practices to local law enforcement agencies.
H-17-021	Open— Acceptable Response	TO THE NATIONAL HIGHWAY TRAFFIC SAFETY ADMINISTRATION: Work with the Governors Highway Safety Association, the International Association of Chiefs of Police, and the National Sheriffs' Association to develop and implement a program to increase the adoption of speeding-related Model Minimum Uniform Crash Criteria Guideline data elements and improve consistency in law enforcement reporting of speeding-related crashes.
H-17-022	Open— Acceptable Response	TO THE NATIONAL HIGHWAY TRAFFIC SAFETY ADMINISTRATION: Work with the Federal Highway Administration to update the Speed Enforcement Camera Systems Operational Guidelines to reflect the latest automated speed enforcement (ASE) technologies and operating practices, and promote the updated guidelines among ASE program administrators.
H-17-023	Open— Acceptable Alternate Response	TO THE NATIONAL HIGHWAY TRAFFIC SAFETY ADMINISTRATION: Work with the Federal Highway Administration to assess the effectiveness of point-to-point speed enforcement in the United States and, based on the results of that assessment, update the Speed Enforcement Camera Systems Operational Guidelines, as appropriate.
H-17-024	Open— Acceptable Alternate Response	TO THE NATIONAL HIGHWAY TRAFFIC SAFETY ADMINISTRATION: Incentivize passenger vehicle manufacturers and consumers to adopt intelligent speed adaptation (ISA) systems by, for example, including ISA in the New Car Assessment Program.
H-17-025	Open— Acceptable Alternate Response	TO THE NATIONAL HIGHWAY TRAFFIC SAFETY ADMINISTRATION: Collaborate with other traffic safety stakeholders to develop and implement an ongoing program to increase public awareness of speeding as a national traffic safety issue. The program should include, but not be limited to, initiating an annual enforcement mobilization directed at speeding drivers.

Appendix. (Continued)

Implement A Comprehensive Strategy To Reduce Speeding-Related Crashes		
Recommendation #	Overall Status	Subject
H-17-026	Open— Acceptable Response	TO THE NATIONAL HIGHWAY TRAFFIC SAFETY ADMINISTRATION: Establish a program to incentivize state and local speed management activities.
H-17-027	Open— Acceptable Response	TO THE FEDERAL HIGHWAY ADMINISTRATION: Revise Section 2B.13 of the Manual on Uniform Traffic Control Devices so that the factors currently listed as optional for all engineering studies are required, require that an expert system such as USLIMITS2 be used as a validation tool, and remove the guidance that speed limits in speed zones should be within 5 mph of the 85th percentile speed.
H-17-028	Open— Acceptable Response	TO THE FEDERAL HIGHWAY ADMINISTRATION: Revise Section 2B.13 of the Manual on Uniform Traffic Control Devices to, at a minimum, incorporate the safe system approach for urban roads to strengthen protection for vulnerable road users.
H-17-029	Open— Acceptable Response	TO THE FEDERAL HIGHWAY ADMINISTRATION: Work with the National Highway Traffic Safety Administration to update the Speed Enforcement Camera Systems Operational Guidelines to reflect the latest automated speed enforcement (ASE) technologies and operating practices, and promote the updated guidelines among ASE program administrators.
H-17-030	Open— Acceptable Response	TO THE FEDERAL HIGHWAY ADMINISTRATION: Work with the National Highway Traffic Safety Administration to assess the effectiveness of point-to-point speed enforcement in the United States and, based on the results of that assessment, update the Speed Enforcement Camera Systems Operational Guidelines, as appropriate.
H-17-031	Open— Await Response	TO THE SEVEN STATES PROHIBITING AUTOMATED SPEED ENFORCEMENT (MAINE, MISSISSIPPI, NEW HAMPSHIRE, NEW JERSEY, TEXAS, WEST VIRGINIA, AND WISCONSIN): Amend current laws to authorize state and local agencies to use automated speed enforcement.
H-17-032	Open— Await Response	TO THE TWENTY EIGHT STATES WITHOUT AUTOMATED SPEED ENFORCEMENT LAWS (ALABAMA, ALASKA, CALIFORNIA, CONNECTICUT, DELAWARE, FLORIDA, GEORGIA, HAWAII, IDAHO, INDIANA, IOWA, KANSAS, KENTUCKY, MASSACHUSETTS, MICHIGAN, MINNESOTA, MISSOURI,.
H-17-033	Open— Await Response	TO THE 15 STATES WITH AUTOMATED SPEED ENFORCEMENT RESTRICTIONS (ARIZONA, ARKANSAS, COLORADO, ILLINOIS, LOUISIANA, MARYLAND, NEVADA, NEW YORK, OHIO, OREGON, RHODE ISLAND, SOUTH CAROLINA, TENNESSEE, UTAH, AND WASHINGTON): Amend current laws to remove operational and location restrictions on the use of automated speed enforcement, except where such restrictions are necessary to align with best practices.

End Alcohol And Other Drug Impairment		
Recommendation #	Overall Status	Subject
H-17-034	Open—Acceptable Response	TO THE GOVERNORS HIGHWAY SAFETY ASSOCIATION: Work with the National Highway Traffic Safety Administration, the International Association of Chiefs of Police, and the National Sheriffs' Association to develop and implement a program to increase the adoption of speeding-related Model Minimum Uniform Crash Criteria Guideline data elements and improve consistency in law enforcement reporting of speeding-related crashes.
H-17-035	Open— Await Response	TO THE INTERNATIONAL ASSOCIATION OF CHIEFS OF POLICE: Work with the National Highway Traffic Safety Administration, the Governors Highway Safety Association, and the National Sheriffs' Association to develop and implement a program to increase the adoption of speeding-related Model Minimum Uniform Crash Criteria Guideline data elements and improve consistency in law enforcement reporting of speeding-related crashes.
H-17-036	Open—Acceptable Response	TO THE NATIONAL SHERIFFS' ASSOCIATION: Work with the National Highway Traffic Safety Administration, the Governors Highway Safety Association, and the International Association of Chiefs of Police to develop and implement a program to increase the adoption of speeding-related Model Minimum Uniform Crash Criteria Guideline data elements and improve consistency in law enforcement reporting of speeding-related crashes.
H-12-034	Open— Await Response	TO THE 45 STATES, THE COMMONWEALTH OF PUERTO RICO, AND THE DISTRICT OF COLUMBIA, WHICH HAVE LOW REPORTING RATES FOR BAC TESTING: Increase your collection, documentation, and reporting of blood alcohol concentration (BAC) test results by taking the following actions, as needed, to improve testing and reporting rates: (1) enact legislation, (2) issue regulations, and (3) improve procedures used by law enforcement agencies or testing facilities.
H-12-035	Open— Await Response	TO THE 45 STATES, THE COMMONWEALTH OF PUERTO RICO, AND THE DISTRICT OF COLUMBIA, WHICH HAVE LOW REPORTING RATES FOR BAC TESTING: Once the National Highway Traffic Safety Administration has developed the blood alcohol concentration (BAC) testing and reporting guidelines recommended in Safety Recommendation H-12-32, incorporate the guidelines into a statewide action plan to achieve BAC reporting rates of at least 80 percent of fatally injured drivers and at least 60 percent of drivers who survived fatal crashes.
H-12-036	Open— Await Response	TO THE 50 STATES, THE COMMONWEALTH OF PUERTO RICO, AND THE DISTRICT OF COLUMBIA: Require law enforcement agencies to collect place of last drink (POLD) data as part of any arrest or accident investigation involving an alcohol-impaired driver.
H-12-037	Open— Await Response	TO THE INTERNATIONAL ASSOCIATION OF CHIEFS OF POLICE AND THE NATIONAL SHERIFFS' ASSOCIATION: Inform your members of the value of collecting place of last drink (POLD) data as part of any arrest or accident investigation involving an alcohol-impaired driver.

Appendix. (Continued)

End Alcohol And Other Drug Impairment		
Recommendation #	Overall Status	Subject
H-12-043	Open—Unacceptable Response	TO THE NATIONAL HIGHWAY TRAFFIC SAFETY ADMINISTRATION: Work with the Automotive Coalition for Traffic Safety, Inc., to accelerate widespread implementation of Driver Alcohol Detection System for Safety (DADSS) technology by (1) defining usability testing that will guide driver interface design and (2) implementing a communication program that will direct driver education and promote public acceptance.
H-12-045	Open— Await Response	TO 33 STATES, THE COMMONWEALTH OF PUERTO RICO, AND THE DISTRICT OF COLUMBIA: Enact laws to require the use of alcohol ignition interlock devices for all individuals convicted of driving while intoxicated (DWI) offenses.
H-12-048	Open—Acceptable Response	TO THE AUTOMOTIVE COALITION FOR TRAFFIC SAFETY: Work with the National Highway Traffic Safety Administration to accelerate widespread implementation of Driver Alcohol Detection System for Safety (DADSS) technology by (1) defining usability testing that will guide driver interface design and (2) implementing a communication program that will direct driver education and promote public acceptance.
H-13-001	Open—Acceptable Response	TO THE NATIONAL HIGHWAY TRAFFIC SAFETY ADMINISTRATION: Seek legislative authority to award incentive grants for states to establish a per se blood alcohol concentration (BAC) limit of 0.05 or lower for all drivers who are not already required to adhere to lower BAC limits.
H-13-005	Open— Await Response	TO THE 50 U.S. STATES AND THE COMMONWEALTH OF PUERTO RICO AND THE DISTRICT OF COLUMBIA: Establish a per se blood alcohol concentration (BAC) limit of 0.05 or lower for all drivers who are not already required to adhere to lower BAC limits.
H-13-006	Open— Await Response	TO THE 50 STATES, THE COMMONWEALTH OF PUERTO RICO AND THE DISTRICT OF COLUMBIA: Include in your impaired driving prevention plan or highway safety plan provisions for conducting high-visibility enforcement of impaired driving laws using passive alcohol-sensing technology during law enforcement contacts, such as routine traffic stops, saturation patrols, sobriety checkpoints, and accident scene responses.
H-13-007	Open— Await Response	TO THE 50 STATES, THE COMMONWEALTH OF PUERTO RICO, AND THE DISTRICT OF COLUMBIA: Include in your impaired driving prevention plan or highway safety plan elements to target repeat offenders and reduce driving while intoxicated (DWI) recidivism; such elements should include measures to improve compliance with alcohol ignition interlock requirements; the plan should also provide a mechanism for regularly assessing the success of these efforts. (H-13-07) [This recommendation supersedes Safety Recommendation H-00-26.]

End Alcohol And Other Drug Impairment		
Recommendation #	Overall Status	Subject
H-13-008	Open— Await Response	TO THE 50 STATES, THE COM- MONWEALTH OF PUERTO RICO, AND THE DISTRICT OF COLUMBIA: Take the following steps to move toward zero deaths from impaired driving: (1) set specific and measurable targets for reducing impaired driving fatalities and injuries, (2) list these targets in your impaired driving prevention plan or highway safety plan, and (3) provide a mechanism for regularly assessing the success of implemented countermeasures and determining whether the targets have been met. (H-13-08)
H-13-009	Open— Await Response	TO THE 41 STATES THAT HAVE ADMINISTRATIVE LICENSE SUSPENSION OR REVOCATION LAWS AND THE DISTRICT OF COLUMBIA: Incorporate into your administrative license suspension or revocation laws a requirement that drivers arrested for driving while intoxicated (DWI) use an alcohol ignition interlock on their vehicle for a period of time before obtaining full license reinstatement. (H-13-09)
H-13-010	Open— Await Response	TO THE 10 STATES THAT DO NOT HAVE ADMINISTRATIVE LICENSE SUSPENSION OR REVOCATION LAWS AND THE COMMONWEALTH OF PUERTORICO: Establish administrative license suspension or revocation laws that require drivers arrested for driving while intoxicated (DWI) to use an alcohol ignition interlock on their vehicle for a period of time before obtaining full license reinstatement. (H-13-10)
H-15-038	Open— Acceptable Alternate Response	TO THE FEDERAL MOTOR CARRIER SAFETY ADMINISTRATION: Determine the prevalence of commercial motor vehicle driver use of impairing substances, particularly synthetic cannabinoids, and develop a plan to reduce the use of such substances.
H-15-039	Open— Unacceptable Response	TO THE FEDERAL MOTOR CARRIER SAFETY ADMINISTRATION: Work with motor carrier industry stakeholders to develop a plan to aid motor carriers in addressing commercial motor vehicle driver use of impairing substances, particularly those not covered under current drug-testing regulations such as by promoting best practices by carriers, expanding impairment detection training and authority, and developing performance-based methods of evaluation.
H-15-043	Open— Await Response	TO AMERICAN BUS ASSOCIATION, AMERICAN TRUCKING ASSOCIATIONS, COMMERCIAL VEHICLE SAFETY ALLIANCE, OWNER-OPERATOR INDEPENDENT DRIVERS ASSOCIATION, UNITED MOTORCOACH ASSOCIATION: Inform your members about the dangers of driver use of synthetic drugs and encourage them to take steps to prevent drivers from using these substances.
H-16-008	Open— Unacceptable Response	TO THE FEDERAL MOTOR CARRIER SAFETY ADMINISTRATION: Disseminate information to motor carriers about using hair testing as a method of detecting the use of controlled substances, under the appropriate circumstances.

Appendix. (Continued)

Eliminate Distractions		
Recommendation #	Overall Status	Subject
H-18-035	Open— Response Received	TO THE NATIONAL HIGHWAY TRAFFIC SAFETY ADMINISTRATION: Examine the influence of alcohol and other drug use on motorcycle rider crash risk compared to that of passenger vehicle drivers, and develop guidelines to assist states in implementing evidence-based strategies and counter measures to more effectively address substance-impaired motorcycle rider crashes.
H-18-056	Open— Await Response	TO THE NATIONAL HIGHWAY TRAFFIC SAFETY ADMINISTRATION: Develop and disseminate best practices, identify model specifications, and create a conforming products list for oral fluid drug screening devices.
H-18-057	Open— Await Response	TO THE NATIONAL TRAFFIC SAFETY ADMINISTRATION: Evaluate best practices and countermeasures found to be the most effective in reducing fatalities, injuries, and crashes involving drug-impaired drivers and provide additional guidance to the states on drug-impaired driving in Counter measures That Work: A Highway Safety Countermeasure Guide for State Highway Safety Offices.
H-18-060	Open— Await Response	TO THE STATE OF TEXAS: Conduct an executive-level review of your impaired driving program and implement data-driven strategies that result in a downward trend in the number of fatalities, injuries, and crashes involving alcohol- and other drug-impaired drivers.
H-18-061	Open— Await Response	TO THE TEXAS DEPARTMENT OF TRANSPORTATION: Promote the importance of attending drug-impaired driving enforcement training and increase training access to meet the demands of local and state law enforcement.
H-03-009	Open— Acceptable Response	TO 34 STATES: Add driver distraction codes, including codes for interactive wireless communication device use, to your traffic accident investigation forms.
H-06-029	Open— Await Response	TO 6 MOTORCOACH INDUSTRY, PUBLIC BUS, AND SCHOOL BUS ASSOCIATIONS AND 3 UNIONS: Develop formal policies prohibiting cellular telephone use by commercial driver's license holders with a passenger-carrying or school bus endorsement, while driving under the authority of that endorsement, except in emergencies.
H-11-039	Open— Await Response	TO THE 50 STATES AND THE DISTRICT OF COLUMBIA: (1) Ban the nonemergency use of portable electronic devices (other than those designed to support the driving task) for all drivers; (2) use the National Highway Traffic Safety Administration model of high visibility enforcement to support these bans; and (3) implement targeted communication campaigns to inform motorists of the new law and enforcement, and to warn them of the dangers associated with the nonemergency use of portable electronic devices while driving.

Eliminate Distractions

Recommendation #	Overall Status	Subject
H-11-047	Open— Await Response	TO CTIA THE WIRELESS ASSOCIATION AND THE CONSUMER ELECTRONICS ASSOCIATION: Encourage the development of technology features that disable the functions of portable electronic devices within reach of the driver when a vehicle is in motion; these technology features should include the ability to permit emergency use of the device while the vehicle is in motion and have the capability of identifying occupant seating position so as not to interfere with use of the device by passengers.
H-14-013	Open— Await Response	TO THE FIFTY STATES, THE DISTRICT OF COLUMBIA, AND THE COMMONWEALTH OF PUERTO RICO: Ban the nonemergency use by pilot/escort vehicle drivers of portable electronic devices (other than those designed to support the pilot/escort vehicle driving task), except to communicate hazard-related information to the escorted vehicle.

Strengthen Occupant Protection

H-11-036	Open— Unacceptable Response	TO THE NATIONAL HIGHWAY TRAFFIC SAFETY ADMINISTRATION: Modify Federal Motor Vehicle Safety Standard 217 to require that all emergency exits on school buses be easily opened and remain open during an emergency evacuation.
H-11-038	Open— Unacceptable Response	TO THE NATIONAL HIGHWAY TRAFFIC SAFETY ADMINISTRATION: To cover the interim period until Federal Motor Vehicle Safety Standard 217 is modified as specified in Safety Recommendations H-11-36 and -37, provide the states with guidance on how to minimize potential evacuation delays that could be caused by protruding latch mechanisms on emergency exit windows and by exit windows that require additional manual assistance to remain open during egress.
H-11-045	Open— Response Received	TO THE STATE OF MISSOURI: Revise your bus evacuation regulations to require that pupils traveling to an activity or on a field trip in a school bus or a school-chartered bus be instructed in safe riding practices and on the location and operation of emergency exits prior to starting the trip.
H-12-022	Open— Unacceptable Response	TO THE NATIONAL HIGHWAY TRAFFIC SAFETY ADMINISTRATION: Evaluate the effects of seat spacing and armrests as factors for potential occupant injury, and if safer spacing or armrest configurations are identified, develop and implement appropriate guidelines.
H-13-032	Open— Await Response	TO THE STATES OF CALIFORNIA, FLORIDA, LOUISIANA, NEW JERSEY, NEW YORK, AND TEXAS: Develop: (1) a handout for your school districts to distribute annually to students and parents about the importance of the proper use of all types of passenger seat belts on school buses, including the potential harm of not wearing a seat belt or wearing one but not adjusting it properly; and (2) training procedures for schools to follow during the twice yearly emergency drills to show students how to wear their seat belts properly.

Appendix. (Continued)

Strengthen Occupant Protection		
Recommendation #	Overall Status	Subject
H-13-033	Open— Await Response	TO THE STATES OF CALIFORNIA, FLORIDA, LOUISIANA, NEW JERSEY, NEW YORK, AND TEXAS: Upon publication of the National School Transportation Specifications and Procedures document, revise the handout and training procedures developed in Safety Recommendation H-13-32 to align with the national procedures as appropriate.
H-13-035	Open— Acceptable Response	TO THE NATIONAL ASSOCIATION OF STATE DIRECTORS OF PUPIL TRANSPORTATION SERVICES, NATIONAL ASSOCIATION FOR PUPIL TRANSPORTATION, NATIONAL SCHOOL TRANSPORTATION ASSOCIATION, SCHOOL BUS MANUFACTURERS TECHNICAL COUNCIL, AND NATIONAL SAFETY COUNCIL, SCHOOL TRANSPORTATION SECTION: Develop guidelines and include them in the next update of the National School Transportation Specifications and Procedures to assist schools in training bus drivers, students, and parents on the importance and proper use of school bus seat belts, including manual lap belts, adjustable lap and shoulder belts, and flexible seating systems.
H-13-036	Open— Acceptable Alternate Response	TO THE NATIONAL ASSOCIATION OF STATE DIRECTORS OF PUPIL TRANSPORTATION SERVICES, NATIONAL ASSOCIATION FOR PUPIL TRANSPORTATION, AND NATIONAL SCHOOL TRANSPORTATION ASSOCIATION: Provide your members with educational materials on lap and shoulder belts providing the highest level of protection for school bus passengers, and advise states or school districts to consider this added safety benefit when purchasing seat belt-equipped school buses.
H-13-037	Open— Acceptable Alternate Response	TO THE SCHOOL BUS MANUFACTURERS TECHNICAL COUNCIL: Develop a recommended practice for establishing and safeguarding the structural integrity of the entire school bus seating and restraint system, including the seat pan attachment to the seat frame, in severe crashes—in particular, those involving lateral impacts with vehicles of large mass.
H-15-010	Open— Acceptable Response	TO THE NATIONAL HIGHWAY TRAFFIC SAFETY ADMINISTRATION: Develop requirements addressing the minimum aisle width for safe evacuation from all buses, including those with moveable seats.
H-15-020	Open— Response Received	TO THE NATIONAL LIMOUSINE ASSOCIATION: Develop and distribute guidelines to your member operators urging them, during pretrip safety briefings, to (1) direct passengers to use seat belts where required by law and strongly encourage passengers to use seat belts where not required by law, and (2) encourage passengers to use properly adjusted head restraints.

Strengthen Occupant Protection		
Recommendation #	Overall Status	Subject
H-15-042	Open— Await Response	TO THE FIFTY STATES, DISTRICT OF COLUMBIA, AND PUERTO RICO: Enact legislation that provides for primary enforcement of a mandatory seat belt use law for all vehicle seating positions equipped with a passenger restraint system. (Safety Recommendation H-15-042 supersedes Safety Recommendation H-97-2)
H-17-001	Open— Await Response	TO MOTOR COACH INDUSTRIES INTERNATIONAL, INC.: Evaluate and, if appropriate, modify the driver and passenger floor struc-ture design on new motorcoaches to prevent driver seat separation during crashes.
H-17-008	Open— Await Response	TO THE AMERICAN BUS ASSOCIATION AND THE UNITED MOTORCOACH ASSOCIATION: Encourage member passenger-carrying companies to (1) establish procedures to ensure that the seat belts on all buses are regularly inspected to maintain their functionality and accessibility, and (2) provide pretrip safety briefings emphasizing the benefits of seat belt use.
H-17-012	Open— Acceptable Response	TO GREYHOUND LINES, INC.: Provide pretrip safety briefings at all stops prior to departure when taking on new passengers, which describe the use of the emergency exits and the benefits of wearing seat belts.
H-17-061	Open— Acceptable Response	TO THE FEDERAL MOTOR CARRIER SAFETY ADMINISTRATION: Work with SAE International and the National Highway Traffic Safety Administration to improve truck-tractor side-mounted fuel tank crashworthiness to prevent catastrophic tank ruptures and limit post collision fuel spillage, and develop and promulgate an updated standard.
H-17-062	Open— Acceptable Response	TO THE NATIONAL HIGHWAY TRAFFIC SAFETY ADMINISTRATION: Work with SAE International and the Federal Motor Carrier Safety Administration to improve truck-tractor side-mounted fuel tank crashworthiness to prevent catastrophic tank ruptures and limit post collision fuel spillage, and develop and promulgate an updated standard.
H-17-065	Open— Await Response	TO SAE INTERNATIONAL: Work with the Federal Motor Carrier Safety Administration and the National Highway Traffic Safety Administration to improve truck-trac- tor side-mounted fuel tank crash- orthiness to prevent catastrophic tank ruptures and limit post collision fuel spillage, and develop and promulgate an updated standard.
H-18-009	Open— Await Response	TO THE STATES OF FLORIDA, LOUISIANA, NEW JERSEY, AND NEW YORK: Amend your statutes to upgrade the seat belt requirement from lap belts to lap/shoulder belts for all passenger seating positions in new large school buses in accordance with Federal Motor Vehicle Safety Standard 222.

Appendix. (Continued)

Strengthen Occupant Protection		
Recommendation #	Overall Status	Subject
H-18-010	Open— Await Response	TO THE STATES OF ALABAMA, ALASKA, ARIZONA, COLORADO, CONNECTICUT, DELAWARE, GEORGIA, HAWAII, IDAHO, ILLINOIS, INDIANA, IOWA, KANSAS, MAINE, MARYLAND, MICHIGAN, MINNESOTA, MISSISSIPPI, MISSOURI, MONTANA, NEBRASKA, NEW HAMPSHIRE, NEW MEXICO, NORTH CAROLINA, NORTH DAKOTA, OHIO, OKLAHOMA, OREGON, RHODE ISLAND, SOUTH CAROLINA, SOUTH DAKOTA, TENNESSEE, UTAH, VERMONT, WASHINGTON, WEST VIRGINIA, WISCONSIN, AND WYOMING; THE COMMONWEALTHS OF KENTUCKY, MASSACHUSETTS, PENNSYLVANIA, AND VIRGINIA; THE DISTRICT OF COLUMBIA; AND THE TERRITORY OF PUERTO RICO: Enact legislation to require that all new large school buses be equipped with passenger lap/shoulder belts for all passenger seating positions in accordance with Federal Motor Vehicle Safety Standard 222.
H-18-058	Open— Await Response	TO THE NATIONAL TRAFFICS SAFETY ADMINISTRATION: Amend Federal Motor Vehicle Safety Standard 210 to increase the minimum anchorage spacing for individual seat belt assemblies, taking into account the dynamic testing of seat belt designs, seat belt fit, and vehicle configuration.
H-18-059	Open— Await Response	TO THE NATIONAL TRAFFIC SAFETY ADMINISTRATION: Amend Federal Motor Vehicle Safety Standard 208 to require lap/shoulder belts for each passenger seating position on all new buses with a gross vehicle weight rating of more than 10,000 pounds but not greater than 26,000 pounds.
H-18-062	Open— Await Response	TO MEDIUM-SIZE BUS MANUFAC-TURERS ARBOC SPECIALTY VEHICLES, LLC; COACH & EQUIPMENT MANUFACTURING CORPORATION; REV GROUP, INC.; DIAMOND COACH CORPORATION; FOREST RIVER, INC.; GIRARDIN BLUE BIRD; SVO GROUP, INC.; AND THOMAS BUILT BUSES: Install lap/shoulder belts in all seating positions as standard, rather than optional, equipment in all newly manufactured medium-size buses.
H-18-063	Open— Response Received	TO THE SEAT MANUFACTURERS FREEDMAN SEATING COMPANY AND HSM TRANSPORTATION SOLUTIONS: Supply seating systems equipped with lap/ shoulder belts as standard, rather than optional, equipment for medium-size buses.
H-96-014	Open— Acceptable Response	TO THE 50 STATES, THE 5 US TERRITORIES, AND THE DISTRICT OF COLUMBIA: Review existing laws and enact legislation, if needed, that would: ensure that children up to 8 years old are required by the state's mandatory child restraint use law to use child restraint systems and booster seats.

Strengthen Occupant Protection		
Recommendation #	Overall Status	Subject
H-99-009	Open—Unacceptable Response	TO THE NATIONAL HIGHWAY TRAFFIC SAFETY ADMINISTRATION: Revise the Federal Motor Vehicle Safety Standard 217, "Bus Window Retention and Release," to require that other than floor-level emergency exits can be easily opened and remain open during an emergency evacuation when a motorcoach is upright or at unusual attitudes.
H-99-049	Open—Unacceptable Response	TO THE NATIONAL HIGHWAY TRAFFIC SAFETY ADMINISTRATION: Expand your research on current advanced glazing to include its applicability to motor-coach occupant ejection prevention, and revise window glazing requirements for newly manufactured motorcoaches based on the results of this research.
H-99-050	Open—Unacceptable Response	TO THE NATIONAL HIGHWAY TRAFFIC SAFETY ADMINISTRATION: In 2 years, develop performance standards for motorcoach roof strength that provide maximum survival space for all seating positions and that take into account current typical motorcoach window dimensions.
H-99-051	Open—Unacceptable Response	TO THE NATIONAL HIGHWAY TRAFFIC SAFETY ADMINISTRATION: Once performance standards have been developed for motorcoach roof strength, require newly manufactured motorcoaches to meet those standards.
Increase Implementation Of Collision Avoidance Systems In All New Highway Vehicles		
H-15-004	Open—Unacceptable Response	TO THE NATIONAL HIGHWAY TRAFFIC SAFETY ADMINISTRATION: Develop and apply testing protocols to assess the performance of forward collision avoidance systems in passenger vehicles at various velocities, including high speed and high velocity differential.
H-15-005	Open—Unacceptable Response	TO THE NATIONAL HIGHWAY TRAFFIC SAFETY ADMINISTRATION: Complete, as soon as possible, the development and application of performance standards and protocols for the assessment of forward collision avoidance systems in commercial vehicles. (Safety Recommendation H-15-005 supersedes Safety Recommendation H-01-006)
H-15-006	Open— Acceptable Response	TO THE NATIONAL HIGHWAY TRAFFIC SAFETY ADMINISTRATION: Expand the New Car Assessment Program 5-star rating system to include a scale that rates the performance of forward collision avoidance systems.
H-15-007	Open— Acceptable Response	TO THE NATIONAL HIGHWAY TRAFFIC SAFETY ADMINISTRATION: Once the rating scale, described in Safety Recommendation H-15-6, is established, include the ratings of forward collision avoidance systems on the vehicle Monroney labels.
H-15-008	Open— Acceptable Response	TO PASSENGER VEHICLE, TRUCK-TRACTOR, MOTORCOACH, AND SINGLE-UNIT TRUCK MANUFACTURERS: Install forward collision avoidance systems that include, at a minimum, a forward collision warning component, as standard equipment on all new vehicles.
H-15-009	Open— Acceptable Response	TO PASSENGER VEHICLE, TRUCK-TRACTOR, MOTOR-COACH, AND SINGLE-UNIT TRUCK MANUFACTURERS: Once the National Highway Traffic Safety Administration publishes per- formance standards for autonomous emergency braking, install systems meeting those standards on all new vehicles.

Appendix. (Continued)

Increase Implementation Of Collision Avoidance Systems In All New Highway Vehicles		
Recommendation #	Overall Status	Subject
H-18-008	Open— Response Received	TO THE NATIONAL HIGHWAY TRAFFIC SAFETY ADMINISTRATION: Require all new school buses to be equipped with collision avoidance systems and automatic emergency braking technologies.
H-18-019	Open— Response Received	TO BLUE BIRD CORPORATION, COLLINS INDUSTRIES, INC., IC BUS, STARCRAFT BUS, THOMAS BUILT BUSES, INC., TRANS TECH, AND VANCON, INC.: Install a collision avoidance system with automatic emergency braking as standard equipment on all newly manufactured school buses.
H-18-029	Open— Response Received	TO THE NATIONAL HIGHWAY TRAFFIC SAFETY ADMINISTRATION: Incorporate motorcycles in the development of performance standards for passenger vehicle crash warning and prevention systems.
H-18-043	Open— Response Received	TO THE NATIONAL HIGHWAY TRAFFIC SAFETY ADMINISTRATION: Incorporate pedestrian safety systems, including pedestrian collision avoidance systems and other more passive safety systems, into the New Car Assessment Program.
H-18-044	Open— Response Received	TO THE NATIONAL HIGHWAY TRAFFIC SAFETY ADMINISTRATION: Develop a detailed pedestrian crash data set that represents the current, complete range of crash types and that can be used for local and state analysis and to model and simulate pedestrian collision avoidance systems.
Reduce Fatigue-Related Accidents		
H-09-009	Open— Await Response	TO THE AMERICAN BUS ASSOCIATION AND THE UNITED MOTORCOACH ASSOCIATION: Inform your members through Web sites, newsletters, and conferences of the circumstances of the Mexican Hat, Utah, accident. The prepared information should encourage charter operators to develop written contingency plans for each charter to ensure that trip planning is in place in the event of driver fatigue, incapacitation, or illness or in the event of trip delays necessitating replacement drivers to avoid hours- of-service violations and inform drivers of their trip's contingency plans. The prepared information should also provide information about the risks of operating in rural areas without wireless telephone coverage and advise members to carry mobile cellular amplifiers or satellite-based devices to communicate emergency events.
H-09-010	Open— Acceptable Response	TO ARROW STAGE LINES: Develop written contingency plans for each charter to ensure that trip planning is in place in the event of driver fatigue, incapacitation, or illness or in the event of trip delays necessitating replacement drivers to avoid hours-of-service violations and inform drivers of their trip's contingency plans.

Reduce Fatigue-Related Accidents		
Recommendation #	Overall Status	Subject
H-12-029	Open—Unacceptable Response	TO THE FEDERAL MOTOR CARRIER SAFETY ADMINISTRATION: Establish an ongoing program to monitor, evaluate, report on, and continuously improve fatigue management programs implemented by motor carriers to identify, mitigate, and continuously reduce fatigue-related risks for drivers. (This safety recommendation supersedes Safety Recommendation H-08-14.)
H-12-030	Open—Unacceptable Response	TO THE FEDERAL MOTOR CARRIER SAFETY ADMINISTRATION: Incorporate scientifically based fatigue mitigation strategies into the hours-of-service regulations for passenger-carrying drivers who operate during the nighttime window of circadian low.
H-15-022	Open— Acceptable Response	TO WALMART STORES, INC. (ORIGINALLY ISSUED TO WALMART TRANSPORTATION LLC): Develop and implement a fatigue management program based on the North American Fatigue Management Program guidelines.
H-17-056	Open— Response Received	TO THE UNITED STATES DEPARTMENT OF LABOR: Develop and disseminate guidelines and training material for agricultural employers and farm labor contractors on the dangers of driving while tired and on strategies for managing driver fatigue.
Require Medical Fitness—Screen For And Treat Obstructive Sleep Apnea		
H-09-015	Open—Unacceptable Response	TO THE FEDERAL MOTOR CARRIER SAFETY ADMINISTRATION: Implement a program to identify commercial drivers at high risk for obstructive sleep apnea and require that those drivers provide evidence through the medical certification process of having been appropriately evaluated and, if treatment is needed, effectively treated for that disorder before being granted unrestricted medical certification.
H-09-016	Open— Acceptable Response	TO THE FEDERAL MOTOR CARRIER SAFETY ADMINISTRATION: Develop and disseminate guidance for commercial drivers, employers, and physicians regarding the identification and treatment of individuals at high risk of obstructive sleep apnea (OSA), emphasizing that drivers who have OSA that is effectively treated are routinely approved for continued medical certification.
H-17-049	Open— Acceptable Alternate Response	TO THE FEDERAL MOTOR CARRIER SAFETY ADMINISTRATION: Make the 2016 Medical Review Board/Motor Carrier Safety Advisory Committee recommendations on screening for obstructive sleep apnea (OSA) easily accessible to certified medical examiners, and instruct the examiners to use the recommendations as guidance when evaluating commercial drivers for OSA risk.

Ms. NORTON. Thank you for your testimony.

Vice Mayor Jones of Neptune Beach, Florida, on behalf of Transportation for America.

Mr. JONES. Good morning, Chairman DeFazio, Ranking Members, and distinguished members of the committee.

Thank you for the opportunity to testify on behalf of Transportation for America this morning.

My name is Fred Jones, and in addition to representing the citizens of Neptune Beach as their vice mayor, I also work as a professional transportation planner for Michael Baker International and also serve on the advisory board for the National Complete Streets Coalition.

Complete Streets, for those that are unfamiliar with the term, is a street that is designed to be safe and convenient for all users, be they drivers, transit users, pedestrians, and cyclists.

Unfortunately, my community is part of the six most dangerous metropolitan areas in the country in which to walk and bike. In fact, the State of Florida is the most dangerous State in the Union for cyclists and pedestrians, and these safety trends are going in the wrong direction.

If you, in fact, were to visit and join my family on the streets that I walk and bike on a daily basis, I think you would agree that they are not dangerous by accident, but dangerous by fundamental design.

Part of the problem is that for the better part of the half century we have been focused on building bigger, faster roadways with wider lanes and development that is set back from the road to make our drivers more comfortable as they move quickly through our communities, all at the cost of human lives.

In fact, roadways are often designed for travel speeds that are 10 to 15 miles an hour faster than what the posted speed limit is, and we do know that drivers will follow this design cue.

We know that speed leads to more deadly crashes, especially for the children that are walking to school or a bus patron that is walking to their stop on their way to work, who lacked the protection of thousands of pounds of steel and aluminum.

What is particularly frustrating is our acceptance of this level of danger and the loss of human life. We have a cure, but we just do not want to use it.

I do want to preface that there are many States and communities across the country, and namely, the Florida Department of Transportation, that should be applauded for adopting robust Complete Street policies and initiatives to change these unsafe paradigms.

However, what we are seeing is a major disconnect between what we think are feel-good policy frameworks and the actual implementation of safe roadways.

As an illustration, there was a State road in my area where the district safety office had recommended actually removing a lane to reduce the crossing distance for pedestrians and make it safer.

Well, what ended up happening, there was a little bit of community pushback, and so the agency conceded by growing the forecasted traffic rates and essentially killed what should have been a legacy project, and all in the nature of future traffic congestion.

And even in instances when the traffic volumes are low enough to warrant building a Complete Street, we will often hear excuses that the road is a parallel reliever to an interstate or it is an evacuation route or, in fact, we are too far along in the design process to do anything different.

Yet there are many roadways in our community where you could probably roll a bowling ball down the road on any given day and not hit anything.

Nationally, Congress communicates its Federal priorities through spending, and while we do spend $40 billion in Federal funds annually in the highway program, less than $1 billion of this is often reserved for pedestrian and cyclist infrastructure, and only $2.3 billion is dedicated to safety.

If you visit this committee's website, the issue profiled is the cost of congestion, and I get it. Congestion is very inconvenient and annoying. But the cost of congestion is roughly equivalent to the cost of the 37,000 lives that were lost on our roadways in 2017, a cost of over $356 billion, and that does not include the cost of injuries, which we know number in the millions. Yet safety spending represents a mere fraction of the money that is spent on the congestion.

In 2012, Congress created a less than optimal performance management system that required MPOs and DOTs to set these performance safety targets, including for cyclists and pedestrians.

Yet in 2017, 18 States have set performance targets forecasting more deaths for cyclists and pedestrians on the roadways. Simply put, we do know how to do better.

In Orlando, for example, the Florida Department of Transportation redesigned Edgewater Drive by taking a travel lane and reconfiguring the road to make it more safe for pedestrians and cyclists.

What were the results? Total collisions dropped 40 percent. Injury rates declined 71 percent. Pedestrian counts increased 23 percent. Cycling increased by 30 percent, and traffic actually dropped 12 percent before returning to original levels.

Most significantly, the corridor gained 77 new businesses and 560 jobs, while the value of property along this corridor rose 80 percent.

Unfortunately, these projects more often than not are the exception. Engineers often have to get special approval to implement them in a process that can take more than 1 year. So why would we not want this to be the rule?

As we bring up reauthorization, we are strongly urging Congress to lead a discussion about what it is that we plan to achieve, not just how much we are going to spend. We need to set specific measurable goals, particularly in terms of safety and livability benefits and hold decisionmakers accountable for reaching them.

Above all, this program needs to be oriented to create a safer transportation system for all users.

Thank you again for your leadership and inviting me to testify today, and I look forward to working with you in the next upcoming reauthorization bill.

[Mr. Jones' prepared statement follows:]

Prepared Statement of Hon. Fred Jones, Vice Mayor, City of Neptune Beach, Florida, on behalf of Transportation for America

Good morning Chairman, Ranking Member and distinguished members of the committee. Thank you for the opportunity to testify today on behalf of Transportation for America, a national nonprofit dedicated to creating a transportation system that moves people, safely and affordably, to jobs and services by all means of travel with minimal impact to the community and the environment.

My name is Fred Jones. I represent the citizens of Neptune Beach, Florida as Vice-Mayor on the City Council, and I also work as a transportation planner for Michael Baker International. Additionally, I serve on the advisory board of the National Complete Streets Coalition. Neptune Beach is a small, quiet coastal community nestled on the northeast coast of Florida between Atlantic Beach and Jacksonville Beach. While there are many wonderful things about my community—the beaches, our vibrant town center, the high quality of life, to name a few—we, unfortunately, are also part of the sixth most dangerous metropolitan area in our country in which to walk or bike. The state of Florida, which is the most dangerous state in the Union for bicyclists and pedestrians, is also home to the #1, #2, #3, #4, #5, #6, #8 and #9 most dangerous cities. And these numbers are going in the wrong direction, in Florida and across the nation.

Over the past 10 years, 5433 people in the state of Florida, including 419 people in the Jacksonville, were struck and killed trying to walk or bike to work, school, running errands or going to a friend's house. These are the streets that I walk, bike and drive on. It is important that we recognize that these roadways are not dangerous by accident: they are dangerous by design.[47]

Some of the problem is that many people do not understand how small changes in roadway design and development patterns affect safety. Wider lanes and broader streets with buildings set back from the road signal to the driver that speed is allowed and encouraged—no matter what your posted speed limit is. In fact, often roadways are designed for traffic speeds 10-15 miles per hour faster than the posted speed. When we talk about roadway design, it's important to emphasize context. We are not talking about limited access freeways but, rather, the misapplication of limited access freeway engineering and design solutions and parameters to local road ways.

While transportation agencies claim that this is done for "safety reasons," the underlying message is that they expect drivers to speed and want to clear space for those speeding drivers to make mistakes and correct them without crashing. This accommodation to drivers, in the name of "safety," creates more danger to those outside of the car because the driver naturally interprets these roadway design cues to go at the higher design speed, inducing the speeding behavior that the design engineers are trying

---

[47] https://smartgrowthamerica.org/dangerous-by-design/.

to head off. And we know that speed leads to mistakes and more deadly crashes, especially for those that don't have thousands of pounds of steel and aluminum surrounding them.

These issues—along with un-signaled crossings, long blocks and multiple driveways—create inherently dangerous conditions for people who walk or bike. All of these designs are put in place for the convenience of drivers and to move vehicles at a high rate of speed, which is the real underlying priority of our national trans- portation program, whether that was our intention or not. But most of all they all put people outside of a car in jeopardy.

What is particularly frustrating to me is the acceptance of this level of danger and loss of human life. It is not a problem that we don't know how to solve. This isn't a problem that we are powerless to address. We have a cure. But for whatever reasons, just don't want to use it.

Two cities that have adopted one major cure, known as Vision Zero, have seen traffic fatalities fall significantly. Vision Zero emphasizes matching speeds of roadways based on the surrounding context. In other words, in populated areas, drivers should have an expectation that they will move slower than in the wide-open countryside or on limited access highways. The results speak for themselves: in New York City fatalities are down 28 percent since 2014. San Francisco is down 41 percent. If you just look at pedestrians, the decrease is 46 percent in New York City and 34 percent in San Francisco. Fortunately, several local cities in my home state have also begun to join this movement, including Tampa, Orlando, West Palm Beach and Miami.

N. Flamingo and Pines Boulevard in the Miami area, a typical example of a major intersection in Florida.

Arterial roadways (not limited access highways) in Miami areas. N. Okeechobee Road and Hialeah Gardens Boulevard is one of the most dangerous intersections in Florida today.

Despite knowing how to fix the problems, many of our transportation agencies are often concerned about the ramifications—often political—of making safety their top priority. To make space for people outside of a car, we sometimes have to take space from the cars. Even where doing so would create very minor delays—as in seconds— for drivers, it is enough to throw the option out. This resistance to change can be found at all levels—from local public works agencies to Congress and from broad policy to bureaucratic procedure and culture.

I want to preface that there are many states and communities, and particularly the Florida DOT, that should be applauded for adopting robust complete street policies and initiatives to change this paradigm. However, there is a major disconnect or cultural barrier that exists between the policy framework around safety and complete streets and the actual implementation of innovative design solutions and projects that would provide better outcomes. Our success requires moving beyond a feel-good policy discussion to meaningful culture change, political will and leadership, and shifting priorities away from speed and capacity at all costs.

I'm going to next provide a few examples and illustrations of the difficulties in building safer roads for all. In terms of procedure, every road project is designed around a standard that most people have never heard of, called Level of Service. This is a measure of how quickly cars can move and how easily they can maneuver through a roadway with little congestion or delay. A wide-open street with free flowing traffic on is considered LOSA. Congested, stop and go traffic is LOSF. As a result, your most economically productive corridors are considered failures in the transportation world, while those that are underutilized get an A. What is the equivalent safety standard that we use to design roads, you may ask? We don't have one. We respond to clusters of crashes, we don't design to avoid them.

In terms of culture, you can find the focus on traffic speeds over safety everywhere. Highway engineers have historically been trained to build highways to maximize capacity, speed and vehicle throughput. This ideal has in turn been misapplied to all roadways, from highways to arterial roads to local, neighborhood streets. DOTs sometimes don't believe that the federal government will permit them to implement a design that would slow traffic. Or they will claim that they aren't allowed to use funding that way. Whether that is true or not (and in spite of several directives from (FHWA) Administration saying it isn't true), they regularly blame the federal government for tying their hands. The excuse for failing to design a roadway for all users varies based on the type of road.

On a state road in my metro area, the local DOT district safety office previously recommended a road diet or lane elimination to reduce the crossing distance for pedestrians and improve overall safety. There was some pushback, so the DOT immediately conceded and raised the forecasted traffic volumes and misapplied other traffic analyses to make a great project that would have provided a sense of arrival on a college campus look infeasible. Two things to take from this story. One, traffic projections and analyses are often overestimated and DOTs have a lot of discretion on how they are established. Computer models used to generate such analyses are only as good as their inputs, and there's nothing easier than tweaking such inputs to get desired outputs. Two, if there is traffic that might be impacted by accommodating pedestrians or cyclists, even if it is minor, it is often considered too much.

If traffic volumes are not high enough to justify refusing to build a complete street, DOTs often will often provide other reasons for not changing the roadway such as claiming that the road is a parallel reliever to an Interstate or highway and that giving up space to pedestrians would impact drivers if a problem on the highway requires traffic to move to that roadway. On one street near downtown Jacksonville, traffic is not the problem. You could roll a bowling ball down the road at nearly any time of day and not hit anything. In this case, the local agency said they couldn't give up a lane because even though the road is well below capacity, it is an evacuation route. There was also a recent instance, when planning for an innovative, autonomous transit service was only supported with the condition that no state roads could be considered for lane elimination. So instead of repurposing a portion of the roadway to support enhanced cycling and walking and transit, things that the local community desire, they insisted that it be left alone—and empty.

It isn't just happening in Florida. It is happening in all of our states. For example, Beach Park, Illinois, has been trying to get better pedestrian protection along a state route that has seen four pedestrian fatalities over the last 15 months. In the most recent crash, the driver said he could not see the victim, but Illinois DOT has been slow to respond to the community's call for visibility improvements. The response has been so slow and lackluster that the city is considering making the improvements on their own and paying penalties for failing to get the required permits.[48]

In terms of broad policy, Congress communicates federal priorities to the state departments of transportation (DOTs) and for metropolitan planning organizations (MPOs) through spending. While we spend over $40 billion in federal funds per year in the highway program, less than $1 billion of that is reserved for the Transportation Alternatives program, which is targeted to bicycle and pedestrian infrastructure, and only $2.3 billion is dedicated to safety improvements.

Even in the messaging from Washington, DC, the convenience for drivers is primary. If you go to this committee's website, the issue profiled is the cost of congestion. And I get it: congestion is annoying and inconvenient. I don't like to sit in it either. But the cost cited on your website for congestion is roughly equivalent to the cost of the $37,133 lives lost on our roadways in 2017, a cost of $356,476,800,000.[49] That doesn't include the cost associated with those injured on our roads, which number in the millions of people each year. Yet safety spending is a small fraction compared to all the money we spend to address congestion.

In 2012, Congress required DOTs and MPOs to set performance targets in federal priority areas. Several of those targets are safety related, including overall fatalities and serious injuries as well as nonmotorized fatalities and serious injuries (i.e., bicyclists and pedestrians).

While this approach is referred to as "performance management" in the law, it is really simply performance tracking. Instead of setting targets and orienting spending around those targets, the program allows states to set priorities and report the safety results. If those targets are ambitious, wonderful. But Congress allows them to be negative too. As a result, in 2017, eighteen states set performance targets to kill more bicyclists and pedestrians on their roadways.

You can find this information if you know where to go deep on the FHWA's webpage to find them. There you must dig through 55 reports that are 60-70 pages each to find this information to compare across states. That's better than the repair and other targets, which aren't available on FHWA's site at all. This is seven years after Congress required performance tracking. That is what passes for accountability in the federal transportation program.

---

[48] https://www.chicagotribune.com/suburbs/lake-county-news-sun/news/ct-lns-beach-park-pedes- trian-fatals-st-0111-20170110-story.html.

[49] Based on the 2016 Revised Value of a Statistical Life Guidance set by the US Department of Transportation of $9.6 million per life.

Bill Deatherage, of the Kentucky Council of the Blind, walking along Louisville, KY's Brownsboro Road before and after sidewalk construction. Photo by Anne M. McMahon.

I have heard many people claim that the focus on congestion mitigation is important for the economy. As a local elected official, I can promise you that an empty roadway, while uncongested, is hardly an example of a healthy economy. Corridors that are full of cars and people are usually our highest performing economic centers. The National Complete Street Coalition analyzed 37 Complete Streets projects in across the nation and found that employment levels rose after Complete Streets projects—in some cases, significantly. Communities reported increased net new businesses after Complete Streets improvements, suggesting that Complete Streets projects made the street more desirable for businesses. In eight of the ten communities with available data, property values increased after the Complete Streets improvements.[50]

In fact, Redfin found, based on more than 1 million homes sold between January 2014 and April 2016, that one walkscore point can increase the price of a home by an average of $3,250, or 0.9 percent. While the majority of home buyers were looking for homes in walkable neighborhoods, Redfin found that they make up just 2% of active listings.[51] As we all know, when something is in high demand and low supply, it can push the price of that item substantially upward. As a result, walkable neighborhoods can become very expensive and are often out of reach for those that are most reliant on walking and transit for their daily activities. And the cost premium created by this low supply is created by restrictions in development and housing policy, but also by transportation programs. Much like the cost of diamonds is elevated by restricting supply, government is increasing the cost of walkable neighborhoods by blocking the market

---

[50] https://smartgrowthamerica.org/resources/evaluating-complete-streets-projects-a-guide-for- practitioners/.
[51] https://www.marketwatch.com/story/how-walk-score-boosts-your-homes-value-2016-08-11.

response to the everincreasing demand for them. A design that would save thousands of lives every year.

Some fear that making space for people walking and biking requires something to be taken from drivers. But when we build roads to move everyone, everyone does better. In Grandview, Missouri, a project was implemented to reinvigorate Main Street by improving the pedestrian accommodations along several blocks. The result was an increase in all modes: pedestrians by 900 percent, bicyclists by 40 percent and automobiles by 20 percent, although it remained uncongested. There were also 90 percent fewer crashes after the changes. The city's investment of $5 million has led to a return of $375 million. This amounts to approximately 1.5 times of the cities entire assessed property evaluation.[52]

In Charlotte, North Carolina, the state DOT redesigned East Boulevard from five lanes to three, adding new sidewalks and bike lanes back in 2006. As a result, they saw a dramatic reduction in crashes, more efficient traffic operations, a drop in speeding, and a 47 percent increase in non-residential property values that raised annual tax revenues by $530,000.[53]

---

[52] http://www.marc.org/Government/GTI/Academy-for-Sustainable-Communities/Sustainable- Success-Stories-Honorees/2016/Grandview-Gateway.
[53] https://www.completestreetsnc.org/project-examples/ex-eastblvdroaddiet/.

In my home state of Florida, we know how to do this right when we want to. In Orlando, Florida DOT redesigned Edgewater Drive by taking a travel lane and reconfiguring the road to make space for pedestrians and bicyclists. Total collisions dropped by 40 percent, injury rates decline 71 percent, pedestrian counts increased by 23 percent and bicycling increased by 30 percent traffic dropped 12 percent before returning to original levels. Additionally, the corridor has gained 77 new businesses and 560 jobs, while the value of property along the corridor rose 80 percent.[54]

Yet these projects are the exception. Engineers actually have to get special approval to implement them, a process that can take more than a year. Why wouldn't we want this to be the rule?

As we consider the next six years of our national surface transportation spending, Congress should update the program to better protect all users. Congress should strengthen existing Complete Streets language to require states and metropolitan regions to plan, design, fund, and maintain safer streets. Congress should fund more Complete Streets projects. And Congress should create real accountability for roadway safety. States should not be allowed negative safety targets. If they are expecting more deaths then investments or changes need to be made to their programs. For years, we have heard about the need for more money. But it's really not about the amount, but rather how it's being prioritized and spent. Shouldn't we ensure that federal funding goes to projects that improve safety, improve traffic operations and create the communities that people want? Every single dollar spent to resurface roadways could include a redesign that saves lives. But when a resurfacing project is developed, stakeholders and the community that might want Complete Streets are told that DOT will have to "study the matter" and then by the time the design concept is reviewed by the traffic division, the project is at 60 percent

---

[54] Edgwater Drive Fact Sheet: https://www.google.com/url?sa=t&rct=j&q=&esrc=s&source=web&cd=2& ved=2ahUKEwjgq2w2rnhAhVDnOAKHZ1cDGUQFjABegQIAhAC&url=http%3A%2F%2Famericas.uli.or g%2Fwpcontent%2Fuploads%2Fsites%2F2%2FULIDocuments%2FEdgewaterDriveOrlandoFL.pdf&usg= AOvVaw0iqKJscXyNniFKC6V8gN.

development and the DOT says they are too far into the process to consider the change. We are choosing bureaucratic, status quo procedure over human life.

Florida DOT, particularly in resurfacing projects, claim they have little flexibility in federal funding rules to support enhancements outside of their right of way jurisdiction. And often this may be a sidewalk or transit stop outside of their right of way jurisdiction. This results in safety and complete street gaps whereby a sidewalk or resurfacing project avoids needed improvements on private or other agency property that would result in a safe, seamless project. We are choosing to leave this part of the transportation system out and it is killing people.

After a road is built or resurfaced, we are told there is no money for retrofits. Even when there is, it is a fraction of the funding they are using to create the problem. It is like building an addition on your house while ignoring a gas leak.

Moreover, as we enter this reauthorization, I look to you all on this committee to set clear goals about what we, the American people, will get for the investment. There is a lot of talk on Capital Hill about raising taxes and putting more funding into the surface transportation program to stabilize it over the long run.

As we bring up reauthorization, Congress should lead a discussion about what we plan to achieve, not just about what you are going to spend. We need to set specific, measurable goals and hold decision-makers accountable for reaching them. There should be rewards for doing well and penalties for failure. And above all, this program should be oriented to create a safer transportation system for all users. Doing so will save lives while creating the economically vibrant, livable communities that Americans want.

Thank you very much for inviting me to testify today. I look forward to working with you to do more for safety in the coming reauthorization bill.

Ms. NORTON. Thank you very much, Vice Mayor Jones.

I am going to next ask the chief of police for the city of Alexandria, Michael L. Brown, to offer his testimony. Five minutes, please.

Mr. BROWN. Thank you, Madam Chairwoman and also members of the committee.

I am going to try and cover the high points in the written testimony I submitted, and principally what I was looking at and trying to offer or was asked to offer was the lens of law enforcement in trying to deal with the traffic safety implications across this country.

In my testimony, we recognize in the profession that clearly the major issues were outlined by the chair regarding impaired driving, speeding, distraction, and the pedestrian conflicts occurring across the country.

I would also add the issue of occupant protection as well because occupant protection speaks directly to the survivability should you get involved in a crash.

But from the law enforcement perspective and the lens we look at the world, frankly, in terms of the competing interests that are placed upon law enforcement, and a lot of those interests come from the local level. The local demand of our neighborhoods in our communities tell us what we need to prioritize on.

And, quite frankly, in some communities like the one in which I work, traffic and even parking is a significant issue.

But that is not across the Nation, and so we need to be flexible in the way we look at creating an authorization that accounts for the local law enforcement and the local expectations that the law enforcement leaders and the officers who do the work are confronted with on a daily basis.

I have included in my testimony a number of general recommendations, especially regarding incentivizing involvement of law enforcement. The current incentives for the national campaigns and those kinds of things that you find in the FAST Act and in previous editions of reauthorization provide an opportunity for law enforcement to engage in campaigns. It is a capacity-driven thing so that it could be coordinated on a national level.

But that does not happen on a day-to-day basis, and as you have heard testimony by law enforcement officials across this country, there are times where that capacity is drawn upon by other commitments and other challenges that law enforcement faces, aside from the fact that we are in an issue in some parts of the country where it is very difficult to recruit people and to fill the ranks of law enforcement.

So this competition takes place within these incentives. General overtime programs we suggest should be continued for a variety of reasons, especially if they drive for capacity at the local level.

The other thing that would be interesting in terms of trying to do this is to raise the awareness through these incentivization programs of traffic safety within the local political establishment.

One of the things that I have suggested is develop a national narrative. The current national narrative in many cases, NHTSA does a good job, but it focuses on a lot of the specific things that we are looking at in our major campaign.

The fact of the matter is most of the crashes that are occurring are directly related to bad behavior on the part of the participants, whether it be a bicyclist, a pedestrian, or some motorists. Very few of them are related to mechanical issues.

People make bad choices, and people get hurt, and in some cases, they die. So what we were trying to do at least in the city that we have and in other parts and communities across the country is to elevate that discussion to something more than just the numbers, something more than just a campaign, trying to get out there and engage in the activity, making a traffic stop, not necessarily making a citation, but looking for the teachable moment that is going to change behavior and get people to voluntarily comply with the laws.

That is taking place across the country at varying levels for the same kind of conditions that we talked about at the local level.

I would suggest that we continue to focus on these key areas, but I would also suggest that in the new authorization we build in as much flexibility for a local government to establish the priorities that they are facing in their local issues. What happens in Alexandria is not the same it is going to be in L.A. It is not going to be the same as Salina, Kansas.

And so we need to be able to provide them the opportunity to address their traffic safety issues, and I would also argue that the traffic safety issues are not accidents. They are crashes, and it is not just deaths. People who survive crashes, and we see them every day, in many cases have lifelong, lasting issues that change their life forever.

So, Madam Chair, thank you very much for the opportunity. I look forward to any questions the committee may have.

[Mr. Brown's prepared statement follows:]

Prepared Statement of Michael L. Brown, Chief of Police, Alexandria (Virginia) Police Department

Mr. Chairman and members of the committee, I am honored to come before you and represent the law enforcement perspective on traffic safety and law enforcement's role in addressing this important issue. My testimony is offered to underscore the importance of traffic safety in our country and some of the challenges we face in addressing it.

Traffic safety is often defined by the number of crashes that have occurred and by the number the fatalities that have resulted from these crashes. While these are important measures, law enforcement deals with it on a much more personal level. Law enforcement officers respond to crash calls, investigate and deal with individual needs of those involved. This occurs thousands of times a day in our country. The level of law enforcement engagement is shaped by local capacity, community interest and political will. The role of the officers and the service they provide is often lost in national level discussions of traffic safety. My testimony will address major policy level issues it and it is also offered to you through this lens.

Traffic Safety Is a Critical Issue for America

The sheer number of crashes in this country illustrates traffic safety is a critical issue that affects millions of people, however, it is frequently under prioritized in the context of other national priorities. Clearly, crashes that involve a fatality or a life changing issue have an impact on individuals and their families. I would also argue that involvement in crashes resulting in minor injuries or mere property damage also complicate the lives of people on a daily basis. Law enforcement officers know this and deal with this every day. Unfortunately, the latter situations are frequently "overlooked" in traffic safety discussions.

Law enforcement is often called upon to deal with traffic safety issues. Each day, we receive many calls or complaints about specific traffic safety which we have to prioritize with our other calls for service. The public call us because they expect law enforcement to enforce traffic laws and mitigate their issue. This is based upon the premise that the real or perception of officers actively or potentially enforcing traffic safety laws will lead to some level of voluntary compliance by individuals in a specific area. Law enforcement acknowledges this expectation and perspective. Law enforcement agencies and their officers respond by prioritizing traffic safety along with the other expectations a community may place upon them, e.g.; crime responses, mental health calls, etc.).

Law enforcement agencies understand the importance of traffic safety in the context of a community's "quality of life". Many agencies have understood this for a long time. Others came to understand that perspective even better during the 1990's. The 1994 Crime Bill required participating law enforcement agencies to conduct 'town hall' meetings with their communities across the country. One of the quality of life issues repeatedly raised in these meetings was traffic safety and traffic management. It became so prevalent that the U.S. Department of Justice's COPS Office developed publications to help law enforcement agencies in responding to traffic safety issues. Today, law enforcement's conversations with the public still include the traffic safety issue. The challenge remains—law enforcement is constantly balancing traffic safety as a community priority alongside more traditional policing issues. Community expectations for policing and traffic safety issues are local community based and the law enforcement response to these expectations vary by community across the nation. That said, there are some specific challenges for law enforcement that surface so often they deserve national discussion and attention. My following comments will cover some of the specific challenges that are high priority.

Impaired Driving

Driving under the influence is a major issue for the nation and its communities. While there has been a significant reduction in fatalities and a reported change in public acceptance of driving impaired, about 1/3 of all traffic fatalities are directly related to problem. Much of this success on this issue can be attributed to the efforts of MADD, law enforcement, and other community groups. The National Highway Traffic Safety Administration (NHTSA) and others have also developed a robust toolkit to deal with this issue including impairment presumption levels, national enforcement campaigns, ignition interlock programs, DUI courts and others. However, local participation in these efforts varies across the nation. This variation can be attributed to local capacity and local political will. We need to remember that law enforcement's response to impaired driving will be governed by these local conditions.

The national approach to this issue should continue and incentivize the use of the current toolkit as these tools have been proven effective in dealing with impaired driving. However, there should be a renewed interest in engaging groups other than law enforcement more effectively in addressing impaired driving. Substance abuse is a major underlying cause of impaired driving and repeat offenders are a prime example of the substance abuse issues that law enforcement confronts in dealing with impaired driving. Law enforcement is not in the substance abuse treatment business and increased access to substance abuse (public health) programs to deal with this issue should be promoted as an intervention measure.

Law enforcement recognizes the importance of enforcing impaired driving laws and accepts its role as evidenced by the number of people they arrest for driving impaired. The evolution of impaired driving law over the years has led to officers completing incredibly long, detailed reports and other protocols which result in a major commitment of the officer's time. I will not say this discourages officers from making DUI arrests nor am I suggesting the development of shortcuts which affect the rights of the arrested individual. The reality for the officer is that, in some cases, a misdemeanor DUI report can be as complicated as a criminal felony homicide case. There must be a way to develop a standardized national methodology which simplifies these reports which appropriately balances the needs of prosecutors and the rights of the arrestee.

Finally, I must address the specific concerns of law enforcement over the impact of driving under the influence of drugs. The country has acknowledged that drug abuse is a public health issue and has many programs to deal with it in this framework. Law enforcement and prosecutors have successfully enforced impaired driving statues for many years and will continue to do so. That said, there is considerable concern within law enforcement over the potential public safety implications for impaired driving and the interests to increase public access to marijuana. Law enforcement is closely monitoring the experience of states and communities that have increased this legal access but the current debate can be confusing and alarming. For the officer, they recognize the absence of credible technology and informative research to assist them in assessing driver impairment during an impaired driving enforcement contact involving drugs. It is critical that these issues are addressed immediately to help guide officers in their impaired driving enforcement efforts.

Occupant Protection

This issue remains a major issue for our nation. About half of the nation's fatal crash reports indicate that one or more vehicle occupants are not wearing their safety belts. This proportion has also been relatively consistent for decades. The same observation can be found in national injury crashes. Again, NHTSA has developed a toolkit to get people to wear their seatbelts but the engagement of law enforcement varies across the nation due to local conditions and political will.

The discussions of seatbelt enforcement often include concerns over the police overstepping their authority and/or over prioritizing the importance of seatbelt enforcement. Officers frequently still hear the response "don't you have more important things to do" when they enforce seatbelt laws. Officers and their leaders are very aware of these conversations and positions and it can also have a 'chilling' effect on actual seatbelt enforcement. The nation needs to change the perspective on the importance of seatbelt laws to improve public compliance. Seatbelt enforcement needs to be viewed as a lifesaving effort not as a tactic used by officers to 'pick on' people.

This is a problem which could also be fixed at some level over time through engineering and design. The use of seat belt interlocks for example could improve this behavior without the need for law enforcement.

Speeding

Nobody likes getting a speeding ticket and yet speed continues to be an issue in most crashes in America. In many cases, it is the principle reason behind the crash. It is also a major factor in the severity of the crash and occupant survivability which relates to the principles of physics. Speed enforcement is a traditional enforcement activity in many police agencies and officers do it every day. Unfortunately, there are many more speeders than there are officers and voluntary compliance by motorists is often dependent upon the motorist's perception that they will be caught speeding. Many motorists like the odds of not being caught and choose to speed. Speed limit compliance could be enhanced by incentivizing law enforcement efforts to speed enforcement at a national level. The increased use of automated speed enforcement technology could also prove useful providing such programs are implemented for traffic safety reasons and not revenue generation. Such programs must be implemented to avoid any challenges to police legitimacy.

Distraction

Distraction is a very real threat to the safe use of our transportation system. Law enforcement acknowledges that and where possible enforces the laws that are available to them. All transportation system users need to pay attention when using these systems. The emerging data is illustrating that this issue is growing especially with our reliance on some technology. Many of the current laws focus on drivers and not other users like pedestrians and bicyclists while in the roadway. When this topic is discussed the issues surrounding police harassment and the ability of officers to detect distraction frequently surface. Some of the existing laws also make the law difficult for officers to enforce e.g.; manipulating a device or texting language. Officers will tell you of many instances where they see drivers, pedestrians, bicyclists and other transportation system users not paying attention and jeopardizing their own personal safety and the safety of others. This will continue unless the nation acknowledges this to be a problem. There should be a national effort to develop hands free laws which are applicable to all system users. There should also be a national priority assigned to this traffic safety threat and a more uniformed enforcement/compliance approach that is acceptable to the states and local authorities.

Pedestrian and Bicycle Safety

There is a growing concern in many communities over the safety of bicyclists and pedestrians. Law enforcement understands these concerns and responds to local traffic safety complaints on these issues on a daily basis. This is particularly important in urban centers and those communities that encourage these travel options. In many discussions on this issue there are references to pedestrians and bicyclists as 'vulnerable' populations which are understandable especially when they share the road with cars. From the law enforcement perspective, there is plenty of blame to share as to what creates this conflict. At times it is the motor vehicle operator that does not recognize or ignores the laws and protections provided to pedestrians and cyclists. Yet, there are also many occasions where these same pedestrians/cyclists involved in these potential conflicts will position the argument so that they are the victim instead of acknowledging that each contributes to the traffic safety issue. This makes it difficult for officers when they take enforcement action involving pedestrian and cyclists. Like some of the other traffic safety issues I have discussed, the narrative needs to change on this issue so that traffic safety is a personal responsibility and all the players must follow the rules.

Other Important Law Enforcement Considerations

There are other issues which I must bring up which can impact the role of law enforcement in performing its traffic safety responsibilities. These issues are real for law enforcement and the communities they serve and provide context for traffic safety enforcement. They include:

Calls for Service and Officer Initiated Activity

At one time in my career I was told by a federal official that "law enforcement will do what we tell them to do". Sadly, other federal officials that were present found that comment humorous at the time. Unfortunately, that perspective is a counterproductive to encouraging law enforcement participation and clearly ignores the daily realities of our officers.

Traffic enforcement occurs when officers are on routine patrol and when they are responding to a specific traffic safety complaint from the community. The latter is treated like a call for service (e.g.; a 911 call) and the officer's discretion to engage in enforcement may be affected. The officers still have discretion to give a warning or a citation but there is an expectation that they respond to the problem area and at least look for violations. Officers on routine patrol have greater discretion to engage in traffic enforcement. Patrolling officers may be more interested in other local policing priorities or their own specific policing interests rather than traffic safety. This has been and will continue to be a challenge for law enforcement leadership. Officers who acknowledge a public safety priority tend to respond to that priority. As such, it is important to develop a national narrative which elevates traffic enforcement as a community public safety threat which deserves the attention of the individual officer. The national narrative needs to be supported with messaging and incentives designed to promote officer engagement in this enforcement effort.

Law Enforcement as an Intervention

Enforcement is often portrayed as the key intervention for improving traffic safety. That is most likely the basis for the number of traffic enforcement call/requests law enforcement agencies receive each day. Research has demonstrated that good enforcement can have an impact on changing some behavior in traffic safety. In some cases, there are more profound foundational issues which dictate the need for other interventions. My coverage of impaired driving included some discussion of other intervention needs when substance abuse behavior is present. There are other disciplines which can be applied. Vehicle design, engineering, and other technologies can be useful in developing interventions which might stop problematic behavior.

Interlock systems for impaired driving and seatbelts are examples of design interventions.

While law enforcement plays a critical role in changing traffic safety behavior many issues require a more complex intervention to effectively deal with any poor behavior. I do believe the role of law enforcement is significant in this effort but we should avoid defaulting to law enforcement as the entity that has sole responsibility for changing behavior that causes crashes.

Officer Discretion and Legitimacy

It is the individual officer that makes the decision to engage in traffic enforcement. Therefore, we must also acknowledge that officers are very aware of the climate in which they work and the public acceptance of their enforcement efforts. Officer decisions to engage involve the professional discretion they have during the performance of their duties. There is considerable research on officer discretion and it has shaped agencies policies. Law enforcement agencies have many policies to control the use of discretion but the myriad of fact patterns an officer confronts while performing their duties make it difficult to develop policy for every situation. That is one reason why law enforcement agencies commit so much time, energy, and money into selecting and training individuals that can exercise good judgment in the use of officer discretion. I would argue that, in practically every case, the competence and motivation of today's officers is at a much higher level than ever before. Legitimacy is a foundational factor in policing and the police will not be effective without it. There have been past concerns and debates about law enforcement actions and legitimacy. There have also been some comments that these concerns and debates have resulted in fewer officers engaging in traffic enforcement as a result. While this may be the case in some communities, I have not seen research that conclusively proves that this is occurring on a national level. That said, it is important for law enforcement and political leadership to create an environment which suggests that officers should engage in traffic law enforcement to respond to community quality of life and public safety issues in a manner which promote police legitimacy within the community the officer serves. This may not be occurring in some communities and should be addressed in a manner which supports officers doing traffic enforcement for the right reasons—protecting the public. A development of a national position which encourages this environment would be useful for improved traffic law enforcement.

Incentives for Law Enforcement

I have referenced incentives in my testimony on several occasions. The incentives that are traditionally offered through the federal government relate to providing enforcement capacity. Providing funding is important for law enforcement agencies that lack the capacity to participate in national traffic safety enforcement efforts. Some approaches result in individual officers performing this enforcement on an overtime basis which, for some officers, may be incentive. Recently, there have been repeated reports within the law enforcement community that overtime details do not often sufficiently encourage officers to perform specific activities including traffic safety enforcement. This may be attributed to the many uses of overtime details to address non-traffic related issues. These other details may compete with traffic enforcement details for available officers to participate. Some law enforcement agencies also argue overtime is not a sufficient high priority or driving factor with some officers. Agencies often advise that filling these overtime details can be difficult as a result. Another reason for the difficulty in getting officers to participate in these details may also be the degree of importance officers assign to traffic safety. Many officers may not recognize their role in traffic safety and enforcement of traffic laws as being that important to their community.

National Narrative

My testimony also makes several references to developing a national narrative outlining the importance of traffic safety and committing the resources to change the belief structures in the country relating to safety on and around our roadways. There are examples where this has worked in this area like the changed attitudes on impaired driving which was initiated by MADD. Other individual groups within the traffic safety community have made similar efforts to change attitudes and culture in specific areas with varying degrees of success. To me, this seems to be 'chipping away' at the essential need for all of us in this country to change our behavior and improve our quality of life as it relates to all aspects of traffic safety.

A national traffic safety improvement narrative would also be useful in getting law enforcement behind the traffic safety issue. Officers and their agencies have a history of responding to recognized threats to public safety. The drug and gang activity in the 1980's, the homeland security effort following 9/11 and, more recently, the issues related to mental health and opioid overdoses are prime examples of a motivated law enforcement response. What is missing today for law enforcement is the commitment to making traffic safety a high priority for our nation.

Conclusion

I have offered a number of perspectives and suggestions in my testimony to assist the committee in its legislative deliberations. The issues surrounding traffic safety are complex and will require leadership to effectively change the behaviors that cause crashes in this country. We currently have individuals that provide that leadership in certain areas of traffic safety but a nationwide comprehensive commitment designed to make this issue a high priority for our country has been missing for some time.

Within our communities are individuals who have personnel stories of how they were affected by a crash. Law enforcement officers make personal death or serious injury notifications to families and friends following a traffic crash on a daily basis. Officers who have done this, including me, will tell you the impact these notifications have on these family and friends as well as the officer are significant. The personal loss, the shock, and the feelings encountered by the officers are the same for traffic crashes as they are those notifications made following a major felony not related to traffic. I have said many times—it doesn't matter if the injury or death is caused by a car fender or a bullet to loved ones.

Our communities want a sustainable and safe quality of life. They want to feel safe in their communities and reduce all threats to safety. Law enforcement's experience has shown this includes their expectations on traffic safety. The committee can play a key leadership role in raising the profile of traffic safety as a public safety issue across our nation. I am confident elevating the issue to a serious, high priority public safety issue will also lead to increased support from law enforcement. This effort may move our nation to a better and safer place than we currently find ourselves.

Thank you for giving me the opportunity to offer my thoughts on this very important policy issue.

Ms. NORTON. Thank you, Chief Brown. Mr. Jay Bruemmer.

Mr. BRUEMMER. Chairwoman Norton and members of the subcommittee, thank you for the opportunity to testify to you today on behalf of the American Traffic Safety Services Association.

ATSSA represents the manufacturers and installers of roadway safety infrastructure devices, such as guard rail and cable barriers, traffic signs, pavement markings, and work zone safety devices, among others.

Our mission is to advance roadway safety and reduce fatalities and serious injuries to zero.

Professionally, I have worked for K&G Striping for 34 years, a Missouri contractor who installs pavement markings, traffic signs, and traffic control.

It is appropriate to be here discussing roadway safety during National Work Zone Awareness Week, as we honor those who lost their lives in work zones around the country, including nearly 800 the previous year.

My first project on an interstate quickly taught me the importance of roadway safety. While striping in a work zone on I–70 nearly Lawrence, Kansas, I looked up to see a semi-truck knocking over cones and headed right at me. I only had enough time to take one step back before I was blown off my feet by the wind.

I was fortunate to go home that day to my family, but tragically many others are not so lucky. Please slowdown in work zones.

Mitigating driver behavior is a perennial challenge for transportation leaders, and knowing this, the roadway safety infrastructure industry has innovated and deployed costeffective countermeasures to combat negative driver behavior. Here are a few examples.

Wrong-way driving crashes are often catastrophic when they occur, especially on highways and high-speed roads. Intelligent transportation systems in conjunction with signage combat wrong-way driving. These systems detect a wrong-way driver and inform both the driver and law enforcement about the incident so law enforcement may intercede within minutes.

Systematic devices like barriers are critically important to the safety ecosystem of a roadway network. This is particularly true in rural areas where 30 percent of total vehicle miles traveled occur, yet 50 percent of roadway fatalities occur.

The Minnesota Department of Transportation installed cable median barrier along 150 miles of road. In the 3 years prior there were 19 fatal cross-median crashes. In the 3 years following, there were zero.

We know that wider pavement markings have positive safety benefits, especially for older drivers. They also prove beneficial for machine-driven vehicles. Under adverse conditions, wider markings consistently improve machine vision detection.

In 2017, nearly 6,000 pedestrians were killed in roadway crashes, and the previous year saw 840 cyclists killed. There are roadway safety infrastructure solutions that help protect both vulnerable users and motorists, including dedicated bike lanes with green pavement markings and delineators, as well as innovative retroreflective crosswalks for pedestrians.

Thirty-seven thousand one hundred and thirty men, women, and children being killed on U.S. roads annually, we cannot allow safety to ever become an afterthought.

None of these safety priorities can be achieved without a solvent, robustly funded Highway Trust Fund.

ATSSA strongly supports increasing user fees to address the long-term viability of the trust fund. This includes indexing gas and diesel taxes and eventually moving towards the vehicle miles traveled user fee system.

The Highway Safety Improvement Program, or HSIP, is the sole Federal highway program focused on roadway safety. States— which are responsible for the safety on all public roads—are able to use these funds for eligible activities.

However, States are allowed to transfer up to 50 percent of their HSIP allocations. Given the importance of safety, ATSSA calls on Congress to eliminate or at the very least reduce the percentage of funds that can be transferred out of HSIP.

Congress has previously ensured that funds from HSIP can only be used for roadway safety infrastructure projects. We urge the committee to continue this language as part of the FAST Act reauthorization and infrastructure packages.

ATSSA calls on Congress to double the size of the Highway Safety Improvement Program to at least 10 percent of the overall core Federal-aid Highway Program so it can aggressively combat fatalities and serious injuries on U.S. roads and expand the use of costeffective, lifesaving roadway infrastructure countermeasures.

In conclusion, we must not let safety slip as our top priority. Roadway safety infrastructure and the Highway Safety Improvement Program are key pieces of the safety puzzle.

And ATSSA looks forward to working with the subcommittee to reduce fatalities and serious injuries on our Nation's roads to zero. Thank you for the opportunity, and I look forward to any questions.

[Mr. Bruemmer's prepared statement follows:]

Prepared Statement of Jay Bruemmer, Vice President, K&G Striping, Inc., on behalf of the American Traffic Safety Services Association

Chairman Holmes Norton, Ranking Member Davis, and members of the Subcommittee, thank you for the opportunity to testify today on behalf of the American Traffic Safety Services Association (ATSSA) on how investing in and improving the safety of America's roadway system impacts each and every one of us. I currently serve as Chairman of ATSSA's Government Relations Committee. I am also a past member of the ATSSA Board of Directors, past President of the ATSSA Chapter Presidents' Council and past President of the Heart of America Chapter of ATSSA (comprised of Kansas and Missouri). ATSSA is a 1,500+ member international trade association which represents the manufacturers, installers and distributors of roadway safety infrastructure devices and services such as guardrail and cable barrier, traffic signs, pavement markings, rumble strips, high friction surface treatments, and work zone safety devices, among others. Our mission is to Advance Roadway Safety and reduce fatalities and serious injuries on U.S. roads toward zero.

Professionally, I am the Vice President of K&G Striping Inc., a Riverside, MO-based contractor focused on pavement marking, traffic sign installation, and traffic control. K&G Striping has been a contractor in the Midwest since 1982, incorporated in 1989, and now serves Johnson County, Jackson County and the greater Kansas City metro area. If you're driving through western Missouri and find yourself in a roadway work zone, chances are you will see our trucks doing the work. In fact, Ranking Member Sam Graves represents our office here in Congress.

Congratulations to Chairman DeFazio, Ranking Member Graves, Chairman Holmes Norton, and Ranking Member Davis on your new leadership positions on the Committee and Subcommittee, and thank you for holding this critically-important hearing. The timing of this hearing coincides with National Work Zone Awareness Week, honoring those who have lost their lives in roadway work zones and spreading awareness for the need to enhance safety in work zones around the coun- try. In 2017, 799 people were killed in work zones, which includes both motorists and workers.

We hear it almost every single day—that transportation safety is the number one priority. Members of Congress, the Executive Branch, businesses, states, local governments and users of the transportation system all talk about the importance of safety programs. But sometimes, the need to invest in safety infrastructure is easy to overlook or take for granted. But with more than 37,000 men, women and children being killed on U.S. roads annually, and from personal experience of working in roadway work zones, we cannot allow safety to ever become an afterthought or second priority. Period.

According to the National Highway Traffic Safety Administration (NHTSA), 37,133 individuals were killed in motor vehicle crashes in 2017. This is truly a horrifying statistic; however, the glimmer of hope is that this was a reduction from 2016 by approximately 2%.[55] Additionally, preliminary 2018 data indicates that this decline in fatalities is potentially continuing.[56] For me and the men and women employed by K&G Striping, this number hits very close to home, especially when you consider that in 2017, 799 of those fatalities occurred in work zones. Imagine yourself working on a road construction project, and passenger vehicles and motor carriers are traveling at 50, 60, 70+ miles per hour only feet from where you are working. You might be protected by a steel or concrete barrier, but you might just have some plastic cones and barrels

---

[55] NHTSA 2017 Fatality Data—https://www.nhtsa.gov/press-releases/us-dot-announces-2017- roadway-fatalities-down.
[56] NHTSA Preliminary 2018 Fatality Data—https://crashstats.nhtsa.dot.gov/Api/Public/ ViewPublication/812629.

separating you from thousands of pounds of speeding steel. I know from personal experience how terrifying this can be.

When I was 18 years old, one of my first projects working on the interstate was on I-70 between Lawrence and Topeka. We were installing temporary pavement markings behind a lane closure to prepare to switch traffic to head to head on the eastbound lanes. While putting down reflective markers, I looked up to see a semi-truck, which had not seen the lane closure in time, knocking over channelizers in the taper and headed directly toward me. I had just enough time to stand up, and take one step back before the wind blew me off my feet. When I stood back up, I saw the tire tracks through the tar I had put down for the next marker I was going to install. Had I not been lucky enough to look up when I did, the outcome would have been catastrophic. At the age of 18, I learned firsthand two incredibly important lessons: that I was not invincible and the importance of safety while working on the road. Years later when I became the owner of our business, I repeatedly used this experience to remind myself that the safety of my employees must be my primary concern.

In 2005 as part of the SAFETEA–LU legislation, Congress authorized the Highway Safety Improvement Program or HSIP, and subsequently reauthorized that program in 2012 in MAP–21 and again in 2015 under the FAST Act. The HSIP program is the sole federal highway program focused on roadway safety infrastructure. Over the lifetime of the FAST Act, HSIP is authorized at approximately $12.5 billion, including set asides for the Work Zone Safety Grant and the Railway-Highway Crossings Program. States—which are responsible for the safety on all public roads, not only state-owned roads—are able to utilize these funds for eligible activities under HSIP. However, states are also allowed to transfer up to 50% of their HSIP allocations to other core federal-aid highway programs—such as the National Highway Performance Program, Surface Transportation Block Grant Program, Transportation Alternatives, National Highway Freight Program, and the Congestion Mitigation and Air Quality Improvement Program and vice versa.

And states have opted to utilize these transfer provisions. Under MAP–21 and the FAST Act—as of September 30, 2018—24 states transferred HSIP funds to other programs, totaling approximately $1.2 billion. Given the importance of safety and the need for safety to remain a priority area of investment, ATSSA calls on Congress to eliminate, or at the very least, reduce the percentage of funds that can be transferred out of HSIP to ensure that roadway safety infrastructure funds are being utilized on roadway safety infrastructure projects.

Additionally, in MAP–21, Congress ensured that funds from the Highway Safety Improvement Program (HSIP) could only be used for eligible roadway safety infrastructure projects under HSIP. We urge the committee to continue this language as part of the FAST Act reauthorization.

Mitigating driver behavior is a perennial challenge for transportation leaders; however, the roadway safety infrastructure industry has innovated and deployed cost-effective countermeasures to combat negative driver behavior. Here are a few examples.

Wrong-Way Driving

Although not incredibly frequent, wrong-way driving crashes are often catastrophic when they do occur, especially on highways and high-speed roads. There are several countermeasures that work to address this issue, namely signage, markings and LED lights on signs. However, road owners can also opt to utilize intelligent transportation systems, in conjunction with signs, to combat wrong-way driving. These systems detect a wrong-way driver and inform both the driver and law enforcement about the incident.[57]

High Friction Surface Treatment

High friction surface treatments (HFST) are an example of an infrastructure safety countermeasure that does not require the driver to make behavioral changes in order to have a positive safety impact. These treatments are applied to high risk crash locations such as intersections or curves. Durable aggregate (usually bauxite) is applied to the road surface and bonded using a polymer binder. In 75 locations in Kentucky where HFST were applied, roadway departure crashes decreased by 91% in wet conditions and 78% in dry conditions.[58]

Pedestrian and Bicycle Safety

In 2017, 5,977 pedestrians were killed in roadway crashes across the United States. In 2016, there were 840 bicyclists killed in roadway crashes. There are roadway safety infrastructure solutions that help protect both vulnerable users and motorists, including dedicate bicycle lanes with green pavement markings and flexible delineators as well as retro-reflective crosswalks for pedestrians. One countermeasure focused on pedestrian safety is the Leading Pedestrian Interval Plus (LPI+), which allows the pedestrian to begin crossing the street before traffic is allowed to move. Studies have shown that LPIs can reduce vehicle-pedestrian crashes by as much as 60%.[59]

Smarter Work Zones

As I mentioned, this week being National Work Zone Awareness Week, it is a crucial moment to talk about safety in work zones. Work zones are inherently dangerous areas, and the safety of the men and women working on the road is paramount. Making work zones smarter, safer, and more efficient will decrease fatalities and serious injuries for

---

[57] "Improving Driver Behavior with Infrastructure Safety Countermeasures" ATSSA case study publication, 2015.
[58] "Improving Driver Behavior with Infrastructure Safety Countermeasures" ATSSA case study publication, 2015.
[59] "Traffic Control Device Innovations to Improve Pedestrian and Bicycle Safety at Signalized Intersections" ATSSA case study publication, 2019.

both drivers and workers. Smarter work zones can mean intelligent transportation systems, data collection and usage, project coordination, and stakeholder engagement, among many other activities. In Washington, DC, the District Department of Transportation (DDOT) realized that multiple road construction projects in the city were having interrelated impacts on road users. So in response, DDOT created a comprehensive, software-based work zone project management system which brought together roadway, utility, and developer construction activities which identified and lessened public right-of-way conflicts. The top goals of this approach were to minimize work zone location conflicts and impacts and improve safety and mobility within the work zones. A web-based work zone tracking application was used to gather all the data and then send that data to project coordinators to alert them of possible conflicts.[60]

Barrier

Barrier is used either in a median or on the roadside to protect vehicles from leaving the road and impacting other fixed objects or oncoming traffic. Systemic devices such as barrier are critically important to the safety ecosystem of a road network. This is especially true in rural areas where, according to 2016 Federal Highway Administration (FHWA) data, 30% of total vehicle miles traveled occurred, yet 50% of roadway fatalities also occurred. Fatalities on rural roads are disproportionately high. Over a four-year period, the Minnesota Department of Transportation installed cable barrier in 31 segments along 150 miles of roadway. In the three years prior to installation of the cable barrier, there were 19 fatal cross-median crashes. In the three years following installation, there were zero.[61]

We know that these countermeasures work. Through the use of dashboard cameras, we can see how effective roadway safety infrastructure can be. For example, this website shows footage from a camera affixed to a tractor-trailer truck on a highway. The video captured the image of another tractor-trailer truck nearly colliding head-on but the crash being mitigated by cable barrier. https://drive.google.com/file/d/1L-5egeInhrJgB9pZO14PtObM7tYQkI1D/view

Wider, High Visibility Pavement Markings and Cavs

Some countermeasures are seemingly commonsense, but they have lasting positive impacts not only for today's human drivers, but also for connected and automated vehicles into the future. A Texas A&M Transportation Institute (TTI) study found that wider pavement markings in Michigan reduced fatal and injury crashes by nearly 25%, nighttime crashes by nearly 40% and nighttime crashes in wet conditions by more than 33%.[62] A 2011 study of Missouri roads found that wider pavement markings had a

---

[60] Smarter Work Zones: Project Coordination and Technology Applications, ATSSA case study publication, 2016.
[61] "Preventing Vehicle Departures from Roadways" ATSSA case study publication 2015.
[62] "Improving Driver Behavior with Infrastructure Safety Countermeasures" ATSSA case study publication, 2015.

positive safety impact in reducing fatal and serious injury crashes, including: a 46% reduction on rural, multilane undivided highways; a 38% reduction on urban, two-lane highways; and a 34% reduction on rural, multilane divided highways.[63]

We know that wider pavement markings have positive safety benefits, especially for older drivers. But the question arises of whether or not wider markings assist vehicles equipped with machine vision/connected and automated vehicles (CAVs). A separate TTI study finds that the answer is yes. In February 2017, BMW's President and CEO-North America testified that clear lane markings were a critical component to a transportation network that was ready to deploy CAVs.[64] Additionally, TTI undertook a separate study in 2018 which looked at wider pavement markings and CAVs. This study found that wider markings, under adverse conditions, consistently improved machine vision detection. Adverse conditions include: crack seal, pavement seams, scarring, "ghost" lines from previous markings, and glare.[65]

With that said, we believe that full deployment of CAVs is still some time away. The average age of a vehicle in the U.S. is 11.5 years old, and according to 2017 data, the median household income in the United States is $61,372.[66] In each congressional district, there are families who make below this average income line. And even for families who have a household income above the median, we need to recognize the fact that most families will not want to purchase a new car until they feel it is time for them to do so. It is hard to believe that, even once CAVs are readily available, families will be able to or necessarily want to immediately rush to their car dealer to purchase one of these new CAVs. It is important that we understand these realities when planning for the expanded deployment of these technologies.

Safety Funding

None of these safety priorities can be achieved without a solvent, robustly-funded Highway Trust Fund. Continuing to spend more from the Highway Trust Fund than is collected through taxes and fees is not a long-term solution. We need to address these deficiencies. In that regard, we strongly support an increase to user fees to address the long-term viability of the Highway Trust Fund, which include increasing and indexing the motor fuels user fees, an eventual move towards a vehicle miles traveled user fee system, and where it makes sense, the use of public private partnerships (P3s).

We view P3s as a separate issue from the Highway Trust Fund solvency. Increasing the use of P3s does not address the underlying fiscal cliff of the Highway Trust Fund. As we consider an infrastructure package and a FAST Act reauthorization, the

---

[63] "Innovative Safety Solutions with Pavement Markings and Delineation" ATSSA case study publication, 2016.
[64] https://www.enotrans.org/article/two-decades-congress-still-pushing-21st-century-infrastructure/.
[65] "Evaluation of the Effects of Pavement Marking Width on Detectability by Machine Vision: 4-Inch versus 6-Inch Markings" October 2018 Texas A&M Transportation Institute.
[66] U.S. Census Bureau Data—https://www.census.gov/library/stories/2018/09/highest-median-household-income-on-record.html.

Administration and Congress must grapple with the fact that increased direct federal investments are crucial to the rebuilding and safety of America's roadway network.

With any increase in revenue for the Highway Trust Fund, ATSSA calls on Congress to double the size of the Highway Safety Improvement Program to at least 10% of the overall core federal-aid highway programs so that we can aggressively combat fatalities and serious injuries on U.S. roads and expand the use of cost-effective, life-saving roadway safety infrastructure countermeasures.

In conclusion, as a nation, we have made great strides in all aspects of roadway safety: behavioral, vehicle, emergency response, and infrastructure. As we move into the third decade of the 21st century, we must continue to press forward with safety and not let it slip from our top priority. Roadway safety infrastructure and the Highway Safety Improvement Program are a key piece of the safety puzzle, and this Subcommittee has the opportunity and responsibility to lead the charge in reducing fatalities and serious injuries on our nation's roads.

Thank you again for the opportunity to testify today. I look forward to answering any of your questions.

Ms. NORTON. And thank you for your testimony.

We want to hear next from Mr. Mike Sewell here on behalf of the League of American Bicyclists.

Mr. SEWELL. Thank you, Chairwoman Norton as well as distinguished members of this subcommittee.

I am very happy to be here to answer your questions about pedestrian/bicycle safety.

My name is Mike Sewell. I am from Louisville, Kentucky, where I work as a professional engineer. I also serve as the Active Transportation Service Line Leader and one of the owners of Gresham Smith. It is an architecture and engineering consulting firm.

I am representing not only the engineering profession today, but also the League of American Bicyclists, where I serve on their board of directors.

But most importantly today, I come to you as a daily bicycle commuter. As little as a decade ago, I would be a very highly unlikely candidate to be talking to you about bicycle and pedestrian safety. However, as fate would have it, I found myself stuck in a car in construction traffic watching pedestrians and bicyclists move across a Second Street bridge passing me, and so in a fit of frustration I decided I would abandon my car on the side of the road and attempt to join them.

Something serendipitous happened about halfway across that Second Street bridge though. I heard a bicycle bell, and as I looked over my shoulder, a bicyclist said, "It is a beautiful day, is it not?" And in my current state of mind, I had a hard time matching his enthusiasm, and at that point I had an epiphany. My choice of transportation that morning was negatively influencing my ability to enjoy myself.

So I decided right then and there I was going to bike to work the next day. That was almost 8 years ago, and I am pleased to say I have biked to work about every day since, and I now have a far better understanding of what it means to be joyful in a commute. But me as an engineer, that decision made me challenge myself in the decisions I was making and our public right-of-way that might impede or allow other folks to have a similar epiphany and enjoy themselves in their commute.

And as most engineers will do, we dug into data, and what I found was quite alarming. Between 2008 and 2017, we saw pedestrian deaths increase by 35 percent while pedestrians as a mode share only increased by 1 percent.

What that tells me is that pedestrian deaths make up a vastly disproportionate amount of fatalities on our roadway.

Bike fatalities are at their highest level since the early 1990s, with a 3-year average increase of 14.7 percent.

There are also direct ties to equity issues in our transportation network that relate also to fatalities. What we found is older adults, people of color, or people attempting to walk and bike in lower income communities are far disproportionately represented in fatalities as well.

Part of this fix is education, and thankfully, the League of American Bicyclists has formal training programs that educate about 60,000 bicycle riders about how better to engage in transportation in our corridors, stay visible, and ride with confidence.

They have also formalized a bicycle-friendly driver program to better educate drivers on what to expect from bicyclists.

However, education alone is not enough. Congress has a critical role in addressing policy and funding that allows people like me, engineers, to proactively design safer transportation systems.

Nationwide bicycling and walking make up approximately 12 percent of trips. They roughly make up 18 percent of fatalities. Yet less than 1 percent of HSIP dollars are spent focusing on better bicycling and pedestrian infrastructure type projects to address these fatalities.

Part of the reason is the way HSIP is set up. States were required to prioritize hot spots, basically pinpoints on a map that categorize how fatal accidents are happening in a location.

But what we found, too, is that it is a straightforward approach, but it does not tell the entire story. There are other factors that determine if a pedestrian is going to be safe or a bicyclist is going to be safe, such as roadway classification, speed differential, geometry, as well as land use. All of these can be used for a data-driven approach to determine where safety issues are likely to occur or where future users will likely encounter them.

This is also not just an urban problem. We found that our rural areas also have a lot of difficulty implementing meaningful and safe multimodal connections.

Today I would like to suggest adding a special rule to HSIP that requires States to address vulnerable user safety where there is a high rate of fatalities related to vulnerable users.

Despite increases in bicyclist and pedestrian fatalities nationwide, there are some good stories that come out of this. In some locations, States and cities are seeing decreases. Oregon, for instance, is a great example, having nearly a 31-percent decrease in the number of fatalities for bicyclists over the course of 2007 to 2016, despite a 46-percent increase in bike commuter trips.

These results can be replicated through proactive policy, appropriate funding, education, and better engineered streets for all users.

I appreciate your time, and thank you for this opportunity. I look forward to answering any questions you may have.

[Mr. Sewell's prepared statement follows:]

Prepared Statement of Mike Sewell, Active Transportation Service Line Leader, Gresham Smith, on behalf of the League of American Bicyclists

Thank you, Chairman DeFazio, Ranking Member Graves, and distinguished members of this committee for the invitation to present my perspectives on bicycle and pedestrian safety. My name is Mike Sewell. I am from Louisville, Kentucky where I work as a professional engineer. I also serve as the Active Transportation Service Line leader and one of the owners of Gresham Smith, an Architecture, Engineering and design practice. Gresham Smith is an active member of the American Council of Engineering Companies (ACEC), the business association of the engineering industry representing more than 5,600 engineering firms and 600,000+ engineers, surveyors, architects, and other specialists nationwide.

I am representing not only the engineering profession today, but also the League of American Bicyclists where I serve on their board of directors. Most importantly, today I come to you as a daily bicycle commuter. Since beginning to bike to work, I have ridden more than 7,000 miles and explored dozens of U.S. cities by bike and experienced both the fear and the joy of being a bicyclist on American roads.

Background

The League of American Bicyclists has been a presence on Capitol Hill since 1880, when the first bicycle advocates rode to Washington, D.C. They presented a petition on a bicycle wheel demanding paved roads, which would be safer and more enjoyable for the rising number of bicyclists in America. Then, just as now, we wanted the voices of bicyclists to be heard in the design and future of our transportation system. As most people who bicycle will tell you, though, today's roads certainly do not feel like they have been designed to make it easier to get to work by bike or get to work safely by bike.

It has only been since 1991 that Congress has made funding for bicycling and walking projects part of federal transportation programs. In the intervening 28 years, we have seen a significant increase in bicycling for both transportation and recreation. More recently, state and local governments have begun promoting bicycling as a transportation option to reduce congestion and improve public health with the proliferation of bike share systems, separated bike lanes, and state and local initiatives with significant investments in bicycling networks. In places like Minneapolis, New York and Virginia, rates of bicycling have increased significantly and these gains have often been accompanied by better safety outcomes for all road users.

Metro Nashville Division Street Extension—Nashville, TN.

Geography/Local Background

Slightly more than 20% of all bike commuters can be found in just 10 cities, including New York City where nearly 50,000 people choose to travel to work by bike. When those in Washington think about someone bicycling for transportation, the image that might come to mind is a young person on Pennsylvania Avenue coming to work from Columbia Heights, benefiting from urban density and local bike amenities.

But bicycling is by no means confined to first tier cities. Louisville, Kentucky, my hometown, is a strong example of how a midsize city has also benefited from prioritizing bicycle facilities:

- Over the last decade, Louisville has made a concerted effort to improve our bicycling options, and is now certified as a Silver-level Bicycle Friendly Community by the League of American Bicyclists.
- Louisville is a member of the Road to Zero Coalition and Kentucky supports the national movement Toward Zero Deaths, focusing on how engineering roads can prevent deaths of people walking or biking.

- These efforts have paid off: while nationwide the number of people killed while biking reached a 25-year high in 2016, Louisville saw a decrease in bicyclist fatalities in recent years even while biking to work increased significantly.
- Bicycling in Louisville is not just an urban solution, but is a way to help people experience the city, countryside and places in between.
  - I personally am involved in projects dedicated to creating safe bikeways within the urban core, as well as a project linking the city to the countryside. That 22-mile project will increase safe, healthy transportation options to nearby residents.
- As a Gold Level Bike Friendly Business, Gresham Smith, actively pursued building space adjacent to better bicycle and pedestrian infrastructure as well as adjacent land uses that allow our employees access to more restaurants and shop that are also bike friendly.

Town Branch Commons—Lexington, KY.

Bicycling is also an important part of transportation in many rural states. In Montana, people bike to work at a rate more than twice the national average. In North Dakota, more people bike to work than use public transit. And in Northwest Arkansas, the construction of 163 miles of trails and paths over the last 10 years has led to a 24% average annual increase in bicycling.

Town Branch Commons—Lexington, KY.

Equity

There is no denying that bicycling is an affordable and economical means of transportation and isused by a wide range of people to make a living. The money people save on transportation allows them to spend more in the local economy, as well as afford housing, education, and other necessary expenses. In fact, bicycling is integral to getting employees to and from work. According to data from the 2017 National Household Travel Survey, people from households with incomes of less than $25k per year took nearly 25% of all the nation's bike trips. Similarly, the same survey said that 20% of bike trips were to earn a living, which is 4% higher than the percentage of trips to earn a living for all modes of transportation [https://nhts.ornl.gov/vehicletrips].

Safety

When I work with communities interested in increasing active transportation, one of their major concerns is safety. No community wants to lose a mother, father, son, daughter, or neighbor in a fatal crash. While multiple surveys show Americans want to bike more, it is often their concern about safety that stops them.

The concern for safety is one of both perception and reality.

- Improvements in traffic safety over the last quarter century have not been evenly distributed; people in cars have been the main beneficiaries, while people biking and walking represent an increasing percentage of traffic fatalities.
- But the data also shows increasing fatalities of people biking and walking, with more people being killed while biking in 2016 than in any year since 1991.
- On a per trip basis, bicycling is just slightly more dangerous than walking and it is safer than walking on a per mile basis.

You might be thinking we are seeing higher fatalities among bicyclists as a result of more people bicycling. However, the inverse is true. For example, despite their overall disparity in population size, more people bike to work in Oregon than in Texas, but in 2016 Oregon had 55 fewer bicyclists die on its roads than Texas. This difference in safety can be explained by at least two reasons:

- Oregon has a long history of investing in safe bicycling infrastructure, meaning that more people are likely riding on safe infrastructure. Oregon has had a Complete Streets law since 1971 and makes bicyclist safety an emphasis area in its Strategic Highway Safety Plan.
    - In comparison, Texas adopted a Complete Streets policy in 2011 and does not make bicyclist safety an emphasis area in its Strategic Highway Safety Plan.
- The number of people biking in Oregon leads to an effect known as "safety in numbers." This effect has been found in numerous studies. The more people who bike leads to more driver awareness of bicyclists, more predictable behavior by bicyclists and drivers, and improved safety through better behavior.

A reimagined Broadway in Louisville, KY with a complete street approach.

The League's Theory of Safety

While there is limited data to pinpoint the reasons for increasing bicyclist fatalities, we know that bicyclists' perceptions of safety and safety outcomes are shaped by drivers and the built environment. According to a 2012 NHTSA survey [https://www.nhtsa.gov/sites/nhtsa.dot.gov/files/811841b.pdf], the most common reason that a bicyclist felt their safety was threatened was due to a motorist's action—usually driving too close. In keeping with that data, improving bicyclist safety should also be about improving driver behavior, like limiting distractions, and implementing infrastructure that reduces or mitigates opportunities for drivers to threaten bicyclists.

To improve bicyclist safety the League has pursued three strategies:

- Increasing bike infrastructure and networks, especially protected bike infrastructure. According to AARP [https://www.aarp.org/livable-communities/getting-around/info-2016/why-bicycling-infrastructure-is-good-for-people-who-dont- ride-bikes.html], in New York City, injuries for motorists, pedestrians and bicyclists declined [http://www.streetsblog.org/2014/09/05/new-dot-report-shows-protected-bike-lanes-improve-safety-for-everybody/] by 20% on streets with pro- tected bike lanes.
  - Bicycle infrastructure can include a variety of solutions based on different community needs. My written testimony includes pictures of some examples.
- Promoting Complete Streets policies and practices. Earlier, I noted how Oregon's early adoption of Complete Streets has led to decades of road design that have resulted in better safety outcomes for cyclists. That is because Complete Streets policies consider all users in the planning, design and construction phases of roads. By adopting policies and practices that assume consideration for all users, the costs of bicycle lanes can be reduced by up to 40% according to data from the FHWA [https://www.fhwa.dot.gov/environment/bicyclepedestrian/publications/resurfacing/resurfacingworkbook.pdf].
  - Complete Streets can encompass a variety of street designs, safety improvements, and planning and operational practices. My written testimony includes picture of some examples.
- Adopting and enforcing safe passing laws, which require drivers to give cyclists at least three feet of clearance when they are passing. According to the National Conference of State Legislatures [http://www.ncsl.org/research/transportation/safely-passing-bicyclists.aspx], 32 states, including Kentucky have this type of law.
  - According to data from NHTSA, a person is most likely to be killed while biking when hit from behind despite this being a relatively rare collision type.

The League believes that improving bicyclist safety will take dedicated pursuit of those three strategies and more. Congress should consider whether more proactive safety legislation—which might improve vehicle designs, provide incentives for advanced and automated vehicle safety systems, and create performance standards for in-vehicle and device-based distraction—are appropriate to supplement the strategies discussed here.

Federally-backed initiatives that embrace the goal of zero traffic deaths, such as the Road to Zero Coalition and Towards Zero Deaths national safety strategy have attracted wide support, but some safety efforts require congressional leadership.

> *"...the most common reason that a person bicycling felt their safety was threatened was due to a motorist's action..."*

Taking off my bike helmet and speaking as an engineer, the trend we are seeing in the engineering industry is toward a "safe systems" approach. The basic idea is that humans will continue to make mistakes and/or choose risky behaviors (e.g., distracted driving, speeding, driving while impaired, not wearing a seatbelt, etc.) so the transportation infrastructure should be designed to reduce fatalities when accidents do occur.

Using a data driven, analytical approach, engineers are deploying a variety of proven countermeasures and design strategies—such as corridor access management, adding turn lanes, medians and pedestrian crossing islands, and road diets/ reconfigurations, among many others—to control vehicle speeds, calm traffic, and thereby manage the kinetic energy transfer among road users in accidents. These factors, in addition to traditional design criteria such as sight distance, intersection design to reduce conflicts, and roadside improvements on horizontal curves, can enhance safety of all roadway users and adapt the structure and function of the system to accommodate the complexities of human behavior.

Louisville Metro Urban Bike Network—Louisville, KY.

HSIP ASK

One area where Congress can make a difference in the lives of people who bike and walk is the Highway Safety Improvement Program (HSIP). HSIP [https://www.fhwa.dot.gov/fastact/factsheets/hsipfs.cfm] is a congressionally authorized road safety program that distributes more than $2 billion each year based on where data shows funding could improve road safety.

First, I would encourage the committee to increase funding for HSIP commensurate with an overall increase in the federal-aid highway program. Safety elements are included in other apportionments, but HSIP is a primary tool for the kinds of enhancements we are discussing and cannot be neglected.

Despite the data and safety outcome focus of the program, because the algorithms are written with blind spots, funding does not flow to places where bicyclists and pedestrians are dying. Currently, Congress requires HSIP funding to go to "hot spots" and leaves it up to state Departments of Transportation to write the formulas for where those hot spots occur.

- For instance, the New Jersey DOT has a stated policy that its HSIP funding should be spent on pedestrian improvements in the same proportion of fatalities that are pedestrians.
- However, despite over 30% of roadway fatalities in New Jersey being pedestrians, the state reports spending NONE of its HSIP on pedestrians. The "data-driven" formula cannot identify a hot spot for these pedestrian fatalities and so 1 in every 3 roadway fatalities in New Jersey goes unaddressed by HSIP.

Bicycling and walking make up 12% of transportation trips, 18% of roadway fatalities, and receive less than 1% of HSIP investments. In 10 states where bicyclist and pedestrian fatalities averaged more than 15% of all traffic fatalities in the last 5 years, the state reported spending $0 of HSIP funding on bicyclist and pedestrian safety projects during that time.

To effectively improve pedestrian and bicyclist safety through HSIP, Congress needs to provide leadership to state DOTs.

- Pedestrian and bicyclist fatalities do not usually occur in "hot spots" but do predictably occur along corridors that can be identified using alternative analyses. Often these corridors are arterial roadways with commercial and residential development and high observed speeds.
- Speed is incredibly important for the safety of people biking and walking.
    - If you are driving 45 mph and hit a bicyclist or a pedestrian, there is a 90% chance you will kill them. At 35 mph the chances of death drop to 50%, at 25 mph there is 85% chance of survival.

The growing number of Vision Zero communities has found a vast majority of fatalities happen on a small percentage of roads with similar contexts.

- For instance in San Francisco, 75% of severe and fatal traffic injuries occur on just 13% of its streets[67].
- In Denver, 50% of traffic fatalities occur on 5% of the roads[68].

Louisville Metro Urban Bike Network—Louisville, KY.

Congress plays a critical role in leading the nation towards sustained improvements for people biking and walking through the Highway Safety Improvement Program. In past transportation bills, such as MAP–21 and the FAST Act, Congress has taken steps to improve the safety of people biking and walking, including:

- Removing the requirement to focus only on hot spots.
- Requiring more attention to bicycling and pedestrian crashes.
- Allowing states to use HSIP on roads that have dangerous features, before fatalities occur. Allowing proactive systematic approaches to safety.

---

[67] Vision Zero SF 2019 Action Strategy.
[68] Denver Vision Zero Action Plan. https://www.denvergov.org/content/dam/denvergov/Portals/705/documents/visionzero/Denver-Vision-Zero-Action-Plan-draft-July2017.pdf. Pg.5.

Metro Nashville 28th-31st Avenue Connector—Nashville, TN.

Those changes were necessary and we applaud them. However, many states have not yet significantly addressed the crisis of safety for people who bike and walk.

At this time, we are not asking states to change their HSIP formulas, but rather are proposing supplementing those formulas. We don't want to throw out the good work done to address hot spots, but want to stop the perpetuation of blind spots and encourage states to slow down and take a harder look at what they might not be seeing.

- In areas where vulnerable user fatalities are above a certain threshold, such as MPOs, regional planning areas, tribal lands, and other jurisdictions that receive federal funding, HSIP funds should be directed to vulnerable user safety projects and protections in those areas.
  - Such a change dovetails with changes in the FAST Act which requires states to consider all users when constructing and reconstructing on non-interstate Federal Highway System roads. These roads are often the arterials and connectors where bicyclist and pedestrian fatalities happen.
  - Vulnerable user safety projects could include separated bicycle infrastructure, improved at-grade crossings including medians, grade-separated connections across high speed and high volume roads, and wider shoulders on rural roads. Many of these projects are already recommended by the FHWA.

Recognize Past Changes

The changes we want for HSIP also dovetail with non-infrastructure changes made by Congress, which recognized the need for education and enforcement to complement safe infrastructure for people biking and walking.

The League believes that traffic safety goes beyond infrastructure and vehicle standards. While my professional career is about building complete streets and better infrastructure for all road users, I am also a strong believer in the role of education in improving the safety of bicycling.

- As a certified League Cycling Instructor, I have been trained to teach adults and children safe bicycling practices, including obeying traffic laws, practicing defensive bicycling techniques, and ensuring your bike is safe to ride.
- Since the 1970s the League has trained more than 6,000 cycling instructors, and these instructors train an average of 60,000 bicyclists each year. Our materials have been translated into seven languages.
- The League is also rolling out a Bicycle Friendly Driver curriculum. It is a program developed in Fort Collins, Colo., to teach drivers why bicyclists ride like we do and create a shared understanding of how we use the road.
- As a lifelong learner in the transportation industry, programs like these help people better respond to the changes we are seeing on our roads and can better support people who choose or depend on biking and walking.

On enforcement, the League celebrated Congress's decision in the FAST Act to create the 405(h) program that funds education and enforcement around state laws pertaining to bicyclists and pedestrians in those states where bicyclist and pedestrian fatalities are more than 15% of all traffic fatalities.

Since its creation in the FAST Act, every eligible state has applied for the available funding and that funding has been used for a variety of education and enforcement campaigns.

- In Georgia [https://www.nhtsa.gov/sites/nhtsa.dot.gov/files/documents/gafy2018 lar.pdf], 405(h) funds were used to publish bicycle safety messages, reaching over 14 million contacts by leveraging existing bicycling-related groups, and to distribute more than 17,000 bicycle safety guides to agencies and others.
- In Oregon [https://www.nhtsa.gov/sites/nhtsa.dot.gov/files/documents/or/fy2018 lar.pdf], 405(h) funds were used to fund minigrants to localities to implement an "Oregon Friendly Driver" program.
- In Florida [https://www.nhtsa.gov/sites/nhtsa.dot.gov/files/documents/fllfy18 lar.pdf], 405(h) funds were used to develop a four-hour classroom based training course to improve the effectiveness of officers taking part in High Visibility Enforcement to support pedestrian and bicycle safety in Florida.

The 405(h) program shows how directing funding to change the culture around how we view the safety of people biking and walking can be successful. Through these programs, Congress has demonstrated attention to the safety of people biking and walking as well as encouraged continued actions to promote the safety of all people who use our nation's roadways.

In closing, I would like to again emphasize the need for updates to the Highway Safety Improvement Program so that it directs funding to the needs of all roadway users. As currently implemented, HSIP all too often has blind spots for the safety of people walking and biking. Just as we ask drivers to do, the program needs to check your blind spots for people you may not have seen.

We appreciate the steps Congress has taken in the last two transportation bills on improving education regarding bicycle and pedestrian laws, and believe Congress should build on those steps by improving HSIP so that the transportation system's most vulnerable users are not overlooked in its data-driven process.

Ms. NORTON. Thank you, Mr. Sewell.

Next, Nicholas Smith for the National Safety Council.

Mr. SMITH. Good morning, Chairwoman Norton, Ranking Member Spano, and Chairman DeFazio, as well as the members of the subcommittee. Thank you for inviting me to testify today on improving the safety on our Nation's roadways.

My name is Nick Smith, and I am the interim president and CEO of the National Safety Council, and I am also the chair of the Road to Zero Coalition, which is focused on reaching zero fatalities by 2050.

Last year, the coalition, which is over 900 strong, representing transportation organizations, government, businesses, academia, safety advocates, including those organizations represented here today on this panel, issued this report [indicating a document], a framework to help us get to zero deaths on our roadways by the year 2050.

Together we call out three steps to reach the goal of zero deaths on our roadways. One, we believe doubling down on what works through proven evidence-based strategies.

Two, accelerate advanced lifesaving technology in vehicles and in infrastructure.

And three, prioritize safety by adopting a safe systems approach and creating a positive safety culture.

My full testimony mentions specific steps for each of these. Today I will focus on prioritizing safety, which is the third step we call out.

Today over 100 people will die in crashes on our roadway. Yesterday over 100 people died in crashes, and tomorrow over 100 people will die again in motor vehicle crashes. But there is no outrage. In every other mode of transportation this committee oversees, there is a different expectation of safety.

For example, after two airplane crashes, countries across the world grounded all Boeing 737 Max 800 and 900 airplanes. In less than a week, a coordinated global action was taken to address a potential risk to millions of people.

This committee rightly held hearings to determine causation and next steps. We can all agree that this was the right decision, but every 72 hours, we lose 328 people, nearly the equivalent of these 2 airplane crashes on U.S. roadways.

Where is our outrage over these deaths? And where is our urgency to prevent them? We must demand safety for all no matter how they are mobile.

Now for the good news. We know how to prevent these fatalities from happening. We just have not had the will to prioritize these actions.

The culture around traveling on the roadways is very different from the airways. We require safety management systems and safety training for people who work in our airway system, and we even have a safety briefing for passengers before every flight.

When things go wrong, this committee demands answers. Several Federal agencies send people to investigate, and a plane can be grounded. Simply put, we have a strong safety culture when it comes to aviation.

So how do we raise the bar on safety on our road? The reauthorization of the FAST Act provides you an opportunity to do so today. While prioritizing safety, the reauthorization bill should encourage States to pass strong laws to implement proven countermeasures to save lives, like automated enforcement and lowering the blood alcohol concentration.

Also, the bill should support safer roadway designs that provide for the safe movement of all roadway users and incorporates safety no matter if in a rural, suburban, or urban area. We know that drivers are human and we make mistakes and errors, and safer designs can help make sure those errors do not become fatalities.

These are only a few examples of how to prioritize safety and move toward our goal to zero deaths on our roadway system.

I have with me a letter from the Road to Zero Coalition asking Congress to prioritize safety. This bill should not be about more miles of pavement only. It must include safety in every aspect of the bill.

I urge you to use this report as a framework to prioritize safety in our transportation system.

I hope you will join me in saying enough is enough. The value of life should not depend on whether you are sitting on an airplane or behind the wheel of a car. It is time to bring the culture of safety on our roadways to levels we have achieved in the air. We know how to get there. We just need the will to do so.

I look forward to discussing more with you today. Thank you. [Mr. Smith's prepared statement follows:]

Prepared Statement of Nicholas J. Smith, Interim President and Chief Executive Officer, the National Safety Council

Chairwoman Norton, Ranking Member Davis and members of the Subcommittee, thank you for inviting me to testify today on improving the safety of our nation's roadways.

It is an honor to be with you today. My name is Nicholas Smith, and I am the Interim President and CEO of the National Safety Council (NSC) and the Chair of the Road to Zero Coalition. It is nice to be back in Washington, as I previously lived and worked here at the Department of Homeland Security and for Majority Leader Bill Frist.

The National Safety Council is a 100-year-old nonprofit committed to eliminating preventable deaths in our lifetime by focusing on reducing fatalities and injuries in workplaces, on the road and in homes and communities. Our more than 15,000 member companies represent employees at more than 50,000 U.S. worksites. Not only do we work with companies but also with organized labor, who share our dedication to keeping workers safe on and off the job. These members are across the United States and are likely in each district represented on this Committee.

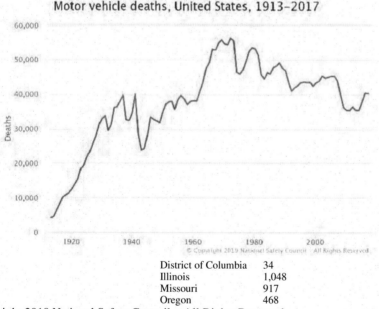

District of Columbia	34
Illinois	1,048
Missouri	917
Oregon	468

Copyright 2019 National Safety Council—All Rights Reserved.

The National Safety Council estimates that over 40,000 people were killed in motor vehicle crashes in 2018.[69] Included here are the number of people killed in motor vehicle

---

[69] https://www.nsc.org/in-the-newsroom/2018-marks-third-straight-year-that-motor-vehicle- deaths-are-estimated-to-have-reached-40-000.

crashes in 2018 from the Chairs' and Ranking Members' states, and a complete overview of all states is included with my testimony.

These are the lives of your constituents. These mothers, fathers, sisters, brothers, aunts and uncles contributed to the communities in which they lived. Yet, our national outrage at these losses is conspicuously absent, particularly when you compare to deaths in other forms of transportation, such as aviation. These crashes and deaths on our roadways not only have a human toll, but there is an annual cost to the American economy of over $433 billion.[70]

The United States has consistently avoided the hard choices needed to save lives on the roadways. The reauthorization of the Fixing America's Surface Transportation (FAST) Act is an opportunity for us to start making the right choices, and I appreciate the opportunity to talk with you today about how to do more to save lives, because we know that all of these deaths are preventable.

What disappoints many of us in the safety community is that the main causes of motor vehicle fatalities—lack of seat belt use, alcohol-impaired driving, and speed—have remained the same for decades.

- 50% of people who die in motor vehicle crashes are unbelted [71]
- 30% of people who die in crashes are involved in alcohol-impaired wrecks [72]
- 27% of the fatalities are speed-related[73]

The solutions to these problems are simple and clearly known, but we need the political and societal will to widely implement them.

Recently, "zero" language has been incorporated into the goals on our roadways. This has been commonplace in other settings like workplaces, where NSC has been involved since its beginning, and it has had meaningful results. NSC is so committed to a zero goal on the roadways that we lead the Road to Zero Coalition, a diverse group of over 900 members committed to eliminating roadway fatalities by 2050. Over the past two and a half years, the coalition has grown to include members from across the country representing transportation organizations, businesses, academia, safety advocates and others, the first time so many organizations have collaborated to put forth a plan to address fatalities on our roads.

The centerpiece of our work together has been the creation of the Road to Zero report, a comprehensive roadmap of the strategies necessary to achieve our goal by 2050. One year ago this month, the coalition issued our report with three primary recommendations.

---

[70] https://injuryfacts.nsc.org/motor-vehicle/overview/introduction/.
[71] https://crashstats.nhtsa.dot.gov/Api/Public/ViewPublication/812662.
[72] https://www.responsibility.org/alcohol-statistics/drunk-driving-statistics/drunk-driving-fatal- ity-statistics/.
[73] https://crashstats.nhtsa.dot.gov/Api/Public/ViewPublication/812451.

1. Double down on what works through proven, evidence based strategies
2. Accelerate advanced lifesaving technology in vehicles and infrastructure
3. Prioritize safety by adopting a safe systems approach and creating a positive safety culture

Double Down

We know what works. Enacting evidence-based laws related to seatbelts, alcohol impairment and speed shows we are ready for change, and education about the laws combined with strong enforcement delivers on the change. We urge legislators to look at these and the many other laws that, if enacted, enforced and promoted would drive down fatalities. While many of these laws require state action, the federal government should consider incentives in the reauthorization bill to accelerate state adoption and enforcement.

The data and research tell us that primary seat belt laws, lowered blood alcohol content laws, and better speed management efforts would have meaningful impact.

Seatbelts

Regardless of other causal factors, the lack of proper occupant restraint continues to increase the severity and lethality of motor vehicle crashes. While 89.6% of American drivers and vehicle occupants used seat belts in 2018, more than 1 in 10 continued to put their lives at unnecessary risk, with tragic consequences. Almost half (47%) of people killed in motor vehicle crashes in 2017 were unbelted.[74] Yet despite these data, only 34 states and the District of Columbia have primary enforcement of their seatbelt laws—meaning law enforcement may stop vehicles solely for belt law violations. Of the other 16 states, 15 have secondary laws—requiring police to have another reason for a traffic stop—and one, New Hampshire, has no belt law. Primary seatbelt laws are proven to increase the rate of belt use and save lives. In 2018, 90.6% of passenger vehicle occupants were belted in states with primary laws, while only 86.4% of occupants were belted in states with secondary or no seatbelt laws.[75] There should only be one acceptable level of safety. Public education and high-visibility enforcement campaigns such as Click It or Ticket have increased public awareness of the dangers of driving unrestrained, but will only be most effective when accompanied by strong laws.

In 2016, the National Highway Traffic Safety Administration (NHTSA) estimates that the use of seat belts in passenger vehicles saved 14,668 lives and if all drivers and passengers had worn their seatbelts, an additional 2,456 lives would have been saved.[76] In

---

[74] https://crashstats.nhtsa.dot.gov/Api/Public/ViewPublication/812662.
[75] https://crashstats.nhtsa.dot.gov/Api/Public/ViewPublication/812662.
[76] https://crashstats.nhtsa.dot.gov/Api/Public/ViewPublication/812454.

Oregon and Illinois, 16 and 52 lives respectively could have been saved with 100% seat belt use.[77] Similarly, the Center for Disease Control and Prevention provides the Motor Vehicle Prioritizing Interventions and Cost Calculator for States (MV PICCS) to help policymakers determine the lives saved and costs of implementation of 14 different evidencebased motor vehicle laws. When comparing Oregon and Illinois again, seat belt enforcement campaigns could save 16 and 35 lives respectively.[78]

Impairment

Another leading cause of roadway deaths is alcohol impairment. Every day, almost 30 people die in alcohol-impaired crashes in the United States—one every 48 minutes.[79] Despite these data, our culture does not prioritize safety, with more than 1 in 10 drivers admitting to driving in the prior year when they thought they were close to or over the legal blood alcohol content (BAC) limit.[80]

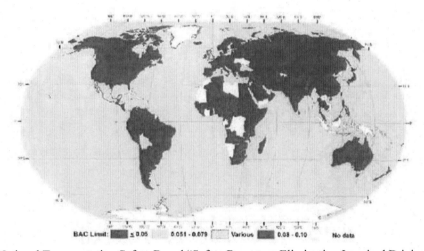

Source: National Transportation Safety Board "Safety Report on Eliminating Impaired Driving (2013)."

The data are clear: drivers are four times more likely to crash at .05 than if they had nothing to drink.[81] Most other industrialized countries have implemented a BAC of .05 or lower, changes which have been followed by decreasing numbers of fatalities from alcoholimpaired crashes. Lowering the BAC limit from .08 to .05 is proven to save lives on the roadways, and in the U.S. could save as many as 1,500 lives if implemented

---

[77] Ibid.
[78] https://www.cdc.gov/motorvehiclesafety/calculator/index.html.
[79] https://www.nhtsa.gov/risky-driving/drunk-driving.
[80] http://tirf.us/wp-content/uploads/2018/12/RSM-TIRF-USA-2018-Alcohol-Impaired-Driving-in- the-United-States-3.pdf.
[81] Blomberg RD, Peck RC, Moskowitz H, Burns M, Fiorentino D: The Long Beach/Fort Lauder- dale relative risk study; J Safety Res 40:285; 2009..

nationally.[82] Utah is the first state in the U.S. to pass a law lowering the BAC to .05. NSC supports other states attempting to implement such legislation, and hopes to see federal legislation introduced to this end.

Speed

The United States has a fatal problem with driving too fast. Just last week, the Insurance Institute for Highway Safety (IIHS) estimated that increasing speed limits over the past 25 years have led to 37,000 deaths.[83] Nearly 27% of roadway fatalities include speed as a causal factor, a factor that is even more deadly for our growing population of vulnerable road users such as pedestrians and bicyclists.

Image: Seattle Department of Transportation

As illustrated, at 20 miles per hour, 9 out of 10 pedestrians would survive being struck by a vehicle, but if you double that speed, 9 out of 10 pedestrians would be killed.

It is not only pedestrians and other vulnerable road users impacted by excess speed, but also 9,242 motor vehicle drivers and occupants who died in 2017 in speed-related crashes.[84] One evidence-based proven countermeasure for speed is automated enforcement. Automated enforcement is proven to reduce speed and save lives, but implementation must be done properly, with safety—not revenue—as the primary objective. NSC, AAA, the Advocates for Highway and Auto Safety and IIHS created the attached checklist to provide guidance to communities as they deploy automated enforcement. As you can see, the guidance encourages transparency and grace among enforcement actions given and dedication of the funds to safety, trauma care or similar purpose.

There are other deadly problems on our roadways, like distraction, that we can do more to solve as well, and these issues should not be overlooked by this Committee.

---

[82] Fell, J.C., and M. Scherer. 2017. Estimation of the potential effectiveness of lowering the blood alcohol concentration (BAC) limit for driving from 0.08 to 0.05 grams per deciliter in the United States. *Alcoholism, Clinical and Experimental Research*. doi: 10.1111/acer.13501.

[83] https://gallery.mailchimp.com/6bedee967fbeb62935e59055b/files/63d3f7b0-3f00-446b-9613-031039a61d02/iihslnewsl040419lemb.pdf?mclcid=5154c704bc&mcleid=ab62186d28.

[84] NSC analysis of NHTSA FARS data.

Advance Technology

Technology is an important disrupter that will continue to transform roadway safety well into the foreseeable future. To reach zero deaths, we need to encourage the development of innovations that address human failures and road design failures and, once proven, establish mandates for adoption of technologies that work. Further, this regulatory certainty and defined standards should drive interoperability and ensure meaningful outcomes. Additionally, data collection on serious and fatal crashes should be required in order to share consistent and verified information, and testing on public roads should be reported to the jurisdictions in which the tests occur. This level of transparency will help consumers better understand the technology and how to operate in it, with it and around it.

Establishing performance standards and common nomenclature for the automated vehicle (AV) technology will also help encourage better understanding. Earlier this year, AAA released a report about the lack of consistency. In it, they found adaptive cruise control has 20 different names and lane keeping assistance has 19 unique names.[85] The trend continued with other technologies. These different names do not aid consumer understanding and acceptance. In fact, AAA also found that over 70% of consumers are afraid of fully automated vehicles.[86] This reauthorization bill should help establish more standards for technology by building the necessary frameworks to support our desired outcomes to reduce deaths on the roadways, and it should include commercial motor vehicles too.

As we sit here today, automakers, technology firms and others are developing partially and fully automated vehicles. The potential safety benefits of automated vehicles could be incredible. When ready, these vehicles will not glance down at their phone, speed through a red light or have an alcoholic beverage before getting behind the wheel—all mistakes that we as human drivers continue to make over and over again, with deadly consequences. To be clear, it will be decades before we have meaningful fleet penetration on U.S. roadways of AVs. In the meantime, there are significant technologies available in vehicles today, Advanced Driver Assistance Systems (ADAS) that can prevent or mitigate crashes. Consumer education about these technologies is key.

While standards are essential, public education is also important. The National Safety Council is working to expand consumer education around these new technologies. NSC and the University of Iowa created a website, MyCarDoesWhat.org, to help. When a person visits MyCarDoesWhat.org, he or she learns about dozens of existing safety features such as lane departure warning, blind spot monitoring, backup cameras, automatic emergency braking and more. The MyCarDoesWhat team has developed videos, infographics and other informational pieces to help drivers understand how these

---

[85] https://www.aaa.com/AAA/common/AAR/files/ADAS-Technology-Names-Research-Report.pdf.
[86] https://newsroom.aaa.com/2019/03/americans-fear-self-driving-cars-survey/.

technologies work and what they are capable of doing. The purpose of MyCarDoesWhat is to educate the public about these assistive safety features in order to maximize their potential lifesaving benefits.

Additionally, the National Safety Council was a founding member of PAVE (Partners for Automated Vehicle Education), which launched in January. PAVE is a broad-based coalition that includes automotive and technology companies, safety and mobility advocates and community partners. PAVE members believe that in order to fully realize the benefits of self-driving technology, policymakers and the public need factual information about the present and future state of such technology. PAVE enhances public understanding through a variety of strategies including an educational website at PaveCampaign.org; "hands-on" demonstrations allowing the public to see and experience driverless technology; and workshops to help policymakers understand the technology. In the future, PAVE will produce educational toolkits for car dealers to help them communicate more effectively with customers about their vehicles' capabilities and limitations.

When it comes to technology, the U.S. prioritized safety years ago by dedicating spectrum for safety purposes to prevent crashes. Today, other groups would like to take the spectrum for streaming services. I urge this committee to direct the U.S. DOT, the Federal Communications Commission, the Department of Commerce and others to maintain the spectrum for roadway safety purposes allowing vehicles to communicate with each other, infrastructure, pedestrians and others to prevent crashes. This spectrum provides a safety margin that we should not give away.

Prioritize Safety

By prioritizing safety, we commit to changing our nation's safety culture. This means we have to accept that any life lost is one too many. Once we accept that one death is too many, we will begin thinking about how to take a "safe systems" approach to our roadways. Fully adopted by the aviation industry, this means building failsafe features that anticipate human error and developing infrastructure with safety margins.

With the understanding that people will make mistakes, the built environment or infrastructure can be more forgiving to eliminate fatalities. Some of these changes may include engineering greater safety into a design. For example, in the pictures below, a multilane intersection with a red light in Scottsdale, Arizona was replaced with a roundabout. With the intersection, there are 32 potential points of failure, but with a roundabout, that is engineered down to only 8.[87] Speeds are decreased, and if crashes do occur, they occur at angles that are not as violent.

---

[87] https://safety.fhwa.dot.gov/intersection/innovative/roundabouts/presentations/safe-tylaspects/long.cfm.

Every Life Counts 93

Successful infrastructure redesign can also look like the picture below from New York City. The picture on the left shows two roads merging together without an area for pedestrians, and the lane lines are non-existent. However, the reworked merge incorporates clearly marked lanes of travel, large sidewalks and areas of less exposure to vehicles for pedestrians.

These infrastructure changes are just as important in rural areas. Rumble strips on the center line or edge of roadways can prevent the roadway departure crashes that account for 52% of fatalities in the U.S.[88] Cable median barriers can also provide a margin of safety to redirect people in to their lane of travel, and high friction surface treatments can decrease vehicle stopping distance on roadways. These are all tools we have available today.

Infrastructure changes can be expensive, but they do not have to be. Through the Road to Zero Coalition, NSC has awarded grants to groups across the country working in communities of all sizes. In the first year of grants, the National Complete Streets

---

[88] https://safety.fhwa.dot.gov/roadwayldept.

Coalition, which is testifying today too, worked with three communities: Lexington, KY, Orlando, FL, and South Bend, IN. Each city was provided only $8,000 dollars from the grant for temporary infrastructure changes that you can see below to measure results. Each city had measurable improvements to safety even with a small dollar investment.

The biggest and hardest change is the shift to truly prioritize safety by changing safety culture on the roads. We cannot be complacent when it comes to losing so many people each and every day on our roads. We need leaders in this area, and I can think of none better than the members of this Committee and Subcommittee. The reauthorization is the vehicle to accomplish this change. We have changed safety culture in workplaces, around child passenger safety and in other areas. We can do it here too with your help.

Other Provisions

There are specific provisions in the FAST Act that can be improved to prioritize safety. These include:

- Altering the "Section 405" programmatic funds that largely go unused by reworking the program to give states different options
- Expanding the use of Highway Safety Improvement Program

Preliminary motor vehicle annual fatality estimates
State motor-vehicle deaths and percent changes

State	Number of Months Reported	2018	2017	2016	2017 to 2018	2016 to 2018
TOTAL U.S.	12	40,000	40,231	40,327	-1%	-1%
Alabama	12	948	914	1,044	4%	-9%
Alaska	12	80	77	84	4%	-5%
Arizona	12	1,013	970	950	4%	7%
Arkansas	12	489	491	545	< 0.5%	-10%
California	12	3,651	3,564	3,680	2%	-1%
Colorado	12	624	630	605	-1%	3%
Connecticut	12	297	284	307	5%	-3%
Delaware	12	111	119	119	-7%	-7%
Dist. of Columbia	12	34	30	28	13%	21%
Florida	12	3,325	3,087	3,037	8%	9%
Georgia	12	1,497	1,528	1,540	-2%	-3%
Hawaii	12	117	107	119	9%	-2%
Idaho	12	233	242	253	-4%	-8%
Illinois	12	1,048	1,080	1,078	-3%	-3%
Indiana	12	859	910	820	-6%	5%
Iowa	12	319	331	403	-4%	-21%
Kansas	12	404	462	431	-13%	-6%
Kentucky	12	721	775	830	-7%	-13%
Louisiana	12	777	792	756	-2%	3%
Maine	12	127	171	159	-26%	-20%
Maryland	12	487	525	490	-7%	-1%
Massachusetts	12	357	360	399	-1%	-11%
Michigan	12	962	1,041	1,064	-8%	-10%
Minnesota	12	382	358	398	7%	-4%
Mississippi	12	633	685	670	-8%	-6%
Missouri	12	917	932	939	-2%	-2%
Montana	12	182	186	190	-2%	-4%
Nebraska	12	230	226	217	2%	6%
Nevada	12	331	305	327	9%	1%
New Hampshire	12	146	102	137	43%	7%
New Jersey	12	565	638	607	-11%	-7%
New Mexico	12	387	375	398	3%	-3%
New York	12	873	928	953	-6%	-8%
North Carolina	12	1,457	1,404	1,435	4%	2%
North Dakota	12	104	113	113	-8%	-8%
Ohio	12	1,071	1,179	1,129	-9%	-5%
Oklahoma	12	627	646	668	-3%	-6%
Oregon	12	468	436	495	7%	-5%
Pennsylvania	12	1,244	1,141	1,189	9%	5%
Rhode Island	12	59	84	53	-30%	11%
South Carolina	12	1,034	983	1,015	5%	2%
South Dakota	12	129	132	116	-2%	11%
Tennessee	12	1,047	1,040	1,042	1%	< 0.5%
Texas	12	3,597	3,721	3,751	-3%	-4%
Utah	12	264	272	280	-3%	-6%
Vermont	12	68	68	64	0%	6%
Virginia	12	817	839	750	-3%	9%
Washington	12	541	554	536	-2%	1%
West Virginia	12	295	303	269	-3%	10%
Wisconsin	12	577	603	592	-4%	-3%
Wyoming	12	111	123	112	-10%	-1%

NOTE: Deaths are reported by state traffic authorities. ALL FIGURES ARE PRELIMINARY. To ensure proper comparisons, 2016 and 2017 figures are preliminary figures covering the same reporting period as those for 2018. The totals for 2016 and 2017 are from the National Center for Health Statistics.

States in bold: States with a decrease in deaths from 2017 to 2018.

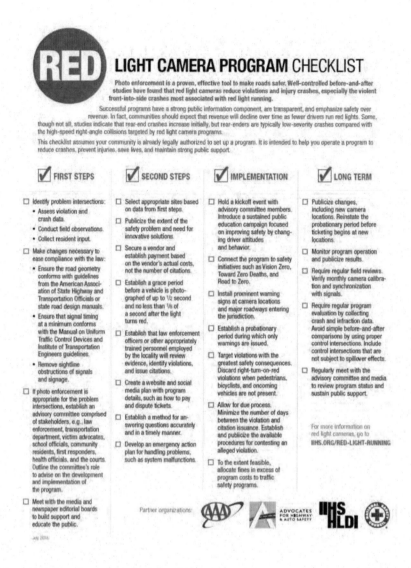

Additionally, the National Safety Council believes we can use data to better target roadway areas for safety improvements. Identifying and prioritizing dangerous areas of roadways for safety improvements can save lives.

Several states have provided estimates to the U.S. Department of Transportation that the fatalities in their states will increase. Focusing the spending in those states on safety to prevent this projection from coming true should be a priority for Congress.

There are evidence-based safety solutions that federal dollars are prohibited to purchase or federal safety programs that have been cut, but there are several communities that would like to employ a range of options that will improve safety. Allowing flexibility in federal spending for evidence-based safety improvements can save lives, and I urge this committee to reevaluate some of those restrictions on technology like automated enforcement and other programs.

NSC looks forward to working with this Committee to fully develop these provisions.

Conclusion

You have an opportunity in front of you to prioritize safety, and the National Safety Council is committed to working with you to reach zero fatalities on our roadways. I hope you will join me in saying enough is enough and start down the Road to Zero. It is not impossible. It just hasn't been done yet.

Ms. NORTON. Thank you very much, Mr. Smith.

And I want to thank all of you for your testimony today.

We will now move on to Members' questions. Each Member will be recognized for 5 minutes of questions.

I now recognize myself.

And this is a question for all of the witnesses. This is frustrating to hear this testimony. Congress has spent some considerable funds to reduce highway deaths, and yet we hear that it has not, in fact, gone much below 35,000 a year since the 1950s.

I mean, this is a country used to making some progress. Now, I recognize that much of this lies with local and State authorities, but I would like to ask all of you, and I will begin with Ms. Homendy, but it is a question for all of you.

What in your view, and I recognize that there are many things that each of you think should be done, but I am trying to focus on major things now; what is the single most important thing that you think Congress can do to reduce the number of roadway fatalities, bearing in mind the State and localities are where the action is? So could I start with Ms. Homendy and just go on down the line?

Ms. HOMENDY. Thank you very much for the question.

And it is hard for the NTSB to pick one thing over another. So something I will say is it is a comprehensive approach.

From our standpoint, it is effective guidance to the States. It is enforcement, high-visibility enforcement, education for drivers and others, and engineering, and that includes vehicle technologies, other technologies like collision avoidance systems, speed limiters, and better data.

Ms. NORTON. Yes, sir, Mr. Jones, Vice Mayor Jones? Mr. JONES. Thank you.

Again, I think it has a lot to do with priorities and accountability. I think there are a lot of great tools in the toolbox to do good design. We have great examples of where we have retrofitted our streets to make them accessible and safe for all users.

But again, I mentioned there is this disconnect between these large policy frameworks and the actual implementation. Sometimes I think it has a lot to do with just the culture. You know, engineers are often trained and their priorities are about moving cars as quickly and efficiently through communities as possible.

And I think there needs to be a greater focus in on sort of changing the paradigm a little bit and prioritizing funding to do things like Complete Streets.

I mean, Florida DOT, for example, the State has a wonderful Complete Streets policy, but what ends up happening is by the time it gets down to the local or the district level, a lot of times it falls by the wayside.

And I think what we need is some more accountability to say, "Look. We can do these projects. Let's put a pot of funding that is dedicated solely to this effort and start to do more demonstration projects so people can see the benefits of these types of improvements in retrofit.''

Ms. NORTON. Chief Brown?

Mr. BROWN. Very briefly, I would say that, frankly, we should really change the narrative from the standpoint, and I put this in my written comments, to drive home the importance of what we are talking about.

A lot of times the threat to the public and the individual road users, whether they be pedestrians, bikes or motorists, is lost in the discussion of the authorization regarding roadway use and construction and everything else.

I put in my testimony a comment that I truly believe and I have said many times over. When you knock on a door and you wake somebody up and you tell them they have lost a loved one or a friend, it does not matter if it is bullet or a fender. The same shock is there.

Our officers across this country deal with that on a daily basis, as do professionals in the medical field and do it at a hospital, and yet we ignore this as a national issue.

What we compete with in the law enforcement arena are other public health and public safety issues. The opioid task issue is a huge issue across this country. We are dealing with it, but no one says it with the same loud depth and a voice as it applies across this country, and yet it affects so many people and so many families.

That is the national narrative, I think, that frankly Congress could tee up and charge all of us to do better at.

Ms. NORTON. Mr. Bruemmer?

Mr. BRUEMMER. The Highway Safety Improvement Program requires data-driven results from State DOTs. DOTs have data on where accidents happen. They lack the funding a lot of times to combat the problem. I think that is probably one of the most useful systems that Congress has at its disposal, is the ability to identify where crashes happen, where fatalities happen, and the ability to take action and provide results.

Ms. NORTON. Mr. Sewell?

Mr. SEWELL. I would like to echo a lot of what Mr. Jones has said. We have great tools currently as engineers and planners of our transportation network. The biggest issues are the data sets that we are using to identify where those issues could occur, and then the funding is always an issue.

So I think for Congress to show leadership on both how we are attacking these to be more proactive and keep people safe as well as the pot of money that can be allocated towards safety projects are the two biggest things for me.

Ms. NORTON. I'm going to allow Mr. Smith to answer briefly.

Mr. SMITH. Of course. I certainly agree with everything that has been said here on the panel, and it really comes back down to the culture and addressing the culture. We would not accept this in the aviation industry, and we cannot accept it on the roadways.

Ms. NORTON. Thank you very much.

I am going to now recognize the ranking member, Mr. Spano. Mr. SPANO. Thank you, Madam Chair.

I represent a district, as I think maybe many of the Members on the dais do, that has urban areas and rural areas, and so you know, the differences in terms of the needs and the guidelines vary so greatly.

So how does the next surface transportation reauthorization bill address the differing needs between rural and urban areas? That is the first question.

And then how do you create or fashion a comprehensive bill that maybe is necessary to obtain compliance while still giving local folks some authority and wiggle room to best use those directions or directives to suit the needs of their local area?

I know that is a big question, but maybe you could each address that.

Ms. HOMENDY. Thank you.

And from our perspective, we have a number of safety recommendations we have issued. For NHTSA we have 108 safety recommendations that are open that we would urge Congress to address in the upcoming reauthorization.

And from our standpoint, those issues regarding safety, it does not discriminate whether you are on a highway, whether you are on a rural road. They are critical safety issues that need to be addressed like impairment, adopting .05 instead of having .08; addressing speeding.

There are a number of pedestrian safety issues that could also be addressed that we can get into in this hearing, but I think addressing those big safety issues would be critical because, like I said, it does not matter if you are on a highway or on a smaller road. These are still critical safety issues.

Mr. SPANO. And if I might interject, Chief Brown, I think you more so than any of the other members on the panel stressed the need for some local input, control in terms of the decisionmaking process.

So how do you square some of the broader requirements with the need to have that flexibility?

Mr. BROWN. That is an excellent question, and quite frankly, there is a framework in the FAST Act that allows you to do some of that, but it gets down to the implementation of it. Nobody should be just given a block grant for traffic safety activity, but I think you can certainly use the FAST Act ideas and concepts to justify the need for it and tailor it to the local issue.

And then the other key is to fund it. Unfortunately, oftentimes there is influence in that process as far as the allocations go where some projects do not get funded and some do.

And in some cases, it is discouraging for some local law enforcement, and frankly, some local communities may not have the capacity to drive even the grant application process, to be real frank, even today.

I would say that the more we provide an opportunity and a framework that is more detailed, but provides the flexibility to address the local issues, I think you can incorporate the same things that we are talking about here on this panel.

The major issues are mostly across the country to one degree or another.

Mr. SPANO. Vice Mayor? Mr. JONES. Thank you.

And that is a great question, and it really points to the issue of context. And when we talk about Complete Streets, they certainly do look much different in a rural context than, say, in very urban areas, but yet they are still complete.

And, again, I want to emphasize here that we are not talking about freeway design but rather what often happens is that sort of mentality ends up going to the local issue. So there is this mismatch where we think about how we design a freeway, and then we might apply it to what should be a local street with maybe two lanes and an opportunity for cyclists and pedestrians.

And I think when it comes to addressing the issue of incentives, I think the more that we can offer to local jurisdictions, you know, in terms of additional funding when they actually meet the performance standards, that is an issue. It is really about accountability.

So if local jurisdictions can show that they are doing these projects, improving safety, reducing the loss of life, then perhaps they should be getting more money.

Mr. SPANO. Mr. Bruemmer?

Mr. BRUEMMER. Engineers have said that we are on the cusp of the largest revolution in surface transportation since the switch from horse and buggy. I think technology moves us forward and changes a lot of the dynamics that differentiate local versus rural. I think there needs to be a coalition of manufacturers from auto industry to surface transportation industry that create a cohesiveness between what we do moving forward. Things that most people do not think about that I think about every day are pavement markings. The auto industry has said what we need to drive our cars machine-wise is good pavement markings.

I think the discussion needs to be brought from industry to make it all work so that we make the right steps moving forward.

Mr. SPANO. I apologize, Mr. Sewell and Mr. Smith. I do not have any time remaining.

Madam Chair.

Ms. NORTON. Thank you, Mr. Spano. Mr. Carbajal.

Mr. CARBAJAL. Mr. Chairman, Madam Chair.

And thank you to all of the witnesses for being here today.

Mr. Bruemmer, according to the National Safety Council, injuries from motor vehicle incidents totaled more than 4.6 million in 2017. The National Highway Traffic Safety

Administration estimates that over 37,000 people lost their lives in accidents on U.S. roadways in that same year.

In my district, Highway 46 is sadly known as Blood Alley due to the countless fatal crashes over the years. As we begin our work on a surface transportation reauthorization, what are some concrete actions Congress can take to make our roads safer?

And, two, as we make greater strides in artificial intelligence and self-driving vehicle technologies, how can we start integrating this technology into our road planning?

Mr. BRUEMMER. Thank you.

As I mentioned before, I think technology is moving at a rapid pace from the auto industry. Unfortunately, they have kept their cards close to their vest from our side of the industry, but as we move forward, the discussion is now becoming more open that how does technology act with infrastructure. How does V2I move the conversation forward?

I think that in the very near term, I think that progress can be seen. At the national level from Congress, I think it is focused on you are already aware of the major problem that you have on Highway 46. That is the start.

Now the problem is talk to the engineers. Talk to the DOT. How do we fix this problem? And how do we bring a package from Congress that can help the State best rectify this problem?

Mr. CARBAJAL. Thank you.

Ms. Homendy, in your testimony you reference the "most wanted list" of recommendations for highway safety. One of NTSB's recommendations is for the Department of Labor to develop and disseminate guidelines on the dangers of driving while tired.

While it seems obvious, I want to ask you. Why are these guidelines necessary?

Ms. HOMENDY. Thank you for the question.

And if you do not mind me adding one thing to what the gentleman said on technology, there are safety technologies available today which are the building blocks to automated vehicles that you could use to save lives today. So we do not have to wait until those are on the road.

So I just want to put that out there.

On fatigue, a lot of the work that has been done by the NTSB has focused on commercial motor vehicles and not on autos, and a lot of that is focused on needing science-based hours-of-service standards, no exemptions to those standards, having fatigue management plans in place, implementing and using electronic logging devices, and screening diagnosis and treating of sleep apnea for FMCSA to do rulemaking in that area, and installation of collision avoidance systems which could help combat fatigue.

Mr. CARBAJAL. Thank you very much. Madam Chair, I yield back.

Ms. NORTON. Thank you.

And I want to call next Mr. Gallagher. Mr. G_{ALLAGHER}. Thank you very much.

I thought it would take me 30 years to get up here at the top, but——

[Laughter.]

Mr. GALLAGHER [continuing]. You know it is only going to last a couple of minutes. So I just want to savor it for a second.

[Laughter.]

Mr. GALLAGHER. Ms. Homendy, forgive me if I am mispronouncing that. In your opening statement, you noted that pedestrian deaths on our roadways have been increasing since 2010. In 2016, nearly 6,000 pedestrians died in collisions with highway vehicles in the U.S. That is an average of 16 per day.

And according to NTSB's 2018 special investigation report, roughly 28 percent of those deaths occur on rural roads.

My district in northeast Wisconsin has a lot of rural roads, and I know this was talked about a little bit before, but could you expand on whether there is a difference in NTSB safety recommendations for urban versus rural roads?

Ms. HOMENDY. For the pedestrian safety study, we did find that there were more fatalities in urban environments and that 18 percent of the fatalities occurred at intersections, 72 percent at non-intersections, and 10 percent at other locations.

Mr. GALLAGHER. I appreciate that.

And for anyone on the panel, can you comment perhaps on the impact that commercial trucking has on pedestrian and nonpedestrian fatalities, if at all?

I do not know who wants to volunteer. Who is brave? Sir, you look eager. If not eager, reluctantly willing to step up.

Mr. BROWN. If I could, sir, I am not so sure that that is a high- priority issue in terms of the representation in fatalities and injuries. Unfortunately, when those incidents occur, because you are dealing with the principle of physics, a bigger vehicle against a human being is not going to come out well for the human being. But generally speaking, I am not aware of a significant change in that kind of an environment under the scenario that you suggested.

Mr. GALLAGHER. Well, let me perhaps ask it a different way and sort of reveal what I am getting at here.

So commercial trucks following local laws in 29 States are barred from using the Federal interstate which then forces them in many cases to stay on winding secondary roads where there are a lot of pedestrian crossings, bicycles, school crossings, traffic lights, and other obstacles, right?

So in 2009, we in Congress authorized a pilot program in Maine that found that allowing these commercial trucks on the interstate even for short distances actually decreased fatalities by 37 percent, which makes sense, right?

If you have these trucks sort of off the rural winding roads where there are a lot more pedestrians, perhaps they would avoid that unfortunate encounter that you referenced.

So I just would ask particularly those who are representatives at the State and local level: would you in theory support States having the option of allowing some of these commercial trucks to use the Federal interstate for short distances in order to reduce highway fatalities?

Mr. BROWN. It would depend upon what type of commercial vehicle we are talking about. Commercial vehicles are very broad. You can have those that involve the transportation, for example, of certain hazardous commodities, whether they are interstate or intrastate. There is a difference in that as far as title 49.

Mr. GALLAGHER. Yes.

Mr. BROWN. In addition to that, there is also the concerns about what our local communities want in their backyard.

We do have bypass traffic because of congestion and congestion mitigation efforts made by commercial drivers at times. But I think you will find that most local folks would love to have the local control over what is migrating through their cities.

But whether or not those vehicles should be allowed on an interstate vis-a-vis through sort of thing, it would depend upon what they are trying to move, quite frankly.

Mr. GALLAGHER. Yes. And for us in northeast Wisconsin, logging is a big issue. You can imagine logging trucks, giving them the ability to for a short distance, 150 miles, use the Federal interstates.

I do not know if anyone has dealt with any of these issues and wants to chime in.

Mr. SEWELL. If I may real quickly, what you are speaking about is very closely tied to land use.

Mr. GALLAGHER. Yes.

Mr. SEWELL. And when you are trying to provide access not only to commercial vehicles or you name it type of vehicle to get to a place they have to do business and you couple that with where we are focused on multimodal pedestrian and bicycle safety, establishing clear context for corridors and then assigning certain vehicles to allow access to places that eliminate conflicts and minimize, as was mentioned, that speed differential between higher moving vehicles and pedestrians or slower moving vehicles is a great idea. Mr. GALLAGHER. Yes. Well, thank you all for being here today.

And I yield the balance of my time.

Ms. NORTON. Thank you, Mr. Gallagher.

And I do want to note that the subcommittee will be having a hearing on trucking and truck safety will be included in that. It is an important issue.

Mrs. Craig.

Mrs. CRAIG. Thank you so much, Chairwoman Norton.

Ms. Homendy, your testimony particularly spoke to me. My step-sister lost her life in one of those intersections in Portland, Oregon. So she left a kindergartner to be raised by his dad and a family that was changed forever.

So you know, I appreciate that the title of this hearing is "Every Life Counts." I grew up in a family where that life was lost. So thank you all for being here.

What I want to follow up on is just this comment about the rural areas. I come from Minnesota's Second Congressional District, and according to the 2016 Federal Highway Administration data, rural areas account for 30 percent of total vehicle miles traveled. Yet 50 percent of roadway fatalities take place in rural areas.

As Mr. Bruemmer noted, over a 4-year period, the Minnesota DOT installed cable barriers in 31 segments along 150 miles of roadway. In the 3 years prior to installation, there were 19 fatal cross-median crashes, and in the 3 years following, there were zero. I would love to hear from you about those types of policy recommendations. Obviously, that is infrastructure investment.

You also talked about speed and alcohol use. Is there any difference in these rural areas?

And what recommendations would you make? Perhaps maybe start with Mr. Brown.

Mr. BROWN. Yes, ma'am. The solution or the proper way to address many of the things that you are talking about in the rural areas does require a little bit of a combined approach actually.

I have seen over and over again where infrastructure like center divider medians, Jersey walls, things to prevent crossovers will increase survivability in the case of a crash.

But a lot of it has to do with behavior. So a lot of the things that you see in an urban environment involving impaired driving and the like we will see in a rural area.

I have had the privilege in my career of working in rural areas, and I know exactly what you are talking about in terms of, you know, the tragedies sometimes are even worse because of the speed that is involved in those kinds of situations.

It is kind of hard to go downtown in Alexandria at 85 miles an hour. It is much easier in a rural area, and that will complicate survivability in many cases.

Mrs. CRAIG. Does anyone else have a thought on any of those factors in rural areas? Anything to add?

Yes, sir.

Mr. SEWELL. Thank you for the question.

I will tack on, too. It is very difficult to engineer bad decisions out of drivers, but one of the things that we can do is better influence user behavior.

There is an infamous NHTSA quote. I believe it is 95 percent of errors everywhere in our transportation system are human error. I think there is a role in engineering and planning that you can eliminate user error or cut it down by positively influencing user behavior, by designing predictable, safer transportation connections.

Mrs. CRAIG. Thank you.

Madam Chair, I yield the remainder of my time. Ms. NORTON. Thank you very much.

I would like to call next on Mr. Palmer.

Mr. PALMER. Thank you, Madam Chairwoman.

I grew up in a rural area of northwest Alabama and unfortunately saw several fatal highway accidents, and the thing that gets me about a lot of drivers is how many people do not wear seatbelts. There was a report that came out in 2002 that indicated there were 43,005 traffic fatalities, and of that, 19,103 were not wearing seatbelts. I think a later report said we would average saving over 4,200 lives a year if just 90 percent of occupants wore seatbelts.

I do not know what we can do. I know in Alabama we have seatbelt laws. If you do not have a seatbelt on, you get a ticket, but that just seems to be one of the most commonsense, easiest things you can do to increase your survivability of an automobile accident.

Do you have anything to add to that, Ms. Homendy?

Ms. HOMENDY. Yes. The single greatest defense against death and injury is the use of effective safety equipment. So whether that is seatbelts or age appropriate restraints for younger children, those are things that the NTSB has recommended, but also for all seating positions in a vehicle, not just in the front seats.

And we have encouraged States to adopt primary enforcement laws so that when law enforcement officers pull a motor vehicle over that they can issue a ticket for not wearing seatbelts, not that you have to have another reason.

Alabama does have a primary enforcement law, but some of the other States do not. You have to have another reason to issue a ticket for not wearing a seatbelt in some of the States.

Mr. PALMER. Yes. Chief Brown, first of all, I want to commend your department on its response to the shooting at the baseball field. I was there. I was 20 steps from the guy. So I really am grateful for the courage of the officers who responded that day.

Also, I would say the issues with impaired driving and the texting, and there is a big push for that, too. Is your department writing many tickets dealing with that?

Mr. BROWN. First of all, sir, thank you very much for the compliments of our officers. We were very proud to serve that day. It was a very difficult day for us as well.

If I may also add, in terms of the seatbelt issue, it ties in with these others as well. There are a lot of assumptions made, I think, by motorists and others that it is not going to be them.

And in the case of occupant protection, your survivability in a crash is entirely dependent upon, especially with airbags, on the use of that seatbelt. It is an integral part of the engineering that goes in there. And people do not wear their seatbelt and they get severely injured.

In impaired driving and also in speeding and all the topical issues that have been mentioned on this panel and by the chair are addressed daily across this country with law enforcement.

The real question is: what are they having to compete with at the same time they are addressing those issues? And the demands upon law enforcement in this Nation right now are incredible.

The mental health requirements that we are having to deal with, the issues related to that, the drugs, opioids are high-priority issues for our communities. Traffic in some communities is high priority. It is in our city, but it is not that way across the country, and somehow that needs to change.

Mr. PALMER. There is just one other issue I want to address, and that is the corporate auto fuel economy standards that impose the miles per gallon standards, which necessarily resulted in a lot of smaller, lighter vehicles being made.

I think there is the safer, affordable fuel-efficient vehicles rule that is going to retain the 2020 model year standards, and they are estimating that that could save $500 billion in societal costs and save almost 13,000 lives.

I am concerned as the father of two girls and one son. My first daughter, I bought her what I called a rolling airbag because of concerns for vehicle safety.

But as we go to more electric vehicles, you are going to have a disproportionate problem there with weight if that vehicle is involved with a lighter vehicle.

I just want your thoughts on retaining the 2020 model year standards.

And what are we doing to compensate in vehicle manufacturing? Because even my pickup truck now gets almost 21 miles per gallon on the road. It is lighter than the truck I had before.

Any thoughts on that, Ms. Homendy?

Ms. HOMENDY. We have not looked at—that is not something we have looked at in CAFE standards. So——

Mr. PALMER. In terms of overall——

Ms. HOMENDY. In terms of mass, I mean, there—when it comes to crashes, we have looked at crashes, obviously, involving different motor vehicles, trucks with motor vehicles. So the mass of the vehicle definitely impacts what occurs in the tragedy, but it is not something that we have really focused on, the difference in the light vehicles versus heavy vehicles, to my——

Mr. PALMER. Mr. Jones, did you want to respond to that?

Mr. JONES. Yes. I just wanted to say, you know, being from northeast Florida, there is definitely a culture in terms of where we drive larger trucks. And, I mean, just traveling around I can see the difference. Every day when I am driving, probably 80 percent of the vehicles that are on the road are F–150s and larger SUVs, and that is part of the problem that we are seeing. And pedestrians and cyclists and other folks are really at a severe disadvantage when it comes to that. So that is——

Mr. PALMER. As are the smaller—— Mr. JONES. That is a tradeoff, yes.

Mr. PALMER [continuing]. Smaller vehicles.

I have gone over my time, Madam Chairwoman, I thank you for your patience with me, and I yield back.

Ms. NORTON. Thank you very much. Mr. Garcia?

Mr. GARCIA. Thank you, Madam Chair, as well as Ranking Member Davis, for holding this hearing.

The statistics are very sobering and stark with respect to people who were killed on U.S. roadways in 2017: 37,000 and 4.6 million people were injured in 2017. I also marked a high in Chicago roadway fatalities. We went from 119 traffic-related deaths in 2016 to 132 in 2017. Many of the areas that I represent in the city of Chicago are considered high crash corridors, according to Chicago's Vision Zero plan. And many of them are in areas that have commercial strips, retail commercial strips in them.

I would like to ask a question of Ms. Homendy. In Illinois we have had a dozen vehicle crashes where vehicles that were stopped—involving law enforcement stops, where—this happened in January, an Illinois State trooper, Christopher Lambert, stopped to assist with a crash and was struck and killed by a passing motorist. He is now 1 of 16 Illinois State troopers that have been killed in accidents starting the beginning of this year.

I understand that the automatic emergency braking, or AEB, could help to prevent these crashes, and the NTSB has recommended the installation of this technology on all new passenger motor vehicles. Despite this recommendation, the AEB is not standard equipment in all new passenger vehicles. Why has the NTSB made such a recommendation, and what are the benefits of the recommendation, and why should AEB be standard equipment for all new vehicles?

Ms. HOMENDY. The NTSB has issued several recommendations regarding collision avoidance, including AEB and forward collision warning, to prevent deaths such as the one that you mentioned in your statement just a minute ago.

The National Highway Traffic Safety Administration has not implemented those recommendations, and they are crucial for preventing fatalities and injuries. And so we are hopeful that they will move forward on those.

Mr. GARCIA. Thank you.

For Mr. Smith, according to Forbes, 10 automakers will be equipping half of their vehicles in 2018. In fact, NHTSA Administrator Heidi King recently said, "Technologies like automatic emergency braking can help make cars safer on roads, which means Americans are safer when traveling."

Are AEBs a sensible step in the right direction? And why should they be considered for large and heavy trucks, as well?

Mr. SMITH. The work that we have done indicates that, in fact— that important technology. And we would suggest looking at all the technologies that are out there being developed. But this is a particularly important one to help reduce the rate of fatalities. And we would also encourage it being looked at in our commercial vehicles, as well, as an important way to reduce those fatalities. So we certainly think this is one of—as you think about those big impacts, one of those areas where you can have big impact, in terms of reducing fatalities.

Mr. GARCIA. Is it your sense that we are on the cusp of a significant breakthrough in safety, if recommendations like those you have made are actually implemented?

Mr. SMITH. I think that those are going to help us on the path. The reality is as we convert the fleet of total vehicles on cars, it is going to be a slow process, just because of the turnover and the average age of cars, and things like that. But it is important we start implementing those things as the technology is proven today, recognizing there is that lag with respect to the integration into the broader fleets.

Mr. GARCIA. Thank you, Madam Chair. I yield back my time.

Ms. HOMENDY. Can I add one thing to that, Congressman? Mr. GARCIA. Sure.

Ms. HOMENDY. Those technologies are available today, and we know from research that they are proven to save lives. And so what the NTSB has said is that they should be standard on all vehicles. Unfortunately, in many vehicles you have to pay for safety upgrades. In our view, safety is not a luxury. Those should be standard on all new vehicles, whether it is a heavy truck, a passenger vehicle, a motorcoach, or a schoolbus. They can and should be implemented today.

Mr. GARCIA. Thank you for interjecting.

I yield back, Madam Chair.

Ms. NORTON. And thank you, Mr. Garcia. Mr. Webster?

Mr. WEBSTER. Thank you, Madam Chair.

Ms. Homendy, I listened to your testimony and you talked about ending alcohol and other drug impairments in transportation. You said in 1990 you first started printing statistics in that area about different modifications that could be done. I listened to that.

I was in the State legislature then. I passed a law raising the drinking age to 21, lowering the blood alcohol to .08 and, for those under 21, .02. There was an open container law that we banned, and boots for repeat offenders on their vehicles, and some other things that we did. And I know those had an effect. I know those helped. And now you have got .05.

To me the statistics seemed to prove that many of the problems come from substance abuse, or alcohol. And yet, when you get into really changing the system, you can do those, those are certainly laws that can be passed, and I was in full favor of those. But when it gets down to really limiting what you can consume, there is a strong lobby against that. And so if you try to do dram shop legislation, which keeps a bartender from serving somebody visibly intoxicated, it is going to be killed every single time, and other things. I just think if you picked out one thing, I would say impairment, especially from external sources, has got to be a major, major issue that, even though we have scraped the edges and done some things, not really hitting the core. Have you got any ideas about that?

Ms. HOMENDY. Yes. Impairment is a significant issue. Ten thousand people lose their lives annually due to alcohol-impaired-related crashes—or more than 10,000.

The NTSB has recommended reducing the BAC limit from .08 to .05 or lower. What we say, though, is it is not about stopping consumption. You can consume alcohol, you just can't drive in addition to it. And impairment, from all the research we have looked at, begins at the very first drink. There are significant challenges, a decline in visual functions,
at .02; reduced coordination at .05. And so, when you talk about .08, then that makes the situation even worse.

And so, from our standpoint, it is reducing the BAC limit to .05, requiring ignition interlocks for all offenders, not just repeat offenders.

One thing that we found in the research is that by the time a first-time offender is convicted, they have driven impaired more than 80 times. And so we believe ignition interlocks for all offenders. And then, of course, invehicle technologies, which exist today, to prevent drivers from operating motor vehicles while impaired.

Mr. WEBSTER. So there is other substances. You mentioned marijuana, and yet we just marched down this road of saying it is fine, nothing wrong with it. And yet have you seen any statistics related to that?

Ms. HOMENDY. The data on marijuana is just not there. Unfortunately, we know how alcohol affects the human body, we just don't know how marijuana does. For one— and we—and because of that we don't have an impairment standard.

And so, to determine impairment is so difficult because you have to look at how it is ingested, whether it is ingested, whether it is smoked, how frequently it is used. It changes, based on body factors. So we have recommended that NHTSA issue guidance to States to inform law enforcement officers when they should require testing, how they should do testing, what methods the laboratories should use, and cut-off levels. Because right now States are handling it all very differently.

Mr. WEBSTER. OK, thank you. My time is out. Thank all of you for appearing. I yield back.

Ms. NORTON. Thank you very much. Mr. Espaillat?

Mr. ESPAILLAT. Thank you, Madam Chair. I want to thank the witnesses for your testimony. The safety of roads is incredibly important for New York City, so much so that it was one of the first issues our mayor, Bill de Blasio, took on when he announced Vision Zero, a very ambitious program.

Just this week I reintroduced legislation, the Stopping Threats on Pedestrians Act, or STOP Act, that will help localities install bollards in highly trafficked areas with many vulnerable users. Bollards in Time Square, New York City, were specifically cited as having prevented further deaths when a driver tried to use his vehicle to attack nearby pedestrians.

The lack of bollards, some may argue, unfortunately, didn't prevent the terrorist attack that occurred on October 31st, 2017, when a pickup truck went on the Hudson River bike path and killed many tourists that were in the area. I think that, in many ways, including this bill can help local governments address safety issues head on.

Mr. Sewell, your testimony recommends changes to the Highway Safety Improvement Program to ensure that States spend funding on infrastructure improvement in proportion to the specific types of safety problems the State encounters. Could you elaborate a little bit more on that?

And particularly with regards to the use of bollards and the prevention of potential terrorist attacks, how do you see that playing out? Do we need to fund these very specific programs that can save lives?

Mr. SEWELL. Well, I appreciate your question. And in the example that you gave, the use of bollards in certain settings is a proven countermeasure for restricting the flow of larger vehicles on certain designated routes. So on the greenway that you just mentioned, the installation of bollards in restricting the flow of those could be an absolute, you know, lifesaver.

In terms of the HSIP and redirecting, you know, to fund proactively the fixes that you just mentioned, I believe it is a good idea. I think that if you look at the percentage of accidents that happen—or not accidents, but crashes that happen, and the loss of lives that happened, I think it should be an equity-based—we should have a proportionate amount of money dedicated to saving those lives.

So yes, I agree with you completely.

Mr. ESPAILLAT. And do you support providing local governments more control over how the program should be funded, and where to implement these new strategies to prevent death? I mean I think there seems to be—local governments really know where these hot spots are at, right? And do you feel there should be more leverage, more flexibility in terms of how the funding is used?

Mr. SEWELL. Yes, and I could not agree more. I think giving local municipalities where—if they are rural or urban settings, they are going to know best their constituents, what their local people are engaging and how they are engaging on their transportation network. And I absolutely think they would be the best to direct the funds in an appropriate manner, yes.

Mr. ESPAILLAT. Madam Chair, let me just stress again the importance of these initiatives and the ability for municipalities to be able to determine where to spend the funding, and they get a fair share of funding to install bollards and other strategies that could prevent terrorist attacks.

We have seen how, in New York City, that was tragic, and we also saw in Times Square how the bollards helped prevent deaths there, as a driver, a reckless driver, tragically went on the sidewalk and basically ran down people.

But we must consider local opinions about where to place these. I think local law enforcement is also well equipped to let us know here in Washington where the hot spots—how we can spend the money and how we can save lives.

Any additional comment?

Mr. SEWELL. One quick one. On Times Square, in particular, that is a great example of a proactive fix. It was identified that it is a heavily used pedestrian area, and so it was decided to invest in place-making for that locale. And you see the result, in terms of not only adjacent businesses reaping the benefit of having a nice, fun place to interact, but, as you mentioned, the restriction of motor vehicular traffic reduces that conflict to basically zero. So I think that is a great example. I wanted to tack that on. Thank you.

Mr. ESPAILLAT. Thank you, Madam Chair. Ms. NORTON. Thank you very much.

Mr. LaMalfa?

Mr. LAMALFA. Thank you, Madam Chair. A lot of ideas here today. What I don't hear often enough is, to me, happy drivers are drivers that are moving and getting to where they want to go. When you have happy drivers, less frustration, all that, things go better.

Just coming in from the airport yesterday we saw a road rage thing break out because the two guys tried to occupy one spot on the on-ramp. And you know, so the infrastructure emphasis, I think, is really important, that we can actually have systems that move traffic better. Most of the time I hear the solutions are ways to corral people and make them where they can't go where they want to go, and that is just highly frustrating.

Some of the emphasis I have heard in the committee today is the impairment. I think that is extremely important that we get after people that are driving incompetently, whether it is under influence of alcohol. And this marijuana thing, you know, we have State after State just rushing to legalize this for normal use.

When I was in the California State Legislature it was interesting. There was a bill early on for, basically, where you couldn't discriminate against people that were on medical marijuana— where it was only medical at the time was supposedly legal—and the list of exemptions to where you couldn't discriminate against an employee were all the important things, like operating equipment and being trusted with large amounts of money, and things like that. And so the areas where you didn't want people acting that— being under that influence were actually the important ones. And so we have next to zero data on marijuana, yet there is research out there that I think we can point to that would start to get a baseline for what you could do with marijuana-influenced people, because everybody, I think, intuitively knows that marijuana influence does slow down your thinking ability and your ability to process more than one thing at a time. And people are amazing at how they can drive and think about 10 other things—you know, not necessarily good, but we see the distractions that are out there. We got to do a lot more on the marijuana situation.

But coming back to traffic that is flowing is happier traffic, and, I mean, just around this town, one more example is that every single stoplight here seems like it is timed. You are sitting there for 60 seconds at 10 o'clock, or 11 o'clock, or midnight, waiting for nothing, instead of the ones that have a sensor to allow you to go. And the amount of time you spend at stop lights and waiting for elevators in your life is really frustrating.

But that said, in my own district in northern California, an area that I share with Mr. Garamendi, we have Highway 70 that travels between, basically—well, the key area we are talking about is Oroville and Marysville, you know, the Chico area. And we have had 40 deaths in that area, just since 2010—what we have here. And that is a traffic flow issue. So many times you are pent up behind vehicles going 45 miles an hour, people get frustrated, they pass where they shouldn't. We have issues with the Oroville Dam spillway crisis and the evacuation there, the fires we have had in the area. We have a lot of frustration and a lot of pentup traffic there.

I just throw it to you, Ms. Homendy, with Chief Brown, Mayor Jones. Wouldn't one of the greatest ways to improve is take away the frustration, and allow traffic to flow, and get these projects done, rather than limiting people and frustrating more? Please.

Ms. HOMENDY. I think I might need a little bit more clarification on the question.

Mr. LAMALFA. OK. I think most people want to see traffic flow. But we hear a lot about how to impede what they are doing. How could we greater emphasize traffic flow in our conversations?

Ms. HOMENDY. Well, part of it is road design, and we have to have road—right now, with road designers and engineers, the focus is on motor vehicle traffic, but not on the complete traffic, which is everything from pedestrians to bicyclists to everything on our Nation's roads. So we have to have a comprehensive view on how we do road design from our traffic engineers.

Mr. LAMALFA. All right. So roads designed in the 1940s or 1950s that are now accommodating triple the traffic, you know, that is the frustration.

So Chief Brown, what would you touch on with an urban area like you have?

Mr. BROWN. Well, I would add—actually, I am very familiar with the area you are from. I, frankly, grew up in Sacramento, so I know that area very well.

My issue is that I think you need to have proper road design, and you need to keep it current. That is balanced against whatever the competing issues are that you are looking at at the local level, in terms of design.

It doesn't matter if it is an urban area or an external area; there are frustrations that take place within the driver's world, based upon design. And sometimes they will—it will cause them to do things they would not ordinarily do, like blocking the box, following too close in an urban area, maybe crossing and passing when it is inappropriate. I have seen that from my own professional experience.

Mr. LAMALFA. Yes, a left turn light that sits there red when there is nobody coming for a mile, and you are waiting there for what, right?

Mr. BROWN. But it doesn't take away from that decisionmaking that that individual has, whether or not to go into that direction, make that call, place themselves and others in jeopardy. And I think we also have to keep that in mind. It is a behavioral thing in most cases with the crashes that we see.

Mr. LAMALFA. Yes, thank you. I will yield back.

Mr. JONES. I——

Mr. LAMALFA. Thank you, Madam Chairwoman. Mr. JONES. I was going to——

Mr. LAMALFA. Oh, you wish to—OK.

Mr. JONES. I did want to add on. I think that, again, this issue here is this happy drivers versus happy pedestrians and cyclists is something that we will continue to deal with. And again, it does boil it down to context. I think for so long that we have been designing the roadways to minimize the delay on drivers, actually— I mean I would say more often than not signals are optimized to reduce and minimize the delay of drivers. And sometimes that does come at the expense of pedestrians and cyclists.

I would say, you know, we will talk about the frustration of, well, we have to add 3 seconds to that signal. But say there is a lady or a person that is trying to walk across the street to get to their destination. We may add 10 minutes to their delay, because they have to walk down to the closest signalized intersection.

So it is always going to be a balance there, and I think there is some context where, certainly, minimizing—or allowing or maximizing vehicular throughput is going to be the most important thing we can do. But there are a lot of contexts, particularly in cities and urban areas, where we have to allow for a greater accommodation of——

Mr. LAMALFA. Thank you.

Mr. JONES [continuing]. Pedestrians.

Mr. LAMALFA. I would yield—need to yield back, thank you. Ms. NORTON. Thank you very much, Mr. LaMalfa.

Mr. Garamendi?

Mr. GARAMENDI. Thank you, Madam Chair.

Mr. Smith, in your testimony you emphasize the need for us to build a true culture of safety. Are there any areas in the traffic safety where you have seen success in doing this? If so, how could we translate those lessons to a broader cultural shift towards roadway safety habits?

Mr. SMITH. Through our chairmanship of the Road to Zero Coalition we have been able to provide grants to local communities and through different organizations that have innovation, and bringing it to the forefront.

We have seen some of the local communities integrate some of these grant dollars in a way that has addressed some of their key pain points. But what they have done is brought the community together as part of solving the solution. And so it is really about doing the design element of it, and bringing the community together, so that we aren't just doing it in a vacuum, and understanding why the particular changes are being made.

And I think there is just more we need to do, from an education perspective, quite frankly, across the country, why do we do some of what we need to do, and why do we need to fund what we are looking to do, particularly when it comes to some of the new augmentation technologies in our vehicles to make it safe, and to understand that it may have some limiting challenges for us, as we traditionally operate our vehicle, but also when it comes to some of the infrastructure, as well. Helping people understand, I think, is what is going to be critically important, and that is where we have seen some case examples where—with some of the grant dollars.

Mr. GARAMENDI. I remember an example of that in California, Mothers Against Drunk Driving. The effort they made some 30 years ago. I think you were in Stockton at the time, Chief, maybe as a young child. But nonetheless, it was very, very successful in developing the laws.

Along that same line, it appears that nearly 30 percent of all fatalities are associated with impaired driving, mostly alcohol, but now, as the discussion has gone here, with marijuana and other drugs. Yet, at the same time, over the last 25 years or so, arrests for impaired driving are down, significantly down, according to the FBI statistics.

So do we have an enforcement issue here? And if so, what do we do about it? And I will leave that open. I start with you, Chief, and then run down the line until I am out of time.

Mr. BROWN. I will be happy to respond to that, and I did kind of address that in my comments. There are a number of reasons we think that that may be taking place. Frankly, if you are from the officer's lens, if you will, the complexities that we currently have in terms of arrests and prosecuting for driving under the influence have grown significantly over that period of time.

When I was a young officer in the 1970s I was in California. We could get done on a four-page piece of paper. Now that document is 27 pages long. There are homicide reports that are prepared that are shorter than some DUI cases, and we are talking about a misdemeanor. There are opportunities to streamline that and still provide and protect the rights of the individual. If we could come up with a way—and this is where—I think, positioned to do that.

The other piece is the competing interests and demands on law enforcement. Right now law enforcement is challenged in ways that it was not challenged 25 years ago. If you go out in a patrol car today you will see officers responding to calls that they did not respond to 25 years ago, so they don't have that discretion because they don't have that ability and that time, if you will, the opportunity to engage in it.

Mr. GARAMENDI. If you will excuse me for a second—because I am going to be out of time in a moment—but then the issue is really a lack of enforcement. Many reasons for that, but is it really an enforcement issue, that we need the police to be enforcing these laws?

Mr. BROWN. I think it gets down to capacity more than anything else.

Mr. GARAMENDI. OK. So that is, again, capacity. Ms. Homendy?

Ms. HOMENDY. It is also a training issue. In a recent accident in- vestigation that we looked at in Concan, Texas, we saw some issues with the training of law enforcement.

Basic training for law enforcement is standardized field sobriety testing. But NHTSA has a couple of great programs called the Advanced Roadside Impaired Driving Enforcement program, or ARIDE, which provides 16 hours of training for law enforcement officials, and the Drug Recognition Expert Training, which is substantially more, 72 hours of classroom training and 60 hours of field training. And those law enforcement officers become highly skilled at detection and identification of impairment.

So we urge—very few of them are trained at those levels, and we are urging more training.

Mr. GARAMENDI. Good. We are—I am almost out of time, and I just want to wrap up. If you look at the statistics here, 29 percent alcohol impaired and 26 percent speeding, it seems to me that both of these are both information, as in Mothers Against Drunk Driving, but also enforcement. And that probably means money.

I yield back my time. Ms. NORTON. Thank you. Mr. Balderson?

Mr. BALDERSON. Thank you. This is something—two subjects that I am very passionate about: bicycles and motorcycles. In fact, my friends say, "What are you going to ride today, Troy, a bike or a motorcycle?" So thank you all, and I appreciate some of your testimony that I have heard.

Mr. Sewell, my first question for you is—and taking the time for being here today, and I appreciate the need for adequate safety and protections for our fellow bikers. The State of Ohio has a safe passing law in place, which requires drivers to give cyclists at least 3 feet. I cosponsored that and really tried to raise awareness of that. In your experience—and that law has passed in the last general assembly—in your experience, how has the implementation of such laws impacted bike safety is the first question.

If you would follow up with that, do you believe the common driver might be aware of such laws? I have an answer for that, and I think you know that response. And, if not, how can we improve the awareness?

Mr. SEWELL. Absolutely. Well—and, first and foremost, I appreciate your support for the 3-foot passing law. I think it is an important law, but it is also coupled directly with education.

I think you are correct, if I am assuming—your response to that second part of your question. It is important when drivers are educated about what it means. And I think there is some great demonstrations that you can help to educate drivers about what it means if you are a cyclist and you get buzzed, how terrifying that can be. I am a biker, too, of course, and so I have been in Columbus, and I have biked around, and I remember hearing when that came through. It is a great idea to have that, but it has to be coupled with education.

Mr. BALDERSON. I totally agree with that. I appreciate your response, and I would love to work with you in trying to figure out how we can address that issue, and make sure that drivers are aware of it. And they love to see how close they can get those mirrors to us on the road.

So my next question is for Ms. Homendy, and thank you very much for being here, and your testimony. My other passion, with the motorcycles—in your testimony you mentioned your safety report from 2018 regarding motorcycle crashes and recommendations for improving, preventions such as the need for enhanced braking and stability control systems on motorcycles.

I myself have a model 2007 that already had that antilock brake system on it, but also the controlled—I mean it is similar to what you are talking about with the stability control. Have you seen an increase of where in the motorcycle community—of such needs that this report has—when it was released?

Ms. HOMENDY. Sorry about that. Yes. We agree that we need antiock braking and stability control systems, and we recommend that they be standard on all motorcycles and that, again, safety is not a luxury, and we don't feel that motorcyclists or auto drivers should have to pay more for vehicles for safe technology. And so we recommend that they be included as standard on all motorcycles.

Mr. BALDERSON. Most manufacturers today, just so you know, are making it standard. In the 2017 BMW that I have, it was standard equipment—— Ms. HOMENDY. Great.

Mr. BALDERSON [continuing]. With antilock brakes. Now, to touch on that, though, the—and I have done all the motorcycle training, all the way through. At one time I was even going to be an instructor, and that is kind of what is going to lead me to that— but the one place I got to try that antilock brakes—I mean it is one thing to do it in a car, but antilock brakes on a motorcycle are completely different than they are a car. So I don't think we have the pleasure of allowing motorcyclists to enact that antilock brake system to actually see what it is going to do. So I am going to try to encourage more and more manufacturers to offer their own input training.

But I get an email every week on motorcycle training and the lack of instructors. How can we encourage to get more members of the motorcycle community—and anybody can answer this—to come out and help us with—I mean whether it is a free oil change, from—I mean I don't know what that—but do you all have any ideas how we can encourage more motorcycle instructors to participate and help us train fellow motorcyclists?

Ms. HOMENDY. Yes, I mean, you know, from our standpoint, you know, when it comes to safety—and I was just in Connecticut, testifying on the importance of motorcycle safety, and talked to some of the motorcyclists, and I think it is crucial to encourage them to get more training, and to have more instructors.

And I think, from NTSB's standpoint, it is just getting out there and encouraging people to improve safety and motorcycle safety, and trying to encourage them to get adequate training.

Mr. BALDERSON. My time is up. I would love to continue this conversation. I yield back, or can—go ahead, sir.

Ms. NORTON. Thank you very much.

Mr. JONES. I just wanted to add more Harley-Davidson dealerships offering incentives for the instructors to come out.

If you don't mind, I did want to talk about the 3-foot rule, if that is possible.

Ms. NORTON. Time is expired. Mr. JONES. OK.

Ms. NORTON. Mr. Lowenthal?

Mr. LOWENTHAL. Thank you, Madam Chair. You know, I am struck by reports that individuals with obstructive sleep apnea are twice as likely to be involved in motor vehicle accidents than are the general public. And we know that interventions like CPAPs can dramatically reduce the incidents of these accidents.

I raise this because within the last 6 months one morning my wife says to me, "You know what, Alan? You are not breathing at night."

I said, "I don't know, what are you talking about? I am breathing at night."

She said, "No, I timed it. I woke up. You go sometimes 7, 8 seconds without breathing."

So I went to George Washington University Hospital and had a screening and found out I have serious sleep apnea, which I was not even aware of. And I will tell you, by using a CPAP, I am much more alert. I do—that is why I can ask you questions now. I would have been——

[Laughter.]

Mr. LOWENTHAL. I never would have been able to ask any of these questions.

So the reason I raise this is for years that the NTSB and other stakeholders have been concerned that Federal agencies haven't implemented clear guidelines to ensure drivers and other transportation workers are screened for sleep apnea, yet in 2017 the Federal Motor Carrier Safety Administration and the Federal Railroad Administration withdrew efforts to update sleep apnea screening standards.

So, Ms. Homendy, can you tell us more about the NTSB recommendations, and how great a safety risk is posed by sleep apnea?

Ms. HOMENDY. It is a significant issue. And as you—so my husband has sleep apnea, didn't even know it.

Mr. LOWENTHAL. Me too, didn't know.

Ms. HOMENDY. Until I told him I was tired of him snoring and he had to go get help.

Mr. LOWENTHAL. I just stopped breathing. At least he was snoring, you know.

[Laughter.]

Ms. HOMENDY. Hopefully—so, you know, we have issued—we have investigated a number of accidents involving fatigued drivers, whether it is in motor vehicles or large trucks or also in the rail industry, with operators of trains. And we have issued a number of recommendations on the screening, diagnosis, and treatment for sleep disorders like sleep apnea.

I do know that some of the carriers and the railroads are doing some of that. But without a rulemaking it won't occur, industrywide. So we are pushing that FMCSA and FRA adequately address this and issue a rulemaking to require screening, diagnosis, and treatment.

Mr. LOWENTHAL. Well, thank you. I am going to ask Mr. Smith. What is your perspective at the National Safety Council?

Mr. SMITH. Sure. Well, you know, we know that according to the AAA, over 328,000 drowsy driving crashes happen every year; 109,000 of those resulted in injury, and 64,000 resulted in fatalities. So this clearly is a big issue, and it is a concern for us, and we definitely recognize that fatigue has been a challenge.

We represent over 15,000 work employers who are dealing with fatigue, as well, in the workplace, and some of those instances it connects to some of the workplace safety.

Where we see a big issue also comes from those shift workers, as well, that are six times more likely to be in an incident based on this drowsy driving. So certainly we think, in the commercial space, obviously we want to see the support for continuing to——

Mr. LOWENTHAL. And so I don't have a lot of time, so I want to ask you.

Mr. SMITH. Sure.

Mr. LOWENTHAL. So you do not support the withdrawing of efforts by the FMCSA or FRA? They just withdrew this.

Mr. SMITH. Yes, we do not support that, correct.

Mr. LOWENTHAL. Thank you. And, well, I yield back. Thank you, Madam Chairwoman.

Ms. NORTON. Thank you very much, Mr. Lowenthal. Mr. Woodall?

Mr. WOODALL. Thank you, Madam Chair.

Ms. Homendy, let me begin with you. You were talking about hours of service earlier, and I thought you said you support hours of service with no exemptions or exceptions. I am thinking about a recent rulemaking for ready-mix concrete trucks, for example, that I would argue brings greater safety and more common sense to the industry. Could you tell me what you mean about no exceptions and no exemptions?

Ms. HOMENDY. We do support science-based hours-of-service standards, and we don't support exemptions to those standards. But we also support fatigue management plans as an adjunct to Federal standards.

Mr. WOODALL. And when I am talking to dispatchers, they will say, "Rob, I am going to do what I have to do to fit within Federal hours of service, but I know the guy I am sending out is worn out. But I can't—I don't have the flexibility to let him do something different that works with his schedule and his needs. If he feels tired, he still has to stay on the road because if he doesn't he is not going to get his hours in today."

Would you support some sort of flexibility for dispatcher and drivers? Or do you believe where we have those rules today, they need to sit right there?

Ms. HOMENDY. And let me clarify exemptions, meaning we believe people should have adequate rest. We don't support allowing them to continue driving if they are not fit for duty.

Mr. WOODALL. Though that would be moving hours of service in a more restrictive direction. I am talking about providing more flexibility, but it is—your position is let——

Ms. HOMENDY. Correct.

Mr. WOODALL. We have as much flexibility as you would like to see us have at the——

Ms. HOMENDY. Well——

Mr. WOODALL. At current——

Ms. HOMENDY. We would not support less off-duty time and more work time, that is correct.

Mr. WOODALL. Thinking about some of the opportunities to partner with industry and safety, there has been some conversation about speed limiters today, there has been some conversation about moving trucks onto interstates. I don't believe we have to have a winner and a loser in a safety conversation, it is just all win, win, win, right? We are all moving in the right direction.

When you are thinking about the safety from—particularly from a bicyclist's perspective, sir, to focus on the folks you represent, do you have the flexibility from your members to say, yes, we are going to make this gain on behalf of bicyclists? And what we will do, then, is we will also put more trucks on the Interstate Highway System, which may make your interstate drive different, but we are going to improve your bicycle drive. Or is it a single-sided conversation when you are speaking on behalf of your members?

Mr. SEWELL. No, I think you nailed it. I think you have to think of all users when you are designing any roadway. So you don't want to do anything that would—and the other question that came earlier was one of frustration, from a motorist's standpoint.

We have to design systems that work for all users. That is part of the engineer's creed. You are doing it for public betterment. And that includes drivers. And so, you have to think through, if you do move a mode of transportation to a different mechanism for transport, is that going to negatively impact safety for other users on that roadway, too?

So yes, I think you said it very eloquently. It is a balancing act between all of these modes of transportation.

Mr. WOODALL. Chief, let me ask you. I see your members more often than I would like to see them, but thank you for keeping my roads safe in that way. I am thinking about cameras on the roads. Do we utilize those cameras to also enforce our distracted driving and our seatbelt regulations?

Mr. BROWN. Not so much with the seatbelt because, quite frankly, you need to be able to observe it, and it is difficult to get the placement. We do use them for red lights. In some communities they use them for speed enforcement.

The key with the cameras, from my personal standpoint, is you need to make sure that it is for problems, not necessarily for the generation of revenue. That is a debate that becomes problematic for law enforcement, when they administer those programs. But if you identify problem areas and you deploy that type of technology, it will have an impact, to some extent, on some of the behavior, and you will get better compliance.

It also increases capacity. But I will also tell you it also results in a number of complaints, because people don't like to see those tickets coming in the mail.

Mr. WOODALL. I share that distaste for those tickets coming in the mail.

[Laughter.]

Mr. WOODALL. But at some point, either the law is the law and we have to enforce it—you don't have enough cops on the beat to cover every cell phone user. You don't have enough cops on the beat to make sure that everybody is wearing their seat belt. And if the law is not evenly and aggressively enforced, my behavior is going to reflect that.

Mr. BROWN. And not all the States allow it. And so that is a national thing. I am not sure exactly where some of the other Federal agencies may be. But frankly, there is—in the Commonwealth, for example, there are a number of communities that would be interested in having the flexibility of applying it for problem areas. Alexandria is one of them. I know that is true across the country, but not all the States allow for that, or they have limited applications that are appropriate.

Mr. WOODALL. All right. I thank you all for being here. Madam Chair, I yield back.

Ms. NORTON. Thank you, Mr. Woodall. Mrs. Napolitano?

Mrs. NAPOLITANO. Thank you, Madam Chair. I have questions for all of you, and this is another—it is public safety. Thank you for being here today.

But of particular concern is the growing number of assaults on bus drivers. Not only are they heinous acts perpetrated on public servants, they also pose a great danger to passengers, pedestrians, and other vehicles, as some of these assaults happen while the driver is operating his vehicle.

My bill, H.R. 1139, Transit Worker and Pedestrian Protection Act, has 100 bipartisan cosponsors, would provide FTA funds for transit agencies to install barriers to protect the driver and keep the bus operating safely.

It also addresses the issue of blind spots in modern buses with large bus frames and sight mirrors that prevent them from—it blocks their view of pedestrians crossing the street. This has led to multiple severe accidents around the country. Some buses in the and many buses in Europe do not have this impediment, those large visual obstructions for the driver. It requires a transit agency to address and remove significant blind spots from the bus driver work station. And I have personally recommended that before they buy any buses, they talk to the manufacturer for those changes on the buses.

Do you have any concerns about the assaults on bus drivers, and the blind spots and the transportation safety hazard? And should we address this issue in Congress?

Ms. HOMENDY. Thank you, Chairwoman. I appreciate the question. The NTSB has not looked at assaults on rail or transit operators. But any injury or fatality is a concern to us, of course.

We have issued recommendations on collision avoidance systems like automatic emergency braking or forward collision avoidance, which could help with other issues. But we haven't specifically looked at the particular issue you are talking about.

Mrs. NAPOLITANO. Would you mind looking at it? We had—— Ms. HOMENDY. Absolutely.

Mrs. NAPOLITANO [continuing]. People coming, bus drivers actually tell us all the heinous acts committed on them.

Ms. HOMENDY. Yes. And, in fact, we are meeting with a few folks in a few days on that.

Mr. BROWN. Mrs. Napolitano, from the standpoint of just being a cop, that is a felony, it is a criminal act, and that always causes us concern. The implications for that, should the bus—should the driver be operating a bus, are huge, because there are implications for all the passengers that are maybe on that bus, let alone the size difference on the vehicles.

There are some communities that have had problems in that area. Not everyone has that same kind of a problem, that I could see from the stats. We have actually looked at that a little bit as it applies to the national capital region to see if it had implications for us and our city.

But the potential jeopardy for the community is huge that is on that bus.

Mrs. NAPOLITANO. Thank you.

Mr. BRUEMMER. I think the transportation of the future certainly relies on multimodal integrating, how does transit operate with other sources: pedestrian, bikes, and regular vehicles. I think infrastructure, as we move forward, needs to change to accommodate those areas so that we do have separation between that. And certainly, you know, it is a major concern when you get pedestrian traffic moving across in front of a large vehicle.

Mrs. NAPOLITANO. They can't see them.

Mr. BRUEMMER. There needs to be a—there is a concern there that they need to be able to integrate with each other.

Mrs. NAPOLITANO. Anybody else?

Well, it is a problem. I have met with the Los Angeles Transportation Department, and they tell me—I met with the drivers and they tell me that it has happened more often than not, especially on routes that are in neighborhoods that are questionable, and especially if they have new drivers assigned to those areas that are less knowledgeable about the area.

There is another question I would like to have. Mr. Sewell, your testimony talks about the importance of designing a built environment through policies such as Complete Streets to consider all road users. You note that engineering is moving to safe system approach to designing for structure.

Is the Federal highway policy currently set up to advance a systems approach and related policies, or do we need to make adjustments to ensure that States and cities design projects that prioritize safety?

Mr. SEWELL. I appreciate your question. And I was recently in L.A., and there is—I think it is a great example of rapid evolution happening in the transportation network, and us poorly responding to it.

And I think it goes back to—to answer your question more specifically—giving local control over how those transportation systems can respond to changes in how people want to move is the way to go. I think that that would have been a great help to a city like Los Angeles in responding to the emergence of scooters, and things like that.

Mrs. NAPOLITANO. Well, thank you for the answer. One of the things I would recommend, especially in California, you have the public access system, and you talk about information, training for the public, like in motorcycle training, you should develop or encourage the industry to do that. And go—free for public safety would be a tremendous help to the public. Thank you.

Ms. NORTON. Thank you very much, Mrs. Napolitano. Mr. Babin?

Dr. BABIN. Yes, ma'am. Thank you, Madam Chair, I appreciate that, and appreciate every one of you experts being here today.

The first question that I have is for Ms. Homendy. Thank you very much for being here. I was just briefed by your Chairman, Robert Sumwalt, and he said to tell you hello. He knows you are going to do a great job.

Ms. HOMENDY. No pressure. [Laughter.]

Dr. BABIN. Thank you. For a good part of my life, born and raised in southeast Texas—I represent the 36th District, from Houston to Louisiana—I have slowly watched Highway 59, U.S. 59, transition and change to become a part of the new Interstate 69.

Now I am leading efforts to try to expand the newly authorized Interstate 14 that will be running east and west through my district.

And with the support of a number of my colleagues, I have, in fact, the bill language right here, Madam Chair, if I could enter this into the record. Would that be possible?

Ms. NORTON. So ordered. [The information follows:]

H.R. 2220

To amend the Intermodal Surface Transportation Efficiency Act of 1991 with respect to high priority corridors on the National Highway System, and for other purposes.

In the House of Representatives

Mr. BABIN (for himself, Mr. Johnson of Louisiana, Mr. ABRAHAM, Mr. GUEST, Mr. PALAZZO, Mr. BRADY, Mr. CONAWAY, Mr. FLORES, Mr. WILLIAMS, Mr. CARTER of Texas, and Mr. WEBER of Texas): introduced the following bill; which was referred to the Committee on Transportation and Infrastructure.

A Bill

To amend the Intermodal Surface Transportation Efficiency Act of 1991 with respect to high priority corridors on the National Highway System, and for other purposes.

Be it enacted by the Senate and House of Representatives of the United States of America in Congress assembled-

Section 1. Short Title

This Act may be cited as the "I-14 Expansion and Improvement Act of 2019".

Section 2. High Priority Corridors on National Highway System

(a) IDENTIFICATION.—

(1) CENTRAL TEXAS CORRIDOR.—Section 1105(c)(84) of the Intermodal Surface Transportation Efficiency Act of 1991 is amended to read as follows:

"(84) The Central Texas Corridor, including the route—

"(A) commencing in the vicinity of Texas Highway 338 in Odessa, Texas, running eastward generally following Interstate Route 20, connecting to Texas Highway 158 in the vicinity of Midland, Texas, then following Texas Highway 158 eastward to United States Route 87 and then following United States Route 87 southeastward, passing in the vicinity of San Angelo, Texas, and connecting to United States Route 190 in the vicinity of Brady, Texas;

"(B) commencing at the intersection of Interstate Route 10 and United States Route 190 in Pecos County, Texas, and following United States Route 190 to Brady, Texas;

"(C) following portions of United States Route 190 eastward, passing in the vicinity of Fort Hood, Killeen, Belton, Temple, Bryan, College Station, Huntsville, Livingston, Woodville, and Jasper, to the logical terminus of Texas Highway 63 at the Sabine River Bridge at Burrs Crossing;

"(D) following United States Route 83 southward from the vicinity of Eden, Texas, to a logical connection to Interstate Route 10 at Junction, Texas;

"(E) following United States Route 69 from Interstate Route 10 in Beaumont, Texas, north to United States Route 190 in the vicinity of Woodville, Texas; and "(F) following United States Route 96 from Interstate Route 10 in Beaumont,

Texas, north to United States Route 190 in the vicinity of Jasper, Texas.".

(2) CENTRAL LOUISIANA CORRIDOR.—Section 1105(c) of the Intermodal Surface Transportation Efficiency Act of 1991 is amended by adding at the end the following:

"(91) The Central Louisiana Corridor commencing at the logical terminus of Louisiana Highway 8 at the Sabine River Bridge at Burrs Crossing and generally following portions of Louisiana Highway 8 to Leesville, Louisiana, and then eastward on Louisiana Highway 28, passing in the vicinity of Alexandria, Pineville, Walters, and Archie, to the logical terminus of United States Route 84 at the Mississippi River Bridge at Vidalia, Louisiana."

(3) CENTRAL MISSISSIPPI CORRIDOR.—Section 1105(c) of the Intermodal Surface Transportation Efficiency Act of 1991, as amended by this Act, is further amended by adding at the end the following:

"(92) The Central Mississippi Corridor commencing at the logical terminus of United States Route 84 at the Mississippi River and then generally following portions of United States Route 84 passing in the vicinity of Natchez, Brookhaven, Monticello, Prentiss, and Collins, to the logical terminus with Interstate Route 59 in the vicinity of Laurel, Mississippi and continuing on Interstate Route 59 south to United States Route 98 in the vicinity of Hattiesburg connecting to United States Route 49 south following to Interstate Route 10 in the vicinity of Gulfport following Mississippi Route 601 southerly terminating near the Mississippi State Port at Gulfport."

(b) INCLUSION OF CERTAIN SEGMENTS ON INTERSTATE SYSTEM.—Section 1105(e)(5)(A) of the Intermodal Surface Transportation Efficiency Act of 1991 is amended in the first sentence—

(1) by inserting "subsection (c)(84)," after "subsection (c)(83),"; and

(2) by striking "and subsection (c)(90)" and inserting "subsection (c)(90), subsection (c)(91), and subsection (c)(92)".

(c) DESIGNATION.—Section 1105(e)(5)(C) of the Intermodal Surface Transportation Efficiency Act of 1991 is amended by striking "The route referred to in subsection (c)(84) is designated as Interstate Route I-14." and inserting "The route referred to in subsection (c)(84)(A) is designated as Interstate Route I-14 North and the State of Texas shall erect signs, as appropriate and as approved by the Secretary, identifying such route as future Interstate Route I-14 North. The route referred to in subsection (c)(84)(B) is designated as Interstate Route I-14 South and the State of Texas shall erect signs, as appropriate and as approved by the Secretary, identifying such route as future Interstate Route I-14 South. The routes referred to in subparagraphs (C), (D), (E), and (F) of subsection (c)(84) and in subsections (c)(91) and (c)(92) are designated as Interstate Route I-14 and the States of Texas, Louisiana, and Mississippi shall erect signs, as appropriate and as approved by the Secretary, identifyiug such routes as segments of future Interstate Route I-14.''

Dr. BABIN. OK. And I want to—with this in mind, I want to ask about safety in regards to converting a highway or State road to an interstate highway.

In your experience with the NTSB, have you seen a correlation between improving roadway safety and updating existing roads, whether U.S. highways or State highways, in order to meet the interstate standards and grades? If you could, maybe elaborate your thoughts on that.

Ms. HOMENDY. I apologize. On that question I will have to get back to you for the record and talk with some of our experts back——

Dr. BABIN. OK.

Ms. HOMENDY [continuing]. In the office. Dr. BABIN. All right.

Ms. HOMENDY. But I will respond, and also contact your office on that.

Dr. BABIN. OK, that would be fine. Does anybody else want to take a stab at that? I will just wait and get back—if you will get back with me, Ms. Homendy.

All right, this is for—the next question is for Mr. Bruemmer, if you don't mind. Thank you for being here today, as well. You said it best in your testimony, that we cannot allow safety to ever become an afterthought or a second priority, period. I couldn't agree with you more on that.

And you know it better than most, that so much of the work this committee did on the FAST Act was to help stimulate innovation, improve safety through data-driven performance-based approaches, and allow our States the flexibility they need to create programs unique to their needs for both motor and non-motorized users. The data has clearly shown a reduction of motor vehicle fatalities, high-lighting that safety programs all over the country are indeed working successfully.

Could you share with the committee where you see the next generation of roadway safety moving, and where do you see innovative and creative ideas, and where they are taking us through the next decade in terms of safety and smart investment? Yes, sir.

Mr. BRUEMMER. Thank you, Congressman. I think, as you look forward, you know, technology is really kind of the front-runner of this. Vehicles are becoming smarter. How does infrastructure react to the vehicles?

From my experience what you look at is pavement markings that are now becoming more recognizable by machine-driven vehicles. You have signs which machines can read. They have got, basically, a QR code inset in them, so that the vehicle comes up and can tell what the sign reads.

Dr. BABIN. Right.

Mr. BRUEMMER. So I think as we look 5, 10 years down the road, how do we make that step from purely a human-driven world to integrating that technology, and we go forward. So that transition period is going to be difficult. I think we need to have a strong map forward of where do we want to be 20 to 25 years from now.

Dr. BABIN. Right. OK. Thank you very much.

And you know what? I don't—unless anybody else has something they would like to add to that, thank you, Madam Chair, I will yield back.

Ms. NORTON. Thank you, Mr. Babin. Dr. BABIN. Yes, ma'am.

Ms. NORTON. Mr. Stanton?

Mr. STANTON. Thank you very much, Madam Chair. An excellent presentation today on an incredibly important topic: safety on our roadways and our highway systems.

And as we plan a significant infrastructure bill through this committee, we need to make sure that safety is at the forefront, and it is equally as important, if not the most important investment we can make in this country is on roadway safety, particularly supporting cities and municipalities across the country, things like Complete Streets and Vision Zero and other programs that are successful models.

The Federal Government can better support those cities, and hope that State legislatures don't preempt cities who have a lot of innovative ideas. I say that as a former mayor of a city.

And the specific issue I want to talk today about has to do with wrong-way drivers. Sadly, that is an issue that my community, the Greater Phoenix, Arizona, community, is confronting in a significant and sad way right now.

In January of 2015 a dispatcher with the Phoenix Fire Department was on her way home from a late shift when she was killed on the I–17 in central Phoenix by a wrong-way driver. Megan Lange was 26 years old, a wife, a mother of two young boys. When the firefighters arrived at the scene of the accident, they knew that she was one of their own, because she was still in her uniform.

Megan's death shook our community, and especially her fellow city employees. I was mayor at the time, and I will never forget taking that call. Her tragedy, unfortunately, was one of a series, part of a pattern of wrong-way drivers that our cities, counties, and State have to work hard to correct.

Two out of three wrong-way crashes are caused by impaired drivers, often drivers with blood alcohol levels more than twice the legal limit. One-quarter of all wrong-way crashes are fatal, compared to just about 1 percent for other highway crashes. And though, nationally, the number of and rate of fatal crashes have been falling for decades, the number of fatal wrong-way crashes continues to creep upward. And that is something that we have to confront.

So I will open up to all the panel, but particularly Mr. Bruemmer. Can you talk a little bit about what we can be doing, as Congress, to better support you and other safety-related organizations to decrease and even stop the epidemic of wrong-way crashes across our country?

Mr. BRUEMMER. Thank you, Congressman. There are innovations coming out, as far as infrastructure, which improve the possibility that someone can't go the wrong way: sensors, which activate lights to notify the driver; also relaying messages to law enforcement, so that they can respond quickly, knowing that there is someone going the wrong direction; pavement markings which are visible as you enter a ramp that, from one direction, say "Do Not Enter," the other way they look normal. So I think that it is an infrastructure question.

People get confused and lost, unfortunately, make a wrong turn up the wrong ramp, and it is catastrophic. How do you avoid that? And I think, really, infrastructure has to combat that at a one-on- one level.

Mr. STANTON. Excellent. Infrastructure and, of course, continuing with our efforts in terms of drunken driving and other types of driving under the influence.

I will leave it—I will open up to other witnesses. What can we do, as Congress, Members of Congress, to better support efforts to reduce and end wrong-way driving?

Mr. BROWN. Mr. Stanton, if I could, the National Transportation Safety Board—I am going to steal your thunder a little bit—did a report.

Ms. HOMENDY. That was my answer. Mr. BROWN. There you go. [Laughter.]

Mr. BROWN. Don Carroll was the one that authored it. He used to be with the California Highway Patrol, did a work on wrong-way drivers. And most cops know that you have a disorientation issue, and largely it comes from impairment of some level. And also, it comes with, to some extent, with people who have developed some kind of limiting capability with their mind.

There are ways to deal with that as intervention. So MADD has the interlock, they have been promoting the ignition interlock as an example. There are other ways to deal with the impairment issues, so that those people don't get in a car and drive.

As far as the issues involving capacity, mental capacity, that is where the DMVs can come in and try to deal with those issues. And certainly that would be within the purview of an authorization act, should that be an issue.

Mr. STANTON. Thank you very much.

Ms. Homendy, did the chief accurately represent NTSB perspective?

[Laughter.]

Ms. HOMENDY. He did. And the person he references, actually, is a former law enforcement official who is on staff at the NTSB. So we did a wrong-way special investigative report in 2012, and looked at six crashes. We had recommendations on improving road designs, having better signage, and then addressing impairment.

And the NTSB's views on impairment is reducing the legal BAC limits from .08 to .05 or lower; requiring ignition interlocks for all offenders, not just repeat offenders, including first-time offenders; stronger enforcement; and then also in-vehicle technology to prevent impaired drivers from getting in the vehicle and driving.

Mr. STANTON. Thank you. I yield back. Ms. NORTON. The gentleman yields back. Mrs. Miller?

Mrs. MILLER. Thank you, Chairwoman Norton. West Virginia has been successful throughout the implementation of the Governor's highway safety program. We have received millions of dollars through the National Highway Traffic Safety Administration to help implement several different programs in all 55 counties of my State.

In my region of southern West Virginia, one of the largest challenges we face is impaired driving. Over 50 percent of impaired driving arrests in southern West Virginia counties have been identified as drug-related. Southern West Virginia has been ravaged by the opioid epidemic, especially as the economy in the region collapsed, due to the war on coal. The economic hopelessness faced by so many in my community has been hard to fathom.

I have learned very quickly, since being in Congress, that we are very fluid in our movement, and in and out of committees, and in and out of chairs. So Ms. Homendy, I hope this question has not been asked to you before.

Programs committed to stop drunk driving have been successful across the country. What programs are in development to stem the tide on drug-impaired driving?

Ms. HOMENDY. Well, I know NHTSA has focused on drug-impaired driving.

From the NTSB's perspective, we have investigated a number of crashes involving impaired drivers. The difficulty with drugs is there is no impairment standard. And so we have recommended that DOT work with HHS to develop a standard. In the meantime, we have recommended that NHTSA issue guidance to States that tells law enforcement officers when to test, what drugs to test for, how to test, and cut-off levels to help determine impairment.

In addition, we need advanced training for law enforcement officials, so that they can recognize when a driver is impaired.

Mrs. MILLER. Thank you. West Virginia is a hub for transportation, and our highways are a crossroads of trade and shipping.

Commercial trucking is essential for our economy, but has not seen the same decrease in accidents that passenger automobiles have.

Mr. Jones, are there any programs in development aimed to protect our Nation's commercial truckers, in particular?

Mr. JONES. I am going to defer that answer, if maybe Ms. Homendy has some more perspective on that. I can't speak about the commercial trucking industry directly.

Mrs. MILLER. OK.

Ms. HOMENDY. I mean for commercial driving, I would say fatigue. I mean, from our perspective, it is strong hours-of-service standards, no exemptions to those standards, strong fatigue mitigation, management plans, implementation of electronic logging devices, and then screening, diagnosis, and treatment for sleep apnea. So fatigue, we would say, is the major issue.

Mrs. MILLER. OK. Does anyone else have any comments on that? Mr. BROWN. Yes, at one point the Federal Motor Carrier Safety Administration also brought up the issue of distraction as a major issue with regards to—within the cockpit of the vehicle. And I would think that that would probably still ring true today. Mrs. MILLER. What type of distraction?

Mr. BROWN. Basic distraction, in terms of the operating of the commercial vehicle, people manipulating cell phones, working on automated electronic logs, things of that nature, not paying attention to their driving.

Mrs. MILLER. OK, thank you. I yield back my time.

Ms. NORTON. Thank you very much, Mrs. Miller. Finally, our Ranking Member Davis.

Mr. DAVIS. Finally bringing up the rear, huh? Pretty long hearing. You guys thought you were done, and then we keep walking back in, right?

[Laughter.]

Mr. DAVIS. Ms. Homendy, great to speak with you yesterday. I hear, because I am late, that some of my other colleagues asked about technology. I was going to channel Don Young [referring to nameplate swap]. Come on, what are you guys doing? The dean of the delegation, the dean of the House.

[Laughter.]

Mr. DAVIS. In all seriousness, Ms. Homendy, you mentioned that the technology is not there yet. For States like Illinois that will be on a path to legalize marijuana, you know, my concern is how do we get technology up to the forefront to be able to do tests, a roadside test, just like we do with impaired drivers due to alcohol consumption.

And you mentioned in your response that the technology is not here yet, but others are working on it. Right? Do you have anything else to add?

Ms. HOMENDY. Right. We have recommended that DOT and HHS work together to provide additional testing mechanisms like oral fluid testing and hair testing.

And in addition to just the testing, in the meantime, NHTSA can issue guidance to States, as I mentioned, for law enforcement officers to clarify when people should be tested, what types of drugs they should be tested for, and cut-off levels for testing. That guidance has not gone out yet.

But in addition, training for law enforcement officers. I mentioned a couple of programs to you yesterday that NHTSA has for advanced training for law enforcement officers. Basic training is the standard field sobriety testing for law enforcement officers, but NHTSA has two programs, one called the ARIDE program and one called DRE—it is an Advanced Roadside Impaired Driving Enforcement program and the Drug Recognition Expert training—which provide 72 hours of classroom training and 40 to 60 hours of field training, which makes them highly skilled at detection and identification of impairment. And very few officers are trained at those levels, so we encourage additional training.

Mr. DAVIS. Right, thank you. And I apologize, my team forgot the WWE belt I promised you yesterday.

Ms. HOMENDY. I was hoping to wear it for my opening statement. Mr. D$_{AVIS}$. My apologies to you and your entire team.

Chief, first off, I want to say thank you. And if you could please relay my thanks and the thanks of many of my teammates for the courageous actions of your three officers who saved us all one fateful morning in Alexandria a few years ago. So thank you for that. And please, again, relay our thanks to them. I don't think they get enough credit for that.

Mr. BROWN. Thank you, sir. I will.

Mr. DAVIS. Thank you. In my home State of Illinois, Chief, we have had 15 officers struck this year already while outside of their vehicles. We have a law called Scott's Law in Illinois that protects our law enforcement officials, our Good Samaritans, and even our tow truck drivers who are on the side of our roadways, trying to help motorists who are stranded. We are looking to expand Scott's Law in Illinois, and I noticed this isn't a law in every State.

What type of activities would you recommend we do at the national level to stop the carnage that we have seen of our law enforcement officers and our Good Samaritans and tow truck drivers that we are seeing in Illinois?

Mr. BROWN. Well, actually, NHTSA has actually taken a position of supporting the move over, at least in concept.

But you are right, there are a lot of differences between the States. My former agency, the California Highway Patrol, just lost a sergeant just a couple of days ago over this very same thing.

That is actually a disincentive in some cases for law enforcement to engage in traffic safety, because oftentimes they are exposed when they go out there. And so any way we can protect the highway worker—and that is not just the cop and the tow truck officers, and it is, in many cases, the person from DOT who is working on the road to repair a roadway. It is a paramount issue.

Moreover laws work. They are difficult to enforce sometimes because, you know, usually there is congestion or other issues around it. But if you can get some level of compliance, it provides a buffer. And I think that would be appropriate to put into some authoriztion to encourage that at some point.

Mr. DAVIS. Well, thank you. This is something that we have not experienced at this level in my home State before. It has happened for many years, and it is something that, obviously, we need to address, especially with distracted driving and other issues that have caused these terrible, tragic accidents, especially in the wake of technology and technological advances in our automobiles.

I rented a car this weekend, and was driving around, and it notified me every time it thought I went outside the lane. I mean at some point we have got to recognize technological advances to assist in saving the lives of the brave men and women who wear that same uniform you do.

Thank you for your time to each and every one of you, and I yield back no time that I have.

Ms. NORTON. I want to thank the ranking member, and I particularly want to thank all of you who have come. You have given us new information, you have given us very helpful information on a very serious subject, where our country is badly in need of the contributions you have made today.

I ask unanimous consent that the record of today's hearing remain open until such time as our witnesses have provided answers to any questions that may have been submitted in writing.

And I ask unanimous consent that the record remain open for 15 days for any additional comments and information submitted by Members or witnesses to be included in the record of today's hearing.

Without objection, so ordered.

This hearing is adjourned. Thank you very much. [Whereupon, at 12:25 p.m., the subcommittee was adjourned.]

SUBMISSIONS FOR THE RECORD

Prepared Statement of Hon. Steve Cohen, a Representative in Congress from the State of Tennessee

Thank you, Chairwoman Norton for putting together this important hearing, and thanks to all the witnesses for being here today.

According to the National Highway Traffic Safety Administration (NHTSA), 37,133 people lost their lives in accidents on U.S. roadways in 2017, or 100 people died each day in motor vehicle crashes.

We must do better.

Fortunately, I believe there are several commonsense, bipartisan steps that Congress can take to improve highway safety. They include, the DUI Reporting Act, the School Bus Safety Act, the Stop Underrides Act, and the Horse Transportation Safety Act.

Dui Reporting Act

The DUI Reporting Act (H.R. 1914) would stop the dangerous practice of charging repeat drunk drivers as first-time offenders.

Just a few years ago, two teenagers from Memphis were killed when the car they were driving was struck by a drunk driver who had accrued seven DUI charges since 2008 and had been allowed to plead guilty five times to a first-offense DUI. Congressman Steve Chabot and I introduced legislation to stop this by creating an incentive for local law enforcement to report DUI arrests to the National Crime Information System, so prosecutors will know if a defendant is a repeat offender. This bipartisan bill has been endorsed by Mothers Against Drunk Driving, and I hope this committee will consider it soon.

School Bus Safety Act

I hope this committee will also consider the School Bus Safety Act, a bill I am planning to reintroduce with Senator Tammy Duckworth, to implement several of the National Transportation Safety Board's recommendations to improve school bus safety.

Specifically, the bill will ensure that there are seat belts at every seat and buses are equipped with safety measures like stability control and automatic braking systems.

In November 2016, there were two high-profile school bus accidents in Chattanooga, Tennessee, and another in Baltimore, Maryland, that left 6 school-aged children robbed of their futures.

These are chilling reminders that Congress needs to act.

Stop Underrides Act

I hope this committee will also take action on the Stop Underrides Act (H.R. 1511/ S. 665).

In 2014, my constituents Randy and Laurie Higginbotham lost their 33-year-old son Michael, like thousands of others have, when his car crashed into a semi-truck trailer and ended up under it. Unfortunately, truck underride is not a new issue. It has been on the highway safety radar for decades, yet action has not been taken. That is why I introduced the Stop Underrides Act with our Transportation Committee colleague Mark DeSaulnier, and Senators Kirsten Gillibrand and Marco Rubio, to require all large truck trailers to have front, side, and rear underride guards.

This bill will save lives and I encourage my colleagues to support it.

Horse Transportation Safety Act

I hope this committee will also take action to protect the lives of both horses and humans as horses are transported on our nation's highways.

In 2007, fifteen horses died when a double deck trailer carrying 59 Belgian draft horses overturned on Route 41 in Illinois. Unfortunately, accidents like this are not uncommon.

Drivers can currently exploit a loophole in current regulation banning the transport of horses in double deck trailers, thus giving drivers an incentive to inhumanely transport horses to assembly points then reload them into single level trailers just outside their final destination.

This practice is not only dangerous and inhumane to the horses, but to the traveling public, as well.

That is why I introduced the bipartisan Horse Transportation Safety Act (H.R. 1400) along with Representatives Peter King, and Transportation Committee members Dina Titus and Brian Fitzpatrick, to ensure the humane and safe transportation of horses.

If enacted, it would prohibit interstate transportation of horses in a motor vehicle containing two or more levels stacked on top of one another. It would also create civil penalties of at least $100 for each horse involved.

These bills will help save lives, and I hope this committee will take action on them. I once again thank the chair for holding today's hearing and yield back.

Prepared Statement of Hon. Frederica S. Wilson, a Representative in Congress from the State of Florida

Thank you, Chairwoman Norton.

Improving safety on our roadways is a top priority for my constituents and me.

Seemingly every day, I see a fresh news story about a traffic collision that either claimed lives or caused injuries in my community.

On November 8, 2018, my longtime friend and neighbor, Alvin Watson, was fatally struck by a vehicle while jogging near his home. He was a beloved husband, father, colleague, and friend.

In January, seven people, five of whom were children, lost their lives on their way to Disney World after their church van collided with three other vehicles.

Just last month, a father and his six-year-old son were struck as they walked to school. While they weren't seriously injured, this was still an extremely traumatic event for them.

In 2017 alone, more than 3,100 people, including 654 pedestrians, died on Florida roadways.

As pedestrians, Floridians face a risk of fatality that's incomparable to any other state.

Shockingly, of the 20 most dangerous metropolitan areas for pedestrians in the nation, 9 are in Florida.

In fact, the stretch of I-95 that runs through Miami-Dade County, which I represent, had more fatal accidents than any other part of the nearly 2000-mile interstate highway in 2015.

Suffice it to say, traffic safety reforms are desperately needed in my state and district. We can and must do better.

As we consider legislation to reauthorize the FAST Act and invest in our infrastructure, I will advocate for robust investments and policies to reduce traffic fatalities and strongly prioritize pedestrian safety.

I have a few questions.

Letter from Shailen P. Bhatt, President and CEO, Intelligent Transportation Society of America, Submitted for the Record by Hon. Norton

April 8, 2019.

Hon. Eleanor Holmes Norton
Chair
Subcommittee on Highways and Transit, Committee
on Transportation and Infra- structure
U.S. House of Representatives
Washington, DC 20515

Hon. Rodney Davis
Ranking Member
Subcommittee on Highways and Transit, Committee
on Transportation and Infrastructure
U.S. House of Representatives
Washington, DC 20515

Dear Chair Norton And Ranking Member Davis:

In anticipation of the Subcommittee on Highways and Transit upcoming hearing entitled "Every Life Counts: Improving the Safety of our Nation's Roadways," the Intelligent Transportation Society of America (ITS America) writes to underscore how new and developing Vehicle-to-Everything (V2X) technology that depends on the 5.9 GHz band is allowing us to finally address the lives lost and ruined on our nation's roads. Vehicle-to-Vehicle (V2V), Vehicle-to-Infrastructure (V2I), and Vehicle-to-Pedestrian (V2P)—collectively referred to as Vehicle-to-Everything (V2X)— have incredible potential to dramatically improve the safety, accessibility, and operational performance of our road infrastructure and vehicle safety.

Safety is the top priority of the nation's transportation system. According to the
U.S. Department of Transportation's National Highway Traffic Safety Administration (NHTSA), 37,133 people lost their lives in motor vehicle crashes in 2017, which roughly breaks down to just over 100 fatalities per day. Examples of V2V deployments available today include systems that provide emergency braking and the

ability to be the "eyes and ears" of other vehicles. Non-Line-of-Sight awareness, as it's known, means that drivers and vehicles can see around corners and receive information about hazards in the roadway, even if they cannot see the hazard. V2V communications help move traffic more efficiently with demand responsive traffic signaling and allow emergency response vehicles to preempt signals.

V2I provides vehicles and drivers information about infrastructure operations—weather and pavement condition, how signals are directing traffic, and even the location of potential hazards at intersections and other critical road safety hotspots. V2I applications include red light violation warnings, reduced speed zone warnings, curve speed warnings, and spot weather impact warnings. V2I soon will support other applications that will disseminate the condition of the infrastructure, such as bridge integrity and collect data from cars that describe pavement condition. V2I technology helps drivers safely negotiate intersections and prevent intersection crashes. Another connected vehicle safety application that helps drivers with left turns at intersections could help prevent left-turn crashes. NHTSA estimates that safety applications enabled by V2V and V2I could eliminate or mitigate the severity of up to 80 percent of non-impaired crashes, including crashes at intersections or while changing lanes.

V2X will enable us to deploy safety solutions to protect vulnerable users of the system, which will be transformational. By allowing vehicles to communicate with these users through sensors or vehicle to device communication (V2P), we can significantly reduce the number of pedestrians killed on our roadways.

Public sector agencies can also reap the benefits of V2X. Increasingly, vehicles will rely on digital formatting of roadway information to process roadway rules. ITS America member Regional Transportation Commission of Southern Nevada recently became first in the world to put roadway information into a digital format. As connected vehicles drive over the roadway, they can pick up differences between the "digital" road and the actual road. This could eliminate the need for agencies to manually examine roadways for striping or automatically report potholes instead of waiting for enough drivers to incur tire damage before fixing them. These vehicles will also give an up-to-the-minute snapshot of the system—how it is performing, are there any incidents, live weather conditions, etc. Millions of dollars have already been invested in this effort, including incorporating connected vehicle technologies into infrastructure by states and cities. Eighty-four communities in the United States are deploying or planning to deploy connected vehicle technology. Of that number, 54 sites are operational, and 30 are in development. Nearly every state has at least one connected vehicle deployment. V2I deployments include expansions of the Safety Pilot Model Deployment in Ann Arbor (MI), large pilot deployments in New York City, Tampa, and Wyoming, and the Smart City Challenge in Columbus (OH).

These technologies can also enhance automated driving systems, which can provide numerous economic, environmental, and societal benefits, such as decreased congestion and fuel consumption, and increased access for older adults and people with disabilities.

However, V2X communications are by no means guaranteed. The 5.9 GHz band for V2X is being targeted by cable companies and their supporters who are seeking additional spectrum for enhanced WiFi experience and are aggressively pressuring the Federal Communications Commission (FCC) to force V2X to share this spectrum with unlicensed consumer broadband devices. Speed matters when safety information is involved. Sharing the band could compromise the speed and put lives at risk. What if a driver knew, in fractions of a second, that an airbag deployed in a car in front of him/her? Alternatively, that the car in front, around the next curve, was sliding on black ice? Or a pedestrian is around the next corner? Thanks to V2X technology, that driver would react—and avoid a crash. Deploying life-saving technologies that allow cars, buses, trucks, bicycles, pedestrians, motorcycles, street lights, and other infrastructure to talk to each other will ensure more people arrive home safely.

ITS America supports preserving the entire 5.9 GHz band for existing, new, and developing V2X technologies. We want to make sure all three phases of testing for the 5.9 GHz band are complete before the FCC rules on whether the spectrum can be shared between V2X operations and unlicensed devices like WiFi. Any unlicensed use in the band should be done without harmful interference to the incumbent technology or other intelligent transportation systems technologies. Finally, ITS America requests a report from the U.S. Department of Transportation (USDOT) on the outcomes of the FCC studies. USDOT must ensure Congress and transportation stakeholder that transportation safety will not be compromised in the 5.9 GHz band.

Sincerely,

Shailen P. Bhatt
President and CEO, Intelligent Transportation Society of America

cc: House of Representatives Subcommittee on Highways and Transit Committee on Transportation and Infrastructure

Ron Thaniel
ITS America Vice President of Legislative Affairs

STATEMENT OF CATHERINE CHASE, PRESIDENT, ADVOCATES FOR HIGHWAY AND AUTO SAFETY, SUBMITTED FOR THE RECORD BY HON. NORTON

Introduction

Advocates for Highway and Auto Safety (Advocates) is a coalition of public health, safety, and consumer organizations, insurers and insurance agents that promotes highway and auto safety through the adoption of federal and state laws, policies and regulations. Advocates is unique both in its board composition and its mission of advancing safer vehicles, safer motorists and road users, and safer roads. We respectfully request that this statement be included in the hearing record.

Deaths and Injuries on Our Nation's Roads Remain Unacceptably High

In 2017, more than 37,000 people were killed and 2.7 million were injured in motor vehicle crashes.[89] Crashes impose a financial toll of over $800 billion in total costs to society and $242 billion in direct economic costs, equivalent to a "crash tax" of $784 on every American. This incredibly high level of carnage and expense would not be tolerated in any other mode of transportation.

Moreover, fatal truck crashes continue to occur at an alarmingly high rate. In 2017, crashes involving large trucks killed 4,761 people. This is an increase of 9 percent from the previous year and an increase of 41 percent since 2009. The number of 2017 fatalities in crashes involving large trucks is also the highest since 2007. Additionally, 149,000 people were injured in crashes involving large trucks in 2017. In fatal two-vehicle crashes between a large truck and a passenger motor vehicle, 97 percent of the fatalities were occupants of the passenger vehicle. The cost to society from crashes involving commercial motor vehicles (CMVs) was estimated to be $134 billion in 2016.

Available Commonsense and Cost-Effective Solutions

While far too many lives are lost and people are injured on our Nation's roads each year, proven solutions are currently available that can help to prevent or mitigate these senseless tragedies. The National Highway Traffic Safety Administration (NHTSA) currently values each life lost in a crash at $9.6 million. Each one of these senseless

---

[89] Statistics are from the U.S. Department of Transportation unless otherwise noted.

tragedies not only irreparably harms families and communities, but they also impose significant costs on society that can be avoided.

Proven, Advanced Vehicle Technologies Should be Standard in All Vehicles

Every day on average, over 100 people are killed and 7,500 people are injured in motor vehicle crashes. Nearly a third of all crashes continue to be caused by an impaired driver and speed is a contributing factor in over 25 percent of crashes. Additionally, distracted driving resulted in over 3,000 deaths in 2017 alone. Advanced vehicle technologies can prevent and lessen the severity of crashes and should be required as standard equipment on all vehicles. These include automatic emergency braking (AEB), lane departure warning (LDW) and blind spot detection (BSD) for cars, trucks and buses. These systems can help stop crashes from occurring, as well as reduce the impact of crashes that do occur. The Insurance Institute for Highway Safety (IIHS) has found that AEB can decrease front-to-rear crashes with injuries by 56 percent, LDW can reduce single-vehicle, sideswipe and head-on injury crashes by over 20 percent, and BSD can diminish injury crashes from lane change by nearly 25 percent. However, these safety systems are often sold as part of an additional, expensive trim package along with other non-safety features, or included only in high end models or vehicles. Moreover, there are currently no minimum performance standards to ensure they perform as expected.

Recommendation: Advanced vehicle technologies that have proven to be effective at preventing and mitigating crashes, including AEB, LDW and BSD, should be standard equipment on all cars, trucks and buses.

Commonsense Regulation of Experimental Driverless Car Technology is Essential

Autonomous vehicles (AVs), also known as driverless cars, are being developed and tested on public roads without sufficient safeguards to protect both those within the AVs and everyone sharing the roadways with them without consent. Numerous public opinion polls show a high skepticism and fear about the technology, and for good reason. At least six crashes resulting in four fatalities have occurred in the U.S. involving cars equipped with autonomous technology that are being investigated by the National Transportation Safety Board (NTSB).

While AVs have tremendous promise to meaningfully reduce traffic crashes, fatalities and injuries as well as increase mobility, once they are proven to be safe, they must be subject to minimum performance standards set by the U.S. Department of Transportation (U.S. DOT). These standards should include, but not be limited to, cybersecurity, vehicle electronics, driver engagement for AVs that require a human driver to take over at any point, and a "vision test" for driverless cars to ensure they can properly detect and respond to their surroundings. Additionally, minimum performance requirements and protections will be especially critical as autonomous systems are deployed in commercial motor vehicles (CMVs). Large trucks and buses should always have an appropriately-trained and licensed driver behind the wheel, and introduction of automated systems should never be used as a rationale for weakening operational rules such as hours of service, driver training and other important requirements.

The recent crashes involving the Boeing 737 MAX airplane tragically highlight the catastrophic results that can occur when automated technology potentially malfunctions and is not subject to thorough oversight. Reports have indicated that many aspects of the plane's certification were delegated to Boeing. In addition, safety systems that could have assisted the pilots were not required as standard equipment. Lastly, both planes were being operated by experienced pilots that had extensive training. Yet, there are no such federal training requirements for individuals testing or operating automated vehicle technology or for the consumers who purchase these vehicles and are using them on public roads.

Recommendation: AVs must be subject to minimum performance standards set by the U.S. DOT including for cybersecurity, vehicle electronics, driver engagement for AVs that require a human driver to take over at any point, and a "vision test" for driverless cars to ensure they can properly detect and respond to their surroundings.

Crash Data Must be Collected and Available

At a minimum, crash data should be collected, recorded, accessible, and shared with appropriate federal agencies and researchers so that safety-critical problems can be identified. Consumers must also be given essential information about the limitations and capabilities of AVs in the owner's manual and at the point of sale, as well as via a public website searchable by VIN that includes, at a minimum, vehicle information such as any exemptions from federal safety standards and the AV's operational design domain (ODD).

Recommendation: Crash data generated by vehicles should be collected, recorded, accessible, and shared with appropriate federal agencies and researchers so that safety-critical problems can be identified. In addition, consumers must also be given essential information about the limitations and capabilities of AVs in the owner's manual and at the point of sale, as well as via a public website searchable by VIN.

Vulnerable Road Users Must be Protected

Deaths and injuries of pedestrians and bicyclists remain unacceptably high. In fact, in 2016, pedestrian and bicyclist fatalities hit their highest levels in nearly 30 years. Vehicles can be designed, specifically in the front end, to reduce the severity of impacts with pedestrians and/or bicyclists. Additionally, collision avoidance systems for pedestrians, like advanced AEB, have promise to further reduce deaths and injuries. Advocates continues to monitor research on the effectiveness of these systems and will support data-driven solutions to these fatalities. Moreover, the New Car Assessment Program (NCAP) must be updated to include pedestrian crash-worthiness and pedestrian crash avoidance. Upgrades to infrastructure could also offer pedestrians and bicyclists better protection to reduce the occurrence and severity of crashes.

Recommendation: NHTSA should be directed to issue a standard for improved vehicle designs to reduce the severity of impacts with road users. In addition, NCAP must be updated to include pedestrian crashworthiness and pedestrian crash avoidance.

Improving Safety for Older Americans

In 2017, over 6,500 people age 65 and older were killed in traffic crashes—representing 18 percent of all traffic fatalities. Advocates has developed federal legislative proposals addressing both human factors and vehicle design issues to advance the safety of older adults. These recommended improvements include development of a crash test dummy representing older occupants, endorsing revisions to NCAP to include a "Silver Car Rating," and promoting a modification of the injury criteria used in crash tests to address the specific injury patterns suffered by older occupants. Additionally, Advocates supported the need to mandate that hybrid and electric vehicles be manufactured to make sounds when operating at speeds below 18 miles per hour in order to enable child and adult pedestrians and bicyclists, especially those with visual-impairments and older adults, to identify the presence and movement of these very quiet vehicles. This final rule was issued in December 2016 and compliance is required by September 2020.

Recommendation: NHTSA should be required to develop a crash test dummy representing older occupants, revise NCAP to include a "Silver Car Rating'', and modify injury criteria used in crash tests to address the specific injury patterns suffered by older occupants.

The Epidemic of Distracted Driving Must be Addressed

In 2017, crashes involving a distracted driver claimed 3,166 lives. Moreover, crashes in which at least one driver was identified as being distracted imposes an annual economic cost of $40 billion dollars, based on 2010 data. Issues with under-reporting crashes involving cell phones remain because of differences in police crash report coding, database limitations, and other challenges. It is clear from an increasing body of safety research, studies and data that the use of electronic devices for telecommunications (such as mobile phones and text messaging), telematics and entertainment can readily distract drivers from the driving task.

Numerous devices and applications, which pose a substantial danger for distracted driving, are being built into motor vehicles. Yet, NHTSA has issued non-binding guidelines which recommend, but do not require, that clearly unsafe electronic devices should not be installed in vehicles. This does not prohibit manufacturers from installing electronic communications devices that have highly distracting features and will not prevent manufacturers from disregarding the agency guidelines.

Recommendation: NHTSA should issue regulations to strictly limit the use of electronic communication and information features that can be operated while driving, and to prohibit the use of those features that cannot be conducted safely while driving.

NHTSA Must be Sufficiently Funded and Given Additional Authorities

Ensuring NHTSA has adequate resources, funds and staff is a crucial priority. However, the Administration has proposed reducing NHTSA's vehicle safety program by $49 million (26 percent) from the agency's 2019 budget. The Fixing America's Surface Transportation (FAST) Act (Pub. L. 114-94) authorized $214,073,440 for NHTSA's vehicle safety program for fiscal year 2020. The Administration's request is $63 million less than the Congressional authorization. In addition, under the Administration's proposal the enforcement budget, which supports the agency's efforts to identify safety recalls and ensure new vehicles meet federal safety standards, will be cut by $13.5 million (40.9 percent) and the rulemaking budget will be cut by $2.4 million (9.6 percent).

In recent years, millions of motor vehicles have been recalled for serious and sometimes fatal safety defects. NHTSA must have the ability to take immediate action when the agency determines that a defect involves a condition that substantially increases the likelihood of serious injury or death if not remedied immediately. This "imminent hazard" power is needed to protect the public, by allowing the agency to direct manufacturers to immediately notify consumers and remedy the defect as soon as possible. Further, NHTSA must also be given the authority to pursue criminal penalties in appropriate cases where corporate officers who acquire actual knowledge of a serious product danger that could lead to serious injury or death and knowingly and willfully fail to inform NHTSA and warn the public. Under current federal law, many agencies already have authority to pursue criminal penalties including the Consumer Product Safety Commission, the Food and Drug Administration, and the Securities and Exchange Commission. The lack of criminal penalty authority has hampered the agency's ability to deter automakers from safety defect recidivism.

Recommendation: Considering the unacceptably high number of fatalities and injuries on our Nation's roads, the prevalence of recalls, and the new responsibilities incumbent upon the U.S. DOT as AVs are developed and deployed, NHTSA must have additional resources and authorities to effectively oversee vehicle safety.

Commercial Motor Vehicle Safety Must be Improved

Large truck crash fatalities continue to skyrocket. Each day on average, 13 people are killed and more than 400 more are injured in large truck crashes. This preventable fatality toll amounts to a major airplane crash every other week of the year. However, technology currently exists that can help to reverse these grim statistics. They include crash avoidance systems like AEB and speed limiting devices. This equipment should be made standard on all large trucks. Advocates has also recommended mandating comprehensive under-ride guards for large trucks in order to prevent serious injuries and deaths that occur in crashes in which a passenger vehicle goes underneath the rear, side or front of a truck—known as "underride."

Additionally, the lack of uniform adequate training for candidates wishing to obtain their commercial driver's license (CDL) has been a known safety problem for decades. Yet, a rule requiring training for all new CDL applicants issued in 2016 failed to include a requirement that they receive a minimum number of hours of the behind-the-wheel (BTW) training. This type of real world experience is needed to enhance the ability of CDL applicants to operate a CMV safely. In addition to these measures, federal truck safety laws including truck size and weight limits, truck driver hours of service rules, and the age requirement for transporting interstate commerce should not be weakened.

Further, the safety deficiencies of motorcoaches identified in countless recommendations and crash investigations by the NTSB had not been addressed for years, even decades, until deadlines for agency action were enacted in the Moving Ahead for Progress in the 21st Century (MAP-21) Act (Pub. L. 112-141). Even still, NHTSA has yet to complete several of these rulemakings despite a long overdue Congressional deadline of October 2014.

Recommendation: Lifesaving technology including AEB, speed limiting devices and underride guards should be standard equipment on CMVs and trailers. Federal truck safety laws including truck size and weight limits, truck driver hours of service rules, and the age requirement for transporting interstate commerce should not be weakened, and truck driver training requirements should be enhanced. Overdue rulemakings enhancing the safety of motorcoaches must be completed without further delay.

Our Most Precious Passengers Need Enhanced Protections

Every year, nearly 500,000 school buses transport more than 25 million children to and from school and school-related activities according to the NTSB. School bus crashes are similar in many respects to aviation crashes—crashes are infrequent but when they do occur, the results can be catastrophic. Leading safety experts have determined that all school buses should be equipped with safety belts to improve passenger safety. Since 2013, the NTSB has recommended that new school buses be equipped with safety belts. Moreover, the American Academy of Pediatrics has a long standing position that new school buses should be equipped with safety belts. NHTSA also supports requiring safety belts on school buses, and has stated that its goal is to make sure there are no fatalities in school buses. Additional technologies can also make school buses safer. NTSB has recommended that school buses be equipped with both electronic stability control (ESC) and AEB. In addition, motion-activated detection systems that can detect pedestrians located near the outside of the school bus and alert the driver of their presence can improve safety for students boarding and departing a school bus.

Recommendation: Congress should require that important safety advancements be made to ensure the safety of children both inside and outside of school buses.

Conclusion

America's roads are needlessly dangerous. Far too many lives are lost and serious injuries sustained in crashes each year. However, commonsense solutions are at hand that can help to improve the safety of all road users. With bold action from this Committee, these measures can be implemented and lives can be saved.

STATEMENT OF THE AMERICAN ROAD AND TRANSPORTATION BUILDERS ASSOCIATION, SUBMITTED FOR THE RECORD BY HON. NORTON

Chairman Norton, Ranking Member Davis and members of the subcommittee, the American Road & Transportation Builders Association (ARTBA) appreciates the opportunity to submit these comments on a subject that is of primary importance to our organization, the entire transportation construction industry and the American public— *Every Life Counts: Improving the Safety of our Nation's Roadways.*

Established in 1902, ARTBA represents over 8,000 member companies and individuals who design, build and manage the nation's highways, public transit, airports and intermodal transportation systems. The primary goal of the association is to grow and protect transportation infrastructure investment to meet the public and business demand for safe and efficient travel. Accordingly, the jobsite safety of the men and women who build and maintain America's transportation infrastructure— as well as that of those who travel through our work zones and drive on our completed roadways—has been a top priority for ARTBA's membership.

As an example of ARTBA's commitment to roadway safety, in 2016 we launched the Safety Certification for Transportation Project Professionals(tm) (SCTPP). This industry driven program aspires to ensure the safety and well-being of construction workers, motorists, truck drivers, pedestrians and their families by making transportation project sites worldwide zero-incident zones.

The SCTPP credential aims to show employers and peers that credentialed transportation professionals can identify common hazards found on transportation project sites and correct them to prevent safety incidents that could result in deaths or injuries. Earning the professional certification also demonstrates command of internationally-recognized core competencies for safety awareness and risk management on transportation projects.

The program was accredited by the American National Standards Institute (ANSI) in May 2018; well over 300 people have earned the credential. And we are just beginning.

Safer Roads and Work Zones

ARTBA understands highway safety is an intricate balance between the roadway infrastructure, the vehicle and the motorist. That equilibrium is particularly challenged during construction operations where workers labor barely inches away from motorists who are often travelling at high rates of speed. We commend the committee for happening to schedule this hearing during National Work Zone Awareness Week, which for 20 years has promoted safety for all roadway users and construction workers who navigate these potentially hazardous roadway construction zones. ARTBA is particularly concerned with the trend of increasing deaths and injuries on these sites.

Over the past eight years, work zone fatalities have increased significantly, from 586 in 2010 to 799 in2017 (the latest year for which data is available). That is a jump of over 30 percent. The table below represents the number work zone-related fatalities, as tracked by the National Traffic Highway Safety Administration's "Fatality Analysis Reporting System" or FARS:

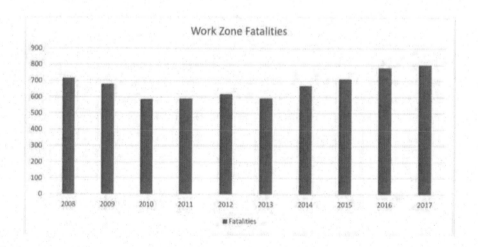

This trend is obviously moving in the wrong direction, and we agree with the committee that a more serious investigation into the cause of work zone fatalities—and all roadway fatalities—is urgently needed.

A Focus on Infrastructure

ARTBA's experience over the past 117 years has led to an understanding that roadway users will make errors. Design, construction and operation of the transportation network should emanate from this premise, allowing for the development of a more "forgiving" roadway system.

In the United States, this principle requires a new paradigm. Today, much of America's basic road safety strategy today is aimed at reducing human error. Most federal efforts focus on reducing the number of crashes by improving motorists' behavior, including the interaction of drivers with pedestrians, cyclists, large trucks and other motorists. ARTBA believes we must turn that premise around by accepting the fact that some motorists will inevitably make mistakes. Too often they pay for their mistakes with their lives—or the lives of innocent bystanders.

On all major routes—and others to the extent practicable—our roadway system must anticipate user error and be designed, constructed, equipped and operated to forgive the errant user and protect the innocent worker, pedestrian, cyclist or other driver.

Severity vs. Frequency

In conjunction with reducing fatalities, ARTBA believes our transportation system must be improved to reduce the severity of incidents. In some situations, such as the use of roundabouts, a possible increased rate in the frequency of accidents may be a viable trade-off for a decrease in the severity of injuries. The U.S. should prioritize the quality of human life and health above the rate of traffic incidents. ARTBA's premise does not remove responsibility from the driver to operate his or her vehicle in a safe and courteous manner. All transportation users have an obligation to follow laws, standards and customs that promote safe and efficient use of the system. At the same time, funds must be provided to give transportation system owners greater opportunities to properly operate their systems.

To date, U.S. policy accepts the fact this is an imperfect system, with a goal to reduce the unsafe consequences of that system. ARTBA believes America's safety goal should be developing a transportation system that features zero predictable crashes with severe consequences—beginning with the major networks through to all other roadways to the extent practicable.

Paradigm Shift

This vision requires a paradigm shift on two parallel tracks:

1. The focus of reducing incidents on America's transportation system must be viewed as reducing severity of injuries as opposed to reducing the number of crashes.

2. The policy anticipates user errors and emphasizes design, construction and maintenance of a system that will be "forgiving" of errant behavior.

This change in philosophy is necessary because system users do not have all the relevant information needed to make critical decisions related to their safety and the safety of other users. For example, drivers are repeatedly reminded: "speed kills," but the problem is not just speed but kinetic energy. Kinetic energy causes the damage in a collision or a crash, yet users are blind to it. They feel safe when they shouldn't. If the transportation system looked dangerous—and hazards were visible in a manner which users could perceive and appreciate—reliance on improved user behavior would be sufficient. The design and operation of America's transportation system must compensate for this information gap and systematically seek to eliminate such invisible hazards.

On April 14, 2010, Dr. Ted Miller of the Pacific Institute for Research & Evaluation (PIRE) offered testimony on this approach before the Senate Committee on Environment and Public Works. He made a remarkable statement to Congress: "The cost of crashes involving deficient roadway conditions dwarf the costs of crashes involving alcohol, speeding, or failure to wear a safety belt . . .Focusing as much on improving road safety conditions as on reducing impaired driving would save thousands of lives and billions of dollars each year." He further estimated "motor vehicle crashes in which roadway conditions is a contributing factor cost the U.S. economy more than $217 billion each year."

Dr. Miller's comments were based on a significant research study commissioned by the Transportation Construction Coalition—a partnership of 31 national construction associations and construction trade unions that is co-chaired by ARTBA and the Associated General Contractors of America. Completed in 2009, the study is entitled, "On a Crash Course: The Dangers and Health Costs of Deficient Roadways." In the report Dr. Miller described several immediate solutions for problem spots including using brighter and more durable pavement markings, adding rumble strips to shoulders, mounting more guardrails or safety barriers, and installing traffic signals and better signs with easier-to-read legends. Dr. Miller emphasized: "More significant road improvements include replacing non-forgiving poles with breakaway poles, adding or widening shoulders, improving roadway alignment, replacing or widening narrow bridges, reducing pavement edges and abrupt drop offs, and clearing more space on the roadside."

Ten years later, the report's findings remain valid, and the state of America's infrastructure may well be in worse condition now than it was a decade ago. ARTBA's April 1 report on the state of U.S. bridges found the pace of bridge repair in the U.S. is slowing. At the current pace, it would take more than 80 years to replace or repair the nation's structurally deficient bridges. That's longer than the average life expectancy of a person living in the U.S. The report, based on an analysis of the recently-released U.S. Department of Transportation 2018 National Bridge Inventory (NBI) database, revealed

47,052 bridges are classified as structurally deficient and in poor condition. The length of America's structurally deficient bridges if placed end-to-end would span nearly 1,100 miles, the distance between Chicago and Houston.

A History of Congressional Support

ARTBA commends Congress for its long-standing support of roadway infrastructure safety. In the MAP-21 and FAST Act surface transportation laws, Congress ensured that funds set aside for the Highway Safety Improvement Program (HSIP) would be dedicated to highway infrastructure safety improvements. The legislation also continued to provide support for the National Work Zone Safety Information Clearinghouse, a public-private partnership dedicated to providing research, information, conferences and many other resources aimed at improving roadway work zone safety. We hope Congress will continue to support these important programs.

A First Step

While there are many needs for roadway improvements—and demands on resources to make those improvements are challenging—some efforts simply require doing that which Congress has already identified as an immediate need. For example, through federal rulemaking after the SAFETEALU surface transportation law and further provisions in both the MAP-21 and FAST Act laws, Congress and previous administrations have expressed in a bipartisan manner the intent to use increased positive separation between workers and motorists on construction projects that present significant hazards to both workers and roadway users. However, the law has not been fully implemented and positive separation is still not used as regularly as Congress intended. New products and technologies are available that make the practice more practical and cost-effective.

Congress should continue to mandate the Federal Highway Administration to strengthen areas of its Subpart K regulation in accordance with the MAP-21 law that requires additional considerations for use of positive separation. It should also institute provisions in the next surface transportation law that allow for greater enforcement and/or consequences for those who violate the law. Congress should also urge FHWA to include **similar positive separation considerations in the agency's Manual on Uniform Traffic Control Devices (MUTCD)**. The law is clear and prescriptive as to when positive protective systems are to be used by the owner/agency and should be followed accordingly.

Conclusion

Improved safety on America's roadways is a critically important goal. With limited resources it is imperative that Congress review all the means available for saving lives and use those resources in a manner that is most effective—both now and in the long term. Investment in improved roadway infrastructure is a proven means to achieve this goal, and will be effective independent of an individual's behavior, whether he or she decides to act responsibly, or chooses to drive impaired, distracted or fatigued.

We have the technology and "know how" to build our roadway system to anticipate user error. It can be designed, constructed, equipped, and operated to forgive the errant user and protect the innocent victim. Sound investment in safe transportation infrastructure is a bipartisan priority. ARTBA encourages T&I Committee members to act in urgency with their colleagues in other House committees and the Senate to complete an infrastructure investment bill that will not only improve transportation operations, but also dramatically reduce the nearly 40,000 lives lost each year on America's roads.

STATEMENT OF THE AMERICAN ASSOCIATION OF STATE HIGHWAY AND TRANSPORTATION OFFICIALS, SUBMITTED FOR THE RECORD BY HON. NORTON

Introduction

The American Association of State Highway and Transportation Officials (AASHTO) welcomes the opportunity to submit this testimony related to safety on this nation's highways. AASHTO represents the state departments of transportation (state DOTs) of all 50 States, Washington, DC, and Puerto Rico.

The State DOTs appreciate the leadership of the House Transportation and Infrastructure Committee, along with your Senate and House peers in partner committees, in shepherding the Fixing America's Surface Transportation (FAST) Act in December 2015. This legislation has ensured stability in the federally-supported passenger rail, freight, safety, highway, and transit programs through 2020.

The safety of all users of the transportation system is a top priority for every state DOT and safety is one of AASHTO's key reauthorization policy areas included as part of our Transportation Policy Form (TPF). Under the direction of the TPF, the state DOTs last year initiated an extensive 18-month effort to develop and adopt reauthorization policy recommendations by October of this year. It is a bottom-up process, where we are currently in the process of gathering expert input from our wide range of technical committees comprising leaders from all state DOTs. We're also seeking our industry partners' input during this process prior to our formal adoption later next year, in order to maximize the inclusivity of perspectives in our policy recommendations to come.

In order to improve the safety of the transportation system for all users, infrastructure owners and operators, such as state DOTs, must take a multidisciplinary and data-driven approach to transportation safety. Transportation safety performance is linked to a variety of elements, including roadway design, traffic law enforcement, road user behavior, and emergency crash response. Therefore, effective transportation safety necessitates a multidisciplinary effort and requires that the infrastructure owners and operators partner with a range of stakeholders and exercise flexibility in how best to use limited funding in order to eliminate traffic fatalities and serious injuries.

As the owners and operators of a significant portion of this nation's roadways, AASHTO members have been at the forefront in ensuring a safe transportation system through safety innovation. In 2012, the Moving Ahead for Progress in the 21st Century (MAP-21) was passed which requires states to use a performance-based management approach to establish targets and then allocate funding to projects and programs that will help a state achieve those targets. The law required the U.S. Department of Transportation (USDOT), to establish a number of national performance measures, of which safety is one of four major groups. The law and subsequent regulations set certain requirements for state DOTs to establish targets and to make progress towards achieving those targets prior to imposing certain consequences. For safety, all state DOTs must establish targets for five safety performance measures:

1. Number of fatalities on all public roads
2. Fatality rate on all public roads
3. Number of serious injuries on all public roads
4. Serious injury rate on all public roads
5. Number of non-motorist fatalities and serious injuries on all public roads

State DOTs are able to establish their own targets for each safety performance measure and must report their targets through their annual Highway Safety Improvement Program (HSIP) report and the Highway Safety Plan (HSP) report. The Federal Highway Administration (FHWA) determines whether a state DOT has made significant progress towards achieving their targets if they meet or exceed four out of five targets or if their final number is better than a baseline value calculated by FHWA. If a state DOT is determined to have not made significant progress towards their safety performance measures, FHWA will impose a number of consequences.

Safety is considered one of the more mature performance management areas since state DOTs have been establishing and reporting on many different safety performance measures through their HSIP, Highway Safety Plans, and Strategic Highway Safety Plans

(SHSP) for nearly ten years. The target-setting process a state DOT uses to establish their targets is very comprehensive and data-driven. It is comprehensive in that it includes many different stakeholders and addresses all public roads and all users of the transportation system. It is data-driven in that numerous sources of data are included in the analysis including the Fatal Accident Reporting System (FARS), law enforcement data, serious injury databases, and roadway design elements. All of this data and information is then used to better understand why crashes occurred where and when they did. Finally, predictive tools and models are used to better understand how best to program funding for specific projects to prevent the crashes from occurring, be it countermeasures, design elements, enforcement efforts, and/or public information campaigns.

Thus, an important aspect to programming funding is *flexibility* both in how funds can be used among engineering, education, enforcement and emergency services efforts as well as within the engineering domain where state DOTs have the most control to identify which engineering solution may be most appropriate to improve safety. In order to make the best engineering decision, state DOTs have pooled their resources to research and develop a number of different design guides that transportation professionals can use to plan and design better and safer transportation systems. The following are examples of the design guides that the state DOTs have developed through AASHTO:

- *Highway Safety Manual*[90]—provides a complete collection of quantitative safety analysis methods to estimate crash frequency or severity at a variety of locations in order to better plan and design safer roadways.
- *Policy on Geometric Design of Highways and Streets*[91] *(also known as the AASHTO Green Book)*—presents a framework for the geometric design of roadways that is flexible, multimodal, and performance-based providing guidance to engineers and designers who strive to make unique design solutions that meet the needs of all highway and street users on a project-by-project basis. The newest edition introduces a set of "contextual" classifications—such as rural, rural town, suburban, urban, and urban core—that will help better guide geometric design efforts to create more "flexible and performance-based" designs for new projects as well as for existing roads. Work has begun on the next edition, which is expected to fully implement a multimodal, performance-based approach for road designers to use to improve safety by meeting the needs of all roadway users.
- *Guide for the Planning, Design, and Operation of Pedestrian Facilities*[92]— provides guidelines for the planning, design, operation, and maintenance of

---

[90] http://www.highwaysafetymanual.org/Pages/default.aspx.
[91] https://store.transportation.org/item/collectiondetail/180.
[92] https://store.transportation.org/Item/CollectionDetail?ID=131.

pedestrian facilities, including signals and signing. The guide recommends methods for accommodating pedestrians, which vary among roadway and facility types, and addresses the effects of land use planning and site design on pedestrian mobility. A new, updated edition of this guide is scheduled to be published this year.

- *Guide for the Development of Bicycle Facilities*[93]—provides detailed planning and design guidelines on how to accommodate bicycle travel and operation in most riding environments. It covers the planning, design, operation, maintenance, and safety of onroad facilities, shared use paths, and parking facilities. Flexibility is provided through ranges in design values to encourage facilities that are sensitive to local context and incorporate the needs of bicyclists, pedestrians, and motorists. Work on a new edition is currently underway.
- *Guide for Geometric Design of Transit Facilities on Highways and Streets*[94]—provides a comprehensive reference of current practice in the geometric design of transit facilities on streets and highways, including local buses, express buses, and bus rapid transit operating in mixed traffic, bus lanes, and high-occupancy vehicle lanes, as well as bus-only roads within street and freeway environments. It also covers streetcars and LRT running in mixed traffic and transit lanes, and within medians along arterial roadways.

All of these guides provide planners, engineers, and designers with significant flexibility in how they ultimately design a transportation project while taking into account the overall safety and operations of the facility. These guides do not establish mandatory requirements for how a project should be designed, rather they emphasize flexibility and encourage planners, engineers, and designers to take into account the unique aspects of each individual project. In fact, state DOTs are adding even more flexibility to these guides while continuing to ensure they remain research-based and peer-reviewed. For example, the next edition of the Policy of Geometric Design of Highways and Streets will include updates to educate engineers and designers on the flexibility inherent in the guide and further emphasize the multimodal nature of our transportation system which includes all users.

Given the comprehensive nature of improving the safety of our transportation system, the remainder of this testimony focuses on three points that have been identified to date through the TPF process that should be addressed in future federal surface transportation authorization laws:

1. Continue to focus on implementation of the performance management regulations;

---

[93] https://store.transportation.org/Item/CollectionDetail?ID=116.
[94] https://store.transportation.org/Item/CollectionDetail?ID=133.

2. The need to add flexibility for the use of HSIP funding; and
3. The need to add eligibility and increased federal share for railway-highway grade crossing projects.

Implementation of Performance Management Regulations

All state DOTs are now in the process of implementing the performance management requirements that were established in law as part of MAP-21 and the FAST Act. The new and updated performance management regulations were developed and published over a six year time period beginning in 2013 and ending in 2018 with the publication of the final rule regarding 23 CFR § 490, National Performance Management Measures, Subpart H and the FTA Safety final rule in July 2018. State DOTs are currently working to implement the first required aspect of these provisions, which is to establish targets for the federal performance measures, incorporate those targets into the planning process, and report on progress towards achieving the targets. Under the current rules, the first comprehensive report documenting and analyzing the results of the first reporting cycle will not be available until CY2022, at the earliest, since the first reporting cycle goes from January 1, 2018 to December 31, 2021[95].

AASHTO members believe the current regulations are working. A case in point is the Missouri DOT (MoDOT) and their current efforts to reduce fatalities and serious injuries on the public roadways. As with all state DOTs, 2017 was the first year for which Missouri had to establish safety targets for the five national-level safety performance measures identified above for CY2018. From the beginning, MoDOT established five-year targets by first establishing a goal for an annual *reduction* in fatalities and serious injuries. MoDOT used their strategic highway safety plan (called the Blueprint) goal of 700 fatalities by 2020, which had the support of many stake-holders statewide, to drive these targets. Their initial 2017 targets for fatalities was a seven percent *reduction*, with a four percent reduction for serious injuries and for non-motorized users. These were considered very aggressive targets since the number of fatalities had increased in 2015 and 2016.

MoDOT, unfortunately, did not achieve their aggressive targets set in 2017 but was encouraged to see a reduction in the number of fatalities nonetheless. For 2018, they continued to pursue their Blueprint target of 700 fatalities by 2020 and set targets even more aggressively at nine percent reduction for fatalities and five percent reduction for serious injuries and four percent reduction for non-motorized users. For 2019, they are proposing even more aggressive targets of 13 percent reduction for fatalities, eight percent reduction for serious injuries and a five percent reduction for non-motorized to

---

[95] https://www.fhwa.dot.gov/tpm/faq.cfm#perf.

continue the course to reach the Blueprint target. Since the beginning of federal safety targets, MoDOT has always set targets based on an anticipated reduction each year. Fatality and serious injury numbers started decreasing consistently in 2017 and continue as of this date.

Because of the data-driven process MoDOT used and setting aggressive targets to improve safety, the Missouri Highways and Transportation Commission allocated an additional $10 million in 2017 for safety projects. MoDOT supported the grass roots Buckle Up Phone Down campaign which took aim at reducing distracted driving. And, in 2017, MoDOT targeted Natural Bridge Road in St. Louis that had three times the number of pedestrian crashes compared to other similar roadways (20 fatalities from 2012-2016). Since the multi-disciplinary efforts of this innovative project started, there has only been one pedestrian fatality, a decrease of 95% While MoDOT is seeing success in their efforts to establish aggressive targets that aim to drive down the number of fatalities and serious injuries we must remember that MoDOT alone cannot be held responsible for a state's ultimate results. MoDOT sets safety targets based on efforts to improve highway safety using the comprehensive approach which includes engineering, education, enforcement, emergency services, and public policy as well as significant engagement with statewide partners, local agencies, and elected officials as part of the solution for reducing fatalities.

The MoDOT story is but one of 52 examples occurring throughout the United States. We believe it is an example of a true success story in the way a data-driven process like performance management can be used to identify areas of concern, agencies can set targets, and then strategies identified to achieve those targets. To this end, AASHTO recommends that no consideration be given to changing existing regulations that would alter the current performance management requirements until after at least two full reporting cycles in order to give the state DOTs time and experience in addressing the regulations which is 2026.

Highway Safety Improvement Program Flexibility

Under current law, HSIP funds are restricted to use on specific activities and cannot be used for education, enforcement, safety research, or emergency medical service safety programs. The legislative change in the FAST Act effectively restricts HSIP eligibility to only 28 strategies, activities or projects listed in the legislation, eliminating the ability to use HSIP funds for public awareness and education efforts, infrastructure and infrastructure-related equipment to support emergency services, and enforcement of traffic safety laws that are identified in the states' Strategic Highway Safety Plans.

Prior to the enactment of the FAST Act, state DOTs had the flexibility to choose safety projects and programs that would lead to the best safety outcome—whether the solutions were roadway safety infrastructure projects or were implemented in combination with non-infrastructure programs. SAFETEA-LU and MAP-21 had provided this flexibility in order to identify: 1) the right solution to fit the unique needs of specific areas or stretches of roadway and to help reverse a trend of increasing fatalities; 2) a systemic approach to address a type of crash state wide; and/or 3) a behavioral issue in a certain area or part of the population. Unfortunately, the FAST Act changed the ability of state DOTs to truly implement a comprehensive and data-driven process since states are limited in how they can use their limited HSIP funding.

Ultimately, the FAST Act changes are inconsistent with the intent of a state's Strategic Highway Safety Plan, which calls for a multidisciplinary approach to reducing highway fatalities and serious injuries on all public roads. The lack of flexibility in safety project selection in the HSIP program, particularly non-infrastructure related activities, stifles innovative safety improvements and partnerships that lead to crash reductions and reduced highway fatalities. AASHTO recommends that Congress restore flexibility for states to use a portion of HSIP funds for non-infrastructure safety programs and for safety research.

Railway-Highway Crossings

Crashes at highway-rail grade crossings are a perennial issue for many state and local DOTs from a safety perspective. According to the U.S. Government Accountability Office, railway-highway crossings are one of the leading causes of railroad-related deaths[96]. According to the Federal Railroad Administration (FRA) data, in 2017, there were more than 2,100 crashes resulting in 273 fatalities. Since 2009 crashes have occurred at a fairly constant rate. And, research sponsored by the FRA identified vehicle driver behavior as the main cause of highway-rail grade crossing crashes and that factors such as train and traffic volume can contribute to the risk of a crash. In addition, over 70 percent of fatal crashes in 2017 occurred at grade crossings with gates. Railway-highway crossings are an important contributor to a state DOT's fatality and serious injury rates and through the 23 USC § 130 program, the federal government provides states funding to improve grade-crossing safety. Within the 23 USC § 130 Program, there are four concerns that the state DOTs have: conflict related to the federal share between 23 USC § 120 and § 130 programs, the need for additional flexibility in the use of railway-highway funds, the need to increase incentive payments for communities, and the eligibility of projects for funding.

Federal Share—For the at-grade rail-highway crossing program, there is a conflict in current law. 23 USC § 120 allows for a 100 percent federal share for certain safety

---

[96] https://www.gao.gov/assets/700/695317.pdf.

projects or projects within Indian reservations, national parks, and national monuments while 23 USC § 130, Railway- Highway Crossing, set the federal share at 90 percent. This difference in what is allowed for the total federal share has resulted in a lot of confusion at both state DOTs and the FHWA. For example, the FHWA allowed thirty-five states plus the District of Columbia to incorrectly authorize 863 projects at 100 percent federal share (per 23 USC § 120) rather than at 90 percent as currently provided in 23 USC § 130. The FHWA is now requiring states to reimburse the federal-aid program for the difference on railway-highway crossing projects authorized above the 90 percent share on or after April 14, 2016, which totals over $26 million.

Unfortunately, decreasing the federal share to 90 percent and requiring state DOTs to reimburse the federal-aid highway program for the difference already approved and spent will be counterproductive to the intent of the law and burdensome to many of the localities where the projects were constructed for two reasons.

First, many of the railway-highway crossing projects that were originally allowed at the 100 percent federal share are located in rural areas that are off the state highway system. And, most of these locations are in small cities and counties that do not have the financial resources to provide the needed ten percent match for the cost of the projects.

Second, if the intent of the law is to improve safety and state DOTs now have to reimburse FHWA for the $26 million, they likely have to take money away from other projects that are also designed to improve safety. Additional flexibility is needed in order to assist rural counties and small cities address their railway-highway crossing safety challenges.

Given the confusion and uncertainty that has been created by the differences in these two sections of Title 23, AASHTO recommends that the two sections be aligned to allow 100 percent participation of 23 USC §130 funds, resulting in the funding being less restrictive to use at the local level where the need is often greatest. AASHTO believes these changes will provide significant safety benefits for rural areas where rail-highway crossings can result in significant safety concerns. In addition, AASHTO believes that the current requirement that states reimburse the federal-aid highway program for the $26 million be rescinded so that states can continue to focus on safety.

Incentive payments—States and railroads may make incentive payments of up to $7,500 for the permanent closure of at-grade railway-highway crossings. Although there are set-aside funds to help incentivize communities to close grade crossings, the $7,500 limit is often not enough to convince local officials to support closing these grade crossings, as the cost of such projects are substantially more expensive than this amount. AASHTO recommends that the $7,500 incentive payment amount be increased to $100,000 in order to encourage the closure of at-grade railway-highway crossings.

Eligibility—The current 23 USC § 130 railway-highway crossing program does not include replacement of functionally obsolete warning devices as an eligible activity. While research shows that a large percentage of crashes occur at railway-highway crossing with gates, the research also shows that modern and updated devices can reduce crashes occurring at railway-highway crossings as well. Thus, AASHTO recommends adding the replacement of functionally obsolete warning devices with modern and innovative devices and techniques to the list of eligible uses of 23 USC § 130 funds.

Conclusion

Every state DOT views a high priority of their work being to provide a safe transportation system to the public. State DOTs have the expertise, data, and analytics to understand where crashes are occurring, how to mitigate the effect of those crashes, and program limited funding to achieve critical safety targets. Ultimately, while the state DOTs are held accountable for the federal performance management safety target achievement, we must remember that state DOTs alone are not solely responsible for achieving the safety targets. Determining how best to mitigate crashes from occurring that result in serious injuries and fatalities must include the ability for all partners to:

- design better infrastructure and vehicles;
- educate the public about safe use of roadways regardless of mode;
- enforce existing laws and/or establish new laws; and
- ensure emergency services are quick to arrive and well equipped if a crash does occur.

Clearly, a state DOT has direct influence over some of these efforts, but certainly not all. Other state agencies, local agencies, elected officials and numerous other stakeholders are all part of the solution for reducing fatalities and serious injuries and the federal laws and regulations must be designed to enable a state DOT to have as much flexibility as possible to focus limited funding on programs and projects that have the potential to reduce the number of crashes as much as possible.

AASHTO members encourage the Committee to continue to provide the necessary funding and program flexibility in order to best meet the safety challenges of today and best prepare for the safety challenges of the future.

LETTER FROM THE ROAD TO ZERO COALITION, SUBMITTED FOR THE RECORD BY HON. NORTON

April 9, 2019.

Dear Chairmen Barrasso and Defazio and Ranking Members Carper and Graves:

The Road to Zero coalition [https://www.nsc.org/roadsafety/get-involved/road-to-zero] believes reaching zero deaths on the nation's roads is not impossible; it just has not been done yet. We are a broad-based diverse group of organizations committed to eliminating roadway fatalities by 2050. Over the past two years we have grown to more than 900 members from across the country representing every facet of the transportation and safety communities. It is the first time so many organizations have collaborated to put forth a plan to address fatalities on our roads, which recently increased after years of decline.

In 2018, the National Safety Council (NSC) estimates more than 40,000 people lost their lives in roadway crashes.[97] Additionally, pedestrian fatalities are at a higher level than any time in the last 25 years. This is unacceptable.

Everyone can do something to reduce fatalities on the roadway—including government leaders, industry, safety experts, transportation planners, engineers, technology providers, health professionals, and advocates. Together, we have awarded eighteen Safe System Innovation Grants for leading safety projects and issued a seminal report, The Road to Zero: A Vision for Achieving Zero Roadway Deaths by 2050, on how to reach this bold objective.

- Double down on what works through proven, evidence-based strategies
- Advance life-saving technology in vehicles and infrastructure
- Prioritize safety by adopting a safe systems approach and creating a positive safety culture

We hope this chapter and the goals in it can help you in your roles, and the Road to Zero Coalition stands ready to assist and show how we are implementing this vision each and every day across the United States.

STATEMENT OF J. SCOTT MARION, PRESIDENT-INFRASTRUCTURE, LINDSAY CORPORATION, SUBMITTED FOR THE RECORD BY HON. LIPINSKI

Mr. Chairman, Members of the Subcommittee, I read the Committee's press release announcing today's hearing, "Every Life Counts: Improving the Safety of our Nation's Roadways," with great interest and respectfully would like to submit the following comments for the record.

---

[97] https://injuryfacts.nsc.org/motor-vehicle/overview/preliminary-estimates/.

For more than six decades, Lindsay Transportation Solutions has been dedicated to developing products and services that help make roads safer. Construction work zones are growing in number around the country. The natural aging of existing roadway infrastructure ensures that more and more maintenance and rehabilitation will be required. Our goal is to reduce traffic congestion and to improve safety forboth motorists and work crews through the use of innovative tools and state-of- the-art technology.

Work zones, by their very definition, create two major issues that must be addressed in some way: safety and mobility. In the United States, highway work zones are responsible for almost 25% of all non-recurring congestion and 10% of overall congestion. According to the National Workzone Safety Information Clearinghouse, there were 799 work zone-related fatalities in the U.S. in 2017—up 4.5% from the previous three-year average of 764.

Vehicle accidents are more common in work zones, and traffic congestion through work zones on urban arterials and freeways is often considered to be "unavoidable." Fortunately, technology is providing new solutions to these problems at an accelerated rate. By combining the best of these new technologies, agencies can effectively reduce injury accidents and mitigate traffic congestion through construction work zones.

The U.S. Department of Transportation (DOT) Strategic Plan for FY 2018-2022 establishes DOT's strategic goals and objectives for Fiscal Year (FY) 2018 through FY 2022. It reflects the Secretary's priorities for achieving DOT's mission through four strategic goals:

- *Safety*: Reduce Transportation-Related Fatalities and Serious Injuries Across the Transportation System.
- *Infrastructure*: Invest in Infrastructure to Ensure Mobility and Accessibility and to Stimulate Economic Growth, Productivity and Competitiveness for American Workers and Businesses.
- *Innovation*: Lead in the Development and Deployment of Innovative Practices and Technologies that Improve the Safety and Performance of the Nation's Transportation System.
- *Accountability*: Serve the Nation with Reduced Regulatory Burden and Greater Efficiency, Effectiveness and Accountability.

As you and your colleagues work to repair America's infrastructure during a time where our roads, bridges and other infrastructure are desperately in need of investment, we must be creative and innovative in addressing these needs in ways that allow every tax dollar to be spent more efficiently and effectively and still meet the Secretary's priorities for achieving DOT's mission through the four strategic goals outlined in the DOT's Strategic Plan.

The utilization of innovative technologies that help manage lanes and construction applications to create "Safe, Dynamic Highways" offering real-time roadway reconfiguration while maintaining positive barrier protection between lanes can assist in meeting the strategic goals outlined in the DOT's Strategic Plan. For instance, to reduce worker exposure, moveable barrier installations can be combined with automated traffic control technology. At the push of a button, traffic advisory signs and lane closure gates can be activated to channel road users into the current lane configuration.

These automated control systems can be operated onsite or remotely, or they can be combined with real time intelligent traffic data that can analyze traffic patterns to determine the best times to reconfigure the roadway. Data from the cloud is sent to automated traffic control as well as the moveable barrier system operators to keep traffic congestion and road closure confusion to a minimum through the work zone. Together, these new technologies will create safer, less congested work zone environments for motorists and provide greater safety for workers by decreasing exposure to vehicles and removing confusion from lane configuration changes.

We welcome the opportunity to work with you and your staff as you begin to consider the scope and reach of an infrastructure bill and we strongly urge the committee to consider the role that innovative technologies, like moveable barriers, can play in assisting Congress in addressing roadway improvements and congestion while improving the safety of our nation's roadways.

LETTERS FROM THE COALITION FOR FUTURE MOBILITY, SUBMITTED FOR THE RECORD BY HON. GRAVES OF MISSOURI

April 10, 2019.

Hon. Peter A. Defazio
Chairman
Transportation and Infrastructure

Hon. Sam Graves
Ranking Member
Transportation and Infrastructure

Hon. Eleanor Holmes Norton
Chair
Highways and Transit

Hon. Rodney Davis
Ranking Member, Highways and Transit

Chairman Defazio, Ranking Member Graves, Chair Norton, and Ranking Member Davis:

In 2017, more than 37,000 lives were lost on U.S. roadways, including approximately 6,000 pedestrians. According to the National Highway Traffic Safety Administration, 94% of all vehicle crashes—including the crashes that take the lives of roadway users—are due to human choice or error.

The Coalition for Future Mobility (CFM), a diverse, multi-stakeholder group representing auto manufacturers, suppliers, repairers, technology and communications companies, mobility providers, state and city governments, safety and national security groups, consumers, seniors, persons with disabilities, and others, writes to underscore the critical role automated vehicles (AVs) could play in helping to reduce the number of crashes and lives lost due human choice or error.

Current federal safety programs focus primarily on behavior—such as incentives to states to increase seat belt use, as well as educating the public about drunk driving or resources to increases enforcement programs, which were established before AV safety technologies were created. We hope that the details uncovered at this hearing serve as a reminder that the status quo of primarily working to support driver behavioral programs alone cannot be expected to eliminate or substantially reduce roadway crashes and fatalities. We encourage you to support legislation and regulatory updates that help to promote safety technologies—including automated vehicle technologies as a way to lessen the more than 37,000 fatalities on our nation's roadways.

Further information on the potential benefits of AV technology and bipartisan AV legislation can be found on the attached letter that our coalition sent to all Members of Congress on February 26, 2019. We at CFM look forward to working with you to help improve safety by lessening the loss of life on U.S. roadways.

THE COALITION FOR FUTURE MOBILITY

Enclosure—Letter from the Coalition for Future Mobility Sent to Congress on February 26, 2019

February 26, 2019.

Hon. Nancy Pelosi
Speaker of the House
U.S. House of Representatives

Hon. Kevin Mccarthy
Minority Leader
U.S. House of Representatives

Hon. Mitch Mcconnell
Majority Leader
United States Senate

Hon. Charles Schumer
Minority Leader
United States Senate

Speaker Pelosi, Minority Leader Mccarthy, Senate Majority Leader Mcconnell, and Minority Leader Schumer:

Roughly two years ago, the Coalition for Future Mobility—a group of key stakeholders that represents a wide cross section of auto manufacturers, suppliers, repairers, technology companies, mobility providers, state and local governments, safety and national security groups, consumers, seniors, and persons with disabilities— was created to highlight the critical need for a federal framework that allows for the safe development, testing, and deployment of automated vehicles (AVs) here in the United States. We write to thank those Members of Congress who were involved in working to pass AV legislation in the 115th Congress and urge you to continue those efforts this year. Without question, Congress is uniquely suited to help provide greater clarity regarding both state and federal authorities that can help when it comes to the safe testing, development, and deployment of AV technologies.

The National Highway Traffic Safety Administration (NHTSA) has found that human choice or error is a factor in approximately 94% of all motor vehicle crashes on U.S. roads—crashes that took the lives of over 37,000 men, women, and children in 2017. By facilitating technology that can potentially eliminate these bad choices and unintentional errors, we can help prevent many crashes from happening and dramatically reduce injuries and fatalities on our roadways.

While safety is a critical component in the drive for the development of AVs, these vehicles can also provide life-changing opportunities for those who are not adequately served by current mobility options, such as seniors, persons with disabilities, and those who require more affordable transportation. Further, the benefits of these vehicles extend to other roadway users. Large-scale AV implementation could also mean less congestion and greater efficiency on our roads.

Last Congress, both the House of Representatives and the Senate recognized the importance of providing a federal framework for AVs. The House of Representatives passed the bipartisan SELF DRIVE Act (H.R. 3388) without a vote in opposition. Shortly after the House acted, the Senate Committee on Commerce, Science, and Transportation unanimously passed similar legislation. In spite of strong, bipartisan support, legislation was unable to receive floor consideration in the Senate. Our coalition encourages you and your colleagues to redouble your efforts to move forward with legislation that will help improve safety, provide a techneutral path forward for private industry to innovate, and ensure clarity for regulators at all levels of government.

The status quo should not be acceptable. Recognizing the potential of this technology to positively impact millions of Americans, we urge you to support a federal AV framework this Congress. Our Coalition members stand ready to work with you.

STATEMENT OF BENJAMIN HARVEY, PRESIDENT, E.L. HARVEY & SONS INC., ON BEHALF OF THE NATIONAL WASTE AND RECYCLING ASSOCIATION, SUBMITTED FOR THE RECORD BY HON. GRAVES OF MISSOURI

Good morning, Chairman Holmes Norton, Ranking Member Davis, and Members of the Committee. My name is Benjamin Harvey and I am the President of E. L. Harvey & Sons Inc. located in Westborough, Mass. E. L. Harvey & Sons is a full-service waste and recycling firm that provides services for commercial and industrial corporations and municipalities throughout eastern Massachusetts, New Hampshire, Rhode Island, and Maine. My company is a member of the National Waste & Recycling Association, also known as NWRA, which I am representing before the committee today in my capacity as the association's chairman.

NWRA is the voice in the nation's capital for the private-sector waste and recycling industry that is essential to maintaining the quality of American life. The delivery of waste and recycling services impacts all residential, commercial, and industrial properties on a daily basis. Apart from the U.S. Postal Service, the waste and recycling industry is one of the few, if not the only other, that travels on every road-way in the country at least once each week.

Association members operate in all 50 states and the District of Columbia and can be found in most, if not all, U.S. congressional districts. Waste and recycling facilities number nearly 18,000 scattered throughout the U.S., mirroring population centers. Our nearly 700 members are a mix of publicly-traded and privately-owned local, regional, and Fortune 500 national and international companies.

The industry directly employs about 420,000 people as of early 2018 with a total payroll of more than $21 billion. It is estimated that the private sector waste and recycling industry accounts for over one million jobs and generates nearly a quarter of a trillion dollars in U.S. GDP.

Tens of thousands of these hard-working men and women in the waste and recycling industry become vulnerable road users everyday as part of their job. The Bureau of Labor Statistics (BLS) has named the waste and recycling collector as the fifth most dangerous occupation (2018).[98] In 2017, "Waste and Recycling" had 33 fatalities, of which 23 were transportation related.[99]

Safety is the number one value for the waste and recycling industry. The goal each day is for every worker and driver to go home safely at the end of their shifts, without a crash, injury or fatality. Our work is focused on making collection, processing, and disposal operations less dangerous by encouraging safety training as well as providing assistance in complying with regulations and company safety rules and policies.

Despite these industry efforts, distracted driving by motorists with whom we share the road puts waste and recycling drivers and workers at risk every day. Many of the transportation related fatalities were caused by inattentive or distracted drivers who failed to yield to waste and recycling collection vehicles. Most of the time, the danger is the same as that experienced by police officers, fire fighters, and tow truck drivers who are stopped along the side of the road.

The private sector of the waste and recycling industry has a commercial motor vehicle (CMV) fleet of more than 100,000 collection trucks and an even greater number of CMV Drivers. These trucks are primarily Heavy-Duty Vehicles as defined by the Federal Highway Administration (FHWA) with a GVWR of more than 26,000 pounds. The industry's fleet includes, but is not limited to, waste and recycling collection trucks, roll-off trucks, post collection tractor trailers, container delivery, and grapple trucks.

The waste (garbage, trash, solid waste) and recycling (paper, plastic, aluminum, metal, compost) collection trucks that service nearly every American household and business are the most recognized part of the industry's fleet. Although waste and recycling collection trucks are virtually identical in most respects, they are significantly different in the means by which the material is emptied into the cargo area (e.g. rear-, front-, automated side-load, etc.).

According to FHWA's 2016 Freight Quick Facts Report, "Waste/Scrap" is the tenth largest commodity by tonnage shipped in the U.S. The industry's truck operations moved 92 percent of the 652.9 million tons transported by all modes in 2015.

---

[98] https://www.bls.gov/iif/oshwc/cfoi/cfch0016.pdf.
[99] Ibid.

Assuming that two-thirds of the industry's trucks are in use on any given work-day, that means approximately 70,000 workers are exposed to dangerous driving situations, such as distracted driving, each workday.

According to the National Highway Traffic Safety Administration (NHTSA), distracted driving is "any activity that diverts attention from driving, including talking or texting on your phone, eating and drinking, talking to people in your vehicle, fiddling with the stereo, entertainment or navigation system-anything that takes your attention away from the task of safe driving." It is estimated that during daylight hours approximately 481,000 drivers are using handheld cell phones while driving, creating significant potential for injury or death.

NHTSA reports that 3,450 people were killed by distracted drivers in 2016 and 562 of these fatalities were not occupants of a vehicle but rather pedestrians, bicyclists, and others including waste and recycling industry employees. In 2015, distracted drivers were responsible for 391,000 injuries in motor vehicle crashes. Teens were the largest age group reported as distracted at the time of fatal crashes. Driving requires the full attention of motorists. Texting in particular poses a danger since sending or reading a text takes one's eyes off the road for an average of 4.6 seconds. Traveling at 55 MPH while texting is the equivalent of driving the length of a football field with your eyes closed.

NHTSA is engaged in several efforts to educate Americans about the dangers of distracted driving including public service announcements, social media campaigns, "Distracted Driving Awareness Month" every April, and partnerships with state and local police departments to enforce laws against distracted driving.

These law enforcement officials are also undertaking the difficult task of enhanced enforcement of distracted driving laws. This is complicated by the need to observe the offense before making a traffic stop since, unlike with impaired driving, the prohibited behavior has typically ended once a driver is pulled over.

So far, 23 states have enacted "Move Over" laws that cover waste and recycling workers. The statutes vary from state to state, but the laws generally require drivers to slow down and yield to collection vehicles, especially when the operator is emptying a cart or walking back to the truck. "Move Over" laws are saving lives by requiring drivers to exercise caution and avoid distractions when they are approaching a collection truck.

NWRA has been at the forefront of efforts to expand state "Move Over" laws to include "amber lighted vehicles" such as waste and recycling, tow trucks, and other similar industries. However, these laws are only effective if the motoring public knows about and law enforcement enforces them.

A 2014 incident in central Florida involving an NWRA-member company is a perfect example. One of their collection workers was injured by a car and the law enforcement officer did not issue a citation to the driver of the vehicle, despite Florida's recently expanded "Move Over" law. When the company's safety director asked for the "Move Over" law to be invoked, the officer stated he did not know about the statute, nor did the command staff of that department. This shows the need to educate both law enforcement and the public about the necessity to move over as well as the consequences of not moving over. NWRA is confident that this situation is not an isolated event.

NWRA urges Congress to use federal infrastructure legislation or surface transportation appropriations as a vehicle to enact incentives for states to adopt "Move Over" laws that include waste and recycling collection workers similar to the incentives it uses to encourage states to set and keep their legal drinking age at 21 years old. This is an opportunity for Congress to make a real difference in improving safety with minimal effort and no additional cost.

Thank you for your consideration of our position. We look forward to working with the committee to improve the safety of our nation's highways. I will be happy to respond to any questions that you may have.

APPENDIX

Questions from Hon. Peter A. Defazio for Hon. Jennifer Homendy, Member, National Transportation Safety Board

Each of your testimonies highlight the dangers of speeding, which increases the likelihood of a crash and the severity of injuries sustained, and nearly guarantees pedestrian death at 40 miles per hour. Mr. Bruemmer, you share your own harrowing story of nearly being struck by a truck in a work zone.

Member Homendy, you cite Federal Highway Administration guidance which emphasizes that States and localities "set speed limits within 5 miles per hour of which 85 percent of vehicle are traveling", known as the 85th percentile rule. This has led to a situation where in 2016, 41 States had maximum speed limits at or above 70 miles per hour, and 7 of those States were at or above 80 miles per hour.

Question 1. Can you comment further on NTSB's recommendation to move away from this 85th percentile approach?

ANSWER. The NTSB recommends that the Federal Highway Administration (FHWA) "revise Section 2B.13 of the Manual on Uniform Traffic Control Devices so that the factors currently listed as optional for all engineering studies are required, require that an expert system such as USLIMITS2 be used as a validation tool, and remove the guidance that speed limits in speed zones should be within 5 mph of the 85th percentile speed'' (H-17-27).

The intent of this recommendation is to deemphasize the use of the 85th percentile speed. The 85th percentile speed is obtained by conducting an engineering study of ideal traffic flows unaffected by inclement weather or traffic congestion. The use of the 85th percentile speed assumes that the majority of drivers are capable of selecting appropriate speeds according to weather conditions, traffic, road ge-metry, and roadside development, and that they operate at reasonable and prudent speeds. Because the research that provided the strongest empirical support of the use of the 85th percentile speed is dated (having been conducted in the late 1950s) and was conducted only on 2- and 4-lane rural highways, it is unclear whether the 85th percentile speed equates to the speed with the lowest crash involvement rate on all road types, such as those in cities. Heavily populated urban areas typically have higher numbers of vulnerable road users, such as pedestrians and bicyclists. Research has clearly shown that these road users have little chance of surviving a collision with a motor vehicle traveling at high speed.

Additionally, the use of the 85th percentile speed has resulted in increasing speed limits among states. For example, the Texas Transportation Code states that the speed limit for certain roads is 70 miles per hour (mph). To increase speed limits, Texas requires an engineering study that follows the Texas Department of Transportation's "Procedures for Establishing Speed Zones,'' which emphasize the 85th percentile speed. Over time, speed limits in Texas have increased from 70 mph to 85 mph, the highest posted speed limit in the United States. In 2012, 35 states had a maximum speed limit of 70 mph, with Texas and Utah at or above 80 mph. Just 4 years later, in 2016, 41 states had a maximum speed limit of 70 mph, with 7 states at or above 80 mph.

Therefore, although assessing roadway operating speed remains important, a more balanced approach to setting speed limits that also considers the vulnerability of pedestrians and bicyclists and crash experience should replace the one that primarily favors vehicular traffic.

Question 2. What policies should Congress look at to reduce speeding? Do you think this can be achieved through education and enforcement alone, or do we also need to look at road design has to slow people down in many contexts?

ANSWER. One of the items on the NTSB's 2019-2020 Most Wanted List addresses speeding by calling for lawmakers, industry, and every American to work together to "implement a comprehensive strategy to reduce speeding-related crashes."

Through research and accident investigations, the NTSB has identified proven countermeasures that must be used broadly to reduce speeding-related crashes. These countermeasures include automated enforcement technology, education campaigns, vehicle technology, and infrastructure design. The NTSB urges Congress to consider actions that (1) encourage data-driven speed enforcement that may include both traditional and automated enforcement technology; (2) urge NHTSA and the FHWA to update and promote best practices for implementing automated speed enforcement; (3) push for social change that makes speeding culturally unacceptable; (4) accelerate the development of performance standards for and industry adoption of advanced speed-limiting technology for heavy vehicles such as trucks, buses, and motorcoaches; (5) create incentive mechanisms to increase adoption of speed-limiting technology for passenger vehicles; (6) emphasize a complete street policy that encourages roadway designs that slow drivers down to the safe speed, such as using road diets, lane narrowing, and curve reconfiguration. Reducing speeding-related fatalities and injuries must include all countermeasures, including road design, education, and enforcement.

Attached is a list of NTSB recommendations that, if implemented, would reduce speeding-related crashes and save lives. These recommendations supplement our Most Wanted List issue item regarding speeding. The NTSB urges Congress to consider them when developing legislation.

Questions from Hon. Frederica S. Wilson for Hon. Jennifer Homendy, Member, National Transportation Safety Board

Member Homendy, congratulations on your appointment to the NTSB. I look forward to working with you.

As you know, in 2017, 26 percent of crashes involved at least one speeding driver. Speeding is a major contributor to fatal accidents in Florida and throughout the nation. In your testimony, you called for "increased leadership and attention" to speeding on the national level.

Question 3. What are some actions this Congress can take to ensure that speeding is being prioritized at a level that reflects its role in fatal accidents?

ANSWER. In interviews the NTSB has conducted, national, state, and local traffic safety stakeholders repeatedly mentioned that—unlike other crash factors such as alcohol impairment or unbelted occupants—speeding is associated with few negative social consequences, and it does not have a leader campaigning to increase public awareness about the issue at the national level. Stakeholders further stated that they thought the dangers of speeding are not well-publicized, and that society therefore underappreciates the risks of speeding. The resulting complacency among drivers has led to speeding becoming a common behavior, even though surveys indicate that drivers generally disapprove of other drivers speeding. Stakeholders also expressed the belief that, to gradually change public perceptions of speeding, safety advocacy groups must launch a coordinated effort, with strong leadership from the federal government.

We have recommended several actions that can be taken at the national level, including implementing an ongoing program to increase public awareness of speeding as a national traffic safety issue, including an annual enforcement mobilization; establishing programs to incentivize state and local speed management activities, for example via federalaid programs such as the National Priority Safety Program; and prioritizing and promoting federal transportation agency efforts to address speeding, such as the work coordinated by the DOT's multiagency Speed Management Team. Attached is a list of our recommendations to reduce speeding-related crashes. These recommendations supplement this issue area on our 2019-2020 Most Wanted List. We urge Congress to consider them when developing future legislation.

Speeding

Member Homendy, in your testimony, you highlight the glaring fact that neither the Highway Safety Program nor the National Priority Safety Program truly incentivize states to address the issue of speeding. You also mentioned that stakeholders cited the lack of a national traffic safety campaign as a key hindrance to increasing public awareness.

Question 4. Can you describe what an effective campaign should include?

ANSWER. An effective campaign to address speeding should be informed by the successes of other highway safety campaigns, such as the long-running "Click It or Ticket" national campaign to increase seat belt usage. "Click It or Ticket" includes an annual high-visibility enforcement mobilization, a robust communications strategy at the national and state levels, legislated incentives to encourage high participation among the states, and dedicated funding. Research has shown that the communications component of a traffic safety campaign increases safety benefits; by using consistent messaging over many years, 85% of the public recognizes the "Click It or Ticket" slogan, according to NHTSA surveys.

Pedestrian Fatalities

Member Homendy, I was pleased to learn that NTSB investigated the recent increase of pedestrians killed in highway crashes. Your investigation found that pedestrian deaths now account for almost one in six highway fatalities.

Question 5. Why are pedestrian deaths so much higher now than they were a decade ago?

ANSWER. In 2008, 4,414 pedestrians died in traffic crashes, representing 12% of all traffic fatalities. In 2017, almost 6,000 pedestrians were killed, comprising 16% of all traffic deaths (based on NHTSA Traffic Safety Facts). There can be a multitude of reasons, and no single factor is causing the substantial increase over the last 10 years. One key ingredient is the rapid increase in urban population. In 2008, 72% of pedestrian deaths occurred in urban areas. In 2017, the percentage reached 80%. Pedestrians and motor vehicles are interacting more in our cities. Because most roadways were designed in an era where vehicular traffic took precedence, moving vehicles from one place to another quickly was favored over the needs of other users, such as pedestrians. Many multilane arterial roadways with high speed limits still snake through our highly populated cities, which is why managing speed is key to tackling pedestrian safety. This requires an integrated approach that includes lowering speed limits, enforcement, education, and road design. Many cities lack adequate pedestrian facilities, such as sidewalks and crosswalks. Pedestrian crashes also appear to be getting deadlier, with deaths per 100 crashes increasing by 29 percent in the last decade (IIHS, 2018). This increase may be the result of changes to the vehicle fleet (for example, more SUVs). In addition, factors like distraction and impairment continue to affect pedestrians and drivers. Accordingly, we have issued recommendations to address vehicle design, roadway design, vehicle speed, impairment, and distraction.

Question from Hon. Brian Babin for Hon. Jennifer Homendy, Member, National Transportation Safety Board

Question 6. During the hearing, Member Homendy committed to providing a response to Representative Babin's question asked at the hearing: In your experience with the NTSB, have you seen a correlation between improving roadway safety and updating existing roads (US/state highways) in order to meet the Interstate standards and grades?

ANSWER. NTSB believes that both new and redesigned highways should be built to the current American Association of State Highway and Transportation Officials and Federal Highway Administration standards in order to incorporate the best available safety technology. Whenever a jurisdiction brings a roadway up to current design standards the result should be an improvement to the safety of the facility because it is using the latest in barriers, signage and a current evaluation of geometric design (in regard to the speed limit). In its investigation of a 2003 highway crash in Hewitt, Texas, we found that the highway (I-35) has been expanded from a US/state highway to an Interstate, but the roadway was not upgraded to meet Interstate standards. In that case, the correlation between improving roadway safety and updating existing roads (US/state highways) in order to meet the Interstate standards and grades was not done. Our investigation cited the poor roadway conditions and inadequate stopping sight distances on I-35 in its determination of the probable cause for that crash.

ATTACHMENT—NTSB RECOMMENDATIONS TO REDUCE SPEEDING-RELATED CRASHES

Implement a Comprehensive Strategy to Reduce Speeding-Related Crashes

Speeding increases the likelihood of being involved in a crash and intensifies the severity of injuries sustained in a crash. Speeding-related crashes kill more than 10,000 people and cost society more than $52 billion annually. **Proven countermeasures—including automated enforcement technology, vehicle technology, infrastructure design, and education campaigns—must be used more broadly to reduce speeding-related crashes.**

RECOMMENDATION NO.   STATUS

Highway

H-05-020   Open–Acceptable Response
TO THE TEXAS DEPARTMENT OF TRANSPORTATION: Install variable speed limit signs or implement alternate countermeasures at locations where wet weather can produce stopping distances that exceed the available sight distance.

H-12-020   Open–Unacceptable Response
TO THE NATIONAL HIGHWAY TRAFFIC SAFETY ADMINISTRATION: Develop performance standards for advanced speed-limiting technology, such as variable speed limiters and intelligent speed adaptation devices, for heavy vehicles, including trucks, buses, and motorcoaches.

H-12-021   Open–Unacceptable Response
TO THE NATIONAL HIGHWAY TRAFFIC SAFETY ADMINISTRATION: After establishing performance standards for advanced speed-limiting technology for heavy commercial vehicles, require that all newly manufactured heavy vehicles be equipped with such devices.

H-17-018   Open–Acceptable Response
TO THE UNITED STATES DEPARTMENT OF TRANSPORTATION: Complete the actions called for in your 2014 Speed Management Program Plan, and periodically publish status reports on the progress you have made.

H-17-019   Open–Acceptable Response
TO THE NATIONAL HIGHWAY TRAFFIC SAFETY ADMINISTRATION: Identify speeding-related performance measures to be used by local law enforcement agencies, including, but not limited to, the numbers and locations of speeding-related crashes of different injury severity levels; speeding citations, and warnings, and establish a consistent method for evaluating data-driven, high-visibility enforcement programs to reduce speeding. Disseminate the performance measures and evaluation method to local law enforcement agencies.

H-17-020   Open–Acceptable Response
TO THE NATIONAL HIGHWAY TRAFFIC SAFETY ADMINISTRATION: Identify best practices for communicating with law enforcement officers and the public about the effectiveness of data-driven, high-visibility enforcement programs to reduce speeding, and disseminate the best practices to local law enforcement agencies.

H-17-021   Open–Acceptable Response
TO THE NATIONAL HIGHWAY TRAFFIC SAFETY ADMINISTRATION: Work with the Governors Highway Safety Association, the International Association of Chiefs of Police, and the National Sheriffs' Association to develop and implement a program to increase the adoption of speeding-related Model Minimum Uniform Crash Criteria Guideline data elements and improve consistency in law enforcement reporting of speeding-related crashes.

H-17-022   Open–Acceptable Response
TO THE NATIONAL HIGHWAY TRAFFIC SAFETY ADMINISTRATION: Work with the Federal Highway Administration to update the *Speed Enforcement Camera Systems Operational Guidelines* to reflect the latest automated speed enforcement (ASE) technologies and operating practices, and promote the updated guidelines among ASE program administrators.

H-17-023   Open–Acceptable Alternate Response
TO THE NATIONAL HIGHWAY TRAFFIC SAFETY ADMINISTRATION: Work with the Federal Highway Administration to assess the effectiveness of point-to-point speed enforcement in the United States and, based on the results of that assessment, update the *Speed Enforcement Camera Systems Operational Guidelines*, as appropriate.

H-17-024   Open–Acceptable Alternate Response
TO THE NATIONAL HIGHWAY TRAFFIC SAFETY ADMINISTRATION: Incentivize passenger vehicle manufacturers and consumers to adopt intelligent speed adaptation (ISA) systems by, for example, including ISA in the New Car Assessment Program.

H-17-025   Open–Acceptable Alternate Response
TO THE NATIONAL HIGHWAY TRAFFIC SAFETY ADMINISTRATION: Collaborate with other traffic safety stakeholders to develop and implement an ongoing program to increase public awareness of speeding as a national traffic safety issue. The program should include, but not be limited to, initiating an annual enforcement mobilization directed at speeding drivers.

H-17-026   Open–Acceptable Response
TO THE NATIONAL HIGHWAY TRAFFIC SAFETY ADMINISTRATION: Establish a program to incentivize state and local speed management activities.

H-17-027   Open–Acceptable Response
TO THE FEDERAL HIGHWAY ADMINISTRATION: Revise Section 2B.13 of the *Manual on Uniform Traffic Control Devices* so that the factors currently listed as optional for all engineering studies are required, require that an expert system such as USLIMITS2 be used as a validation tool, and remove the guidance that speed limits in speed zones should be within 5 mph of the 85th percentile speed.

H-17-029   Open–Acceptable Response
TO THE FEDERAL HIGHWAY ADMINISTRATION: Work with the National Highway Traffic Safety Administration to update the *Speed Enforcement Camera Systems Operational Guidelines* to reflect the latest automated speed enforcement (ASE) technologies and operating practices, and promote the updated guidelines among ASE program administrators.

H-17-030   Open–Acceptable Response
TO THE FEDERAL HIGHWAY ADMINISTRATION: Work with the National Highway Traffic Safety Administration to assess the effectiveness of point-to-point speed enforcement in the United States and, based on the results of that assessment, update the *Speed Enforcement Camera Systems Operational Guidelines*, as appropriate.

H-17-031   Open–Initial Response Received
TO THE SEVEN STATES PROHIBITING AUTOMATED SPEED ENFORCEMENT (MAINE, MISSISSIPPI, NEW HAMPSHIRE, NEW JERSEY, TEXAS, WEST VIRGINIA, AND WISCONSIN): Amend current laws to authorize state and local agencies to use automated speed enforcement.

H-17-032   Open–Initial Response Received
TO THE TWENTY EIGHT STATES WITHOUT AUTOMATED SPEED ENFORCEMENT LAWS (ALABAMA, ALASKA, CALIFORNIA, CONNECTICUT, DELAWARE, FLORIDA, GEORGIA, HAWAII, IDAHO, INDIANA, IOWA, KANSAS, KENTUCKY, MASSACHUSETTS, MICHIGAN, MINNESOTA, MISSOURI, MONTANA, NEBRASKA, NEW MEXICO, NORTH CAROLINA, NORTH DAKOTA, OKLAHOMA, PENNSYLVANIA, SOUTH DAKOTA, VERMONT, VIRGINIA, AND WYOMING): Authorize state and local agencies to use automated speed enforcement.

H-17-033   Open–Initial Response Received
TO THE 15 STATES WITH AUTOMATED SPEED ENFORCEMENT RESTRICTIONS (ARIZONA, ARKANSAS, COLORADO, ILLINOIS, LOUISIANA, MARYLAND, NEVADA, NEW YORK, OHIO, OREGON, RHODE ISLAND, SOUTH CAROLINA, TENNESSEE, UTAH, AND WASHINGTON): Amend current laws to remove operational and location restrictions on the use of automated speed enforcement, except where such restrictions are necessary to align with best practices.

H-17-034   Open–Acceptable Response
TO THE GOVERNORS HIGHWAY SAFETY ASSOCIATION: Work with the National Highway Traffic Safety Administration, the International Association of Chiefs of Police, and the National Sheriffs' Association to develop and implement a program to increase the adoption of speeding-related Model Minimum Uniform Crash Criteria Guideline data elements and improve consistency in law enforcement reporting of speeding-related crashes.

H-17-035   Open–Initial Response Received
TO THE INTERNATIONAL ASSOCIATION OF CHIEFS OF POLICE: Work with the National Highway Traffic Safety Administration, the Governors Highway Safety Association, and the National Sheriffs' Association to develop and implement a program to increase the adoption of speeding-related Model Minimum Uniform Crash Criteria Guideline data elements and improve consistency in law enforcement reporting of speeding-related crashes.

H-17-036   Open–Acceptable Response
TO THE NATIONAL SHERIFFS' ASSOCIATION: Work with the National Highway Traffic Safety Administration, the Governors Highway Safety Association, and the International Association of Chiefs of Police to develop and implement a program to increase the adoption of speeding-related Model Minimum Uniform Crash Criteria Guideline data elements and improve consistency in law enforcement reporting of speeding-related crashes.

Questions from Hon. Peter A. Defazio for Hon. Fred Jones, Vice Mayor, City of Neptune Beach, Florida, on Behalf of Transportation for America

Mr. Jones, your testimony notes that the performance metrics established by Congress in MAP-21 allows States to set their own priorities and targets. States are considered in compliance with performance management requirements as long as they are tracking a particular metric—States do not have to make progress or improve their performance over time. Your testimony reports that in 2017, 18 States set safety performance targets that were worse in terms of fatalities than the previous year.

Question 1. Do you support stronger accountability under the performance management system, to actually require States to demonstrate improvement in a particular metric? Would you support a requirement to shift more funds to build infrastructure projects that reduce fatalities for any State that does not set, or does not meet, a target that is an actual safety improvement?

ANSWER. Yes. While States were granted the flexibility and discretion to set priorities and report their results under the current FHWA performance management system, enabling negative safety targets should be prohibited. In 2017, eighteen states established targets resulting in more bicyclist and pedestrian deaths on their facilities. If the States are to be held to a higher standard of accountability with respect to safety measures, particularly for pedestrians and bicyclists, any State that does not set, or does not meet, such targets beyond reasonable control, may receive less funding for traditional, capacity-based projects or have their allocated funds redirected to safety and complete street projects.

Additionally, we would like to see greater emphasis and reliance on other nontraditional roadway performance metrics such as community and economic development, job creation, health impacts, and resiliency over the conventional use of roadway capacity, level-of-service and delay as the primary metrics for funding and prioritization. This is particularly for States and communities planning and constructing more complete streets and multimodal infrastructure.

Questions from Hon. Frederica S. Wilson for Hon. Fred Jones, Vice Mayor, City of Neptune Beach, Florida, on Behalf of Transportation for America

Mr. Jones, your testimony notes that the performance metrics established by Congress in MAP-21 allows states to set their own priorities and targets. States are considered in compliance with performance management requirements as long as they are tracking a particular metric; they do not have to make progress or improve their performance over time. Your testimony reports that in 2017, 18 states set safety performance targets that were worse in terms of fatalities than the previous year.

Question 2. Do you support greater accountability under the performance management system to actually require states to demonstrate improvement in a particular metric?

ANSWER. Yes. Our transportation agencies' top priority should be safety. We cannot claim that safety is a priority if we are willing to tolerate safety targets—actual goals—for our roads to get less safe. And our current program tolerates just that. Why is that? Because we understand that there are many priorities that need to be addressed, and as a matter of policy Congress has been comfortable if transportation agencies place other priorities above safety. But this should not be the case. In the aviation industry, planes are grounded in order to protect safety. Safety is a goal placed above economics and convenience. Likewise, safety should be the top priority in surface transportation, and that priority should be clear in our program spending so long as there are preventable crashes occurring on our roadways.

There is no world in which we will ever have enough money to address everything that needs to be addressed on our transportation system. That means we have to set priorities. And safety should always be the top one.

Local Choice

Mr. Jones, your testimony provides some good examples of complete streets projects, but also describes what happens when a state DOT does not want to or feels it does not have flexibility with federal funds to pursue a complete streets approach or other design enhancement. The committee has heard from local government stake-holders in past hearings that greater control over project choice at the local government level would help bring about projects in communities that are perhaps not the priority of the state DOT.

Question 3. If Congress expanded the role of local governments in programming federal transportation funding, and you had greater direct control over how federal funds are spent in your community, do you believe this would result in a different range of projects than when the decision making is controlled by Florida DOT?

ANSWER. Yes and that is because state governments have typically overlooked the local trip in spite of the fact that most trips are local. State departments of transportation were formed to build highways that connect cities and towns while the locals have had the responsibility of moving people around that city or town. Also while state departments of transportation have responsibility for roads, the cities are not just trying to move people around but are also trying to create great places and create high quality of life. In the case of Florida, if local governments had more control and decision-making on FDOT facilities, they would likely support different ranges of projects that promote placemaking and quality of life over vehicular throughput, such as reducing speeds, lane widths, or reallocating travel lanes for other travel modes or community spaces.

Bringing more voices into the program can only generate more diversity in terms of the challenges we are trying to address and how we address them.

Mr. Jones, you state in your testimony that "We have a cure" for reducing traffic-related fatalities, "But for whatever reasons, we just don't want to use it."

Question 4. What are some of the "cures" New York and San Francisco implemented that decreased traffic fatalities by 28 and 41 percent, respectively? What are some of the solutions that were specific to pedestrians?

ANSWER. Both cities slowed down traffic speeds. Mistakes are inevitable with humans. But mistakes turn more deadly for people in and outside a car the faster cars are going. True "Vision Zero" cities are lowering speed limits, slimming down lanes, and taking other steps to slow down traffic. There should be an expectation that when a driver arrives in a town or city that they slow-down in order to create a safe environment and to create a great place to spend time in. Other strategies that help are shorter and more visible crossings for pedestrians and bringing front doors for houses and businesses along the road to the sidewalk, creating a canopy that makes the area more comfortable for pedestrians and encourages drivers to slow down.

Questions from Hon. Eleanor Holmes Norton for Michael L. Brown, Chief of Police, Alexandria (Virginia) Police Department

Chief Brown, your testimony calls for a "national narrative" on the importance of traffic safety and committing the resources to carry it out. You note that this would help law enforcement across the nation unite behind traffic safety, much like the response to homeland security efforts following 9/11 and more recently the opioid crisis. You state "what is missing today for law enforcement is the commitment to making traffic safety a high priority for our nation."

Question 1. What can Congress do to promote this national narrative and to demonstrate the Federal commitment improving safety on our roads?

ANSWER. The first step to changing the national narrative on traffic safety would be to raise the level of awareness and driving home the negative consequences of *both traffic deaths and injuries*. The message should be sufficiently powerful to demonstrate the costs to, not only to those involved in crashes, but also to their families, friends, employers, and the nation as a whole. These costs are more than just dollars. There can also be quality of life implications that can last a lifetime, e.g.; permanent disability.

Practically all of the crashes are preventable and predictable. They are caused by poor choices made by individuals that are sharing our roadways. The message should be broad enough to capture the attention of everyone as a quality of life issue in our communities. The current traffic safety messages are good but they focus on individual problems. The ultimate message should transmit a message that this is indeed a public health crisis.

Aside from the message, Congress can make a more dramatic impact through the reauthorization. The reauthorization should provide more flexibility in for law enforcement to address traffic safety issues in their local communities. As I mentioned during the hearing, the issues raised in prior reauthorizations are important but they may not be the highest priority in every community. The new reauthorization could continue to highlight the prior focus areas but it should also provide more flexibility and support for enforcement on the issues that might be facing the communities law enforcement serves. This can be accomplished by setting up an adjusted program providing less restrictive guidance to the states to deliver the assets or funding to law enforcement. Issues like speeding, right of way violations, jay-walking, and similar, often overlooked but important community issues can be addressed.

The design of a traffic safety enforcement program must also recognize that officers will make stops for issues based upon what they see as a legitimate and important violation. When making a traffic stop officers often find other issues relevant to traffic safety. For example, an officer stopping a speeding vehicle may ultimately detect an impaired driver, a driver on a cell phone, or someone not wearing a seatbelt.

Additionally, the practice of "counting tickets" should be avoided in grant activity reports. Citations are but one means of measuring activity and finding teachable moments for those on the road. Sometimes, a verbal warning can be just as effective. Counting tickets can also have a chilling effect on officer engagement and may even depress the level of engagement that is being sought.

The guidance to the state highway safety offices needs to be more specific otherwise it creates the opportunity for differing interpretations in developing projects. These interpretations may also be too restrictive and may result in fewer grant applications or lower levels of officer engagement. Past authorizations have frequently resulted in different interpretations by federal and state officials which can discourage law enforcement participation especially when law enforcement is interested in enforcing local traffic safety issues. Another approach to consider might be a direct appropriation to law enforcement agencies that are interested in working on traffic safety in their community. This would reduce the influence of interpretation issues. Finally, if this is to be serious effort to improve traffic safety it must be accompanied by a substantial increase in funding designed to address local traffic issues. The past reauthorizations have focused on a select group of important issues. More funding for local traffic issues needs to be included to encourage participation in a comprehensive national traffic safety effort. As I mentioned in my testimony, the capacity of law enforcement is already taxed in most communities with non-traffic related issues. The use of overtime grants has been the traditional approaches applied to increase this capacity and this should be continued. However, not every agency can use this approach. It might useful to consider adding traffic safety officer positions to those agencies that can justify an extreme lack of capacity.

Chief Brown, you mention in your testimony that you support expansion of automated speed enforcement, granted that it is used for public safety purposes and not revenue generation. I believe many constituents oppose automated speed enforcement technologies because they assume that revenue would be the real motive behind it.

Question 2. How can we implement automated enforcement in a way which eases these concerns?

ANSWER. The National Highway Traffic Safety Administration (NHTSA) has developed a considerations document which outlines many of the steps law enforcement should consider when looking at automated enforcement. The NHTSA document focuses on problem identification needs to promote the legitimacy of the enforcement efforts and the proper use of the technology that is used.

Another issue of some concern in the public's perspective is whether or not the fines that result from this enforcement are a revenue source. NHTSA addresses this issue in its document but it does not specifically address what a non-law enforcement agency may feel about these fines. Too often, the fine revenue becomes a fiscal revenue stream for communities which feeds the narrative that citations are issued to ease fiscal concerns. Whatever is being considered at the local level the local government and law enforcement agencies should consider all of these issues and the NHTSA guidance is helpful. The use of automated enforcement on a national level will not be possible without encouraging or incentivizing state efforts to adopt legislation that enables this type of enforcement. Automated enforcement is not available in every state or community and its implementation is often inconsistent. This inconsistency does not help with public acceptance. The new authorization could and should address this issue so more agencies can employ automated enforcement technology at the local level across the nation in a consistent manner.

Finally, there should funding to further develop technology to address other traffic safety issues. Currently, there is a focus on running red lights and speeding issues. There should also be challenge to develop technology to identify other traffic safety violations, (e.g.; jaywalking, cell phone use, failure to yield conditions), especially with the emerging technological systems being placed on our roadways and in our vehicles.

Overall, automated enforcement could prove to further enhance compliance with traffic safety laws by increasing the public's perception that violations may be discovered through the use of this technology.

Questions from Hon. Eleanor Holmes Norton for Jay Bruemmer, Vice President, K&G Striping, Inc., on Behalf of the American Traffic Safety Services Association

Mr. Bruemmer, one of the solutions to addressing the dangerousness of work zones is work zone project management software, and you note that it has been employed by the District of Columbia.

Question 1. Can you provide more detail on how this system worked and tell us whether there are any other places you're aware of that are using similar methods? If not, how can we help promote its adoption in other cities?

ANSWER. In responding to your written question regarding the smarter work zone application in Washington, DC, I wanted to point you and the Subcommittee staff to ATSSA's innovation website which is focused on educating departments of transportation and public works agencies on the opportunities that exist for smarter work zones and innovative roadway safety countermeasures generally.[100]

Additionally, I have attached the case study publication entitled, *Smarter Work Zones: Project Coordination and Technology Applications.* This publication is focused on various applications of smarter work zones across the nation, including the application in Washington, DC.[101] Project coordination is a focus for departments of transportation (DOTs) around the country. The Federal Highway Administration (FHWA) created a *Guide to Project Coordination for Minimizing Work Zone Mobility Impacts,* which helps DOTs utilize project coordination in their planning and execution.[102]

Finally, there is additional information on project coordination efforts around the country, including case studies.[103] Local transportation agencies rely on state DOTs and ultimately FHWA to incorporate new technology into projects and provide best practices. FHWA is in the process of developing systems to update their specifications to keep pace with emerging innovation through an update to the Manual on Uniform Traffic Control Devices (MUTCD). We encourage Congress to provide FHWA the resources to promote adoption of this and other new life-saving roadway safety infrastructure countermeasures. As for the Washington, DC-specific example, upon further conversations with the District Department of Transportation (DDOT), DDOT indicated difficulties in moving the project forward due to continuous software maintenance upgrades. That said, project coordination, in general, is important part of work zone safety, and it underscores the need to have guidelines and systems in place to keep up with ever-evolving technology.

ATTACHMENT—CASE STUDY PUBLICATION ENTITLED "SMARTER WORK ZONES: PROJECT COORDINATION AND TECHNOLOGY APPLICATIONS"

[The case study publication is retained in committee files.]

---

[100] ATSSA Innovation Website—http://innovate.atssa.com/innovative-technology-by-state.html.
[101] Washington, DC case study on project coordination—https://www.workzonesafety.org/files/documents/SWZ/DClPClcaselstudy.pdf.
[102] Guide to Project Coordination for Minimizing Work Zone Mobility Impacts—https://·ops.fhwa.dot.gov/publications/fhwahop16013/index.htm.
[103] Project coordination repository—https://www.workzonesafety.org/swz/swzproject-coordination/ outreach/.

Question from Hon. Peter A. Defazio for Nicholas J. Smith, Interim President and Chief Executive Officer, the National Safety Council

Mr. Smith, your testimony raises the specter of the FCC reneging on its initial decision to preserve a small piece of bandwidth for connected vehicles to communicate critical safety information with high speed and accuracy. Today, big telecomm wants to share the spectrum despite the lack of studies that guarantee their transmission will not interfere with vehicle to vehicle communication that will save lives.

Question 1. Should this committee allow the FCC to undercut the opportunity to prevent 37,000 deaths a year so people can download a movie a few minutes faster?

ANSWER. Mr. Chairman, the United States prioritized safety in 1999 by preserving the 5.9 GHz spectrum band for roadway safety communication. Communication between vehicles and other objects over this spectrum has the opportunity to mitigate and prevent crashes that could result in the loss of life. Infrastructure owners and vehicle manufacturers have begun installing 5.9 compatible technology, and the National Safety Council (NSC) would like to see implementation progress and proliferate.

The FCC and the Department of Transportation should exercise vigorous oversight of any testing of unlicensed devices to ensure no interference in the band that compromises safety. NSC urges Congress to monitor this testing as well.

Life-saving technology can operate over this band, including in areas that are often overlooked by other technology buildouts. NSC encourages Congress to preserve this spectrum for safety to help eliminate these preventable deaths.

In: Highway Safety
Editor: Bertha G. Baldwin

ISBN: 978-1-53617-176-1
© 2020 Nova Science Publishers, Inc.

Chapter 2

TRAFFIC SAFETY: IMPROVED REPORTING COULD CLARIFY STATES' ACHIEVEMENT OF FATALITY AND INJURY TARGETS[*]

United States Government Accountability Office

ABBREVIATIONS

DOT	Department of Transportation
FARS	Fatality Analysis Reporting System
FHWA	Federal Highway Administration
HSIP	Highway Safety Improvement Program
HSP	Highway Safety Plan
NHTSA	National Highway Traffic Safety Administration

WHY GAO DID THIS STUDY

Over 37,000 people were killed in traffic crashes on the nation's highways in 2017. Within the U.S. Department of Transportation (DOT), two agencies—NHTSA for behavioral factors and FHWA for highway infrastructure—provide about $3 billion annually to states for programs to improve traffic safety. To ensure that states are held accountable for these funds, NHTSA and FHWA developed performance management

---

[*] This is an edited, reformatted and augmented version of United States Government Accountability Office; Report to Congressional Requesters, Publication No. GAO-20-53, dated October 2019.

frameworks that require states to use performance measures and targets in tracking traffic fatalities and serious injuries.

GAO was asked to review NHTSA's and FHWA's traffic safety performance management frameworks. This report examines the extent to which: (1) states have met fatality and serious injury targets, and NHTSA's and FHWA's approaches to assessing states' achievements, and (2) states have used performance measures and targets to make traffic safety funding decisions. GAO analyzed state-reported targets and NHTSA data from 2014 through 2017—the most recent data available— for all 50 states, the District of Columbia, and Puerto Rico; surveyed these states on the use of performance measures and targets; reviewed requirements in NHTSA's and FHWA's frameworks; and interviewed officials from NHTSA, FHWA, and 10 states, selected to obtain a mix of population sizes, geographic locations, and other factors.

WHAT GAO RECOMMENDS

GAO recommends that NHTSA (1) provide additional direction and clarification to ensure states assess and report progress in meeting fatality targets, and (2) report on states' final achievement of targets. DOT concurred with the recommendations.

WHAT GAO FOUND

From 2014 through 2017, states did not achieve most of the fatality-related targets they set under the National Highway Traffic Safety Administration's (NHTSA) performance management framework (see table), and the number of serious injury targets states achieved during this period is unclear. GAO did not assess whether states achieved targets they set under the Federal Highway Administration's (FHWA) framework because the data were not yet available. State officials we interviewed said that achieving fatality targets may depend on factors outside their control, such as demographic, economic, and legislative changes. GAO's analysis of states' reports showed that nearly half of states did not provide the required assessment of progress to NHTSA on their most recent set of fatality targets. While NHTSA has taken steps to improve its review of these reports, officials acknowledged states are not clear on which target years to assess. Further, NHTSA lacks a mechanism to report whether states eventually achieve these targets. As a result, NHTSA and other stakeholders have limited insight into the results states have achieved from their use of federal safety funds. The extent to which states achieved serious injury targets is unclear because states have changed their definitions of serious injury over time. To ensure the consistency of these data, NHTSA and FHWA established a standard definition for reporting serious injuries, which states are in the process of adopting.

In a survey that GAO administered, officials from a majority of states said that performance measures informed how they selected projects under NHTSA's framework. GAO found, however, that in the 2019 plans submitted by states to NHTSA, less than a third of states reported how performance targets and funded projects were linked. Since the submission of those plans, NHTSA has provided training and guidance to its staff to ensure future plans will more clearly identify these links. Under FHWA's framework, about one-third of states reported in GAO's survey that performance measures influenced their project selection; the remaining two-thirds reported using an alternative data-driven approach, such as cost-benefit analysis. FHWA officials said they are developing guidance to help states integrate performance measures and targets into methods that states are currently using to select highway safety projects.

Selected Traffic Fatality Performance Measure Targets Achieved by States, 2014–2017

Traffic fatality performance measure	Number of states achieving target			
	2014	2015	2016	2017
Motorcycle fatalities	25	20	16	17
Pedestrian fatalities	14	3	8	10
Speed-related fatalities	25	25	17	19

Source: GAO analysis of National Highway Traffic Safety Administration data. | GAO-20-53
Note: States include the 50 states, the District of Columbia, and Puerto Rico.

October 22, 2019

The Honorable Roger Wicker
Chairman

The Honorable Maria Cantwell
Ranking Member
Committee on Commerce, Science, and Transportation
United States Senate

The Honorable Thomas Carper
Ranking Member
Committee on Environment and Public Works
United States Senate

The Honorable Peter DeFazio
Chairman

The Honorable Sam Graves
Ranking Member
Committee on Transportation and Infrastructure
House of Representatives

Over 37,000 people were killed and an estimated 2.7 million were injured in traffic crashes in the United States in 2017, due to persistent safety issues such as speeding, distracted driving, and driving under the influence of alcohol. The U.S. Department of Transportation (DOT)— through the National Highway Traffic Safety Administration (NHTSA) and the Federal Highway Administration (FHWA)—annually provides about $3 billion in federal funds to states to improve highway safety.[1] NHTSA provides grants to state highway safety offices to address behavioral factors that affect safety (such as impaired or distracted driving), while FHWA provides federal-aid highway funds to state departments of transportation for roadway safety improvements (such as rumble strips).

Since the late 2000s, we have highlighted the need for Congress to consider restructuring the nation's transportation programs to move to a performance-based approach in order to improve accountability and help states more efficiently allocate federal surface transportation funding, including funding used to enhance traffic safety.[2] In response to the Moving Ahead for Progress in the 21st Century Act, which established the requirements for a performance-based approach to traffic safety in 2012,[3] NHTSA and FHWA have each established performance management frameworks for traffic safety.[4] Under these frameworks, states use performance measures to track traffic fatality, serious injury,[5] and other metrics, and establish targets annually for those performance measures to evaluate progress. In rulemakings, NHTSA and FHWA indicated an intent for these performance management frameworks to help states select projects to reach their long-term safety goals, such as to reduce fatalities to zero, by directly linking investments to performance outcomes. The consistently high number of traffic

---

[1] In this report, we use the term "states" to refer to the 50 states, the District of Columbia, and Puerto Rico.
[2] See in particular, GAO, *Surface Transportation: Restructured Federal Approach Needed for More Focused, Performance-Based, and Sustainable Programs*, GAO-08-400 (Washington, D.C.: Mar. 6, 2008).
[3] Pub. L. No. 112-141, § 1203, 126 Stat. 405, 524 (2012). In addition, the Fixing America's Surface Transportation Act (FAST Act), enacted in 2015, contained some performance management related provisions. For example, the FAST Act shortened the time for states to make progress toward meeting performance targets under the National Highway Performance Program. Pub. L. No. 114-94, § 1406, 129 Stat.1312, 1410 (2015).
[4] 23 C.F.R. Parts 490, 1200, and 1300. Part 1200 was recodified to Part 1300 for fiscal year 2018 funds and thereafter. According to FHWA and NHTSA, these frameworks reflect an on-going approach to transportation performance management that uses system information to make investment and policy decisions to achieve national performance goals.
[5] In this report, we use the term "serious injuries" to refer to suspected serious injuries. Suspected serious injuries are any injury other than fatal that results in one or more of the following: (1) severe laceration resulting in exposure of underlying tissues, muscle, organs or resulting in significant loss of blood, (2) broken or distorted arm or leg; (3) an injury resulting from a crushing force; (4) suspected skull, chest, or abdominal injury other than bruises or minor lacerations; (5) significant burns, such as second- and third-degree burns over 10 percent or more of the body; (6) a state of unconsciousness when taken from a crash scene; or (7) paralysis. This is consistent with FHWA's and NHTSA's definition of suspected serious injuries in 23 C.F.R. §§ 490.205 and 1300.3.

fatalities—over 30,000 each year since 2007—has raised the question of whether NHTSA's and FHWA's recent application of performance management principles in federal highway safety programs is helping states achieve their safety goals and make the best use of federal funds.

We were asked to review NHTSA's and FHWA's traffic safety performance management frameworks.[6] This report examines: (1) the extent to which states have met fatality and serious injury targets, and NHTSA's and FHWA's approaches to assessing states' achievement of these targets; and (2) the extent to which states have used performance measures and targets to make funding decisions related to traffic safety.

To address both of these objectives, we reviewed laws, regulations, and policy documents related to NHTSA and FHWA's performance frameworks, as well as our body of work on performance management in the federal government and transportation programs. We also interviewed highway safety and state department of transportation officials in 10 states about their approaches to setting targets and selecting projects to fund.[7] We selected states with a diversity of population sizes and geographic locations, among other factors.[8] We applied these criteria to select a non-generalizable sample of states that included states with varying characteristics within and across each criterion. These criteria allowed us to obtain information from officials representing a diverse mix of states, but this information cannot be generalized to all states because the states selected were part of a nonprobability sample. To gather additional information, we also interviewed NHTSA and FHWA officials and representatives of transportation associations.[9]

To evaluate the extent to which states have met the fatality and serious injury targets they set for NHTSA's traffic safety grant programs, we analyzed fatality targets established for NHTSA's Highway Safety Grants Program in states' highway safety planning documents from 2014 through 2017. We selected this time period because 2014 was the first year states were required to submit targets to NHTSA under their framework, and 2017 was the most recent year that fatality data were available during our review. We compared state targets to data on fatalities from NHTSA's Fatality Analysis Reporting System (FARS) and assessed the extent to which states had achieved their

---

[6] The Department of Transportation Reports Harmonization Act also included a provision for us to review states' progress achieving traffic safety performance targets, among other things. See Pub. L. No. 115-420, § 5, 132 Stat. 5444, 5445 (2019).

[7] These states were Alabama, Florida, Maryland, Michigan, Nebraska, Nevada, New York, Oklahoma, Utah, and Washington.

[8] As part of selecting the sample of states, we also included states with varying population densities, miles of public road, numbers of achieved traffic safety targets, and levels of performance management experience. We based the level of performance management experience on recommendations from DOT and national transportation organizations.

[9] Specifically, we interviewed representatives from the American Association of State Highway and Transportation Officials, the Association of Transportation Safety Information Professionals, and the Governors Highway Safety Association.

targets over this time.[10] To assess the reliability of the data, we interviewed NHTSA officials about their methods for collecting and validating FARS data and reviewed related documentation. We determined that the data were sufficiently reliable for the purposes of our reporting objectives. To evaluate the extent to which states have met fatality and serious injury targets under FHWA's performance framework, we analyzed the initial set of fatality targets states established for 2018. We did not assess states' progress in achieving their initial set of FHWA targets because the data for 2018 were not yet available during our review. We also reviewed NHTSA's and FHWA's documents and guidance for establishing serious injury targets, and interviewed officials from these agencies about serious injury data. To evaluate NHTSA's and FHWA's approaches for assessing states' achievement of targets, we reviewed regulations and documents to analyze the approaches NHTSA and FHWA have developed to evaluate states' progress. We then compared NHTSA's and FHWA's approaches to federal internal control standards for information and communication.[11]

To assess the extent to which states have used performance measures and targets to make funding decisions related to traffic safety, we reviewed states' annual highway safety planning and reporting documents. Specifically, for all states, we reviewed the 2018 Annual Reports and 2019 Highway Safety Plans submitted to NHTSA, and the 2018 Highway Safety Improvement Program (HSIP) Annual Reports submitted to FHWA. These were the most recent reports available at the time of our review. We compared the content of reports to requirements in NHTSA's and FHWA's regulations.[12] In addition, from April through May 2019, we surveyed 52 state highway safety offices about NHTSA's performance framework and surveyed 52 state departments of transportation about FHWA's performance framework.[13] We received responses from 50 state highway safety offices (96 percent response rate) and from all 52 state departments of transportation (100 percent response rate).[14] We also reviewed results from an FHWA survey of state departments of transportation from all states on transportation performance management.[15]

---

[10] NHTSA's FARS system contains data on all fatal traffic crashes within the 50 states, the District of Columbia, and Puerto Rico.

[11] GAO, *Standards for Internal Control in the Federal Government*, GAO-14-704G (Washington, D.C.: September 2014).

[12] 23 C.F.R §§ 924.15, 1300.11 and 1300.35. To help ensure the accuracy of the information we collected, two analysts reviewed each report and coded for the presence of required information using a data collection instrument.

[13] We conducted four pretests of the survey to ensure that the questions were clear and did not place an undue burden on officials, that the terminology was used correctly, and that the questionnaire was comprehensive and unbiased. We incorporated the feedback we received from these pre-tests into each survey instrument as appropriate. We then emailed the survey in a Microsoft Word document to recipients, which they completed and returned via email to us.

[14] The complete survey instruments and corresponding results can be found in appendixes I and II.

[15] FHWA conducted the survey of all 50 states, the District of Columbia and Puerto Rico, from December 2018 through February 2019 and received responses from 47 state departments of transportation, a 90 percent response rate.

We conducted this performance audit from October 2018 through October 2019 in accordance with generally accepted government auditing standards. Those standards require that we plan and perform the audit to obtain sufficient, appropriate evidence to provide a reasonable basis for our findings and conclusions based on our audit objectives. We believe that the evidence obtained provides a reasonable basis for our findings and conclusions based on our audit objectives.

BACKGROUND

Reducing transportation-related fatalities and serious injuries has consistently been DOT's top priority. Traffic fatalities and serious injuries may result from unsafe driver behaviors, such as speeding and alcohol- or drug-impaired driving, or from the design or condition of the road and its accompanying infrastructure. Within DOT, both NHTSA and FHWA are charged with reducing fatalities and serious injuries on the nation's highways and, respectively, provide grant funding to states to mitigate the behavioral and infrastructure-related causes of vehicular crashes.[16]

- NHTSA provided over $600 million in fiscal year 2018 to state highway safety offices through the Highway Safety Grants Program for activities designed to improve traffic safety by modifying driver behavior. For example, states may use NHTSA grant funding for efforts to increase seatbelt use, or to reduce impaired driving.
- FHWA provided about $2.6 billion in fiscal year 2018 to state departments of transportation through the Highway Safety Improvement Program (HSIP) for projects to improve safety on all public roads. HSIP funds can be used for infrastructure projects, such as rumble strips, and other projects such as road safety audits, safety planning, and improving safety data. States are allowed to transfer up to 50 percent of their HSIP safety apportionment made available each fiscal year to the other core FHWA highway programs.[17] For example, from 2013 through 2018, 24 states transferred HSIP safety funding totaling over $1 billion to other core programs and three states transferred approximately $600 million into their HSIP safety program from other core programs.

---

[16] DOT also funds safety programs through the Federal Motor Carrier Safety Administration, whose primary mission is to prevent commercial motor vehicle-related fatalities and injuries.

[17] HSIP is one of five core formula programs under the larger Federal-Aid Highway Program. The Federal-Aid Highway Program supports state highway systems by providing financial assistance for the construction, maintenance and operations of the nation's 3.9- million-mile highway network. FHWA is charged with implementing the program in cooperation with the states and local governments. In addition to HSIP, there are four other core Federal-Aid Highway programs: the National Highway Performance Program, the Surface Transportation Block Grant Program, the Congestion Mitigation and Air Quality Improvement Program, and the National Highway Freight Program.

Over the last decade, the federal government has taken steps to move toward a performance-based framework for traffic safety funding. Historically, most federal surface transportation funds were distributed through formulas that often had no relationship to outcomes or grantees' performance. In 2008, we recommended that Congress consider integrating performance-based principles into surface transportation programs such as NHTSA's Highway Safety Grants Program and FHWA's HSIP to improve performance and accountability in states' use of federal funds.[18] In particular, we noted that tracking specific outcomes that are clearly linked to program goals can provide a strong foundation for holding grant recipients responsible for achieving federal objectives and measuring overall program performance. The Moving Ahead for Progress in the 21st Century Act, enacted in 2012, formally required the Secretary of the Department of Transportation to, among other things, establish performance measures for states to use to assess fatalities and serious injuries to ensure further accountability for federal traffic safety funding provided to states.[19] See Table 1 for a complete list of mandatory performance measures.[20]

States are also required to establish targets annually for each of the performance measures and measure progress toward these targets. NHTSA first required states to develop targets for their performance measures as part of their planning for fiscal year 2014, and FHWA first required states to establish targets for their performance measures set in 2017 for calendar year 2018. Starting with these targets, state highway safety offices and departments of transportation were required by both NHTSA and FHWA to set identical targets for the three common performance measures in both frameworks.[21] Both NHTSA's and FHWA's frameworks provide flexibility to states in how they may establish targets and emphasize using data to develop realistic and achievable targets rather than aspirational ones that reflect a long-term vision for future performance. Because the frameworks do not require a specific reduction in fatalities or serious injuries, states may set targets that are higher or lower than their historical averages depending on state-specific factors, such as population increases or economic conditions. As a result, targets may reflect either an anticipated increase or decrease in fatalities or serious injuries.

NHTSA and FHWA require states to submit annual plans and reports to establish targets and describe their use of federal funds to improve safety and the results they have achieved relative to their targets. (See Table 2.)

---

[18] GAO-08-400.
[19] Pub. L. No. 112-141, § 1203, 126 Stat. 405, 524 (2012).
[20] States also have the option to track other performance measures, such as the number of fatalities involving a distracted driver or percentages of children in crashes who were unrestrained.
[21] 23 C.F.R. §§ 1300.11(c)(2)(iii), 490.209(a)(1).

Table 1. National Highway Traffic Safety Administration's (NHTSA) and Federal Highway Administration's (FHWA) Required Performance Measures for Fatalities and Serious Injuries

NHTSA	FHWA
• All traffic fatalities[a] • All traffic fatalities per 100 million vehicle miles traveled[a] • Alcohol-impaired fatalities • Cyclist fatalities • Motorcycle fatalities, all • Motorcycle fatalities, unhelmeted • Pedestrian fatalities • Speed-related fatalities • Unrestrained passenger fatalities • Young driver (under 21 years old) fatalities • All serious injuries[a]	• All traffic fatalities[a] • All traffic fatalities per 100 million vehicle miles traveled[a] • Non-motorized fatalities and serious injuries • All serious injuries[a] • All serious injuries per 100 million vehicle miles traveled

Source: GAO analysis of NHTSA and FHWA and information. | GAO-20-53
[a] Both the NHTSA and FHWA frameworks require these performance measures.

Table 2. National Highway Traffic Safety Administration's (NHTSA) and Federal Highway Administration's (FHWA) Targets and Annual Reporting Requirements

	NHTSA	FHWA
Deadline for states to submit targets	July 1 each year	August 31 each year
Document where targets established	Highway Safety Plan	Highway Safety Improvement Program Annual Report
Unit of measurement for targets	For performance measures shared with FHWA, targets reflect a state's desired 5-year-average for a performance measure ending with the current year.[a] (e.g., targets established for 2020 will reflect the desired average from 2016 through 2020.) For all other performance measures, states may select the years included in their targets, and may express the target as a single year or multi-year average.	All targets reflect a state's desired 5-year-average for a performance measure ending with the current year. (e.g., targets established for 2020 will reflect the desired average from 2016 through 2020.)
Reporting mechanism	Highway Safety Plan Annual Report	Highway Safety Improvement Program Annual Report

Source: GAO analysis of NHTSA and FHWA information. | GAO-20-53
[a] Both the NHTSA and FHWA frameworks require performance measures for all traffic fatalities, all traffic fatalities per 100 million vehicle miles traveled, and all serious injuries.

NHTSA requires that states submit an annual Highway Safety Plan to, among other things, set targets, identify projects they will implement in the upcoming fiscal year, and describe how they will use funds from the Highway Safety Grants Program.[22] States are

---

[22] 23 C.F.R. §§ 1300.11-12.

also required to submit an Annual Report to NHTSA that includes an assessment of the state's progress in achieving safety performance targets in the previous fiscal year.[23] States are required to submit an HSIP report to FHWA that describes, among other things, how they have used federal HSIP funding for highway safety improvement projects during the prior reporting period as well as performance targets for the upcoming calendar year.[24] In addition to the annual requirements, FHWA requires a Strategic Highway Safety Plan from states every 5 years that identifies a state's key safety needs and long-term goals, and guides investment decisions to reduce fatalities and serious injuries.[25] NHTSA and FHWA rely on states and localities to collect and report fatality and serious injury data used in the performance framework. In addition to providing information through annual plans and reports, states report traffic fatalities to NHTSA's FARS database, which tracks all fatal traffic crashes nationwide. When a fatal crash occurs, a state or local police officer completes a crash report form unique to each state. These forms can include a variety of data fields, such as the time of the crash, weather conditions, and the number of killed or injured persons. FARS analysts—state employees who are trained by NHTSA's data validation and training contractors—use the data in crash report forms to compile a record of the fatal crash. However, NHTSA's collection and validation of these data may take up to 24 months following the end of a calendar year before it is finalized. FARS also contains serious injury data associated with fatal crashes, though neither NHTSA nor FHWA maintain a database of all serious injuries. Rather, the agencies rely on states and localities to collect and store records of serious injuries resulting from traffic crashes and report this information to them each year. Based on data the states and localities provide, NHTSA estimates the number of total injuries resulting from crashes to track overall national trends.

STATES' OVERALL ACHIEVEMENT OF FATALITY AND SERIOUS INJURY TARGETS IS UNCLEAR DUE TO INCOMPLETE REPORTING AND DATA LIMITATIONS

States Did Not Achieve Most of Their NHTSA Fatality Targets from 2014 through 2017, and NHTSA and States Do Not Fully Report Progress and Communicate Results

From 2014 through 2017, states did not achieve about two-thirds of the targets they set for the required fatality performance measures, according to our analysis of state-

---

[23] 23 C.F.R. § 1300.35.
[24] 23 C.F.R. § 924.15.
[25] 23 C.F.R. § 924.9. According to FHWA, a state's Strategic Highway Safety Plan provides direction for the HSIP, and states must ensure that funded HSIP projects are consistent with this plan.

reported NHTSA data. In addition, for a majority of the fatality performance measures required by NHTSA, these data show that the number of targets states achieved generally decreased from 2014 through 2017. (See Table 3.) Over this same time, fatalities increased nationwide by 13 percent from about 33,000 in 2014 to over 37,000 in 2017. NHTSA officials said that fewer states achieved their targets over this time because fatalities increased nationwide over the same period due to increases in vehicle miles traveled and corresponding exposure to driving-related risks.[26]

Table 3. States' Achievement of National Highway Traffic Safety Administration (NHTSA) Fatality Performance Measure Targets, Fiscal Years 2014–2017

Number of states achieving target				
Traffic fatality performance measure	2014	2015	2016	2017
All traffic fatalities	26	16	10	9
All traffic fatalities per 100 million vehicle miles traveled	23	18	15	16
Alcohol-impaired fatalities[a]	17	20	13	17
Cyclist fatalities[b]	N/A	19	18	12
Motorcycle fatalities, all	25	20	16	17
Motorcycle fatalities, unhelmeted	26	26	21	23
Pedestrian fatalities	14	3	8	10
Speed-related fatalities	25	25	17	19
Unrestrained passenger fatalities	31	28	17	15
Young driver (under 21 years old) fatalities	30	22	13	15

Source: GAO analysis of NHTSA data. | GAO-20-53
Notes: States include the 50 states, the District of Columbia, and Puerto Rico. Data as of March 2019.
Fiscal years refer to the fiscal year Highway Safety Plan in which the state established the target, and not necessarily the fiscal year measured by the target.
[a] NHTSA estimates the number of alcohol-related fatalities through the use of statistical imputation because blood-alcohol test results are not always known for drivers and passengers involved in a crash. NHTSA does not provide the statistical error associated with these estimates.
[b] NHTSA required states to set a target for the cyclist fatality performance measure beginning in fiscal year 2015.

Officials from the 10 states we selected said that achieving targets often depends on factors outside of their control, such as demographic and economic factors, as well as changes to state laws.

- Demographic factors. Officials from eight of the 10 selected states said that demographic factors such as increases or decreases in population affect traffic safety. For example, officials from one state said that when companies expanded in the state, the population increased rapidly and the economy improved and led to more driving. Officials from another state noted that the increasing population in the state's urban areas has increased the number of pedestrian fatalities.

---

[26] We did not assess states' progress in achieving their initial set of FHWA targets because the data for 2018 were not yet available during our review.

- Economic factors. Officials from seven of the 10 selected states noted that economic factors such as low unemployment can affect traffic safety. For example, officials in one state said that fatalities decreased during the 2009 recession, but when the economy began to improve and more people were employed, fatalities increased. These officials noted that the number of people driving is also affected by gas prices because when prices increase, people drive less.
- Changes to state laws. Officials from eight of the 10 selected states said that changes in state laws can affect whether a state meets its targets. For example, officials from one state said fatalities increased beginning in 2012 when the state legislature passed a law allowing the operation of a motorcycle without a helmet, and continued to increase through 2017 when the state legislature increased the speed limit on some roads from 70 to 75 miles per hour. These officials also noted that they expect fatalities in their state to further increase as a result of the recent legalization of the recreational use of marijuana.

However, the extent to which states achieve targets does not necessarily reflect whether the number of fatalities has increased or decreased over time.

- First, states that achieved fatality targets did not necessarily experience reduced traffic fatalities. For example, for the 2017 targets, state-reported NHTSA data shows that 10 of 52 states achieved their target for the pedestrian fatalities performance measure, but five of these 10 states also experienced an increase in pedestrian fatalities compared to their 2012 through 2016 historical average. These data also show that the remaining 42 states did not achieve their total fatality target.
- Second, some states have experienced a decrease in traffic fatalities while not achieving their targets. For example, state-reported NHTSA data shows that 31 states did not achieve their targets for the speeding-related fatalities performance measure. However, these same data show that 11 of these 31 states decreased the total of number of these fatalities over their 2017 target period compared to their 2012 to 2016 average.
- Further, states that established targets that represented an increase in fatalities from historical averages (increasing targets) were more likely to achieve them than states that established targets that represented a decrease or no change in fatalities compared to their historical averages (decreasing targets), according to state-reported NHTSA data. Specifically, in 2017, for all of the required fatality performance measures, these data show that states that set increasing fatality targets relative to their historical 2012 to 2016 average achieved them at a higher rate than states that set targets that represented a decrease or no change to the

number of fatalities (See Figure 1.) For example, for the total fatality performance measure, eight states set increasing targets relative to their historical 2012 to 2016 average, while 44 states set decreasing or unchanged targets relative to their averages.[27] However, these data show that six of the eight states with increasing targets for the total fatalities performance measure achieved them, while only three of the 44 states with decreasing or unchanged targets achieved theirs.

In response to statute, NHTSA requires states to assess and report progress in achieving targets in the following year's Highway Safety Plan and the NHTSA Annual Reports each year.[28] Such an approach is consistent with federal standards for internal control, which state that agencies should communicate quality information, including about activities and achievements.[29] According to NHTSA officials, state evaluations of their progress in these plans and reports are designed to be an interim assessment of a state's progress. For example, because fatality data can take up to 2 years to be recorded by states in FARS and validated by NHTSA, final FARS data are not available when states are required to report on the achievement of the prior fiscal year's targets in their Highway Safety Plans. Therefore, NHTSA encourages states to use state data to conduct this assessment or provide a qualitative analysis of the progress made in achieving these targets when FARS data are not available. Upon review of these reports, NHTSA publishes them on its website.

While NHTSA has established requirements for states to provide assessments of their progress on achieving the prior year targets in their Highway Safety Plans and Annual Reports, we found that many states have not done so. For example, in the 2019 Highway Safety Plans submitted to NHTSA in July 2018, a third of states (19 of 52) did not provide an assessment of the progress they had made in achieving the fatality targets established in their 2018 Highway Safety Plans. Similarly, in the 2018 Annual Reports, submitted to NHTSA in December 2018, half of states (26 of 52) did not provide an assessment of whether they had made progress toward achieving the fatality targets established in their 2018 Highway Safety Plans. Instead, many of these states assessed progress for an earlier year or performance period. NHTSA officials acknowledged that some states are not clear on which target years to assess in their Highway Safety Plans and Annual Reports.

---

[27] By comparison, under FHWA's framework, in 2017, 27 states established targets for 2018 that decreased the average total fatalities relative to this historical average, while 25 states set increasing targets. NHTSA and FHWA required states to have the same total fatality target under both frameworks beginning in 2017 with the establishment of 2018 targets.

[28] 23 C.F.R. §§ 1300.11, 1300.35.

[29] GAO-14-704G.

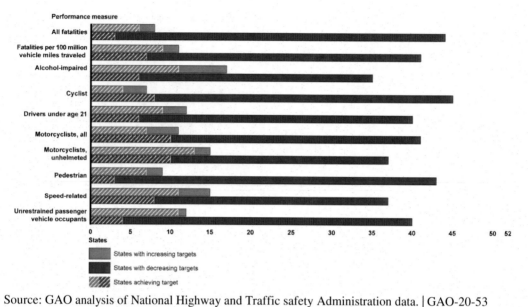

Source: GAO analysis of National Highway and Traffic safety Administration data. | GAO-20-53
Notes: States include 50 states, District of Columbia, and Puerto Rico. We determined each performance measure target developed by states to be increasing or decreasing based on a comparison to the 2012 to 2016 average of fatalities for that performance measure in that state. Decreasing targets include those that neither increased nor decreased compared to the 2012 to 2016 average. Figure includes data available through March 2019, which includes data through fiscal year 2017.
Fiscal year refers to the fiscal year Highway Safety Plan in which the state established the target, and not necessarily the year measured by the target.

Figure 1. States' Achievement of National Highway Traffic Safety Administration (NHTSA) Fatality Targets by Performance Measure and Target Type, Fiscal Year 2017.

NHTSA officials stated that they work closely with states to review the contents of the Highway Safety Plans and Annual Reports. To do so, NHTSA has developed guides to help its staff review Highway Plans and the Annual Reports to ensure states meet requirements to provide assessments of their progress. NHTSA officials stated they expect most states to comply with the requirements to assess progress in future Annual Reports and Highway Safety Plans because states will be more familiar with the reporting requirements. However, NHTSA has had similar requirements for states to provide in-progress assessments in these documents for a number of years. For example, the requirement to report on progress achieving highway safety performance measure targets identified in the Highway Safety Plans in the Annual Report was introduced in 2013.

Similarly, NHTSA's regulations have also required states to include an assessment of their progress in meeting state performance targets in their Highway Safety Plans since 2013.[30] Without additional clarification from NHTSA to states on which target years to assess in their Highway Safety Plans and Annual Reports, NHTSA and other stakeholders may lack a timely understanding of the progress states have made in achieving their targets. NHSTA could provide such clarification through outreach to states, or by providing guidance on NHTSA's website.

Beyond the required interim state assessments of progress contained in the Annual Reports and Highway Safety Plans, NHTSA does not communicate to the public and other stakeholders about whether states eventually achieve their fatality targets. Federal standards for internal control state that agencies should communicate quality information, including about activities and achievements, so that external parties–such as Congress and other stakeholders–can help realize agency goals and objectives.[31] NHTSA officials said that they have reported on states' achievement of fatality targets in the past. For example, NHTSA previously reported to Congress in 2017 on states' achievement of the fatality targets established in the 2014 and 2015 Highway Safety Plans in response to a statutory requirement.[32] However, NHTSA did not provide this report to other stakeholders, and it has not subsequently reported to Congress or the general public on whether states achieved targets. NHTSA officials told us they did not have any plans to develop a similar report in the future because the requirement to report to Congress was repealed in January 2019.[33] NHTSA was directed by statute in January 2019 to provide information on its website on state performance relative to the targets in the Highway Safety Plan. The statute broadly directs NHTSA to report on state performance and does not specifically direct NHTSA to communicate whether states eventually achieve their performance targets. NHTSA officials told us that this effort was in its initial stages and NHTSA is still in the process of determining how to meet the statutory requirement.

By improving external communication of states' achievement of fatality targets, NHTSA could give stakeholders better insight into the results states and NHTSA have achieved in their efforts to reduce fatalities and hold states more accountable for their use of federal safety funds. NHTSA could provide such information to all stakeholders through its planned website or by developing an alternative mechanism to convey this information.

---

[30] These requirements were integrated into NHTSA's performance management approach in NHTSA's regulations in 2013 as part of an interim final rulemaking, and states were required to provide an assessment in their highway Safety Plans beginning in fiscal year 2015. See 78 Fed. Reg. 4986, 5012, 5024 (Jan. 23, 2013) (codified at 23 C.F.R. §§ 1200.35, 1200.11(d); see also 2018 uniform procedures codified at 23 C.F.R. §§ 1300.35, 1300.11(b)). See 83 Fed. Reg. 3466, 3484, 3497 (Jan. 25, 2018).
[31] GAO-14-704G.
[32] 23 U.S.C. § 402(n).
[33] Pub. L. No. 115-420, § 5(a), 132 Stat. 5444, 5445 (2019).

States' Achievement of Serious Injury Targets is Unclear, and Consistent Data will Not Be Available for Some Time

We were not able to determine the extent to which states achieved NHTSA serious injury targets from 2014 through 2017 because states' definitions of "serious injury" have changed over time. As a result, state serious injury data used to set targets and analyze results may not be comparable year to year over this time period. NHTSA officials noted that changes to serious injury definitions can affect the total number of serious injuries recorded by the states. Similarly, officials from the Association of Transportation Safety Information Professionals told us that based on their experience, when there is a change to how serious injury data are defined or collected by states, total serious injury numbers in that state may change by up to 15 percent the following year. In some cases, changes to serious injury totals may be more extensive. For example, in 2016, one state changed its definition as part of implementing a new database to store crash records. After this change, the number of serious injuries nearly doubled from the previous year.

NHTSA and FHWA have taken steps to standardize how states define and report serious injury data. In 2016, both FHWA and NHTSA set out requirements for all states to use a specific definition of serious injury by April 15, 2019, establishing a single national standard definition that will be used under both NHTSA's and FHWA's performance management framework.[34] This standard includes requirements for states to integrate this definition into their practices for collecting and recording serious injury data. According to NHTSA and FHWA, this standard will ensure consistent, coordinated, and comparable data at the state and national levels and will assist stakeholders in addressing highway safety challenges. Moreover, according to officials from the Association of Transportation Safety Information Professionals, adoption of this standard will be an improvement upon the previous approaches used by states to define serious injuries.

However, it will take time for states to adopt this standard and collect consistent data under the new national standard for serious injuries to use in the NHTSA's and FHWA's performance management frameworks.

- First, NHTSA's and FHWA's regulations require that states establish 5-year averages for serious injury targets; however, according to states' most recent reporting, many states have only recently adopted NHTSA and FHWA's national standard for defining serious injuries. Specifically, based on our review of information submitted by states in their 2018 HSIP reports, we found that 18

---

[34] 23 C.F.R. §§ 490.205, 1300.3. FHWA established its requirement in a March 2016 final rule. See 81 Fed. Reg. 13882, 13914-15 (Mar. 15, 2016). NHTSA established the same definition for serious injury in an interim final rule in May 2016, and included the definition in a final rule in January 2018. See 81 Fed. Reg. 32554, 32581 (May 23, 2016); 83 Fed. Reg. 3466, 3483-84 (Jan. 25, 2018).

states had reported that they were fully compliant with the national standard as of the end of August 2018. FHWA officials told us that, based on their review of the information in the 2018 HSIP reports, they estimated that an additional 22 states planned to fully align their serious injury definition with requirements in the national standard by April 2019, and that the remaining 12 states had not indicated if they would be compliant with the national standard by that time. FHWA officials said they would conduct a compliance assessment in fall 2019 to determine whether states fully adopted the national standard.

- Second, data collected under previous, differing definitions cannot be retroactively converted to equivalent data under the definition established by the national standard, and thus it will take time to develop a consistently defined set of serious injury data. Specifically, for those states that have adopted the new standard in the last year, it may be 4 to 5 years until a 5-year average of serious injury data under the new standard can be reported, while the transition period may be longer for those states that have yet to adopt the standard. For example, the American Association of State Highway and Transportation Officials noted that if a state was not currently using the national standard, it would take a lengthy and resource-intensive effort to adopt the standard, including changing reporting processes, guidance, and training. State officials we interviewed also said the costs of updating software and paper forms to collect and store serious injury information, and of training state officials to collect serious injury data using the national standard, could further delay implementation.

NHTSA and FHWA have taken steps to assist states with the transition to the new national standard for serious injuries. For example, in preparation for issuing the regulations, NHTSA and FHWA published state-specific guidance to help states adopt an interim standard before the national standard took effect in 2019. According to NHTSA and FHWA officials, this guidance, which aligned states' existing definitions with a scale for injury severity, helped states provide more consistent serious injury statistics prior to implementing the new national standard in the FHWA rulemaking. While this interim standard helps improve consistency of the definition of serious injury within a state, it does not standardize the specific definition across all states as does the new national standard. In addition, NHTSA and FHWA developed an outreach program and training to help states adapt to the new requirement prior to implementation in 2019.

While the transition occurs and until states have collected 5 years of data under the new national standard for serious injuries, NHTSA and FHWA plan to take different approaches to assessing states' progress toward serious injury targets and communicating the results of their assessments.

- NHTSA officials told us that they would wait to assess progress until the states had adopted a consistent set of data under the national standard for serious injuries. NHTSA officials also noted that they did not assess whether states achieved their serious injury targets in NHTSA's 2015 and 2017 reports to Congress, because of limitations with the data that the new standard seeks to mitigate. However, once the transition to the new national standard for serious injuries is complete, similar to state fatality targets, NHTSA does not have a formal mechanism for communicating whether states eventually achieve their serious injury targets. Communication of states' achievement of both fatality and serious injury targets could help NHTSA hold states more accountable for their use of federal funds.
- In contrast, as directed by statute and regulations, FHWA plans to evaluate whether each state has met or made "significant progress" toward meeting both the fatality and serious injury-related targets by improving upon the state's historical 5-year baseline for four of the five required performance measures. As directed by statute and FHWA's regulations, states that FHWA determines either have not met their 2018 targets or not made significant progress are required to develop an implementation plan to describe how they will achieve targets in future years.[35] Further, these states must use a portion of these states' fiscal year 2021 HSIP funding exclusively for HSIP projects and may not transfer this portion of their HSIP funding to other core highway programs.[36] Once FHWA's evaluation of state progress is complete, it plans to communicate the extent to which states achieve these targets on its website, which contains information on the 5-year averages that make up the baseline, targets, and results, and tracks this information over time.

FHWA officials said that, as states transition to the new national standard for serious injuries, the use of data collected under multiple definitions in a state may occur in future assessments of significant progress as states collect 5 years of data under the national standard.[37] However, FHWA officials said that states will be able to take the limitations in the data into consideration and adjust targets each year as needed to minimize the risk that states' results will vary significantly from their targets. An official from the Association of Transportation Safety Information Professionals said that he expects states may recalculate targets to account for changes in the data over the transition to the national standard for serious injuries, but that states have not expressed concerns about doing so. More broadly, FHWA officials also stated that modifying its approach for the

---

[35] 23 U.S.C. 148(i); 23 C.F.R. § 490.211(d).
[36] 23 U.S.C. 148(i); 23 C.F.R. § 490.211(d).
[37] FHWA officials stated that the transition to the national standard will not affect the assessment of the 2018 targets because states will be evaluated using data under the interim standard, under which most states have had a consistent definition for serious injuries for at least 5 years.

transition period would require additional rulemakings by both FHWA and NHTSA, which could be a lengthy process and thus may not be completed before most states collect 5 years of data under the new standard.[38]

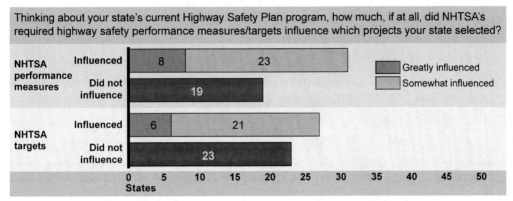

Source: GAO survey results. | GAO-20-53

Figure 2. State-Reported Use of National Highway Traffic Safety Administration (NHTSA) Performance Measures and Targets to Select Projects.

STATES HAVE NOT FULLY INCORPORATED PERFORMANCE MEASURES AND TARGETS INTO TRAFFIC SAFETY FUNDING DECISIONS, BUT NHTSA AND FHWA ARE TAKING STEPS TO ASSIST STATES

Over Half of States Use Performance Measures and Targets to Make Funding Decisions under NHTSA's Framework, and NHTSA Is Taking Steps to Improve Reporting

Officials from a majority of the states we surveyed reported that the performance measures and targets in the NHTSA framework influenced which projects they selected to fund to improve traffic safety and reduce fatalities and serious injuries. (See Figure 2.) For example, officials from two states we surveyed reported that the performance measures helped them identify emerging traffic safety trends, such as higher rates of speeding; as a result, the states directed more funding to projects addressing those issues. Officials from another state noted that the performance measures have led them to

---

[38] In our prior work, we found that rulemakings can range from 1 to nearly 14 years to complete, depending on a number of factors. More specifically, we found that a rulemaking takes an average of 4 years to complete, based on a sample of 16 rulemakings from four federal agencies, including DOT. See GAO, *Federal Rulemaking: Improvements Needed to Monitoring and Evaluation of Rules Development as Well as to the Transparency of OMB Regulatory Reviews*, GAO-09-205 (Washington, D.C.: Apr. 20, 2009).

develop new projects to reduce cyclist and pedestrian fatalities, in addition to their traditional projects targeting impaired driving or seat belt use. In addition, other state officials responded that setting targets influenced their project selection by requiring staff to identify and fund projects that would have a positive effect on the targets established. When NHTSA developed the performance measures for states, it noted that, in addition to helping states monitor and evaluate their progress, performance measures can be used to allocate resources towards the most pressing safety issues.[39]

Officials from 19 states we surveyed said that the performance measures in the NHTSA framework did not influence their project selection. Similarly, officials from 23 states said the targets did not influence their project selection.[40] Officials we surveyed cited a variety of reasons for why they did not use this performance information to select projects. For example, officials from three of these states said their states already had a data-driven or performance-based approach to project selection. Officials from one state explained that the NHTSA performance measures provide them with a general overview of safety trends in the state, but that they rely on more detailed data analysis of safety trends in different localities to select projects. Officials from another state said they do not use the specific targets to select projects, because they look for ways to decrease fatalities, not to achieve a specific number of fatalities in a given year. Officials from another state explained that they receive limited safety funding and therefore select projects to make sure they are eligible to qualify for NHTSA grants.[41] NHTSA officials acknowledged that the performance management framework can pose challenges for some states, but noted that they provide technical assistance and guidance to help states make the best use of their performance information.

State officials reported other safety benefits from NHTSA's performance framework in addition to improved project selection. Specifically, officials from almost three-quarters of states we surveyed said the NHTSA framework helped them to improve highway safety in their state. For example, officials from five states we surveyed reported that the framework has improved how they identify highway safety problems, such as by formalizing a data-driven approach to highway safety in their state. Officials we surveyed also noted that by requiring states to reach agreement on some NHTSA and FHWA targets, the framework helped them to increase collaboration with other highway safety stakeholders in the state. For example, officials from one state reported that the collaboration between the state department of transportation and highway safety office has increased their awareness of how physical road improvements and behavioral projects can work together to improve safety in the state. Officials from the 14 states who

---

[39] NHTSA, *Traffic Safety Performance Measures for State and Federal Agencies* (Washington, D.C.: August 2008).

[40] Officials from 19 states said neither the performance measures nor the targets influenced their project selection.

[41] A state must identify the types of projects that it will conduct in order to qualify for some NHTSA grants. For example, states with a seat belt use rate of under 90 percent must meet additional application requirements in order to qualify for a grant. Specifically, the state may choose to demonstrate compliance with at least three of six criteria to qualify for a grant, such as by conducting sustained seat belt enforcement. See 23 U.S.C. § 405(b)(3)(B).

reported that the framework has not helped them improve safety cited various reasons, including that they used data-driven approaches prior to NHTSA's framework and that the framework has increased their administrative burden. NHTSA officials agreed that the framework imposed some administrative burdens on states, but stated that the benefits of using a performance-based approach to manage state highway safety programs outweighed any costs for states.

To ensure that the framework helps states to improve traffic safety, NHTSA regulations require states to include at least one performance measure (and associated target) for each program area contained in their Highway Safety Plans.[42] These requirements are consistent with federal standards for internal control that agencies should establish and operate activities to monitor the internal control system. Such monitoring activities should be built into the agency's operation.[43] We found 49 states included performance measures with all the program areas in their 2019 Highway Safety Plans.[44] For example, one state uses the number of motorcyclist fatalities and unhelmeted motorcyclist fatalities as performance measures for its motorcycle safety program area. The remaining three states included performance measures for at least 80 percent of their program areas. By requiring states to establish performance measures for their program areas, NHTSA can help ensure states have appropriate performance measures in place to evaluate whether they are achieving the objectives of their highway safety programs.

NHTSA's regulations also require states to describe the linkage between the countermeasure strategies—the safety initiatives a state plans to fund to address highway safety problems—and the performance targets in their Highway Safety Plans.[45] Requiring states to link their funding decisions with their targets aligns with a leading practice for performance management we have previously identified: that agencies should use performance information to allocate resources.[46] We examined the sections of 2019 Highway Safety Plans where states are prompted to provide this linkage, and found, however, that less than a third of states (12 of 52) described all the linkages between their performance targets and the countermeasure strategies in those sections. NHTSA officials noted that states are directed to submit similar information in other locations throughout the plans, and that NHTSA's review of the 2019 plans credited states with making these linkages by considering information in other sections of the plan.

---

[42] 23 C.F.R. § 1300.11(c)(2)(i). A "program area" is defined by regulation as "any of the national priority safety program areas identified in 23 U.S.C. 405 or a program area identified by a state in the Highway Safety Plan as encompassing a major highway safety problem in the State and for which documented effective countermeasure strategies have been identified or projected by analysis to be effective." 23 C.F.R. § 1300.3.

[43] GAO-14-704G.

[44] We did not include states' administrative or traffic records program areas in our analysis.

[45] 23 C.F.R. § 1300.11(d)(1)(ii). "Countermeasure strategies" are a proven effective or innovative countermeasure proposed or implemented with grant funds under 23 U.S.C. Chapter 4 or Section 1906 to address identified problems and meet performance targets. Examples of proven effective countermeasures include high-visibility occupant protection enforcement, driving-under-the-influence courts, or alcohol screening and brief intervention programs. 23 C.F.R. § 1300.3.

[46] GAO-05-927.

NHTSA has taken steps this year to improve states' reporting and its own review of the 2020 Highway Safety Plans. For example, NHTSA officials told us that they have held in-person meetings with state highway safety officials to emphasize the need to provide linkages between their targets and countermeasures in their 2020 Highway Safety Plans. NHTSA officials said they have also held training in 2019 for staff who review these plans to ensure states adhere to reporting requirements. Specifically, during the training, NHTSA officials said they provided guidance to staff on reviewing Highway Safety Plans; this guidance prompts reviewers to check whether states link their countermeasure strategies with targets, and to provide feedback to states that have not provided these linkages. As a result of these actions, NHTSA anticipates that states will more clearly identify linkages in their 2020 plans.

Some States Use Performance Measures and Targets for Funding Decisions under FHWA's Framework, and the Agency Is Developing Guidance to Assist States

While states recently began setting performance measure targets under FHWA's framework in 2017, officials from about a third of states we surveyed reported that performance measures in FHWA's framework influenced their decisions about which infrastructure-based safety projects to fund. (See Figure 3.) Slightly fewer respondents said the targets they set influenced their project selection. These states reported that this performance information influenced their decision making in different ways. For example, officials from one state reported funding more pedestrian and bicycle safety projects as a result of the trends indicated by the performance measures. Officials from another state said they have shifted to selecting projects that can be constructed quickly in order to reach their annual safety targets.

Officials from about two-thirds of states we surveyed said the performance measures and performance targets did not influence their HSIP project selection. Instead, many of these state officials reported that the FHWA performance framework has not changed their project selection methodology, and that they used alternative data-driven approaches to select highway projects.[47] For example, officials from four states reported that they used their 5-year Strategic Highway Safety Plans, which highlight traffic safety issues to guide project selection. In other cases, state officials reported that they continued to use a data- driven approach, such as cost-benefit analysis or crash data analysis, to maximize safety benefits and select the most cost-effective highway safety projects. This approach is consistent with a recent FHWA survey of state departments of transportation, which

---

[47] FHWA officials noted that some states may not have included the safety performance measures in their state transportation improvement plans since the performance framework requirements took effect because they are only required to do so when the plans are updated.

reported that most states used their 5-year Strategic Highway Safety Plans and cost to prioritize projects. Federal guidelines, including those at FHWA, encourage the use of cost- benefit analysis for selecting infrastructure projects.[48] We have also previously reported that such analysis can lead to better-informed transportation decisions.[49] According to FHWA officials, performance management is not intended to supplant the use of other data-driven project selection methods, but to complement and be integrated into existing methods. To help further this synthesis, FHWA officials told us that they are developing a guide to better explain how states can incorporate the use of performance measures into existing methods, such as cost-benefit analysis, to select projects and achieve their safety targets. FHWA officials expect to issue this guide by January 2020.

Overall, a slight majority of states we surveyed (27 of 52) reported that FHWA's performance framework assisted them in improving safety. Officials cited safety benefits beyond improved project selection, such as increased awareness of highway safety issues for state leaders and the public; and increased collaboration with other highway safety agencies within the state. State officials who did not find the framework helpful cited various reasons. For example, some state officials we surveyed said they were already using performance measures prior to FHWA's framework. Other officials surveyed said FHWA's performance framework was not helpful because they have a "Vision Zero" or a "Toward Zero Deaths" policy in their state.[50] According to these officials, under such a policy, the state's goal is to achieve zero traffic fatalities. Officials from a state with such a policy explained that setting a target to achieve any fatalities was not acceptable to the public or the state because it suggests that not every life is important. FHWA officials said that setting annual targets, however, can ensure states are on track to reach their long-term goals, such as to reduce fatalities to zero.

To encourage states to integrate the performance framework into their other safety plans, FHWA regulations require states to link their performance measure targets to the long-term goals in their 5-year Strategic Highway Safety Plans. States must provide a description in their HSIP reports of how each target supports these goals.[51] FHWA has developed and issued a template for the HSIP report that prompts states to describe the link between their targets and their Strategic Highway Safety Plans' goals. However, about half of the states did not describe how all of their targets support their Strategic Highway Safety Plans' goals in their 2018 HSIP report, and thirteen of these states did not describe these linkages for any of their targets. In response to our analysis, FHWA

---

[48] See, for example, Executive Order No. 12893, "Principles for Federal Infrastructure Investments," 59 Fed. Reg. 4233 (Jan. 31, 1994).

[49] GAO, *Highway And Transit Investments: Options for Improving Information on Projects' Benefits and Costs and Increasing Accountability for Results*, GAO-05-172 (Washington, D.C.: Jan. 24, 2005) and GAO, *Surface Transportation: Many Factors Affect Investment Decisions*, GAO-04-744 (Washington, D.C.: June 30, 2004).

[50] "Vision Zero" is a multi-national effort to reduce traffic fatalities to zero. Similarly, "Toward Zero Deaths" is a national highway safety strategy shared by government agencies, safety advocates and safety associations to reduce traffic fatalities to zero.

[51] 23 C.F.R. § 924.15(a)(iii)(B).

officials have taken additional actions to improve states' HSIP reporting. Specifically, FHWA officials provided training to staff and state officials that referenced our analysis that states did not describe the linkages between targets and long-term goals in their HSIP reports. During the training, FHWA officials emphasized the importance of including such information as states prepare their 2019 HSIP reports. Additionally, FHWA officials said they are updating the guide its staff uses to review HSIP reports to ensure states are describing how the targets they set support their Strategic Highway Safety Plan's goals.

CONCLUSION

In light of the large number of fatalities that occur each year on the nation's highways and the billions of federal dollars DOT provides annually to states to improve traffic safety, the ability to assess the outcomes of federal surface transportation safety programs and hold grant recipients accountable for results is critical. NHTSA and FHWA have made great strides over the last decade in moving to a performance-based approach for traffic safety funding to improve accountability for federal funds. The results, however, that states have achieved under these frameworks are not always clear. For example, NHTSA has required states to report on their interim progress achieving targets, but states have not had clear direction on what results to assess. In addition, NHTSA lacks a formal mechanism to communicate whether states have been achieving the targets set under their framework. Without improved communication of progress, Congress will be limited in its ability to hold NHTSA and states accountable for their use of federal funds. Moreover, improved reporting of states' achievements under NHTSA's framework could help provide insight into the effectiveness of the overall federal traffic safety program.

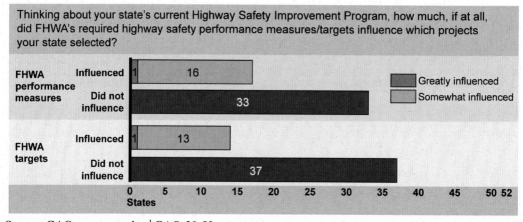

Source: GAO survey results. | GAO-20-53

Figure 3. State-Reported Use of Federal Highway Administration (FHWA) Performance Measures and Targets to Select Projects.

RECOMMENDATIONS FOR EXECUTIVE ACTION

We are making two recommendations to NHTSA:

- The NHTSA Administrator should provide direction and clarification to states to ensure compliance with requirements to assess and report progress made in achieving fatality targets. (Recommendation 1)
- The NHTSA Administrator should develop and implement a mechanism that communicates to Congress and other stakeholders whether states achieve their fatality and serious injury targets. (Recommendation 2)

AGENCY COMMENTS

We provided a draft of this report to DOT for comment. In its comments, reproduced in appendix III, DOT stated that it concurred with our recommendations. DOT also provided technical comments, which we incorporated as appropriate.

We are sending copies of this report to the appropriate congressional committees, the Secretary of Transportation, and other interested parties.

Susan A. Fleming
Director, Physical Infrastructure

APPENDIX I: SURVEY OF STATE HIGHWAY SAFETY OFFICES ON NHTSA'S PERFORMANCE MANAGEMENT FRAMEWORK

The questions we asked in our survey of state Highway Safety Offices and the aggregate results of the responses to the closed-ended questions are shown below. Our survey was comprised of closed- and open-ended questions. We do not provide results for the open-ended questions. We sent surveys to 52 state highway safety offices about the National Highway and Traffic Safety Administration's (NHTSA) performance framework from the 50 states, Puerto Rico and the District of Columbia. We received responses from 50 state highway safety offices, for a 96 percent response rate. For more information on our survey methodology, see page 4 of this report.

Q1a. NHTSA has implemented a performance management framework that requires states to set targets for highway safety performance measures and to track their progress towards meeting those targets. Generally speaking, has NHTSA's highway safety performance framework assisted you in improving highway safety in your state?

Response	Number of responses
Greatly assisted	6
Somewhat assisted	29
Did not assist	14
Don't know	1
No answer/not checked	0

Q1b. Why has NHTSA's highway safety performance framework assisted or not assisted you in improving highway safety in your state?
(Written responses not included.)

Q2a. Each year, states use Highway Safety Plan (HSP) funding and select projects to address identified highway safety problems. How much, if at all, has NHTSA's highway safety performance framework changed your state's current approach to selecting HSP projects?

Response	Number of responses
Changed, a great deal	2
Changed, somewhat	25
Did not change at all	22
Don't know	1
No answer/not checked	0

Q2b. In what ways, if any, has NHTSA's highway safety performance framework changed your state's current approach to selecting HSP projects?
(Written responses not included.)

Q3a. Thinking about your state's current HSP program, how much, if at all, did NHTSA's required highway safety performance measures influence which projects your state selected?

Response	Number of responses
Greatly influenced	8
Somewhat influenced	23
Did not influence	19
Don't know	0
No answer/not checked	0

Q3b. In what ways, if any, have NHTSA's required performance measures influenced which HSP projects your state selected?
(Written responses not included.)

Q4a. Thinking again about your state's current HSP program, how much, if at all, did the specific targets your state set for NHTSA's required performance measures influence which projects your state selected?

Response	Number of responses
Greatly influenced	6
Somewhat influenced	21
Did not influence	23
Don't know	0
No answer/not checked	0

Q4b. In what ways, if any, have the specific targets your state set for NHTSA's required performance measures influenced which HSP projects your state selected?
(Written responses not included.)

APPENDIX II: SURVEY OF STATE DEPARTMENTS OF TRANSPORTATION ON FHWA'S PERFORMANCE FRAMEWORK

The questions we asked in our survey of state departments of transportation and the aggregate results of the responses to the closed- ended questions are shown below. Our survey was comprised of closed- and open-ended questions. We do not provide results for the open-ended questions. We surveyed 52 state departments of transportation about the Federal Highway Administration's (FHWA) performance framework from the 50 states, Puerto Rico and the District of Columbia. We received responses from all 52 state departments of transportation, for a 100 percent response rate. For more information on our survey methodology, see page 4 of this report.

Q1a. FHWA has implemented a performance management framework that requires states to set targets for highway safety performance measures and to track their progress towards meeting those targets. Generally speaking, has FHWA's highway safety performance framework assisted you in improving highway safety in your state?

Response	Number of responses
Greatly assisted	4
Somewhat assisted	23
Did not assist	22
Don't know	3
No answer/not checked	0

Q1b. Why has FHWA's highway safety performance framework assisted or not assisted you in improving highway safety in your state?
(Written responses not included.)

Q2a. Each year, states use Highway Safety Improvement Program (HSIP) funding and select projects to address identified highway safety problems. How much, if at all, has FHWA's highway safety performance framework changed your state's current approach to selecting HSIP projects?

Response	Number of responses
Changed, a great deal	1
Changed, somewhat	17
Did not change at all	33
Don't know	1
No answer/not checked	0

Q2b. In what ways, if any, has FHWA's highway safety performance framework changed your state's current approach to selecting HSIP projects?
(Written responses not included.)

Q3a. Thinking about your state's current HSIP program, how much, if at all, did FHWA's required highway safety performance measures influence which projects your state selected?

Response	Number of responses
Greatly influenced	1
Somewhat influenced	16
Did not influence	33
Don't know	2
No answer/not checked	0

Q3b. In what ways, if any, have FHWA's required performance measures influenced which HSIP projects your state selected?
(Written responses not included.)

Q4a. Thinking again about your state's current HSIP program, how much, if at all, did the specific targets your state set for FHWA's required performance measures influence which projects your state selected?

Response	Number of responses
Greatly influenced	1
Somewhat influenced	13
Did not influence	37
Don't know	1
No answer/not checked	0

Q4b. In what ways, if any, have the specific targets your state set for FHWA's required performance measures influenced which HSIP projects your state selected?
(Written responses not included.)

Appendix III: Comments from the Department of Transportation

U.S. Department of Transportation
Office of the Secretary of Transportation

Assistant Secretary for Administration

1200 New Jersey Avenue, SE
Washington, DC 20590

OCT 0 7 2019

Susan A. Fleming
Director, Physical Infrastructure Issues
U.S. Government Accountability Office (GAO)
441 G Street NW
Washington, DC 20548

Dear Ms. Fleming:

Reducing traffic fatalities and injuries is the top priority for the National Highway Traffic Safety Administration (NHTSA). NHTSA has developed a performance management framework to increase accountability and transparency of actions taken to reduce fatalities and injuries on America's roadways. The agency has made great strides over the last decade in moving to a performance-based approach. Specifically, NHTSA is working closely with State Highway Safety Offices to improve the use of performance measures to focus efforts on evidence-based programs to reduce traffic fatalities and injuries and improve accountability.

NHTSA continues to improve upon its implementation of the performance management framework by:
- Helping to strengthen the collaboration among State Departments of Transportation, Highway Safety Offices and other safety stakeholders on performance measurement and target setting;
- Issuing a rulemaking and working with States to link funding decisions with "data-driven" targets;
- Providing technical assistance to encourage States to develop realistic and achievable targets and use problem identification to direct funding to programs that are proven effective;
- Implementing measures to ensure that, where a State has not met its performance targets, it will describe how it will adjust its upcoming Highway Safety Plan to better meet performance targets;
- Establishing a process for posting State performance targets and achievement on NHTSA's website.

Upon review of the GAO's draft report, we concur with the two recommendations to (1) provide additional direction and clarification to ensure States assess and report progress in meeting fatality targets, and (2) develop a method to communicate to Congress and other stakeholders States' final achievement of targets. We will provide a detailed response to each recommendation within 180 days of the final report's issuance.

We appreciate the opportunity to respond to the GAO draft report. Please contact Madeline M. Chulumovich, Director Audit Relations and Program Improvement, at (202) 366-6512 with any questions or if you would like to obtain additional details.

Sincerely,

Keith Washington
Deputy Assistant Secretary for Administration

In: Highway Safety
Editor: Bertha G. Baldwin

ISBN: 978-1-53617-176-1
© 2020 Nova Science Publishers, Inc.

Chapter 3

FEDERAL TRAFFIC SAFETY PROGRAMS: IN BRIEF (UPDATED)[*]

David Randall Peterman

INTRODUCTION

Driving is one of the riskiest activities the average American engages in. Deaths and serious injuries resulting from motor vehicle crashes are one of the leading causes of preventable deaths. In 2017, 37,133 people were killed in police-reported motor vehicle crashes in the United States, and in 2016 an estimated 3.14 million people were injured.[1] Many of the people who die in traffic crashes are relatively young and otherwise healthy (motor vehicle crashes are the leading cause of death for people between the ages of 17 and 23).[2] As a result, while traffic crashes are now the 13th leading cause of death overall, they rank seventh among causes of years of life lost (i.e., the difference between the age at death and life expectancy).[3]

In addition to the emotional toll exacted by these deaths and injuries, traffic crashes impose a significant economic toll. The Department of Transportation (DOT) estimated that the annual cost of motor vehicle crashes in 2010 was $242 billion in direct costs and

---

[*] This is an edited, reformatted and augmented version of Congressional Research Service, Publication No. R43026, dated October 26, 2018.
[1] Deaths: National Highway Traffic Safety Administration, *Traffic Safety Facts Research Note: 2017 Fatal Motor Vehicle Crashes: Overview*, DOT HS 812 603, October 2018; Injuries: NHTSA, *Summary of Motor Vehicle Crashes: 2016 Data*, DOT HS 812 580, September 2018, Tables 1 & 2. Injury estimates for 2017 were not yet available as of October 2018.
[2] National Highway Traffic Safety Administration, *Traffic Safety Facts Research Note: Motor Vehicle Traffic Crashes as a Leading Cause of Death in the United States, 2015*, DOT HS 812 499, February 2018, p. 2.
[3] Ibid., p. 1.

$836 billion when the impact on quality of life of those killed and injured was included.[4] About one-third of the direct cost came from the lost productivity of those killed and injured; about one-third from property damage; 10% from present and future medical costs; 12% from time lost due to congestion caused by crashes; and the remainder from the costs of insurance administration, legal services, workplace costs,[5] and emergency services.

MEASURING TRAFFIC SAFETY

The most commonly cited measure of traffic safety is the number of annual fatalities. That number held steady from 1985 to 2007 at around 42,000, leading to claims that traffic safety was not improving. But the raw number of traffic fatalities does not take into account increases in the number of drivers, the number of vehicles, or the number of miles being driven. While the number of deaths appeared to show no improvement in traffic safety between 1985 and 2007, the number of fatalities per 100 million vehicle miles traveled (VMT) fell by more than half (see Figure 1).

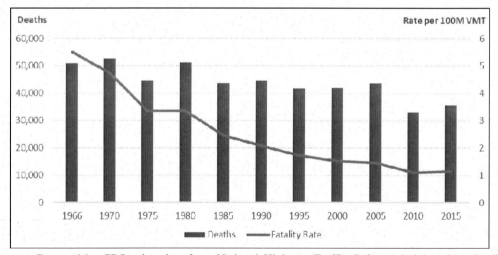

Source: Prepared by CRS using data from National Highway Traffic Safety Administration, *Traffic Safety Facts 2016*, DOT HS 812 554, Table 2.

Figure 1. Traffic Fatalities and Fatality Rate, 1966-2015.

---

[4] National Highway Traffic Safety Administration, *The Economic Impact of Motor Vehicle Crashes 2010*, DOT HS 812 013, May 2015. Direct costs include tangible losses resulting from crashes and those costs required to restore crash victims, as far as possible, to their pre-crash physical and financial status. These include medical costs, lost productivity, legal and court costs, insurance administrative costs, and property damage. The quality-of-life costs reflect the intangible value of death and injury to the victims: in the case of death, the loss of the victims' remaining lifespan, and in the case of serious injury, the resulting impairment and physical pain. See p. 113 of the report cited for more details.

[5] Costs of workplace disruption due to the loss or absence of an employee.

The improvement accelerated between 2007 and 2009, with the number of traffic deaths dropping to around 33,000, and the fatality rate dropping another 15% (see Figure 2). Part of this decline was likely due to weak economic conditions; traffic deaths and injuries typically decline during economic downturns and rise as the economy recovers.[6] Although the decline in traffic deaths after 2007 was heralded by some as evidence that traffic safety interventions were working, the number and rate of fatalities has risen since 2014 as the economy resumed growing. The dramatic improvement in traffic safety numbers from 2007-2014, then, was probably due to broader factors along with federal and state safety initiatives.

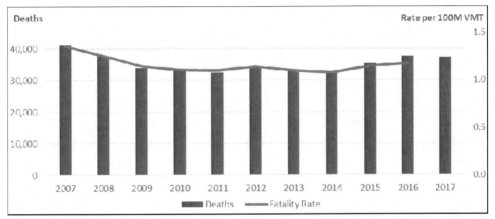

Source: Prepared by CRS using data from National Highway Traffic Safety Administration, *Traffic Safety Facts 2016*, DOT HS 812 554, Table 2, except the 2017 death number is from National Highway Traffic Safety Administration, *Traffic Safety Facts Research Note: 2017 Fatal Motor Vehicle Crashes: Overview*, DOT HS 812 603, October 2018.

Note: Fatality rate for 2017 not yet available.

Figure 2. Traffic Deaths and Fatality Rates, 2007-2017.

FEDERAL EFFORTS TO IMPROVE TRAFFIC SAFETY

Federal traffic safety programs are administered by three separate agencies within DOT. The National Highway Traffic Safety Administration (NHTSA) has responsibility for programs targeting driver behavior and regulates safety-related aspects of vehicle design. The safety of roads falls within the purview of the Federal Highway Administration (FHWA). The Federal Motor Carrier Safety Administration (FMCSA)

---

[6] The explanation for this phenomenon is not clear. The number of vehicle miles traveled (VMT) tends to stagnate or decline during recessions, but the percentage decline in deaths and injuries is typically much greater than the percentage decline in VMT. For example, from 2008 to 2009 VMT declined by less than 1%, but traffic fatalities declined by 9%.

manages a separate set of programs focusing on the safety of commercial drivers and vehicles.

Congress typically amends federal traffic safety programs in the periodic reauthorization of federal surface transportation programs. Recent reauthorizations were enacted in 2012 and 2015; the current authorization expires at the end of FY2020. Occasionally, changes are made in standalone legislation[7] or as part of other legislation such as the DOT appropriations act.[8]

Encouraging Safer Driving Behavior

A significant portion of crashes is caused, at least in part, by drivers behaving unsafely. Prominent among these behaviors are speeding,[9] driving while under the influence of alcohol or other drugs,[10] and driving while distracted.[11] Fatalities are also increased by failure to wear seat belts[12] (or in the case of motorcyclists, helmets).[13] Use of seat belts, among the most effective safety features in a vehicle, has risen from 58% (1994) to 90% (2017).[14] Use of motorcycle helmets, the most effective safety feature for a motorcyclist, has declined from 71% (2000) to 65% (2017).[15]

---

[7] For example, in 2008 Congress passed the Cameron Gulbransen Kids Transportation Safety Act of 2007 (P.L. 110 189), which directed DOT to initiate rulemakings to require that power windows in cars be designed to reverse direction when they encounter an obstacle and to reduce the risk of backing over a child by improving the driver's view of the area behind the vehicle.

[8] For example, the FY2001 DOT appropriations act provided that states that had not passed a law making driving with a blood alcohol content level of 0.08 illegal would have a portion of their federal highway funding withheld beginning with FY2004 (P.L. 106-346, §351).

[9] In 2017, 26% of fatalities involved speeding. National Highway Traffic Safety Administration, *Traffic Safety Facts: 2017 Fatal Motor Vehicle Crashes: Overview*, DOT HS 812 603, October 2018, p. 5 (percentage calculated by CRS).

[10] In 2017, 29% of traffic fatalities involved alcohol-impaired drivers. National Highway Traffic Safety Administration, *Traffic Safety Facts: 2017 Motor Vehicle Crashes: Overview*, DOT HS 812 603, October 2018, p. 4. There is some overlap between the percentages of fatal crashes involving speeding and those involving alcohol-impaired drivers.

[11] Around 9% of fatal crashes in 2017 involved distracted drivers.

[12] In 2017, almost half (47%) of fatally injured passenger vehicle occupants were not wearing seat belts or in child restraints. National Highway Traffic Safety Administration, *Traffic Safety Facts Research Note: 2017 Motor Vehicle Crashes: Overview*, DOT HS 812 603, October 2018, p. 5. Overall seat belt use (by front seat occupants) was estimated at 90% in 2016 and 2017; NHTSA estimated that seat belt use had saved the lives of 14,668 people involved in crashes in 2016, and that another 2,456 lives could have been saved if seat belt use had been 100%. *Traffic Safety Facts Crash Stats: Lives Saved in 2016 by Restraint Use and Minimum-Drinking-Age Laws*, DOT HS 812 454, October 2017, Table 1.

[13] Nationwide use of DOT-compliant motorcycle helmets in 2017 was estimated at 65%; in the 20 states where helmets are required for all riders, the estimate was 87%, versus 44% in the states where helmets are not required for all riders. National Highway Traffic Safety Administration, *Motorcycle Helmet Use in 2017—Overall Results*, DOT HS 812 512, August 2018, Figure 3. Requiring all riders to wear a helmet—a universal helmet law—has been estimated to reduce motorcyclist fatalities by 20% or more. National Cooperative Highway Research Program, *Effectiveness of Behavioral Highway Safety Countermeasures*, Report 622, 2008, p. 41.

[14] National Highway Traffic Safety Administration, *Traffic Safety Facts Research Note: Seat Belt Use in 2017—Overall Results*, DOT HS 812 465, April 2018.

[15] National Highway Traffic Safety Administration, *Traffic Safety Facts Research Note: Motorcycle Helmet Use in 2017—Overall Results*, DOT HS 812 512, August 2018, Figure 1.

Two groups are of particular concern. Young male drivers (aged 16-24) are far more likely to be involved in fatal traffic crashes than any other age-group, including young female drivers.[16] And the fatality rate for motorcyclists (most of whom are male) is over 20 times the rate for occupants of other motor vehicles.[17]

Since driver behavior is the cause of most crashes, regulating driver behavior is a way of reducing the number of crashes. But regulating driver behavior is a power reserved to the states.[18] NHTSA (and Congress) attempts to encourage states to pursue safety initiatives affecting driver behavior either by providing money to states to do certain things (incentive grants) or by withholding money from states that do not do certain things (sanctions).[19] In the most recent reauthorization of highway safety programs, Congress established or renewed incentive grant programs for states that take specified actions to promote seat belt and child restraint use ("occupant protection"), reduce impaired and distracted driving, require graduated licenses for teen drivers, address the safety of motorcyclists, bicyclists, and pedestrians, and improve the quality of state traffic safety information systems.[20]

Vehicle Safety Improvements

NHTSA began establishing minimum standards for passenger vehicles (known as Federal Motor Vehicle Safety Standards, or FMVSS) in the 1960s based on provisions in highway and traffic safety acts passed in that period.[21] Existing standards are amended and new standards are added from time to time at the direction of Congress, at NHTSA's own initiative, or as a result of a request from the public. New standards and amendments to existing standards must go through the federal rulemaking process, which provides for public review and comment on proposed changes. Standards currently under consideration include improved rollover structural integrity for motorcoaches and audible

---

[16] National Highway Traffic Safety Administration, *Traffic Safety Facts 2016*, DOT HS 812 554, Table 62.

[17] In 2016 the fatality rate per 100 million VMT for motorcyclists was 25.85, compared to an overall motor vehicle fatality rate of 1.18. National Highway Traffic Safety Administration, *Traffic Safety Facts 2016*, DOT HS 812554, Tables 2 and 10. In 2017 5,172 motorcyclists were killed.

[18] For example, the federal government can require vehicle manufacturers to put seat belts in vehicles, but cannot require that people use them; only states can make failure to use seat belts a legal offense.

[19] Two of the current traffic safety sanctions are "weak" sanctions; they do not withhold any transportation funding from a state that is not in compliance, but redirect a small portion of a state's federal highway construction funding to its safety programs (including its Highway Safety Infrastructure Program). Many states remain subject to these sanctions. One requires states to prohibit open alcoholic containers in vehicles; 14 states were subject to that sanction in FY2018. Another requires states to impose certain minimum penalties for repeat offenders convicted of driving while intoxicated; 17 states were subject to that sanction in FY2018. In contrast, the sanction that requires states to set a blood alcohol concentration of 0.08 as the legal level of driving while intoxicated is a "strong" sanction; states not in compliance will lose a portion of their federal highway construction funding. Every state is in compliance with that requirement.

[20] P.L. 114-94 (FAST Act), §4005.

[21] These are collected in Part 571 of Title 49 of the *Code of Federal Regulations*.

notifications for rear seat belt usage.[22] NHTSA also tests vehicles for compliance with safety standards, rates the crashworthiness of vehicles, and monitors consumer complaints about vehicles for evidence of safety defects that may necessitate a vehicle recall.[23]

Improvements in vehicle design, such as the use of crumple zones, have made vehicles structurally safer over the past few decades. NHTSA also mandated safety features such as airbags, which have been required in all passenger vehicles since model year 1997. Improved design and safety features have contributed to a reduction in the deadliness of crashes; the percentage of crashes in which vehicle occupants are killed or injured has dropped from around 33% (during the 1990s) to around 28% (2015-2016).[24]

Developments in electronic technology are shifting the focus of vehicle safety research from an emphasis on crashworthiness—a vehicle's ability to protect occupants in the event of a crash—to crash avoidance. For example, electronic stability control systems automatically apply braking force to individual wheels to reduce the risks of skidding or rollover; this has been required on all new passenger vehicles since the 2012 model year. Other technologies, such as adaptive cruise control (which automatically maintains a safe distance from the car ahead), forward collision mitigation (which automatically brakes to prevent the vehicle from striking an object in its path), and lane departure warning, are available as options on some vehicles. The National Transportation Safety Board has recommended that NHTSA add several of these new technologies to the list of safety standards required for all vehicles because of their potential to prevent crashes.[25]

NHTSA and the Insurance Institute for Highway Safety announced in 2016 that 20 automakers, representing 99% of the U.S. auto fleet, had agreed to make automatic emergency braking with forward collision warning a standard feature on all their cars by September 1, 2022. NHTSA said this agreement would result in the near universal availability of this safety feature at least three years sooner than by going through the regulatory process to make it a legal requirement. For the 2017 model year, the first full model year following this agreement, 19% of the vehicles produced by these companies for the U.S. market had this technology as standard equipment.[26]

NHTSA is also beginning rulemakings to develop a safe method of on-road testing of advanced vehicle technologies, such as automated driving systems, and to identify current regulations that may hinder the introduction of advanced vehicle technologies.

---

[22] Department of Transportation, *September 2018 Significant Rulemaking Report*, available at https://www.transportation.gov/regulations/report-on-significant-rulemakings.
[23] Manufacturers typically voluntarily recall vehicles that have a defect, but if necessary NHTSA can order a manufacturer to recall a defective vehicle.
[24] National Highway Traffic Safety Administration, *Traffic Safety Facts 2016*, Table 1: Crashes by Crash Severity.
[25] National Transportation Safety Board, *Most Wanted List: Increase Implementation of Collision Avoidance Technologies*, https://www.ntsb.gov/safety/mwl/Pages/mwl2-2017-18.aspx.
[26] National Highway Traffic Safety Administration, "Manufacturers make progress on voluntary commitment to include automatic emergency braking on all new vehicles," December 21, 2017, https://www.nhtsa.gov/press-releases/nhtsa-iihs-announcement-aeb.

DOT has issued voluntary guidance regarding the introduction of autonomous vehicles, and Congress is considering legislation that would affect the treatment of autonomous vehicles (e.g., H.R. 3388, S. 1885).

Roadway Safety Improvements

The design of roads influences how safe they are. The most dramatic example is the Interstate Highway system; although these roads are heavily trafficked by vehicles traveling at high speeds, they are the safest category of road due to such factors as having no intersections, long sight lines, gentle curves, wide lanes, etc. Road designs change over time as research identifies characteristics that can reduce the likelihood of crashes. One benefit of improved road design is that it reduces the incidence of driver misbehavior.

Roadway design is a particular concern for vulnerable road users for whom there are few other effective options to improve safety, namely pedestrians and bicyclists. Perhaps due in part to increased awareness of the health benefits of exercise, the level of pedestrian and bicyclist activity appears to have risen in recent years. As well, the number of pedestrians and bicyclists killed in traffic crashes has risen: from 4,699 pedestrians (11% of all traffic deaths) in 2007 to 5,987 (16% of all traffic deaths) in 2017,[27] and from 701 bicyclists (1.7% of all traffic deaths) in 2007 to 840 (2.2 % of all traffic deaths) in 2017.[28] Roadway designs to protect these road users include sidewalks, protected bike lanes, crossing islands and raised medians, and other traffic-calming measures.[29]

FHWA supports research and makes grants to states to improve roadway safety. Safety improvements are eligible expenses under most FHWA grant programs, but one of the core grant programs is specifically focused on safety, the Highway Safety Improvement Program. This program distributes more than $2 billion annually to states for road safety improvements. To qualify to use their funding, states must develop highway safety plans that use crash data to identify hazardous road locations or features and identify measures to address the problems.[30] FHWA is encouraging a shift in

---

[27] National Highway Traffic Safety Administration, *Traffic Safety Facts 2016 Data: Pedestrians*, DOT HS 812 493, March 2018, Table 1.
[28] National Highway Traffic Safety Administration, *Traffic Safety Facts 2016 Data: Bicyclists and Other Cyclists*, DOT HS 812 507, May 2018, Table 1.
[29] National Highway Traffic Safety Administration, *Advancing Pedestrian and Bicyclist Safety: A Primer for Highway Safety Professionals*, DOT HS 812 258, April 2016.
[30] These measures may include replacing intersections with roundabouts, adding medians and pedestrian crossing islands to urban and suburban streets, limiting highway access points, and adding rumble strips to two-lane roads. See http://safety.fhwa.dot.gov/ provencountermeasures/ for more information.

emphasis from highway design standards to steps that improve safety as measured by changes in crash data.[31] Projects are chosen by state DOTs.

Commercial Transportation Safety

The federal government lacks authority to regulate the behavior of ordinary drivers, which is under state jurisdiction. However, the behavior of commercial drivers who engage in interstate commerce is a federal matter. For example, Congress has required that commercial drivers satisfy requirements for training, licensing, and medical fitness, and specifies how much time drivers can work each day (generally, no more than 12 hours).

Federal regulations concerning vehicles and drivers are enforced by FMCSA and state authorities, who conduct both on-site and roadside inspections. Enforcement is challenging, given the scale of the industry; there are over 700,000 commercial truck and bus operators with millions of vehicles and drivers. FMCSA inspectors and law enforcement officials have the power to remove a vehicle from service, and FMCSA can order an operator to suspend operations in the event of serious violations. Fines for less severe violations are imposed by state authorities.

One of the most significant opportunities for improvement in commercial vehicle safety is the application of automated driving systems that supplement the role of the driver. NTSB, in calling for greater use of such technologies for commercial vehicles, noted that

> In a 2015 study by the University of Michigan Transportation Research Institute, researchers found that in the large motor carriers they surveyed, [Lane Departure Warning Systems] reduced crashes by 14 percent, electronic stability control by 19 percent, [Forward Collision Warning Systems] by 14 percent, blind spot detection by 5 percent, and vehicle communications systems by 9 percent.[32]

FMCSA plans to issue a request for public comment about Federal Motor Carrier Safety Regulations that may need to be updated, modified, or eliminated to facilitate the safe introduction of automated driving systems-equipped commercial motor vehicles.[33]

In 2010, FMCSA adopted a new enforcement approach called the Compliance, Safety, Accountability program (CSA). CSA is a monitoring program that seeks to make better use of enforcement resources by using data collected through federal and state

---

[31] See, for example, FHWA's Highway Safety Manual website (https://safety.fhwa.dot.gov/ rsdp/hsm.aspx /).

[32] National Transportation Safety Board, 2017-2018 Most Wanted List of Transportation Safety Improvements: Increase Implementation of Collision Avoidance Technologies: Highway, https://www.ntsb.gov/safety/mwl/Documents/2017-18/2017MWL-FctSht-CollisionAvoidance-H.pdf.

[33] Department of Transportation, *September 2018 Significant Rulemaking Report*, entry #44.

inspections and crash data to identify high-risk operators who can then be targeted for interventions. Questions have been raised about the CSA, particularly its Safety Measurement System component, which uses data to identify high-risk carriers, and Congress directed that the program be reviewed by the National Academy of Sciences; its report made several recommendations for improving the effectiveness of the Safety Measurement System.[34]

In December 2011, FMCSA's Motor Carrier Safety Advisory Committee and its Medical Review Board made recommendations regarding screening of commercial drivers for sleep apnea, a medical condition that causes frequent disruption to breathing during sleep, interfering with restful sleep and causing drowsiness during the day. Obesity is linked to sleep apnea, and commercial drivers have above-average rates of obesity, due in part to sitting behind the wheel of a vehicle for up to 12 hours a day, which leaves little time for exercise, as well as often limited options for healthy eating while on the road and often irregular sleep patterns. Sleep apnea can be a medically disqualifying condition for a commercial driver, though there are medical treatments that can permit a commercial driver to continue to drive. The FMCSA committees recommended that medical examiners should routinely test commercial drivers who are extremely obese (BMI 35+)[35] for sleep apnea. FMCSA would have to go through the rulemaking process in order to make that recommendation a requirement.[36]

Since December 2017, in response to a congressional directive, most truckers have had to use an electronic logging device (ELD) to record how many hours they spend on duty and driving each day. Federal hours of service (HOS) regulations have for several decades limited duty and driving hours of commercial drivers in order to reduce the risk of fatigued drivers causing crashes. Surveys indicated that drivers often violated those limits, but since drivers were responsible for keeping track of their own hours in a paper log, it was easy to conceal such violations. Highway safety groups had long called for Congress to require that commercial drivers use an automated system to track their driving time in order to limit violations. Now that most commercial drivers must use ELDs to track their hours, some sectors of the commercial trucking industry, particularly livestock haulers, are objecting that the ELD requirement—which is to say, the improved enforcement of the hours-of-service rules that have been in place for years—makes it hard for them to conduct their business. Congress has granted livestock haulers a temporary reprieve from the ELD mandate, and FMCSA has issued an Advanced Notice

---

[34] The National Academies of Sciences, Engineering, and Medicine, *Improving Motor Carrier Safety Measurement*, 2017, https://doi.org/10.17226/24818.
[35] BMI stands for Body Mass Index, and is essentially a measure of a person's weight divided by his or her height.
[36] In 2013 Congress provided that FMCSA would have to go through the rulemaking process to implement screening, testing, or treatment of commercial drivers for sleep disorders; P.L. 113-45.

of Proposed Rulemaking seeking public input regarding possible revisions to certain HOS rules.[37]

OPTIONS FOR CONGRESS

Congress may review the performance of the current traffic safety measures and consider additional traffic safety measures in the context of the next surface transportation authorization legislation (the current authorization expires at the end of FY2020). Several opportunities exist for Congress to further promote highway safety, although some options may impinge on driver behavior in a way that some people find objectionable.

Speeding, for example, is a violation committed by virtually all drivers at times, and by some drivers routinely. Speeding contributes both to the risk of crashing and to the impact of crashing (all else being equal, the greater the speeds of the vehicles involved in a crash, the greater the destructiveness of the crash). Speed limits are hard for law enforcement officers to enforce because violations are ubiquitous, and it is often dangerous to pull offenders over to issue them a ticket; each year a number of law enforcement officers engaged in roadside stops are struck and killed by passing motorists. Conversely, automated enforcement of speed limits (and of red light running) is relatively low-cost compared to the cost of a human officer, operates around the clock, and does not require stopping the offender to issue a ticket, thus keeping officers out of harm's way. Studies of speed and red light cameras indicate they reduce injuries and deaths, and NHTSA gives them the highest rating for effectiveness.[38] However, Congress prohibits states from using federal-aid highway funding for automated traffic enforcement (except in school zones);[39] in a further disincentive to the use of automated enforcement, Congress requires states in which automated enforcement systems are in operation to conduct a biennial survey of those systems.[40]

Similarly, the single most effective safety measure for motorcyclists is wearing a helmet, but many motorcyclists choose not to do so. Mandatory helmet laws (requiring all riders to wear helmets) have been shown to increase the rate of helmet wearing and to save lives, and are relatively simple to enforce (since violations are easy to see), but only19 states require all motorcyclists to wear a helmet; most require helmets only for

---

[37] Federal Motor Carrier Safety Administration, "Hours of Service of Drivers," *Federal Register* v. 83, p. 42631 (August 23, 2018), https://www.federalregister.gov/documents/2018/08/23/ 2018-18379/hours-of-service-of-drivers.

[38] National Highway Traffic Safety Administration, *Countermeasures That Work: A Highway Safety Countermeasure Guide For State Highway Safety Offices*, Ninth Edition (2017), "Motorcycle Helmets," p. 5-8, https://www.nhtsa.gov/ sites/nhtsa.dot.gov/files/documents/ 812478_countermeasures-that-work-a-highway-safety-countermeasures-guide-.pdf.

[39] P.L. 114-94 (FAST Act), §1401.

[40] P.L. 114-94 (FAST Act), §4002(2).

young riders. Congress does not have the authority to enact mandatory helmet laws, but can influence state legislatures to enact such laws: in the early 1970s the prospect of having a portion of a state's federal highway funding withheld if it did not have a mandatory helmet law led to 47 states adopting such laws. But the penalty provision was then repealed, after which many states repealed their mandatory helmet law. Congress has created a motorcycle safety incentive grant program that emphasizes education, although there is little evidence that educational programs result in improvement in motorcyclist safety. Congress also has prohibited NHTSA from encouraging states to adopt mandatory helmet laws,[41] and has prohibited states from using any federal highway funding to set up traffic checkpoints that target motorcyclists for inspection, or for any program that checks helmet usage.[42]

---

[41] 49 U.S.C. Section 30105. The prohibition on NHTSA urging state legislatures to oppose or adopt legislation is general, but the motivation for this provision, which was enacted in 1998, may have been a video NHTSA produced that supported the use of motorcycle helmets; see https://one.nhtsa.gov/nhtsa/whatsup/tea21/GrantMan/HTML/05e_LobbyMemo_2_9_00.rest.html.

[42] P.L. 114-94 (FAST Act), §4007.

Chapter 4

FEDERAL HIGHWAY TRAFFIC SAFETY POLICIES: IMPACTS AND OPPORTUNITIES[*]

David Randall Peterman

SUMMARY

In 2017, 37,133 Americans were killed in crashes involving motor vehicles. Motor vehicle crashes are a leading cause of death for Americans overall, and the number one cause of death for teenagers. Millions of people are injured in crashes annually, and motor vehicle crashes are estimated to have cost some $242 billion in 2010 in lost productivity, medical costs, legal costs, property damage, and time lost in congestion caused by crashes. As measured by the number of deaths per mile people are driving, the rate at which people are killed in traffic crashes declined significantly from 1929, when records began to be kept, until 2014, but has risen by almost 10% between 2014 and 2016.

Congress has played a role in improving highway safety. Making road travel safer was one of the responsibilities Congress gave to the federal Department of Transportation (DOT) when it created the department in 1966. Congress has directed DOT to improve the safety of automobile design and of road design, as well as to support programs to improve driver behavior.

An oft-cited statistic in traffic safety is that as many as 90% of road deaths are due at least in part to driver error or misbehavior (such as driving too fast for conditions or driving while drunk or distracted). Driver behavior is a state, not federal, matter; in an effort to address it, Congress has enacted programs that encourage states to pass laws to promote safer driving. The role of driver behavior versus road design and traffic management is a subject of debate. Some analysts note that road designs and traffic management arrangements often allow, or even encourage, driver error and misbehavior, and so play a larger role in crashes than is often recognized. One of the core highway

---

[*] This is an edited, reformatted and augmented version of a Congressional Research Service publication R44394, prepared for Members and Committees of Congress dated July 12, 2019.

capital improvement programs authorized by Congress is intended to fund safety improvements to highway infrastructure.

A federal study estimated that half of the improvement in highway fatality rates between 1960 and 2012 was attributable to improvements in vehicle safety technologies, with social and demographic changes, driver behavior interventions, and improvements in road design playing smaller roles. Most of the vehicle safety technologies analyzed in the study increased the likelihood that vehicle occupants would survive a crash. More recently, technological improvement has focused on preventing crashes. While some crash-prevention technologies, such as automatic braking and lane departure warnings, are available now, others, such as vehicle-to-vehicle communication and vehicles that can operate without human intervention, are not yet on the market. Even when these become commercially available, given that most vehicles remain in use for well over a decade, it may be many years before the majority of cars on the road incorporate these technologies.

While U.S. crash and injury rates are no longer declining, and even rising, several other nations have significantly improved their highway safety rates in the past few years, surpassing the U.S. rates. The International Transport Forum's Road Safety Annual Report 2018 found that between 2010 and 2016, 26 of the 32 nations tracked in the report had reduced their number of traffic deaths, some by over 30%; during the same period, the number of U.S. deaths increased by 14%.

Policy options that might further reduce traffic crashes, injuries, and fatalities include encouraging states to adopt stronger laws regarding use of seat belts and motorcycle helmets and encouraging the use of automated traffic enforcement to reduce speeding and failure to stop at red lights and stop signs. While a majority of the population supports mandatory motorcycle helmet laws and automated traffic enforcement, and these measures are demonstrably effective in reducing deaths, these measures provoke opposition from a smaller but vociferous portion of the population.

INTRODUCTION

In 2017, 37,133 Americans were killed in crashes involving motor vehicles. Motor vehicle crashes are a leading cause of death for Americans overall, and the number one cause of death for teenagers. Millions of people are injured in crashes annually, and motor vehicle crashes are estimated to have cost some $242 billion in 2010 in lost productivity, medical costs, legal costs, property damage, and time lost in congestion caused by crashes.[1] As measured by the number of deaths per mile people are driving, the rate at which people are killed in traffic crashes declined significantly from 1929, when records began to be kept, until 2014, but has risen by almost 10% between 2014 and 2016. Although preliminary figures indicate the fatality rate declined slightly in 2017 (from 1.19 to 1.16),[2] that is still higher than at any time since 2008.

Congress has played a role in improving highway safety. Making road travel safer was one of the responsibilities Congress gave to the federal Department of Transportation

---

[1] National Highway Traffic Safety Administration, *The Economic and Societal Impact Of Motor Vehicle Crashes, 2010 (Revised)*, DOT HS 812 013, May 2015 (Revised).
[2] NHTSA, *Traffic Safety Facts Research Note: 2017 Fatal Motor Vehicle Crashes: Overview*, DOT HS 812 603, October 2018.

(DOT) when it created the department in 1966. Congress has directed DOT to improve the safety of automobile design and of road design, as well as to support programs to improve driver behavior.

An oft-cited statistic in traffic safety is that as many as 90% of road deaths are due at least in part to driver error or misbehavior (such as driving too fast for conditions or driving while drunk or distracted).[3] Driver behavior is a state, not federal, matter, as it does not involve interstate commerce (save for commercial truck drivers); lacking direct authority over driver behavior, Congress has attempted to address it by encouraging states to pass laws to promote safer driving.

The role of driver behavior versus vehicle design, road design, and traffic management in improving highway safety is a subject of debate. Some analysts note that road designs and traffic management arrangements often allow, or even encourage, driver error and misbehavior, and so play a larger role in crashes than is often recognized. Responsibility for promoting safety through improved road design is exercised by the Federal Highway Administration; one of the core highway capital improvement programs authorized by Congress is intended to fund safety improvements to highway infrastructure.

This report focuses primarily on the driver behavior aspect of highway safety. Within the DOT, the National Highway Traffic Safety Administration (NHTSA) administers programs that address general driver behavior, and the Federal Motor Carrier Safety Administration (FMCSA) administers programs that address the behavior of commercial truck drivers.

TRAFFIC SAFETY TRENDS

There are several ways to measure traffic safety. Measures include the number of highway fatalities; the number of serious injuries from crashes; the economic loss to people involved in crashes; and the social cost of emergency response and accident-induced traffic delays. To understand these numbers in context, other measures are often applied to produce rates such as number of events (e.g., accidents, injuries, fatalities) per million miles traveled, per million registered drivers, and per million persons in the total population. Similar measures can reveal trends for narrower categories such as vehicle occupants and bicyclists, though the information necessary to produce rates is not always available for narrower categories.

The quality of data is critical to analysis, but changes in data collection methods may result in data that are not comparable to previously collected data. In 2011 the U.S.

---

[3] NHTSA, *Tri-Level Study of the Causes of Traffic Accidents*, DOT HS 805 099, May 1979; NHTSA, *Traffic Safety Facts Crash-Stats: Critical Reasons for Crashes Investigated in the National Motor Vehicle Crash Causation Survey*, DOT HS 812 115, February 2015.

Department of Transportation (DOT) revised the methodology for collecting registration information and vehicle miles traveled by vehicle type. This revision was applied to data from 2007 onwards. In some cases, the revised numbers are significantly different from those for 2006 and previous years.[4] Thus, when examining trend data for specific vehicle types, a break in the trend line may be shown between 2006 and 2007, or trend data may begin at 2007.

The fatality rate per 100 million vehicle miles traveled (VMT) is the most commonly cited measure of traffic safety, due in part to the seriousness of that outcome and in part to the fact that fatalities are closely tracked and unambiguous. Every crash involving a fatality is supposed to be investigated and clearly identified as a vehicle-related incident. In contrast, crashes involving injuries or property damage may be reported inconsistently by local public safety agencies or may not come to the attention of authorities; reported data on the numbers of serious crashes and of crashes involving injuries are estimated based on sampling.

U.S. Fatality Rate Trending Downward Over Time, But Rising Recently

The fatality rate has improved significantly since detailed statistics began to be kept in 1966, dropping from around 5.5 deaths per 100 million VMT to around 1.1 in 2011 (see Figure 1). Since 2014, however, the fatality rate has risen from 1.08 to 1.18, a 9% increase (see Figure 2).[5] As noted by some economists, there have been four periods of abrupt declines in the fatality rate since 1970, all of which coincided with recessions; in each instance, the decline was followed by a period of little improvement or even an increase in the fatality rate as the economy emerged from recession, before the fatality rate resumed its downward trend.[6]

The number of people killed in traffic-related crashes dropped from a high of around 55,000 in 1972 to around 33,000 per year in the 2009-2014 period, against a background of increases in both number of drivers and vehicle miles traveled (see Table 1). From 2014 to 2016, however, the number of fatalities rose 14%, from 32,744 in 2014 to 37,461 in 2016. Preliminary figures for 2017 indicate a decline in fatalities to 37,133 (a decrease of less than 1% from the original 2016 number), the fatality rate also declined to 1.16.[7]

---

[4] For example, the estimated vehicle miles traveled (VMT) for motorcycles went from 12 billion in 2006 to 21 billion in 2007, the first year of the new methodology. VMT is the denominator for one of the most widely cited rates, fatalities per VMT, and greatly increasing the estimated VMT number significantly reduces the fatality rate, which accordingly dropped from 40 per 100 million VMT in 2006 to 24 in 2007. The number of motorcyclist fatalities comes from a different source, police-reported fatal crashes, and the fatality trend was relatively stable. Such a significant drop in the fatality rate is likely to be largely a result of the changed methodology, rendering a trend analysis spanning both periods unreliable.

[5] The preliminary estimate for 2017 is 1.16, but the figure for 2016 was revised upward to 1.19; NHTSA, *Traffic Safety Facts Research Note: 2017 Fatal Motor Vehicle Crashes: Overview*, DOT HS 812 603, October 2018.

[6] Monica M. He, "Driving Through the Great Recession: Why Does Motor Vehicle Fatality Decrease When the Economy Slows Down?" *Social Science & Medicine*, v. 155, April 2016, pp. 1-11. The author notes that the unemployment rate is the primary explanatory variable.

[7] NHTSA, *Traffic Safety Facts Research Note: 2017 Fatal Motor Vehicle Crashes: Overview*, DOT HS 812 603, October 2018. This report also revised upward the number of fatalities and the fatality rate from what was

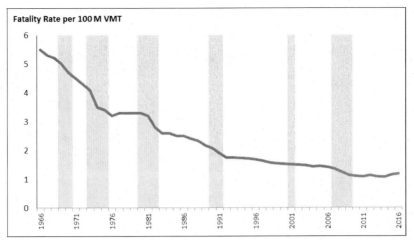

Source: CRS, based on data from National Highway Traffic Safety Administration (NHTSA), *Traffic Safety Facts 2016*, DOT HS 812 554, Table 2.

Notes: Shaded columns are recessions as determined by the National Bureau of Economic Research, US Business Cycle Expansions and Contractions, http://www.nber.org/cycles.html.

Figure 1. U.S. Highway Fatality Rate, 1966-2016. Fatality Rate per 100 million vehicles miles travelled.

Table 1. Traffic Deaths, Licensed Drivers, and Vehicle Miles Traveled, 1972 and 2016

	1972	2016
Traffic deaths	54,589	37,461
Licensed drivers	118 million	222 million
Vehicle miles traveled (VMT)	1.26 trillion	3.2 trillion
Deaths per million licensed drivers	461	169
Deaths per 100 million VMT	4.33	1.18

Source: CRS; data from NHTSA, *Traffic Safety Facts 2016*, DOT HS 812 554, Table 2.

Other highway safety indicators also have deteriorated in recent years. The rate of crashes was higher in 2015 than in 2007 (Figure 3).

Highway safety rates and trends vary by state. Fatality rates tend to be lower in more urbanized states (for example, in 2016 the fatality rate per 100 million VMT in South Carolina, 1.86, was three times that of Massachusetts, at 0.63). In addition, some states have relatively strict laws concerning safety matters, such as enforcement of mandatory seat belt use and requirements that motorcyclists wear helmets, while other states have fewer or less strict safety laws or enforce such laws less vigorously.

---

reported in NHTSA's 2016 edition of the annual *Traffic Safety Facts* report, making the 2017 decline larger (almost 2%) than it is when compared to the original 2016 numbers.

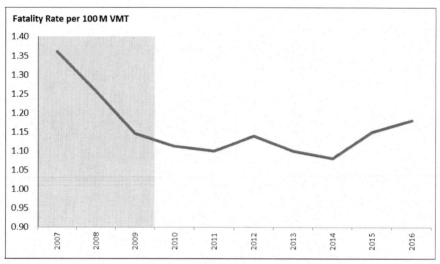

Source: CRS, based on data from National Highway Traffic Safety Administration (NHTSA), *Traffic Safety Facts 2016*, DOT HS 812 554, Table 2.

Notes: The shading for the years 2007-2009 represents the recession as determined by the National Bureau of Economic Research, US Business Cycle Expansions and Contractions, http://www.nber.org/cycles.html.

Figure 2. Fatality Rate per 100 Million Vehicle Miles Traveled, 2007-2016.

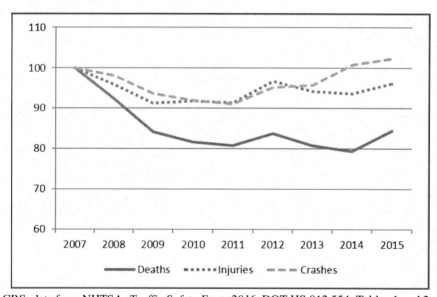

Source: CRS; data from NHTSA, *Traffic Safety Facts 2016*, DOT HS 812 554, Tables 1 and 2.

Notes: Injury estimates are produced on a different timetable than fatality counts; 2016 injury data was not available at the time of the publication of the source, The rates are indexed to their 2007 level for ease of visual comparison. The actual rates for injuries and crashes per 100 million VMT are many times larger than the fatality rate: in 2015, the fatality rate per 100 million VMT was 1.15, the injury rate was 79, and the serious crash rate was 203 (calculated by CRS).

Figure 3. Trends in Rates for Crashes, Injuries, and Deaths, 2007-2015. Index, 2007=100; Incidents per 100 million VMT.

U.S. Fatality Rate Now Higher Than Some Other Wealthy Countries

As Figure 4 shows, certain selected countries have significantly improved their safety performance (as measured in fatalities per billion vehicle-kilometers traveled) since 2000, dropping below the U.S. fatality rate for the first time. Significantly, they continued to show improvement after 2010, when, like the United States, they experienced economic growth after the recession of the late 2000s. This is significant because during periods of economic growth following recessions, road safety in the United States has often gotten worse (as it has done in the past few years) before returning to the long-term trend of improvement. The example of the other countries in Figure 4 shows that experiencing worsening safety figures coming out of a recession may be preventable.

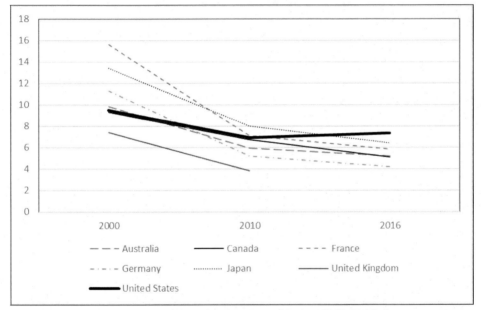

Source: International Transport Forum, *Road Safety Annual Report 2018*, Table 3.
Notes: 2016 data for UK not included in source.

Figure 4. Fatalities per Billion Vehicle-Km, Selected Countries.

Motorcycle Fatality Rates Remain Steady

The fatal crash rates for passenger cars, light trucks, and large trucks have fallen steadily since the 1980s. The same is not true for motorcycles. The fatal crash rate for motorcycles doubled between 1997 and 2005, then fell sharply in 2006. Between 2007 and 2016, there was no further improvement. The motorcycle fatal crash rate in 2016 was higher than in 2007, while the crash rates for other types of vehicles were at or below their 2007 rate (see Figure 5).

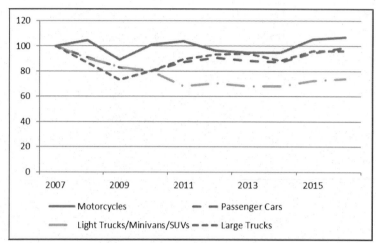

Source: CRS; data from NHTSA, *Traffic Safety Facts 2016*, DOT HS 812 554, Table 3.

Notes: VMT data collection for passenger vehicles and light trucks changed in 2010, and data were recalculated beginning with 2007; this change had the effect of reducing the VMT of passenger vehicles (thus slightly increasing their fatality rate) and increasing the VMT of light trucks (thus slightly decreasing their fatality rate). The data-collection change greatly altered the motorcycle data. This chart thus omits data before 2007. The index of rates given in this figure are based on the number of vehicles involved in crashes relative to their 2007 level, not to the number of individuals involved; in the case of a multivehicle crash, more than one vehicle may be included in the count. Passenger cars are vehicles such as convertibles, sedans, and station wagons; light trucks/minivans/SUVs are trucks under 10,000 pounds, including pickups, vans, truck-based station wagons, and utility vehicles; and large trucks are trucks over 10,000 pounds.

Figure 5. Trends in Fatal Crash Rates by Vehicle Type, 2007-2016. Index, 2007=100.

Motorcyclists are somewhat more likely to be involved in a crash than other drivers on a per vehicle-mile-traveled basis.[8] However, a motorcyclist is much more likely to die as a result of a crash than is a driver of a car or light truck; in 2016 the likelihood of a motorcyclist dying in a crash was more than 27 times that of a passenger car occupant. Figure 6 compares the fatality rate for occupants of motorcycles and passenger cars.

The causes of the recent trend in the motorcycle fatality rate—dropping during the recession, then rising again since 2014 (see Figure 7)—are not clear. Motorcycle registrations increased during this period even as the fatality rate declined immediately after the recession. The median age of motorcyclists has increased from 41 in 2003[9] to 50 in 2018[10]—a change that would be expected to reduce fatality rates, as older drivers are

---

[8] The total crash rate per VMT for motorcycles is estimated to be about 28% higher than for passenger cars. Calculations by CRS based on data from NHTSA, *Traffic Safety Facts 2013*, DOT HS 812139, Table 3, except passenger car VMT from Table 7 and motorcycle VMT from Table 10.

[9] Bureau of Transportation Statistics, U.S. Department of Transportation, *Special Report: Motorcycle Trends in the United States*, SR-014, May 2009.

[10] Kate Murphy, Motorcycle Industry Council's 2018 Stats: Who Are We? RideApart.com, February 6, 2019, https://www.rideapart.com/articles/304226/mic-2018-stats-who-are-we/. The Motorcycle Industry Council's

generally less likely to be involved in crashes than younger ones—but the proportion of motorcyclists over 50 dying in crashes has exceeded the proportion of those under 30 every year since 2009.[11] The proportion of fatally injured motorcycle operators who were riding bikes with an engine size greater than 1,400 cubic centimeters has risen from 1% in the mid-1990s to around 30% today, suggesting that the combination of older riders and larger, heavier bikes may be a factor in rising fatality rates.[12]

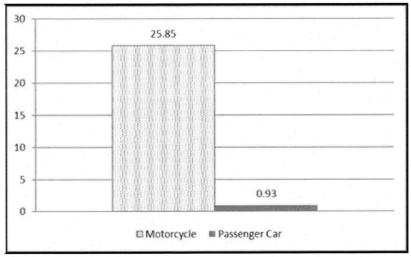

Source: CRS; data from NHTSA, *Traffic Safety Facts 2016 Data: Motorcycles*, DOT HS 812 492, June 2018, Table 2.

Figure 6. Fatality Rate for Motorcycle and Passenger Car Occupants, 2016. Rate per 100 million V.

One factor that appears to be important in motorcycle deaths is alcohol. While 24% of passenger car drivers involved in fatal crashes in 2016 had alcohol in their system,[13] the figure for motorcyclists was 32% (though this was down from 42% in 1995).[14] Another risk factor is wearing, or not wearing, helmets: 39% of motorcyclists (and 55% of motorcycle passengers) killed in crashes were not wearing helmets.[15] Nineteen states, the District of Columbia, and three territories require all motorcyclists to wear helmets (a requirement often referred to as a "universal helmet law"); most other states require

---

annual survey is the source of the age data in the BTS Special Report: Motorcycle Trends in the United States cited at #2.

[11] In 1975, 80% of motorcyclists dying in crashes were under 30, and 3% were over 50; in 2017 28% were under 30 and 36% were over 50. Insurance Institute for Highway Safety, *Fatality Facts: Motorcycles*, "Percentage of motorcyclist deaths by age, 1975-2017," https://www.iihs.org/topics/fatality-statistics/detail/motorcycles-and-atvs.

[12] The role of engine size as a risk factor is contested, with some analysts contending that the power-to-weight ratio of a motorcycle is a greater risk factor.

[13] That is, a blood alcohol content of .01% or more.

[14] National Highway Traffic Safety Administration, *Traffic Safety Facts 2016*, DOT HS 812 554, Table 17.

[15] Ibid., Table 92.

helmets only for motorcyclists under age 18, and three (Illinois, Iowa, and New Hampshire) have no helmet requirement.[16]

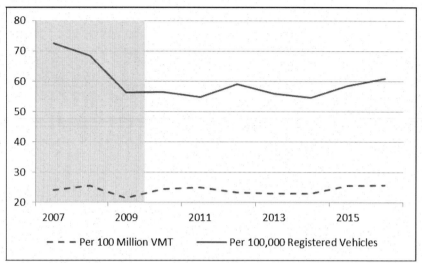

Source: CRS; data from NHTSA, *Traffic Safety Facts 2016*, DOT HS 812 554, Table 3.

Notes: The shading for the years 2007-2009 represents the recession as determined by the National Bureau of Economic Research, US Business Cycle Expansions and Contractions, http://www.nber.org/cycles.html.

Figure 7. Motorcyclist Fatality Rates, 2007-2016. Rate per 100 million VMT.

Large Trucks and Highway Safety

Large trucks—vehicles with a gross vehicle weight rating greater than 10,000 pounds— represented only around 4% of registered vehicles in 2016. But the average large truck is driven far more than the average passenger vehicle, and large trucks are involved in crashes at a rate proportionate to the distance they are driven rather than their proportion of vehicles on the road. Large trucks accounted for 9% of total vehicle miles traveled in 2016 and represented 9% of vehicles involved in fatal crashes.[17] The crash involvement rate of large trucks, like that of most other types of vehicles, has fallen significantly since 1988, but has risen significantly since the end of the Great Recession (see Figure 8).

---

[16] Governors Highway Safety Association, "State Laws: Motorcyclists," https://www.ghsa.org/ state-laws/issues/motorcyclists.

[17] National Highway Traffic Safety Administration, *Traffic Safety Facts: Overview, 2017 Data: Large Trucks*, DOT HS 812 663, January 2019, p. 2, https://crashstats.nhtsa.dot.gov/ Api/Public/ViewPublication/812663.

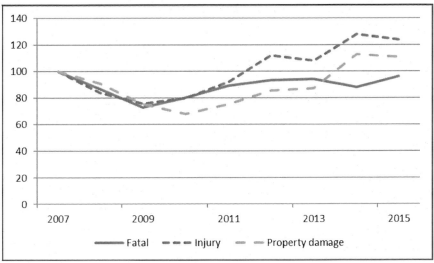

Source: CRS; data from NHTSA, *Traffic Safety Facts 2016*, DOT HS 812 554, Table 3.

Figure 8. Large-Truck Crash Involvement Rate Trend by Type of Crash, 2007-2015. Index, 2007=100.

Table 2. Share of VMT on Interstate Highways by Selected Vehicle Type, 2017

In billions of VMT			
Vehicle Type	**Total VMT**	**Interstate VMT**	**% of VMT on Interstate**
All light-duty vehicles	2,877	688	24%
Single-unit trucks	116	28	24%
Combination trucks	181	95	52%

Source: CRS; data from Federal Highway Administration, *Highway Statistics 2017*, Table VM-1.

Note: "Light-duty vehicles" are passenger cars, light trucks (curb weight under 6,000 pounds), vans and sport utility vehicles.

Large trucks can be divided into two groups: single-unit trucks and combination trucks such as "semi" tractor-trailers. Only around 25% of all large trucks are combination trucks, but these account for 61% of total truck mileage. Combination trucks experience 1.7 fatal crashes per 100 million VMT, compared to 1.1 for single-unit trucks.[18] This is noteworthy, since drivers of combination trucks do most of their driving on the Interstate System (see Table 2), on which crash and fatality rates are far lower than on the local roads on which most single-unit truck mileage is logged.[19]

---

[18] National Highway Traffic Safety Administration, *Large Truck and Bus Crash Facts 2013*, FMCSA-RRA-15-004, April 2015, Figure 7.

[19] A DOT study found that large combination vehicles (combination trucks that are longer or heavier than the standard "semi" tractor-trailer) generally have higher crash rates than standard combination trucks. But the analysis was constrained by data limitations, as most state crash reports do not record a truck's weight or configuration. DOT concluded that nationally representative estimates could not be developed from the available data. U.S. Department of Transportation, *Comprehensive Truck Size and Weight Limits Study: Highway Safety and Truck Crash Comparative Analysis Technical Report*, June 2015.

Fatal large truck crashes often involve multiple vehicles. Over 90% of the persons killed in such crashes (72% of people killed in all types of large truck crashes) are occupants of the other vehicle(s) rather than occupants of large trucks (see Table 3 and Figure 9).

Table 3. People Killed in Crashes Involving Large Trucks, 2017

	Number	Percentage of Total
Occupants of large trucks	841	18%
In single-vehicle crashes	*498*	*10%*
In multiple-vehicle crashes	*343*	*7%*
Occupants of other vehicles in crashes involving large trucks	3,450	72%
Nonoccupants (pedestrians, bicyclists, etc.)	470	10%
Total	**4,761**	**100%**

Source: NHTSA, *Traffic Safety Facts: Large Trucks, 2017 Data*, DOT HS 812 663, January 2019, Table 1.

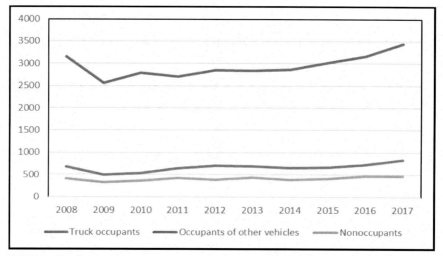

Source: NHTSA, *Traffic Safety Facts: Large Trucks, 2017 Data*, DOT HS 812 663, January 2019, Table 1.

Figure 9. Persons Killed in Large Truck Crashes, 2008-2017.

Driver intoxication is far less frequent in large truck crashes than in crashes involving passenger vehicles; 3% of large-truck drivers involved in fatal crashes had a blood alcohol concentration (BAC) of .08 or higher, above the standard for driving under the influence of alcohol in most states, compared to 21% for passenger car drivers.[20] Of greater concern with respect to drivers of large trucks is fatigue. A 2006 study identified

---

[20] NHTSA, *Traffic Safety Facts: Large Trucks, 2017 Data*, DOT HS 812 663, January 2019, p. 5.

fatigue as a contributing factor in 8% of crashes involving commercial drivers.[21] Where the average noncommercial driver might drive for a couple of hours, divided into two or more periods, on a typical day, a commercial driver might spend up to 12 hours driving. One survey of commercial drivers found that 25% reported having fallen asleep while driving at least once during the previous year.[22] However, fatigue is not a risk confined to commercial drivers with fatigue identified as a contributing factor in 15% of crashes involving passenger vehicle drivers.[23]

In 2018, a congressional mandate took effect requiring that most commercial trucks be equipped with electronic logging devices (ELDs). The purpose was to reduce fatigued driving among commercial drivers through better enforcement of federal hours of service limits. Previously, truckers had been allowed to fill out their time logs by hand, and it was an open secret that drivers often falsified their logs to make it appear that they were complying with the hours of service time limits when they were in fact driving more hours than permitted. The Federal Motor Carrier Safety Administration (FMCSA) estimated that the mandate would prevent 1,844 crashes each year and save 26 lives each year.[24] Data for large truck crash involvement and vehicle miles traveled in 2019 are not yet available to see if these benefits were realized. Other factors, such as variations in large truck VMT, weather conditions, and random variations in crashes from year to year, may obscure the safety effectiveness of ELDs.

Commercial drivers and vehicles are subject to random roadside inspections by law enforcement personnel checking for compliance with federal and state regulations. Each year safety officials sponsor "Roadcheck," a three-day event where roadside inspectors from across North America perform truck and bus roadside inspections of commercial vehicles. The dates the Roadcheck will be conducted are announced months in advance, so while the inspections during that period are still random, drivers and trucking companies could be aware of a heightened possibility of being inspected and prepare. During the 2018 Roadcheck, roughly 68,000 vehicles and their drivers were inspected; 4% of the drivers and 22% of the vehicles were found to have violations so serious that they were placed out of service. The most common cause of out-of-service orders for drivers was violations of hours-of-service regulations; for vehicles, it was brake problems.[25]

---

[21] Federal Motor Carrier Safety Administration, *Large Truck Crash Causation Study: Report to Congress*, 2006, Table 10, https://www.fmcsa.dot.gov/safety/research-and-analysis/report-congress-large-truck-crash-causation-study.

[22] Anne T. McCartt et al., "Factors Associated with Falling Asleep at the Wheel Among Long-Distance Truck Drivers," *Accident Analysis and Prevention*, Vol. 32, no. 4 (July 2000), pp. 493-504.

[23] Federal Motor Carrier Safety Administration, *Large Truck Crash Causation Study: Report to Congress*, 2006, Table 10, https://www.fmcsa.dot.gov/safety/research-and-analysis/report-congress-large-truck-crash-causation-study.

[24] Federal Motor Carrier Safety Administration, Electronic Logging Devices and Hours of Service Supporting Documents; Final Rule, 80 Fed. Reg. 78292 (December 16, 2015).

[25] Commercial Vehicle Safety Alliance, *CVSA Releases 2018 International Roadcheck Results*, September 12, 2018, https://cvsa.org/news-entry/2018-roadcheck-results/.

Some portions of the trucking industry, including the American Trucking Association, a group representing large trucking companies, has long asserted that there is a shortage of commercial drivers, and have asked Congress to lower the minimum age at which drivers are allowed to operate in interstate commerce from 21 to 18 in order to increase the pool of eligible drivers. Other portions of the industry, including the Owner-Operator Independent Driver Association, a group representing drivers who own their own vehicles, assert that any shortage is a result of low pay and difficult working conditions offered by the trucking companies, and that the appropriate solution is not to lower the minimum age for commercial drivers but to make the job more attractive. The industry has sought to lower the minimum age of commercial drivers for many decades, but studies consistently show that young commercial drivers, like young drivers overall, are much more likely to be involved in crashes than their older counterparts.[26] In the Fixing America's Surface Transportation Act (FAST Act, P.L. 114-94), the surface transportation reauthorization enacted in 2015, Congress authorized a pilot program to allow veterans under age 21 who were trained as heavy truck drivers in the military to work as commercial drivers in interstate commerce.

Pedestrians and Bicyclists

Miles-traveled exposure data are not available for pedestrians, so pedestrian fatality rates are typically reported as a proportion of the total population. The pedestrian fatality rate fell by more than half between 1975 (7,516 pedestrians were killed, a rate of 4 per 100,000 population) and 2013 (4,735 pedestrians were killed, a rate of 1.5 per 100,000 population).[27] How much of this reduction is due to safety measures (such as additional sidewalks, pavement markings, and lower speed limits) and how much to a reduction in exposure (as the proportions of workers walking to their workplaces and students walking to school have declined)[28] is not known; in 2016, the rate rose to 1.85 killed per 100,000 population (a total of 5,987).[29] In 2016, 5% of pedestrians killed were children under the age of 16.[30]

Consistent miles traveled exposure data is not available for bicyclists, and highway safety organizations, including DOT's National Highway Traffic Safety Administration

---

[26] Janine Duke, Maya Guest, May Boggess, "Age-related safety in professional heavy vehicle drivers: A literature review," *Accident Analysis & Prevention*, Vol. 42, No.2, March 2010, pp. 364-371.

[27] 1975 rate: U.S. Center for Disease Control and Prevention, "Achievements in Public Health, 1900-1999 Motor Vehicle Safety: A 20th Century Public Health Achievement," *Morbidity and Mortality Weekly Report*, vol. 48, no. 18 (May 14, 1999), pp. 369-374, http://www.cdc.gov/mmwr/preview/mmwrhtml/mm4818a1.htm. May 14, 1999; 2013 rate: National Highway Traffic Safety Administration, *Traffic Safety Facts 2013*, DOT HS 812139, Table 97.

[28] Noreen C. McDonald, "Active Transportation to School: Trends Among U.S. Schoolchildren, 1969–2001," *American Journal of Preventive Medicine*, v. 32 no. 6, June 2007, pp. 509-516.

[29] National Highway Traffic Safety Administration, *Traffic Safety Facts 2016*, DOT HS 812 554, Table 97.

[30] Ibid., calculation by CRS.

(NHTSA), tend to report the number of bicyclist fatalities rather than calculating a rate based on population.[31] The number of bicyclists killed in traffic crashes has generally declined since 1975, and has risen following the Great Recession. Data indicate that 722 cyclists were killed in 2004 (0.25 per 100,000 population), 628 in 2009 (0.20), and 840 in 2016 (0.26).[32] The recent increase may simply be tracking the general increase in vehicle-related crashes and fatalities following the 2007-2009 recession, but it may also be related to increased bicycle usage. Although there are no reliable data on bicycle VMT, the proportion of American workers who bicycle to work rose from 0.4% in 2000 to 0.6% in the 2008-2012 period.[33]

The average age of bicyclists killed in crashes increased from 24 in 1988 to 44 in 2013. At least three in five bicyclists killed in crashes were not wearing helmets. Intoxication is a factor in both pedestrian and bicyclist fatalities; one-third of pedestrians 14 and older[34] and 11% of bicyclists killed in 2016 were legally intoxicated.[35]

SOCIAL FACTORS THAT AFFECT ROAD SAFETY TRENDS

Government policies influence highway safety in important ways. However, some of the change in accident and fatality rates over the past several decades is attributable to factors beyond the scope of federal highway safety policies.

Declining Share of Young Drivers

The risk of a crash is not uniform for all drivers. Drivers under age 25 have significantly higher crash rates and rates of involvement in fatal crashes than drivers 25 or over, and young male drivers have the highest rates of any age group (see Table 4).

In 1975 the proportion of male licensed drivers under 25—those with the highest rate of crashes—peaked at 13%, with 15.8 million males in that cohort. Since then the number has fallen has fallen by nearly 2.4 million, representing 6% of all licensed drivers in

---

[31] This may reflect differences in the extent of walking and bicycling. According to the National Household Travel Survey, in 2009 10.5% of all trips were done by walking, while 1.0% of all trips were done by bicycling. It is likely that the proportion of the population that ever bikes is much smaller than the proportion that ever walks. John Pucher et al., "Walking and Cycling in the United States, 2001-2009: Evidence from the National Household Travel Surveys," *American Journal of Public Health*, v. 101 (July 2011). http://bloustein.rutgers.edu/wp-content/uploads/2014/10/ NHTS_TRB_25Jan2011.pdf.

[32] National Highway Traffic Safety Administration, *Traffic Safety Facts* annual report for 2004, 2009, and 2016, Table 102.

[33] Brian McKenzie, "Modes Less Traveled—Bicycling and Walking to Work in the United States: 2008-2012," Washington, DC: U.S. Census Bureau, May 2014, http://www.census.gov/hhes/commuting/files/2014/acs-25.pdf, p. 3.

[34] National Highway Traffic Safety Administration, *Traffic Safety Facts 2016*, DOT HS 812 554, Table 20.

[35] Ibid, Table 77.

2017.[36] The spread of stricter licensing requirements for the youngest drivers plays some role in this decline, but so do economic factors and personal preferences that lead young people to obtain driver's licenses at later ages or to drive less frequently. The impact of these factors on reducing the number and proportion of the highest risk drivers has likely improved highway safety statistics.

Smaller Share of Drivers in Rural Areas

The proportion of the U.S. population that lives in rural areas declined by seven percentage points, from 26.4% to 19.3%, between 1970 and 2010.[37] Drivers in rural areas have higher fatality rates per 100 million VMT than drivers in urban areas, so a reduction in the proportion of VMT by rural drivers would tend to lower the overall fatality rate. However, some part of the decline in the proportion of rural dwellers resulted not from people relocating to urban areas but from rural areas being reclassified as part of urban areas due to economic and demographic changes,[38] so the smaller proportion of drivers in rural areas may have little impact on overall safety trends.

Increasing Share of Travel on Interstate Highways

Interstate System highways are among the safest roads in the nation due to design characteristics that eliminate intersections and separate opposing lanes by a median or barrier. In 1975, the proportion of all VMT that took place on Interstate highways was 17%; in 2017, it was 26%.[39] All else being equal, the greater share of driving occurring on Interstate highways would be expected to lead to lower accident and fatality rates.

Fuel Prices

Generally, as fuel prices rise, people respond by driving less. This leads to a smaller number of fatalities, but the effect of fuel price changes on the fatality rate is small. One study estimated that a 10% decrease in the price of gasoline is associated with a 1.6%

---

[36] Calculated by CRS using data from FHWA, *Highway Statistics 2017*, Table DL220, Licensed drivers by sex and age group, 1963-2017, https://www.fhwa.dot.gov/ policyinformation/statistics/2017/.

[37] "Urban Percentage of the Population for States, Historical," Iowa State University, http://www.icip.iastate.edu/tables/ population/urban-pct-states.

[38] United States Department of Agriculture, Economic Research Service, Rural America at a Glance, 2017 Edition, Economic Information Bulletin 182, November 2017, https://www.ers.usda.gov/webdocs/publications/85740/eib-12.pdf.

[39] Calculated by CRS; data from Federal Highway Administration, *Highway Statistics* series, various years, Table VM-1: Annual Vehicle Distance Traveled in Miles and Related Data.

increase in fatal crashes.[40] However, another study found that higher fuel prices lead some drivers to shift from cars to motorcycles, leading to an increase in motorcycle VMT, which in turn is associated with a higher fatality rate.[41]

Table 4. Driver Involvement Rates in Fatal Crashes by Age and Sex, 2016

Rate per 100,000 registered drivers in age-group		
Age	Rate	
	Male	Female
16-20	50.24	22.81
20-24	52.68	19.29
All Drivers	34.28	11.84

Source: Adapted from NHTSA, *Traffic Safety Facts 2016*, DOT HS 812 554, Table 62.

Economic Recessions

Periods of economic recession are associated with declines in traffic crashes, injuries, and deaths. VMT also tends to decline in recessions, but the proportional reductions in deaths, injuries, and serious crashes are much greater than the reduction in VMT (see Table 5). Similarly, as the economy emerges from recessions, crashes, injuries, and deaths from vehicle accidents increase at greater rates than the increase in VMT. Studies of the possible causes for the sharp decline in fatalities during recessions find that rising unemployment is associated with reductions in both vehicle miles traveled and the number of crashes per 100 million VMT.[42] The decline in fatal crashes per 100 million VMT during recessions is associated with a decline in fatal crashes involving a drunk driver.[43]

In the late 2000s, the general long-term downward trend in U.S. traffic deaths was punctuated by two consecutive years (2008-2009) of dramatic year-over-year decreases coinciding with the period of the Great Recession and resulting in the lowest fatality rate recorded to that point. The Secretary of Transportation cited the improvement as

---

[40] David C. Grabowski and Michael A. Morrisey, "Gasoline Prices and Motor Vehicle Fatalities," *Journal of Policy Analysis and Management*, Vol. 23, No. 3 (Summer 2004), pp. 575-593.

[41] He Zhu et al., "Rising Gasoline Prices Increase New Motorcycle Sales and Fatalities," *Injury Epidemiology*, vol. 2 (2015), p. 23. The authors estimated that a $1 per gallon increase in gasoline prices would result in the purchase of 295,000 new motorcycles and lead to 233 additional motorcycle deaths annually.

[42] Christopher J. Ruhm, "Are Recessions Good For Your Health?" National Bureau of Economic Research, Working Paper 5570, May 1996. Ruhm found that a 1% increase in a state's unemployment rate was associated with a 2.4% reduction in motor vehicle crash fatalities; he attributed the effect to changes in alcohol consumption and distances driven during recessions.

[43] Chad Cotti and Nathan Tefft, "Decomposing the Relationship between Macroeconomic Conditions and Fatal Car Crashes during the Great Recession: Alcohol- and Non-Alcohol-Related Accidents," *B.E. Journal of Economic Analysis & Policy*, vol. 11, no. 1 (2011), p. 5, http://www.degruyter.com/view/j/bejeap.2011.11.issue-1/ bejeap.2011.11.1.2860/bejeap.2011.11.1.2860.xml.

evidence that DOT's efforts to improve safety were succeeding.[44] The improvement stopped in 2010 and the traffic death and injury rates have risen since 2014. This may raise the question of the effectiveness of DOT safety efforts in the context of larger socio-economic changes. To date, researchers have not found definitive evidence that explains the recent increases in fatality and injury rates.

Table 5. Change in VMT, fatalities, and injuries during the great recession

Percentage change from previous year			
	VMT	Fatalities	Injuries
2008	-1.8%	-9.3%	-5.8%
2009	-0.7%	-9.5%	-5.5%

Source: CRS; data from NHTSA, *Traffic Safety Facts 2013*, DOT HS 812139, Tables 1 and 2.
Note: The "Great Recession" lasted from December 2007 to June 2009, according to the National Bureau of Economic Research.

THE IMPACT OF FEDERAL TRAFFIC SAFETY POLICIES

There are four basic tools available to government to improve traffic safety: engineering, education, enforcement, and emergency response. These tools may be used, in different ways, to achieve three traffic safety goals: reducing the number of crashes; reducing the severity of crashes; and improving medical care for people injured in crashes. As indicated in Table 6, each of these tools is better suited to achieving some goals than others.

Table 6. Categories of Traffic Safety Efforts and Their Effects

	Effect		
	Reduce Incidence of Crashes	Reduce Severity of Crashes	Improve Medical Care for Crash Victims
Engineering (both of vehicles and the roadway)	X	X	
Education of drivers	X		
Enforcement of traffic laws	X	X	
Emergency response			X

Source: CRS.

---

[44] U.S. Department of Transportation, "U.S. Transportation Secretary LaHood Announces Lowest Level Of Annual Traffic Fatalities In More Than Six Decades," http://www.nhtsa.gov/About+NHTSA/Press+Releases/2012/U.S.+Transportation+Secretary+LaHood+Announces+Lowest+Level+Of+Annual+Traffic+Fatalities+In+More+Than+ Six+Decades.

Federal policy efforts fall primarily into the categories of engineering and enforcement. Driver education and emergency response to traffic incidents are handled largely by state and local governments with little federal involvement or funding.

Federal involvement in education and enforcement of safe driving practices has come through funding for state activities. As behavior of passenger car drivers is largely under the authority of states, not of the federal government, Congress is not able to mandate driver behavior. Instead, it has had to rely on both carrots (incentive grants) and sticks (penalties that reduce federal transportation funding) to influence state governments to adopt and enforce traffic safety measures affecting driver behavior. In recent years, Congress has largely restricted itself to using incentives rather than penalties to influence state enforcement efforts.

Engineering

Federal involvement in engineering has proceeded by way of establishing standards for highway and vehicle designs and funding safety-related improvements in highway infrastructure.

Road Design

The way roads are designed has a significant impact on their safety. For example, as noted earlier, the Interstate Highway System, although it typically carries a high density of traffic at high speeds, has relatively few crashes thanks in large part to its design elements, including the absence of intersections and the physical separation of vehicles moving in opposite directions. Reconstructing roads to reduce crash risks can be as simple as adding traffic-calming features such as speed humps or as extensive as adding lanes for passing or turning. Since road design improvements have a continuing effect, in contrast to enforcement efforts, even relatively costly improvements may be cost-effective when considered in light of the number of drivers affected.

The vast majority of federal-aid highway funding is available for road design improvements. One of the core highway formula programs is the Highway Safety Improvement Program, which provides funding to eliminate hazardous road locations or features. In FY2019, the Highway Safety Improvement Program distributed $2.4 billion to the states.[45]

---

[45] Federal Highway Administration, *Notice: Revised Apportionment of Federal-Aid Highway Program Funds for Fiscal Year (FY) 2019*, Table 1, N 4510.831, December 6, 2018, https://www.fhwa.dot.gov/legsregs/directives/notices/ n4510831/n4510831_t1.cfm.

Improvements in Vehicle Design

The fact that injury and fatality rates have fallen much more steeply than crash rates since the mid-1990s suggests that changes in motor vehicle design have improved occupant protection, reducing the probability of a fatality in a serious crash.

The federal government has mandated vehicle safety improvements since 1966, when DOT required seat belts as standard equipment on all passenger vehicles beginning with the 1967 model year. Since then, NHTSA has mandated a number of other vehicle design standards to improve safety. These standards, published in NHTSA's Federal Motor Vehicle Safety Standards (FMVSS), require now-familiar equipment such as airbags, high-mount brake lights, antilock brakes, and electronic stability control. They also govern vehicle design in less obvious ways such as a regulation standardizing headlight placement. NHTSA spent $190 million to oversee motor vehicle design and engineering in FY2019, including defect investigations and recalls.[46]

Estimates of the safety impact of these standards vary, in part because a number of the safety standards were mandated beginning with model year 1967 vehicles, eight years before the establishment of the nationwide system for reporting fatal crashes. Another complication is that it is difficult to differentiate the effects of vehicle improvements from other factors that affect crash and fatality rates. For example, the introduction of safety belts was a significant safety improvement[47]—wearing a safety belt reduces the risk of injury in a crash by around 42%—but safety belts are effective only when worn, and increasing use of seat belts is not always correlated with significant reductions in crash fatalities.[48] One theory to explain this discrepancy is that the type of person who is more likely to wear a seat belt may also be the type of person who is less likely to engage in other risky driving behavior, such as speeding or driving while intoxicated.[49] The theory that vehicle safety improvements lead drivers to drive in a riskier manner—variously called the Peltzman effect, risk compensation, or risk homeostasis—does not appear to apply to seat belt use; studies have found little or no evidence that belted drivers are more likely to be involved in a crash.[50]

---

[46] The comparison of $190 million in federal spending on vehicle design versus $2.4 billion on safe road design understates the impact of federal vehicle regulations; much of the cost of investment in vehicle safety engineering as a result of federal mandates has been borne by automakers and their customers.

[47] Several researchers have suggested that safety belts may be the single most effective safety feature added to vehicles in the 20th century, and certainly the most cost-effective: Rune Elvik and Truls Vaa, *The Handbook of Road Safety Measures* (Oxford: Elsevier, 2004), pp. 615-616, 619-620.

[48] Ibid., pp. 614-615.

[49] Lenard Evans, *Traffic Safety* (Bloomfield, Mich: Science Serving Society, 2004), pp. 290-291, estimated, using crash data from 2002, that unbelted drivers had a crash risk 70% higher than belted drivers.

[50] Alma Cohen and Liran Einav, "The Effects of Mandatory Seat Belt Laws on Driving Behavior and Traffic Fatalities," *Review of Economics and Statistics*, vol. 84, no. 4 (November 2003), pp. 828-843. The Peltzman effect was described by Sam Peltzman, professor emeritus of economics at the University of Chicago.

Yet another complicating factor is that similar vehicle improvements might have become widespread even in the absence of federal standards. Early federal motor vehicle safety standards forced automakers to add equipment that the industry had been resisting, such as seat belts and airbags. More recently, perhaps influenced by the safety rating programs of NHTSA and other entities, automakers have been adding safety features beyond those required by federal standards, such as side-impact airbags, adaptive cruise control, and automatic braking.

Yet another complicating factor is that the safety impact of vehicle improvements is not simply cumulative. For example, by reducing the number of single-vehicle crashes, electronic stability control also reduces the safety impact of safety belts and air bags, which protect occupants from injury in the event of a crash. Thus the total safety impact of a combination of vehicle safety features may be much less than the sum of the impacts of each feature.[51]

NHTSA has estimated that vehicle safety technologies are responsible for roughly half of the reduction in the risk of death for vehicle occupants between 1960 and 2012, with "everything else," which includes social and demographic changes such as those previously discussed, improved road designs, efforts to make drivers drive more safely, and improvements in emergency medical response, accounting for the other half.[52]

The most effective of the initial safety improvements—such as collapsible steering columns that reduced injuries to drivers in head-on collisions, safety belts, and roof crush resistance standards—protected vehicle occupants from the effects of crashes. In recent years the availability of electronic sensors and controls enabled manufacturers to add features that can help to avoid crashes altogether. These include electronic stability control,[53] adaptive cruise control, automatic braking, and, on the horizon, the integration of these and other features to produce a self-driving car. In one study, researchers estimated that improvements made in passenger vehicles after the 2000 model year prevented 700,000 crashes, prevented or reduced the severity of injuries to 1 million vehicle occupants, and saved 2,000 lives in calendar year 2008.[54]

---

[51] Leonard Evans, *Traffic Safety*, pp. 114-115.
[52] C.J. Kahane, *Lives Saved by Vehicle Safety Technologies and Associated Federal Motor Vehicle Safety Standards, 1960 to 2012—Passenger Cars and LTVs—With Reviews of 26 FMVSS and the Effectiveness of Their Associated Safety Technologies in Reducing Fatalities, Injuries, and Crashes*, January 2015, DOT HS 812069, National Highway Traffic Safety Administration, p. xii. This analysis considers safety belts as a vehicle safety technology.
[53] Electronic stability control (ESC) became available on some popular vehicle models in 2000; it was phased in as a federal standard beginning with model year 2009 noncommercial vehicles: 55% of a manufacturer's model year 2009 vehicles had to have ESC, rising to 100% of model year 2012 noncommercial passenger vehicles.
[54] National Highway Traffic Safety Administration, *An Analysis of Recent Improvements to Vehicle Safety*, DOT HS 811572, June 2012, p. 1 (http://www-nrd.nhtsa.dot.gov/Pubs/811572.pdf).

Education and Training of Drivers

Educating and training road users seems an obvious way to improve their safety. But there is little evidence that education is effective in reducing crashes.[55] In large part this is because the vast majority of crashes are due to driver behaviors such as driving while intoxicated, driving too fast for conditions, and becoming distracted, and these are errors of judgment rather than of ignorance or lack of skill. Although motorcycle advocacy groups often call for more education of motorcyclists and of drivers as alternatives to mandatory helmet laws, there is no evidence that such efforts have an effect on motorcycle safety. Safety-related education is primarily the responsibility of state governments, and federal spending for this purpose is minimal.

Enforcement

The establishment and enforcement of rules governing road use, such as limiting speeds, prohibiting driving while intoxicated, and requiring the wearing of safety belts, is a proven method of improving road safety. However, these are areas over which Congress does not have authority with respect to drivers not engaged in interstate commerce; rather, they are under the control of the states. The federal government is directly involved in enforcement with respect to commercial vehicles that operate across state lines, though even in this case most of the enforcement is done by state law enforcement agencies. Federal spending on enforcement, through both NHTSA and the Federal Motor Carrier Safety Administration, which regulates truck and intercity bus safety, came to $1.3 billion in FY2019. Much of this went for grants to states to support their enforcement efforts. Congress has employed two approaches to influence states to act on traffic safety issues: penalties and incentives.

Encouraging State Enforcement—Penalties

Penalties have been of two types: the loss of a portion of a state's federal highway funding (a "strong" penalty), and the transfer of a portion of a state's highway funding to highway safety purposes (a "weak" penalty). Of these two approaches, the strong penalty appears to have been more effective in influencing state legislatures to act.

One example of a strong penalty law, adopted by Congress in 1966, provided that states that did not require motorcyclists to wear helmets within 10 years could lose a portion of their federal highway funds. In response, 48 states adopted such laws between

---

[55] Education has not proved effective in increasing rates of seat belt use or motorcycle helmet use; driver education programs have not been shown to reduce crashes, and, by enabling young drivers to get licenses sooner, may actually contribute to increasing the number of crashes. NHTSA, *Countermeasures That Work* (Ninth Edition, 2017), pp. 5-11, 6-3, 6-19 - 6-21, 7-10–7-13, 9-19.

1966 and 1975. After the threat of losing federal highway funding was removed in 1976, 27 states repealed those laws by 1979, illustrating the power of federal financial sanctions in overcoming state-level opposition.[56] Language in the FY2001 DOT appropriations act provided that states that did not make it illegal to drive with a blood alcohol content (BAC) of .08% or higher would lose a portion of their federal highway funding beginning in 2004.[57] At the time of enactment, 19 states had such laws; by the end of FY2004, every state had such a law (see Table 7).

Strong enforcement, however, can evoke resistance, which may lead to the enforcement effort being scaled back or eliminated. This has occurred at both the federal and state levels. For example, two of the four laws in Table 7 were repealed by later Congresses, and when Congress repealed the penalty for not mandating motorcycle helmets, many states then repealed the universal helmet law they had enacted in response to the prospect of that penalty.

Table 7. Highway Safety Laws Enforced with Loss of Highway Funding

Law	Year Adopted	Number of States Responding	Notes
Mandatory motorcycle helmet law	1966	47	Penalties would have taken effect in 1976; Congress repealed the law in 1975
National maximum speed limit	1973	50	Repealed in 1995
National minimum drinking age	1984	50	The act actually set a minimum age for purchasing or publicly possessing alcohol, not for drinking; 23 U.S.C. §158
National .08% blood alcohol content (BAC) per se law	2000	50	P.L. 106-346, §351; 23 U.S.C. §163

Source: CRS, based on information from the Governors Highway Safety Association and the United State Code.

The "weak" penalty—having a small portion of a state's federal highway funding transferred from other programs to highway safety activities—appears to have less influence on the actions of state legislatures. There are currently two transfer penalty statutes: one requires a state to have a law making it illegal for an occupant of a motor vehicle to have an open container of alcohol; the other requires a state to have a law requiring a repeat offender convicted of driving under the influence of alcohol (DUI) to use an ignition interlock device for one year or have his or her license suspended for at

---

[56] As of July 2019, 19 states had universal helmet laws.
[57] The penalty was 2% of federal highway funding in FY2004, increasing by 2% each year to a maximum of 8% in FY2007 and after, though states that adopted the .08% BAC limit by 2007 would get back all of the funds withheld in the previous years.

least one year. The penalty for a state not having such laws is that, in each case, the Federal Highway Administration will require that a small portion of the state's federal-aid highway funding be used for certain safety-related purposes;[58] there is no overall loss of federal highway funding. These two penalties have been in effect since FY2000.

Table 8. Number of States Complying with Federal Open Container and Repeat Offender Requirements, Selected Years FY1998-FY2016

States Complying with	1998 (Requirements Enacted)	FY2001 (First Transfers Applied)	FY2002 (Second Transfers Applied)	FY2003 (Third Transfers Applied)	FY2019 (Nineteenth Transfers Applied)
Open container requirement (§154)	14	31	35	37	39
Repeat offender requirements (§164)	5	24	28	33	34
Both requirements	3	19	23	25	27

Source: Adapted from General Accounting Office (now the Government Accountability Office), *Highway Safety: Better Guidance Could Improve Oversight of State Highway Safety Programs*, GAO-03-474, April 2003; 2019 data from Federal Highway Administration, "Apportionment of Federal-Aid Highway Program Funds for Fiscal Year (FY) 2019," Notice N 4510.831, December 6, 2018.

Notes: Table includes compliance status of all states and the District of Columbia. Both the Open Container and Repeat DUI Offender requirements were expanded beginning in FY2013, and the number of states penalized increased, though some then changed their laws in response and were no longer penalized in subsequent years. Several states that are penalized have open container and repeat offender laws, but those laws do not comply with federal requirements.

The transfer penalties appeared to have a significant impact initially; almost half the states changed their laws to comply with the federal requirements within the first three years that the transfers were applied (see Table 8). But in the succeeding 13 years, almost none of the remaining states have changed their laws to comply with the requirements. The Government Accountability Office (GAO) interviewed state safety officials in a handful of states about the impact of the transfer penalties; some felt that the penalties had been important in motivating their legislatures to enact laws complying with the federal requirement, but officials in New York State, which had complied with the open container requirement but not the repeat offender requirements, felt that the transfer penalty amount was too small to influence the state legislature.[59]

As of FY2019, 12 states were not in compliance with the requirement concerning open containers, and 17 states were not in compliance with the requirement regarding repeat DUI offenders (see Table 9). This suggests that the "transfer of funding" penalty is

---

[58] Currently, the penalty is 2.5% of the funding from two of the four core federal-aid highway programs; this amounts to roughly 2% of a state's total federal highway funding.

[59] Government Accountability Office, *Highway Safety: Better Guidance Could Improve Oversight of State Highway Safety Programs*, GAO-03-474, April 2003, p. 31. New York State is now in compliance with both requirements.

less effective at influencing state legislators than is the "loss of funding" penalty, although it is possible that the transfer of funding penalty would be more effective if the penalty amount were larger.

Table 9. States Subject to Federal Highway Funding Penalties for Noncompliance with Open Container and Repeat DUI Offender Requirements, FY2019

States subject to both penalties marked with asterisk		
State	**Open Container Penalty**	**Repeat DUI Offender Penalty**
Alaska*	X	X
California		X
Colorado		X
Connecticut	X	
Delaware	X	
Hawaii*	X	X
Indiana		X
Louisiana*	X	X
Maine	X	
Minnesota		X
Mississippi	X	
Missouri	X	
Montana		X
New Mexico		X
Ohio*	X	X
Oregon		X
Rhode Island		X
South Carolina		X
South Dakota		X
Tennessee	X	
Vermont		X
Virginia	X	
Washington		X
Wyoming*	X	X
Total	**12 states**	**17 states**

Source: Federal Highway Administration, "Apportionment of Federal-Aid Highway Program Funds for Fiscal Year (FY) 2019," Notice N 4510.831, December 6, 2018.

Notes: Both penalties began in FY2000. Both the Open Container and Repeat DUI Offender requirements were expanded beginning in FY2013, and the number of states penalized increased, though some then changed their laws and came back into compliance in subsequent years.

Congress has not adopted a new loss-of-funding penalty related to traffic safety since 2000.[60] This may reflect, in part, a growing deference to state discretion on the part of Congress in the area of traffic safety, though there is also evidence against that interpretation; Congress has, for example, taken away state discretion to use federal

---

[60] Congress has made changes to the two existing penalties—for open containers and repeat DUI offenders—since 2000.

highway funding to support automated traffic enforcement, forbidding states to use any of their federal highway funding for that purpose.[61]

Table 10. Number of States Qualifying to Receive NHTSA Safety Incentive Grants, by Program, FY2013, FY2015, and FY2018

Incentive Grant Program	Number of States Receiving Grants		
	FY2013	FY2015	FY2018
Impaired Driving	47	50	49
Ignition Interlock	2	4	5
Occupant Protection	44	47	48
Traffic Data Collection	49	49	50
Distracted Driving	7	1	7
Graduated Driver's Licenses	0	0	0
Motorcycle Safety	46	42	45
Total Grant Recipients	**195**	**193**	**204**

Source: CRS; data from Governors Highway Safety Association, Section 405 National Priority Safety Program, Funding tables; 2018 data from NHTSA Office of Grants Management and Operations, FY 2018 S. 402, 405, 1906 and 154/164 Authorized Grant Amounts, April 19, 2018.

Notes: The District of Columbia and certain territories were also eligible for grants, but are omitted from this table. The criteria for several grant programs were amended in 2015, so the 2018 numbers are illustrative rather than exactly comparable. For example, the decline in distracted driving grants from 2013 to 2015 is partly explained by the fact that the qualifying standard rose over time, so a state that qualified for a grant in FY2013 would not automatically qualify in FY2015; in 2015 Congress amended the standard to make it easier for states to qualify for a grant.

Encouraging State Enforcement—Incentive Grants

The incentive approach has had inconsistent impacts. In the 2012 surface transportation authorization legislation, Congress created or extended seven highway safety incentive grant programs.[62] In the three years following its passage, as Table 10 shows, these incentive programs had little impact in inducing states to enact legislation that would qualify them to receive the grants: in FY2013, states received 195 grants out of a possible 350,[63] while two years later states received 193 grants.[64] Three years later, in FY2018, after changes to several of the grant programs[65] the number of grants received by states out of the possible total rose from 55% in 2015 (193 out of 350) to 58% (204 out of 350).

---

[61] P.L. 112-141, §1533 and §31102(c); P.L. 114-93, §1401.

[62] These programs provide grants to states if the states meet certain criteria specified by Congress; for example, a state may qualify for a grant by having a law that requires that all drivers convicted of driving under the influence be required to have an ignition interlock system installed in their car for a period of time.

[63] Fifty states were eligible for these seven grant programs.

[64] In several grant programs, the qualifications to receive a grant increased over time, which may explain why in some programs fewer states qualified for grants in FY2015 than in FY2013.

[65] In §4005 of the FAST Act, P.L. 114-94.

Federal Policy Efforts on Key Dimensions of Driver Behavior

Occupant Protection/Safety Belts

Federal motor vehicle safety standards have required that lap and shoulder belts be provided in cars manufactured since the 1960s.[66] Seat belts are the simplest way to reduce deaths in traffic crashes; NHTSA estimates that more than 10,000 lives are saved each year because occupants of vehicles in crashes wear safety belts.[67] But safety belts have no safety benefit if they are not used.

Congress created an occupant protection incentive grant program in 2000 to make grants to states that adopt various measures in order to improve the rate of seat belt (or child restraint) use. There was also a one-time grant to encourage states to adopt a primary enforcement law.[68] These programs have granted well over $1 billion to states since 2000. Prior to 2000, 49 states and the District of Columbia had seat belt laws, but only 14 states had primary enforcement laws; as of June 2019, 34 states and the District of Columbia had primary enforcement laws.[69] As the number of states with primary enforcement seat belt laws has increased, the nationwide seat belt use rate has gone up (see Table 11).

Impaired Driving

Alcohol

Almost one-third of traffic fatalities involve an alcohol-impaired driver (one with a blood alcohol content [BAC] above the legal limit, currently .08%).[70] The proportion of drivers involved in fatal crashes who were impaired by alcohol declined from 35% in 1982 to 20% in 1997; since 1999 the proportion has remained around 20% (see Figure 10).

The impact of federal and state DUI-prevention policies on this trend is not clear. During the period of that decline, from 1982 to 1997, changes in a number of factors may have contributed to the decline: the per-capita consumption of alcohol in the United States declined, the number of young drivers decreased, the proportion of female drivers increased, there was increased publicity about the drunk-driving problem, and national

---

[66] All new passenger vehicles were required to have shoulder belts as of 1968 and integrated lap and shoulder belts as of 1974.
[67] NHTSA, *Traffic Safety Facts: Estimating the Lives Saved by Restraint Use and Minimum Drinking Age Laws*, DOT HD 812137, April 2015.
[68] This allows a law enforcement officer to stop a vehicle to issue a citation for failing to wear a seat belt; in states without a primary enforcement law, occupants may be cited for failing to wear a seat belt if the vehicle is stopped for some other violation, but an officer cannot stop a vehicle solely for violation of a seat belt law.
[69] New Hampshire has no seat belt law. Sources: primary law states before 2000 from Centers for Disease Control and Prevention, "Injury Prevention and Control: Motor Vehicle Safety: Intervention Fact Sheets: Primary Enforcement of Seat Belt Laws," Table B.5, http://www.cdc.gov/motorvehiclesafety/calculator/factsheet/seatbelt.html; laws as of 2019 from, Governors Highway Safety Association, "Seat Belt Laws," https://www.ghsa.org/ state-laws/issues/seat%20belts.
[70] NHTSA, *Countermeasures That Work* (Ninth Edition: 2017), p. I-1, "Alcohol- and Drug-Impaired Driving."

citizen activist groups dedicated to eliminating drunk driving were established.[71] There was also a decline in alcohol-related crashes in other countries, so other factors may have played a role as well.[72]

Table 11. States with Primary Enforcement Seat Belt Laws and Nationwide Observed Belt Use

Year	States With Primary Enforcement Seat Belt Laws	Nationwide Observed Seat Belt Use
1995	9	60%
2018	35	90%

Source: NHTSA, *Traffic Safety Facts Research Note, Seat Belt Use in 2018–Overall Results*, DOT HS 812 662, January 2019; 1995 data from NHTSA, *Traffic Safety Facts Research Note, Seat Belt Use in 2014–Overall Results*, DOT HS 812 113, February 2015.
Note: "States" includes District of Columbia.

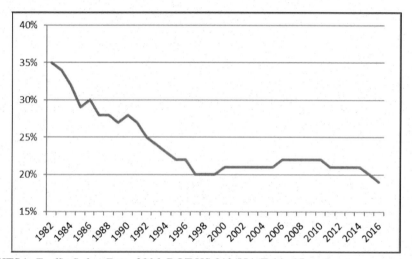

Source: NHTSA, *Traffic Safety Facts 2016*, DOT HS 812 554, Table 15.
Note: Blood alcohol content information was not generally collected before 1982.

Figure 10. Percentage of Drivers Involved in Fatal Crashes Who Were Alcohol-Impaired, 1982-2016. Impaired = BAC .08%+.

Moreover, as Figure 10 shows, while the decline in the proportion of drivers involved in fatal crashes who had high blood-alcohol content was quite significant, the decline stopped around 1996.

Congress does not have the power to directly regulate alcohol consumption by the general public; that is a state authority.[73] Hence federal policies concerning impaired

---

[71] "Remove Intoxicated Drivers" was established in 1978; in 1980, "Mothers Against Drunk Driving" was formed.
[72] James C. Fell, A. Scottt Tippetts, and Robert B. Voas, "Fatal Traffic Crashes Involving Drinking Drivers: What Have We Learned?" Annals of Advances in Automotive Medicine/Annual Scientific Conference 53 (2009), pp. 63-76, http://www.ncbi.nlm.nih.gov/pmc/articles/PMC3256806/.

driving have sought to influence states to regulate alcohol consumption, especially in connection with driving. In 1984 Congress passed the Minimum Drinking Age Act. The act provides that states that do not set a minimum age for purchasing alcohol and for being in possession of alcohol in public will lose a portion of their federal transportation funding. Within a few years every state had such a law. The impact of this law on reducing drunk driving fatalities, while substantial, is difficult to isolate, as many states enacted other supporting laws (for example, laws setting a minimum age for drinking alcohol and making it illegal for an underage person to have any measurable blood alcohol content). Studies estimate that stiffer laws accounted for less than half of the reduction in the proportion of drunk drivers involved in fatal crashes between 1982 and 1997, with demographic factors accounting for the rest.[74]

In 2000 Congress directed that any state that did not have .08% BAC as its per se threshold for driving while intoxicated would lose a portion of its federal transportation funding beginning in FY2004;[75] all states had enacted such a limit by 2005. A statistical analysis suggests this tightening of the legal intoxication standard for drivers may have made a small contribution to lowering the proportion of alcohol-impaired drivers involved in fatal crashes after 2001.[76]

There have been two significant improvements in alcohol-impaired driving crash numbers since 1997; neither, however, is attributed to policies targeting impaired driving. First, the number of teens involved in alcohol-impaired crashes has declined, but that has been attributed to the introduction of graduated driver-licensing laws, which have reduced the rate of teen driving by delaying the age at which teens can get an unlimited license. Second, there was a significant drop in alcohol-impaired fatalities and the fatality rate per 100 million VMT from 2006 (13,491 deaths, a fatality rate of 0.45) through 2011 (9,845 deaths, a fatality rate of 0.33)[77], which paralleled the overall decrease in crashes and fatalities during that period. From 2011 through 2017 the number of alcohol-impaired fatalities and the fatality rate have remained fairly stable around the 2011 level.[78]

Fatality rates due to alcohol-impaired driving vary significantly from state to state, and even from area to area within states. For example, in 2016 the proportion of drivers involved in fatal crashes who had a blood alcohol content of .08% or higher was 19% nationwide; among the states it varied from a low of 12% (Mississippi, Utah) to a high of

---

[73] Congress did have the power to directly regulate alcohol consumption by the general public between 1919, when the 18th Amendment to the Constitution was ratified, and 1933, when it was repealed.

[74] J. N. Dang, "Statistical Analysis of Alcohol-related Driving Trends, 1982-2005," National Highway Traffic Safety Administration, DOT HS 810 942, May 2008.

[75] P.L. 106-346, §351.

[76] Ibid. Prior to Congress's action, a few states already had .08% BAC as their threshold, while most others had .10% as their threshold.

[77] National Highway Traffic Safety Administration, *Traffic Safety Facts: Alcohol-Impaired Driving, 2015 Data*, DOT HS 812 360, December 2016.

[78] National Highway Traffic Safety Administration, *Traffic Safety Facts: Alcohol-Impaired Driving, 2017 Data*, DOT HS 812 630, November 2018.

36% (Montana).[79] DUI crash rates also vary by other factors such as rural versus urban population, road conditions, and economic activity, as well as by state laws and programs and socioeconomic factors.

Marijuana

Eleven states and the District of Columbia, representing over a quarter of the U.S. population, have decriminalized the recreational use of marijuana, and other states are considering doing so as well. As the opportunity for legal use of marijuana grows, there is concern about the impact of marijuana usage ("drugged driving") on highway safety. Advocates of loosening restrictions on marijuana often compare marijuana usage to drinking alcohol, which may contribute to some stakeholders viewing marijuana use's impairment of driving as similar to alcohol's impairment of driving. Eighteen states have enacted laws declaring that a specified concentration of tetrahydrocannabinol (THC, the primary psychoactive component in marijuana) in a driver's body constitutes evidence of impairment and is inherently illegal, similar to the .08% BAC standard of alcohol impairment.

Research studies indicate that marijuana's effects on drivers' performance may vary from the effects of alcohol, in ways that challenge addressing marijuana-impaired driving similarly to alcohol-impaired driving. Research studies have been unable to consistently correlate levels of marijuana consumption, or THC in a person's body, and levels of impairment. Although laboratory studies have shown that marijuana consumption can affect a person's response times and motor performance, studies of the impact of marijuana consumption on a driver's risk of being involved in a crash have produced conflicting results, with some studies finding some increase in risk of crashing after marijuana usage, while others find little or no increased risk of a crash. Levels of impairment that can be identified in laboratory settings may not have a significant impact in real world settings, where many variables affect the likelihood of a crash occurring. Thus some researchers, and the National Highway Traffic Safety Administration, have observed that using a measure of THC as evidence of a driver's impairment is not supported by scientific evidence to date. Nonetheless, federal laws and regulations prohibit marijuana use by transportation safety-sensitive employees and require mandatory drug testing.

If additional states legalize marijuana, the issue of marijuana impairment of drivers is likely to become more prominent. This may increase the relevance of research on the impact of marijuana on driver performance and on measurement techniques for marijuana impairment, as well as training for law enforcement on identifying marijuana impairment.[80]

---

[79] National Highway Traffic Safety Administration, *Traffic Safety Facts 2016*, DOT HS 812 554, Table 118.
[80] For more information on this topic, see CRS Report R45719, *Marijuana Use and Highway Safety*, by David Randall Peterman.

Speeding

Speeding is associated with crashes involving injuries and fatalities, since the faster a vehicle is moving, the more energy is absorbed by occupants during a crash and the greater the likelihood of serious injury. Excessive speed has been shown to increase the likelihood of crashes.

There is currently no federal limit on highway speeds. In 1974, Congress adopted a national maximum speed limit of 55 miles per hour (mph).[81] In 1984, the Transportation Research Board estimated this change to have saved 2,000 to 4,000 lives annually due to reductions in the number and severity of crashes.[82] In 1987 Congress amended the law to allow speeds up to 65 mph on qualified segments of rural Interstate System highways; most states responded by raising rural Interstate speed limits.[83] In 1995, Congress repealed the law entirely. After the repeal most states raised speeds on their Interstate highways. Studies suggest that the elimination of the maximum speed limit resulted in an increase in the number of crashes and deaths, especially on Interstate highways.[84] One study estimated that each 5 mph increase in speed limits resulted in an 8% increase in fatalities on interstates and a 4% increase in fatalities on other roads.[85] Thus reinstituting a national maximum speed limit that was lower than current levels would likely save lives. In addition, such a change would also reduce fuel consumption. However, from a cost-benefit perspective, studies suggest that the cost of the additional travel time imposed by a lower speed limit may outweigh the value of the reductions in crashes, injuries, and fatalities.[86]

Congress has made it harder for states to enforce speed limits by barring the use of federal transportation funding for automated speed enforcement, though states may use their own funds for this purpose. Studies indicate that automated speed enforcement is an effective way to enforce speed limits and reduce deaths and injuries.[87]

---

[81] As with other aspects of driver behavior, Congress does not have the authority to regulate traffic speeds directly, so this was done by cutting highway funding to states that did not adopt a 55 mph speed limit. The original intent was to temporarily reduce speeds to reduce fuel use in the wake of a fuel shortage after the 1973 oil embargo, but when the safety impact of the speed limit became known, Congress made the speed limit permanent.

[82] Transportation Research Board, *55: A Decade of Experience*, Special Report 204, 1984.

[83] P.L. 100-17, §174.

[84] C. M. Farmer, R. A. Retting, and A. K. Lund, "Changes in Motor Vehicle Occupant Fatalities After Repeal of the National Maximum Speed Limit," *Accident Analysis & Prevention*, vol. 31, no. 5 (September 1999), pp. 537-543; D. C. Grabowski and M. A. Morrisey, "Systemwide Implications of the Repeal of the National Maximum Speed Limit," *Accident Analysis & Prevention*, vol. 39, no. 1 (January 2007), pp. 180-189; Lee S. Friedman, Donald Hedeker, and Elihu D. Richter, "Long-Term Effects of Repealing the National Maximum Speed Limit in the United States," *American Journal of Public Health*, vol. 99, no. 9 (September 2009), pp. 1626-1631.

[85] Charles M. Farmer, *The Effects of Higher Speed Limits on Traffic Fatalities in the United States, 1993–2017*, Insurance Institute for Highway Safety, April 2019.

[86] Transportation Research Board, *55: A Decade of Experience*, Special Report 204, 1984; Thomas H. Forester, Robert F. McNown, and Larry D. Singell, "A Cost-Benefit Analysis of the 55 MPH Speed Limit," *Southern Economic Journal*, V. 50, No. 3 (January 1984), pp. 631-641.

[87] Libby Thomas et al., "Safety Effects of Automated Speed Enforcement Programs: Critical Review of International Literature," *Transportation Research Record: Journal of the Transportation Research Board*, No. 2078 (2008), pp. 117-126.

Distracted Driving

Driver distraction is estimated to be a factor in 10% of fatal crashes.[88] Driver distraction is difficult to detect, as it typically leaves no evidence, and there are disincentives (e.g., financial liabilities) to drivers admitting to being distracted. There are many possible sources of distraction, some of which have been around as long as there have been cars, such as eating while driving, talking to passengers, and gazing at objects outside the driving lane ("rubbernecking"). The recent proliferation of cell phones and smartphones and their use by drivers has led to growing concern about driver distraction.

Studies looking at cell-phone records indicate that cell-phone use increases the risk of being involved in a crash by a factor of four.[89] Many states have passed laws prohibiting hand-held cell phone use by drivers, but allowing hands-free usage. Some studies of driver distraction indicate that it is the driver's attention to the conversation—cognitive distraction—rather than the physical encumbrance of driving with one hand while holding a phone that is the primary source of distraction; hands-free phone use is as distracting to drivers as hand-held phone use.[90] Text messaging, which combines cognitive distraction with diverting the driver's eyes from the road, is significantly more distracting than carrying on a conversation.[91] Internet-connected information/entertainment systems in vehicles may present additional sources of driver distraction.

There are as yet few effective countermeasures to drivers engaging in distracting behavior. While surveys indicate that most people are opposed to cell-phone use while driving, they also indicate that most people engage in such behavior at least occasionally. Forty-eight states and the District of Columbia ban text messaging by all drivers, 39 states and the District of Columbia ban cell-phone use by novice drivers, and 19 states and the District of Columbia ban all drivers from using hand-held cell phones while driving.[92] Studies indicate that such laws alone have little impact; intensive enforcement of such laws can be effective in the short term, but it is relatively expensive in terms of the commitment of law enforcement resources required for intensive enforcement. The only countermeasure that has been clearly proven to work is graduated driver licensing—that is, limiting the driving opportunities for teens.[93]

Congress established a distracted driving incentive grant program in 2012 to encourage states to prohibit texting by all drivers, and prohibit cell-phone use entirely for drivers under age 18. To qualify for a grant, states were required to have these as primary

---

[88] National Highway Traffic Safety Administration, *Countermeasures That Work* (Ninth Edition), 2017, p. 4–2.
[89] S. P. McEvoy et al., "Role of Mobile Phones in Motor Vehicle Crashes resulting in Hospital Attendance: a Case-Crossover Study," *British Medical Journal*; 331 (2005), pp. 428-430.
[90] D. L. Strayer et al., *Measuring Cognitive Distraction in the Automobile*, AAA Foundation for Traffic Safety, June 2013, p. 28. Cognitive distraction can also occur when a driver talks with another occupant of the vehicle.
[91] Thomas A. Ranney, G. H. Scott Baldwin, and Ed Parmer, Transportation Research Center Inc.; John Martin, Ohio State University; Elizabeth N. Mazzae, National Highway Traffic Safety Administration, *Distraction Effects of Manual Number and Text Entry While Driving*, DOT HS 811 510, National Highway Traffic Safety Administration, August 2011.
[92] Governors Highway Safety Association, "Distracted Driving Laws," reviewed July 2019.
[93] National Highway Traffic Safety Administration, *Countermeasures That Work* (Ninth Edition), 2017, pp. 4–11.

violations, to have no exception for use while stopped in traffic, and to have a minimum fine for first offenders and an increased fine for repeat offenders. One state, Connecticut, qualified for a grant under this program in FY2014 and FY2015. In December 2015, Congress deleted the requirement for an increased fine for repeat offenders, and established a second distracted driving grant program for fiscal years 2017 and 2018 that included less demanding requirements; these changes were expected to allow more states to qualify for grants.[94] In 2018, four states received grants under the new temporary program and three states received grants under the amended 2012 program.[95]

Motorcycle Safety

Injuries to the head are the most common cause of fatalities among motorcyclists; they are also a common type of nonfatal injury.[96] The only policy approach that has been demonstrated to be effective in reducing motorcycle crash deaths is a law requiring all motorcyclists to wear helmets ("universal helmet law").[97]

As noted above, Congress enacted a penalty for states lacking a universal motorcycle helmet law in 1966, but repealed it in 1975. In 1966, no state had a universal motorcycle helmet law; by 1975, 47 states had adopted such legislation. The motorcycle fatality rate per 100,000 motorcycles declined from 127 (1966) to 67 (1976). After Congress repealed the law in 1976, 27 states repealed their mandatory helmet laws within three years, and the fatality rate per 100,000 motorcycles rose from 67 (1976) to 91 (1979). Universal helmet use legislation was again passed by Congress in 1991, repealed in 1995, and unsuccessfully proposed on occasion since then.

Currently, 19 states, the District of Columbia, and three territories have universal helmet laws; 28 states and one territory require helmets for young riders, and three states have no helmet requirements.[98] The observed use rate for helmets in states varies, but as a group, helmet use in universal helmet law states approaches 100%, while in other states it averages around 50% (see Figure 11). NHTSA has estimated that if every motorcyclist wore a helmet that met the DOT standard, around 650 to 800 motorcyclist deaths would be prevented each year.[99]

---

[94] §4005 of the FAST Act, P.L. 114-94.
[95] National Highway Traffic Safety Administration, Office of Grants Management and Operations, *FY2018 S. 402, 405, 1906 and 154/164 Authorized Grant Amounts*, April 19, 2018, https://www.nhtsa.gov/sites/nhtsa.dot.gov/files/ documents/all-grant-awards-summary-fy2018.pdf.
[96] National Highway Traffic Safety Administration, *Traffic Safety Facts: Bodily Injury Locations in Fatally Injured Motorcycle Riders*, DOT HS 810856, October 2007, available at http://www-nrd.nhtsa.dot.gov/Pubs/810856.pdf.
[97] U.S. Government Accountability Office, *Motorcycle Safety: Increasing Federal Funding Flexibility and Identifying Research Priorities Would Help Support States' Safety Efforts*, GAO-13-42, November 14, 2012, p. 16.
[98] Governors Highway Safety Association, "State Laws: Motorcyclists," https://www.ghsa.org/ state-laws/issues/motorcyclists.
[99] The number varies each year with the number of fatal crashes, but has been between 660850 each year for the past decade; see National Highway Traffic Safety Administration, *Traffic Safety Facts: Lives Saved in 2017 by Restraint Use and Minimum-Drinking-Age Laws*, DOT HS 812 683, March 2019; *Lives Saved in 2012 by Restrain Use and Minimum-Drinking-Age Laws*, DOT HS 811 851, November 2013, Table 1.

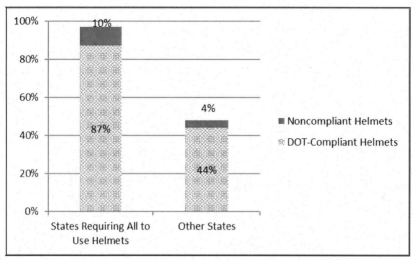

Source: R. Li T. M. Pickrell, *Traffic Safety Facts Research Note: Motorcycle Helmet Use in 2017—Overall Results*, DOT HS 812 512, NHTSA, August 2018, Figure 3.

Figure 11. Motorcycle Helmet Use in 2017, by State Law and Helmet Type.

Some motorcyclists wear helmets that do not comply with the DOT standard; these so-called "novelty helmets" do not offer the same degree of protection in a crash. State enforcement authorities have observed that the existence of such helmets makes it difficult to enforce helmet use laws (which require a DOT-compliant helmet), since "novelty" aren't always easily distinguished visually from DOT-compliant helmets. In 2015 NHTSA initiated a notice of proposed rulemaking to restrict the sale and use of noncompliant helmets;[100] it now plans to withdraw that rulemaking due to "changed circumstances" and is to evaluate other alternatives that might prove effective in reducing novelty helmet availability and use.[101]

Congress has established a motorcycle safety incentive grant program under which DOT "shall award grants to states that adopt and implement effective programs to reduce the number of single- and multi-vehicle crashes involving motorcyclists."[102] States can qualify for a grant by meeting two of the six criteria set by Congress. Two of the criteria are numerical measures (reducing the number of motorcycle deaths and the rate of crashes involving motorcycles compared with the previous year; and reducing the number of deaths and rate of crashes involving impaired motorcyclists compared with the previous year). The four remaining criteria are policy measures

---

[100] 80 *Federal Register* 29458, May 21, 2015.
[101] U.S. Department of Transportation, *June 2019 Significant Rulemaking Report*, #54: FMVSS No. 218 and Enforcement Policy Concerning Novelty Helmets, https://www.transportation.gov/ regulations/report-on-significant-rulemakings.
[102] 23 U.S.C. §405(f)(1).

- offering motorcycle rider training courses;
- having a program to increase motorist awareness of motorcyclists;
- having a statewide program to reduce impaired driving that includes specific measures to reduce the number of motorcyclists riding while impaired; and
- using all fees collected for motorcycle training and safety programs for those purposes.

As noted above, there is no evidence that the types of training programs encouraged by the four policy criteria are effective in reducing crash or fatality rates.[103] The safety policy that has been proven to be effective in reducing motorcyclist deaths—a universal helmet law—is not among the options for qualifying for the motorcyclist safety grant program.

Emergency Response

The key element in emergency response is reducing the amount of time between a crash and the provision of medical assistance to injured victims. This is a growing challenge in rural areas due to the closure of rural hospitals and thus greater distance to travel for emergency medical care.[104] Federal highway safety programs play virtually no role in this aspect of emergency response.

POLICY OPTIONS FOR FURTHER SAFETY IMPROVEMENTS

Although U.S. highway safety statistics have generally improved over the previous decades, there is room for further improvement. After 2010 the reductions in U.S. fatality and injury rates stopped, and between 2014 and 2016 the rates have risen by around 10%. Also, while the U.S. highway safety record was once the world's best, in recent years the highway safety performance of several other industrialized nations has surpassed that of the United States.[105]

---

[103] National Highway Traffic Safety Administration, *Countermeasures That Work* (Eighth Edition: 2015), p. 5–6.
[104] The Sheps Center for Health Services Research at the University of North Carolina tracks rural hospital closures; it reports that as of June 2019 106 rural hospitals had closed since January 2010. https://www.shepscenter.unc.edu/ programs-projects/rural-health/rural-hospital-closures/.
[105] Transportation Research Board, *Achieving Traffic Safety Goals in the United States: Lessons from Other Nations*, Special Report 300, Washington, DC, 2011; International Transport Forum, Road Safety Annual Report 2018.

There are several policy actions Congress could consider that are recommended by safety advocates that they assert to be low-cost but effective interventions. These include actions dealing with seat belt usage, motorcycle helmets, automated traffic enforcement, and implementation of new vehicle safety technologies.

Seat Belt Usage

A survey found that 90% of front-seat occupants wore seat belts in 2018. The rate was 91% in states with primary enforcement seat belt laws, and 86% in states with other laws.[106] Other countries have achieved higher use rates: Australia (96%), England (95%), and Canada (92%).[107] NHTSA estimated that in 2017 an additional 2,549 lives would have been saved if all unrestrained passenger vehicle occupants five years of age and older had worn seat belts.[108] As noted above, the incentive grant program Congress created in 2005 to encourage states to adopt mandatory belt use laws with primary enforcement was judged to have reached its ceiling by 2012, with 34 states and the District of Columbia having adopted such laws for front-seat passengers, and 17 states and the District of Columbia having adopted such laws for all vehicle occupants (front and rear seats). Options available to Congress to increase the number of states with primary enforcement laws for seat belt use by all occupants include an incentive program with a much greater value of incentive, a program that would penalize states that do not adopt such laws, or a combination of the two.

Universal Motorcycle Helmet Laws

NHTSA estimates that use of motorcycle helmets saved 1,872 lives in 2017, and that an additional 749 lives would have been saved if every motorcyclist wore a helmet meeting the DOT standard.[109] Universal helmet laws have been shown to be very effective in promoting helmet usage, because a violation of the law is easily seen. In Australia, for example, the reported helmet use rate by motorcycle operators is 99%.[110] Congress has prohibited NHTSA from lobbying state legislatures to encourage the adoption of universal helmet laws, and it omitted adoption of universal helmet laws from

---

[106] National Highway Traffic Safety Administration, *Traffic Safety Facts: Seat Belt Use in 2018—Overall Results*, DOT HS 812 662, January 2019.
[107] National Highway Traffic Safety Administration, *Documenting How States Recently Upgraded to Primary Seat Belt Laws*, DOT HS 811524, September 2011, p. 6.
[108] National Highway Traffic Safety Administration, *Traffic Safety Facts: Lives Saved in 2013 by Restraint Use and Minimum Drinking Age Laws*, DOT HS 812137, April 2015.
[109] National Highway Traffic Safety Administration, *Traffic Safety Facts: Lives Saved in 2017 by Restraint Use and Minimum-Drinking-Age Laws*, DOT HS 812 683, March 2019, p. 1.
[110] Increasing Motorcycle Helmet Use, http://www.mrasa.asn.au/pdf/who_part_report.pdf.

the list of safety measures required for a state to receive a motorcycle safety incentive grant. In the surface transportation authorization enacted in 2015, Congress prohibited states from using federal highway safety funding to check motorcycle helmet use or to create checkpoints that specifically target motorcyclists.[111]

Automated Traffic Enforcement

Automated traffic enforcement, such as the use of cameras to capture evidence of speeding and running red lights, has several advantages in encouraging compliance with traffic laws. Such tools reduce the risk that officers enforcing traffic laws will be attacked by suspects they approach or be hit by passing cars, allow monitoring of many more intersections and miles of roadway, and may be less costly to deploy than police officers. In numerous studies, red-light cameras have been shown to decrease the number of both red-light violations and crashes involving injuries and fatalities at signalized intersections.[112] A review of 28 studies measuring the effect of speed cameras found that speed cameras reduced the number of crashes in an area, generally from between 14% to 25%, and also reduced the number of crashes resulting in injuries or deaths.[113] A number of other countries have made extensive use of speed cameras in their highway safety programs. For example, in France, use of automated enforcement was a key feature of a highway safety initiative announced in 2002, and resulted in reductions in both average speeds and fatal crashes.[114] Australia introduced such cameras in 1989; 2,300 cameras were in place by 2009. The percentage of light vehicles in free-flowing traffic exceeding the speed limit by more than 10 kilometers per hour (roughly 6 mph) dropped from 36% in 2001 to 10% in 2009.[115] In the United Kingdom, road deaths dropped by 34% from 1990-199, compared to a 6.5% drop in the United States; one study suggested the greater reduction in fatal crashes in the U.K. was due largely to small decreases in the speed of drivers due to the introduction of speed cameras and other speed-calming measures in the U.K, while in the U.S. speed camera use was rare and speed limits were increasing.[116]

---

[111] The Fixing America's Surface Transportation Act (FAST Act), P.L. 114-93, §4007.
[112] A. S. Aeron-Thomas and S. Hess, "Red-light Cameras for the Prevention of Road Traffic Crashes," *Cochrane Database of Systematic Reviews* 2005, Issue 2, Art. No. CD003862.
[113] Cecelia Wilson, Charlene Willis, Joan K. Hendrikz, Robyne Le Brocque, and Nicholas Bellamy, "Speed Cameras for the Prevention of Road Traffic Crashes, Injuries and Deaths," *Cochrane Database of Systematic Reviews* 2010, Issue 11, Art. No. CD004607.
[114] Laurent Carnis and Etienne Blais, "An Assessment of the Safety Effects of the French Speed Camera Program," *Accident Analysis and Prevention*, 51 (2013) 301-309.
[115] Transportation Research Board, *Achieving Traffic Safety Goals in the United States: Lessons from Other Nations*, Special Report 300, Washington, DC, 2011, pp. 77, 81.
[116] Elihu Richter, Lee S. Friedman, Tamar Berman, Avraham Rivkind, "Death and Injury from Motor Vehicle Crashes: A Tale of Two Countries," *American Journal of Preventive Medicine*, vol. 29, no. 5, 2005, pp. 440-449.

In the past two surface transportation authorization acts, Congress prohibited states from using any federal-aid highway funding or highway safety funding for automated traffic enforcement (except in school zones).[117] In what some see as a further disincentive to the use of automated enforcement, Congress requires states in which automated enforcement systems are in operation to use some of their federal safety funding to conduct a biennial survey of those systems.[118]

---

[117] P.L. 112-141 §1533 & §31102; P.L. 114-94 §1401; codified at 23 U.S.C. §402(c)(4). This statute begins by directing states to maintain a highway safety program designed to reduce traffic deaths and injuries, then prohibits using federal funding for this tool for accomplishing those goals.

[118] P.L. 114-94 §4002. The survey is to include a list of the automated traffic enforcement systems in each state, data on the "transparency, accountability, and safety attributes" of each system, and comparison of each system with DOT guidelines for operation of automated enforcement systems.

In: Highway Safety
Editor: Bertha G. Baldwin
ISBN: 978-1-53617-176-1
© 2020 Nova Science Publishers, Inc.

Chapter 5

ISSUES WITH FEDERAL MOTOR VEHICLE SAFETY STANDARDS[*]

Bill Canis

SUMMARY

Federal motor vehicle safety regulation was established more than 50 years ago by the National Traffic and Motor Vehicle Safety Act (P.L. 89-563) to address the rising number of motor vehicle fatalities and injuries. The National Highway Traffic Safety Administration (NHTSA) administers vehicle safety laws and has issued dozens of safety standards, including regulations affecting windshield wipers, hood and door latches, tires, and airbags.

NHTSA has estimated that between 1960 and 2012, federal motor vehicle safety standards saved more than 600,000 lives, and the risk of a fatality declined by 56%. Although dozens of technologies were made subject to federal standards in the decades after federal regulation began, a NHTSA study reported that more than half of the lives saved—329,000—were from use of seat belts. While the federal standard was helpful in reducing fatalities, the study found that the passage of state laws allowing police to issue tickets if a driver or passengers are not wearing seat belts caused the number of lives saved to climb from 800 per year to 6,000 per year.

In addition to promulgating and enforcing vehicle safety standards, NHTSA investigates vehicle defects that affect safety and issues vehicle or parts recalls if safety defects are discovered. In recent years, the number of vehicle and parts recalls has risen significantly, from 16.3 million vehicles and parts in 2013 to 87.5 million in 2015. The rising number of recalls is due to stricter laws and reporting requirements, larger fines, delayed detection of vehicle problems by NHTSA, and several high-visibility cases, including General Motors' faulty ignition switch and Takata airbags.

---

[*] This is an edited, reformatted and augmented version of Congressional Research Service, Publication No. R44800, dated March 24, 2017.

Recalls rarely obtain 100% completion rates, leaving many defective vehicles on the road long after a recall is initiated. A recent study by J.D. Power, a market research company, showed that between 2013 and 2015, recalls of fewer than 10,000 vehicles had a 67% completion rate, while recalls of more than a million vehicles had a completion rate of only 49%. The larger recalls are thought to result in fewer repaired vehicles because of the difficulty in finding and notifying larger numbers of owners, a lengthened repair period due to lack of an adequate supply of replacement parts, and the ability of manufacturers to use more personalized communications, such as telephone calls, in smaller recalls.

Many emerging technologies, such as automatic emergency braking and lane departure warning, are expected to reduce vehicle injuries and deaths in the future. Over time, these separate technologies will be combined as vehicles are built with higher levels of automation. To deal with these rapid changes, NHTSA has broadened the agency's approach beyond the traditional rulemaking to include new means of interacting with manufacturers and other vehicle safety stakeholders, such as voluntary agreements to accelerate use of life-saving technologies.

The 2015 Fixing America's Surface Transportation (FAST) Act included significant vehicle safety provisions, including a new requirement that rental car fleets be covered by recalls, new methods for notifying consumers about recalls, larger penalties for violations, and a longer period for consumers to obtain remedies for defects.

Congress remains interested in motor vehicle safety; proposed legislation calls for used vehicles to be subject to recalls, NHTSA to provide more public access to safety information, civil penalties to be increased, regional recalls to be terminated, and federal standards to be issued to secure electronic motor vehicle data from hackers.

INTRODUCTION

In 1956, the year Congress authorized the Interstate Highway System, there were 37,965 fatalities on U.S. roads—6.05 fatalities for every 100 million vehicle miles traveled (VMT).[1] The construction of limited-access highways spurred travel by automobile, leading to an increase in the number of fatal accidents. Congress responded with a series of laws that have helped reduce the fatality rate by 80% over the past six decades. By 2014, the United States recorded only 1.08 fatalities for every 100 million VMT, although the rate ticked up to 1.13 per 100 million VMT in 2015 (Table 1), and again in the first 9 months of 2016, when fatalities rose to 1.15 per 100 million VMT.[2]

Development of new motor vehicle technologies, investments in building safer highways and educating motorists, and improving emergency medical services all have contributed to reduced fatality rates.[3] Congress has played a significant role in improving highway safety by directing the federal government to impose and enforce safety

---

[1] President Eisenhower signed the Federal-Aid Highway Act of 1956 into law on June 29, 1956.
[2] Motor vehicle traffic fatalities rose by 7% in 2015 and by 8.3% in the first nine months of 2016. NHTSA, *Early Estimate of Motor Vehicle Traffic Fatalities for the First 9 Months of 2016*, DOT HS 812 358, January 2017, https://crashstats.nhtsa.dot.gov/Api/Public/View Publication/812358.
[3] C. J. Kahane, *Lives Saved by Vehicle Safety Technologies and Associated Federal Motor Vehicle Safety Standards, 1960 to 2012*, NHTSA, DOT HS 812 069, January 2015, p. x.

standards for motor vehicles. This effort has been at times controversial, and several large recalls have raised questions about the effectiveness of federal motor vehicle regulation.

Table 1. Motor vehicle traffic fatalities and fatality rates

Year	Total Fatalities	Million Vehicle Miles Traveled (VMT)	Fatality Rate per 100 Million Vehicle Miles Traveled (VMT)
1956	37,965	627,843	6.05
1966	50,894	925,899	5.50
1976	45,523	1,402,380	3.25
1986	46,087	1,834,872	2.51
1996	42,065	2,484,080	1.69
2006	42,708	3,014,371	1.42
2011	32,479	2,950,402	1.10
2012	33,782	2,969,433	1.14
2013	32,893	2,988,280	1.10
2014	32,744	3,025,656	1.08
2015	35,092	3,095,373	1.13

Source: National Highway Traffic Safety Administration.

FEDERAL MOTOR VEHICLE SAFETY STANDARDS

In the early decades of the automobile, U.S. vehicles were lightly regulated by a combination of state and private-sector standards. National regulation was generally not seen as appropriate; in the early 1900s, according to two historians of auto safety, it was widely believed that "the only useful and politically acceptable action Congress might take was to help the states and localities construct more and better roads."[4] The Society of Automotive Engineers (SAE), a professional association founded in 1905, became the primary source of vehicle safety rules for many decades. State governments often used SAE recommendations to set their own standards for vehicle brakes, headlamps, and windshield wipers.

At the same time, the rising number of highway deaths prompted a new interest in vehicle safety: between 1962 and 1964, Congress passed three safety bills into law, including a seat belt regulation.[5] The new laws were only a precursor to broader federal regulation. Two publications also spurred interest in a greater federal role. Ralph Nader's 1965 book, *Unsafe at Any Speed: The Designed-in Dangers of the American Automobile*,

---

[4] Jerry Mashaw and David Harfst, *The Struggle for Auto Safety* (Cambridge, MA: Harvard University Press, 1990), pp. 30-31.

[5] P.L. 87-637 required hydraulic brake fluid used in motor vehicles to meet certain standards established by the Secretary of Commerce; P.L. 88-201 required the Secretary of Commerce to promulgate safety standards for seat belts; and P.L. 88-514 required vehicle manufacturers to meet certain minimum safety standards for vehicles sold to the General Services Administration (GSA) for the federal fleet.

argued that cars were unnecessarily unsafe and that the auto industry should be regulated by a federal agency.[6] Also influential was *Accidental Death and Disability: The Neglected Disease of Modern Society*, a National Academy of Sciences report that documented the impact of accidental injuries, including those by motor vehicles.[7]

Comprehensive vehicle safety legislation was passed in the form of the National Traffic and Motor Vehicle Safety Act of 1966.[8] As approved unanimously by both houses of Congress and signed by President Lyndon B. Johnson, the legislation had two parts:

1) The Highway Safety Act of 1966 mandated that each state put in place a highway safety program in accordance with federal standards to improve driver performance, accident records systems, and traffic control.

2) The National Traffic and Motor Vehicle Safety Act of 1966 directed the Secretary of Commerce (later changed to the Secretary of Transportation when that agency was established in 1967) to issue safety standards for all motor vehicles beginning in January 1967. A National Traffic Safety Agency was established to carry out the provisions of the new law; it was renamed the National Highway Traffic Safety Administration (NHTSA) in 1970.[9]

Since its establishment, NHTSA has issued dozens of safety standards,[10] including regulations affecting windshield wipers, hood latches, tires, brakes, seat belts, and airbags.[11] Proposing and finalizing a NHTSA safety regulation can take many years: all NHTSA regulations follow the Administrative Procedure Act of 1946 (APA),[12] which ensures that proposed rulemaking is publicized in the *Federal Register*, comments are taken and considered, and agency decisions are clearly explained. Court review of standards is allowed, and revisions to federal regulations must also follow the APA.

NHTSA does not verify in advance that motor vehicles and parts comply with its standards. Instead, the law provides that "[a] manufacturer or distributor of a motor vehicle or motor vehicle equipment shall certify to the distributor or dealer at delivery that the vehicle or equipment complies with applicable motor vehicle safety standards prescribed under this chapter.

---

[6] Ralph Nader, *Unsafe at Any Speed: The Designed-in Dangers of the American Automobile* (New York: Grossman, 1965).

[7] National Academy of Sciences and National Research Council, *Accidental Death and Disability: The Neglected Disease of Modern Society*, 1966, https://www.ems.gov/pdf/1997-Reproduction-AccidentalDeathDisability.pdf.

[8] P.L. 89-563. When he signed the law, President Johnson cited the 50,000 people killed on U.S. highways as the biggest cause of death and injury among young Americans. The White House, "Remarks of the President at Signing of the Highway Safety Act and the Traffic Safety Act," press release, September 9, 1966, cited in *National Traffic and Motor Vehicle Safety Act of 1966, Legislative History*, vol. 1, p. 31, published by NHTSA in 1985.

[9] Highway Safety Act of 1970, P.L. 91-605.

[10] The authority for issuing standards is found in 49 U.S.C §30111.

[11] See https://www.nhtsa.gov/staticfiles/rulemaking/pdf/FMVSS-QuickRefGuide-HS811439.pdf.

[12] 5 U.S.C. §551.

Certification of a vehicle must be shown by a label or tag permanently fixed to the vehicle.[13]

Manufacturers are responsible for testing their vehicles and are liable for recalls and penalties if they are later found not to meet NHTSA's Federal Motor Vehicle Safety Standards (FMVSS). After a new model goes on sale, NHTSA buys a sampling from dealers and tests the vehicles at its own facilities to determine whether they comply. If NHTSA determines there is noncompliance, it can encourage the manufacturer to recall the model to correct the problem, or it can order a recall.[14]

In addition to promulgating motor vehicle standards and addressing vehicle defects, NHTSA's mission also includes providing assistance to states on traffic safety issues, such as drunk driving and distracted driving,[15] and maintaining a comprehensive database about motor vehicle crashes.[16]

Estimates of Effects of Federal Safety Standards

A recent NHTSA study estimated that passenger vehicle safety technologies associated with Federal Motor Vehicle Safety Standards (FMVSS) have saved 613,501 lives between 1960 and 2012.[17] The study evaluated the effects of 31 motor vehicle technologies mandated by NHTSA, including dual master cylinders and front disc brakes,[18] electronic stability control, energy-absorbing steering assemblies,[19] seat belts, door locks,[20] airbags, and side door beams.[21] It estimated that the risk of a fatality in 2012

---

[13] P.L. 89-563, 49 U.S.C. §30115.
[14] NHTSA, *Motor Vehicle Safety Defects and Recalls: What Every Vehicle Owner Should Know*, https://www-odi.nhtsa.dot.gov/recalls/documents/MVDefectsandRecalls.pdf.
[15] For a discussion about NHTSA's role in modifying driver behaviors, such as distracted driving, as well as its state assistance programs, see CRS Report R44394, *Federal Highway Traffic Safety Policies: Impacts and Opportunities*, by David Randall Peterman.
[16] NHTSA data analysis and research are managed by the National Center for Statistics and Analysis (NCSA) and the Office of Vehicle Safety Research, https://www.nhtsa.gov/research-data; NHTSA maintains the Fatality Analysis Reporting System (FARS), which records factors of fatal crashes such as location, time and circumstances of the crash, type of vehicle, passengers involved, and vehicles' movements leading to the crash.
[17] The study evaluated technologies in cars, sport utility vehicles (SUVs), pickup trucks, minivans, and full-size vans. C. J. Kahane, *Lives Saved by Vehicle Safety Technologies and Associated Federal Motor Vehicle Safety Standards, 1960 to 2012*, NHTSA, DOT HS 812 069, January 2015.
[18] Dual master cylinders and disc brakes are part of a vehicle's braking system. The single reservoir master cylinder formerly in use provided pressure to both the front and rear systems, but cylinder failure left the motorist vulnerable to loss of all braking power. A dual system splits the car into front and rear, so some brakes should work even if one cylinder fails. Disc brakes, used on the front of a vehicle (with more traditional drum brakes on the back), cool faster, have better overall stopping power, and are less susceptible to warping than drum brakes.
[19] Steering columns are designed to collapse in a frontal collision, reducing the potential head and chest injuries to the driver.
[20] Improvements in door locks, latches, and hinges have reduced door ejections in crashes.
[21] Side door beams are anti-intrusion bars that protect passengers from side impacts.

was 56% lower than in 1960, based on evaluation of the effectiveness of specific technologies in reducing occupant fatalities.[22]

The NHTSA report found seat belts, introduced in the late 1960s, to have been responsible for more than half of all the lives saved, 329,715, and that their effectiveness rose sharply after NHTSA required installation of combined lap and shoulder belts in place of simple lap belts in 1974.[23] However, the study also highlighted the importance of other measures in addition to federal vehicle safety regulation: it estimated that the number of lives saved annually by seat belts rose from 800 to 6,000 after many states allowed police to issue tickets if a driver or passengers were not wearing seat belts. Every state but New Hampshire has enacted laws requiring seat belt use.[24]

The study notes that the full benefits of new federal safety standards may take many years to be felt. The passenger vehicle fleet turns over slowly; nearly half the cars and light trucks on the road are more than 12 years old.[25] And standards can take many years to develop and issue.

Although electronic stability control[26] was introduced as standard equipment on one make of vehicle in 1998 and was subsequently adopted on some other makes, only 22% of light vehicles on the road were equipped with the technology in calendar year 2012. FMVSS required electronic stability control to be included in all new vehicles starting in model year 2012. The study estimates that more than 1,362 lives may be saved annually when all vehicles on the road utilize the technology, but this will not occur for a couple of decades.

In a separate study in 2012,[27] NHTSA evaluated the crashworthiness and crash avoidance performance of passenger cars and light vehicles, isolating the vehicle element in traffic safety improvements from human and environmental effects.[28] The study did not focus solely on FMVSS-regulated technologies, but also included overall vehicle design and improvements initiated by manufacturers. Unlike NHTSA's *Lives Saved by Vehicle Safety Technologies and Associated Federal Motor Vehicle Safety Standards, 1960 to 2012*, this study did not address specific technology and product sources of the improvements.

---

[22] C. J. Kahane, *Lives Saved by Vehicle Safety Technologies and Associated Federal Motor Vehicle Safety Standards, 1960 to 2012*, NHTSA, DOT HS 812 069, January 2015, p. xii.

[23] Centers for Disease Control and Prevention (CDC), *Injury Prevention & Control: Motor Vehicle Safety*, viewed March 9, 2017, https://www.cdc.gov/motorvehiclesafety/calculator/factsheet/seatbelt.html.

[24] Other major technologies and the cumulative lives saved as identified in the NHTSA study were steering wheel assemblies (79,989), frontal airbags (42,856), door locks (42,135), and side impact protection (32, 288). C. J. Kahane, *Lives Saved by Vehicle Safety Technologies and Associated Federal Motor Vehicle Safety Standards, 1960 to 2012*, NHTSA, DOT HS 812 069, January 2015.

[25] The average age of a vehicle on the road is 11.6 years. Jack Walsworth, "Average age of vehicles on road hits 11.6 years," *Automotive News*, November 22, 2016.

[26] ESC helps the driver maintain control of the vehicle during extreme steering maneuvers by keeping the vehicle headed in the driver's intended direction.

[27] Donna Glassbrenner, *An Analysis of Recent Improvements to Vehicle Safety*, National Center for Statistics and Analysis, NHTSA, DOT HS 811 572, June 2012.

[28] Human factors include drunk driving, driving experience, and use of seat belts and similar restraints; environmental factors include traffic signals, left turn lanes, and weather conditions. Ibid., pp. 1-2.

The NHTSA report found that the likelihood of crashing in 100,000 miles of driving had decreased from 30% in a new model year 2000 vehicle to 25% in a new model year 2008 vehicle. The likelihood of escaping a crash uninjured improved from 79% to 82% in the same time period.[29] The report contended that "the nationwide impact of these advancements is substantial" and that vehicle improvements between 2000 and 2008 prevented 700,000 vehicle crashes, prevented (or mitigated) injuries of 1 million occupants, and saved 2,000 lives in calendar year 2008 alone.[30]

TRENDS IN VEHICLE RECALLS

In addition to promulgating and enforcing vehicle safety standards, NHTSA investigates vehicle defects that affect safety.[31] NHTSA's Office of Defects Investigation (ODI) reviews and investigates complaints of alleged defects from vehicle owners, automakers, and other sources. There are several routes a potential recall complaint can take:

- Denial. When NHTSA's analysis of petitions calling for defect investigations leads the agency to decide not to proceed, it publicizes the reasons for the denial in the *Federal Register*.
- Further Review. If NHTSA determines there is reason to open an investigation of alleged safety-related defects, it looks further into the facts and ends with either a recommendation that the manufacturer recall the vehicle or a determination that there is no safety-related defect.

If a safety defect is confirmed by NHTSA, most manufacturers will initiate a recall; if they fail to do so, NHTSA can initiate a recall itself. In addition to the NHTSA investigative process, manufacturers also conduct their own internal investigations; if a manufacturer finds that a vehicle or component does not comply with a federal safety standard, it may issue its own recall to correct a safety defect before accidents are reported.

The law establishing the motor vehicle safety program requires that a manufacturer of a defective vehicle or component notify the vehicle owner and fix the defect without charge.[32] In practice, most recalls are issued by manufacturers, sometimes influenced by a NHTSA defect finding and sometimes solely by a manufacturer upon its own finding of a

---

[29] Donna Glassbrenner, *An Analysis of Recent Improvements to Vehicle Safety*, National Center for Statistics and Analysis, NHTSA, DOT HS 811 572, June 2012.
[30] Ibid.
[31] 49 U.S.C. §30166.
[32] Remedies for Defects and Compliance, 49 U.S.C. §30120.

defect. Of the 1,039 recalls issued in 2016, 92 were issued by manufacturers influenced by a NHTSA finding, and 947 were issued based on a manufacturer's finding alone.[33]

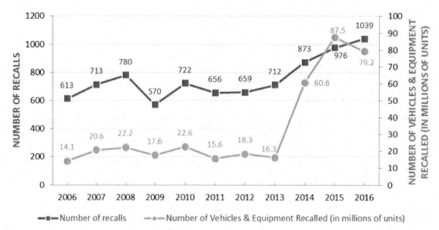

Source: NHTSA, 2016 Annual Recall Report.
Notes: Data include recalls of motor vehicles, motor vehicle parts, tires, and child safety seats. In 2016, out of 79.2 million recalled vehicles and items of equipment, 78.7 million units were of motor vehicles and parts.

Figure 1. Motor Vehicle and Equipment Recalls.

The annual number of recall actions has generally risen in the past decade (except for the recession year of 2009), and the number of vehicles and items of equipment recalled has risen steeply since 2013 (Figure 1). There are several reasons for the rising number of recalls, including stricter laws, larger fines, delayed detection by NHTSA of vehicle problems, and several recent high-visibility cases affecting millions of vehicles.

In 2014 and 2015, two large recalls were issued:

- General Motors (GM) recalled 2.2 million vehicles because of faulty ignition switches, which could slip out of the "run" position and prevent airbags from deploying in crashes. GM acknowledged that the defective switches caused 15 deaths and a number of injuries. NHTSA assessed a maximum $35 million civil penalty against GM.[34] In a separate settlement, the Department of Justice fined GM $900 million in criminal penalties.[35]
- Nineteen manufacturers recalled a total of about 42 million vehicles due to a defect in airbags provided by Takata, a parts supplier. The defect may cause the

---

[33] NHTSA, *2016 Annual Recall Report*.
[34] NHTSA, "U.S. Department of Transportation Announces Record Fines, Unprecedented Oversight Requirements in GM Investigation," press release, May 16, 2014, https://www.nhtsa.gov/press-releases/us-department-transportation-announces-record-fines-unprecedented-oversight.
[35] U.S. Department of Justice, "U.S. Attorney of the Southern District of New York Announces Criminal Charges Against General Motors and Deferred Prosecution Agreement with $900 Million Forfeiture," press release, September 17, 2015, https://www.justice.gov/opa/pr/us-attorney-southern-district-new-york-announces-criminal-charges-against-general-motors-and.

airbags' inflators to explode. The faulty airbags are linked to 16 deaths globally. In the United States, there have been 220 cases of Takata-supplied airbag inflators exploding, with 11 deaths and 184 injuries.[36] NHTSA fined Takata $200 million, with $70 million due in cash; an additional $130 million payment would be demanded if Takata fails to meet its commitments or if additional violations of the law are determined.[37] Separately, the Department of Justice fined Takata $1 billion, including a $25 million criminal fine, $125 million for victim compensation, and $850 million for compensating automakers for a portion of the cost of recalling the vehicles.[38]

In response to the GM ignition switch recall, NHTSA evaluated its procedures, interactions, and communications with General Motors. Its publication *NHTSA's Path Forward in 2015* outlined how the lessons learned from that recall could improve its defect investigation system. The then-NHTSA Administrator, Mark Rosekind, wrote in that publication that

> it is no overstatement to say [the ignition switch recall] was one of the most significant cases in NHTSA's history, not only because of the tragic toll of deaths and injuries, or the technical challenges it presented, but because of the unprecedented steps the manufacturer took to conceal a deadly defect.[39]

Path Forward identified five shortcomings in the recall and NHTSA procedures that affected its handling of the GM ignition switch problem:[40]

1) GM withheld critical information about engineering changes that would have allowed NHTSA to more quickly identify the defect.
2) NHTSA did not hold GM accountable for providing inadequate information.
3) Neither GM nor NHTSA completely understood the application of advanced airbag technology in GM vehicles.
4) NHTSA did not consider alternate theories proposed by internal and external sources.

---

[36] NHTSA, "U.S. Department of Transportation expands and accelerates Takata air bag inflator recall to protect American drivers and passengers," press release, May 4, 2016, https://www.nhtsa.gov/press-releases/us-department-transportation-expands-and-accelerates-takata-air-bag-inflator-recall-0.

[37] NHTSA, "U.S. DOT imposes largest civil penalty in NHTSA history on Takata for violating Motor Vehicle Safety Act; accelerates recalls to get safe air bags into U.S. vehicles," press release, November 3, 2015, https://one.nhtsa.gov/About-NHTSA/Press-Releases/
nhtsa_imposes_record_fine%E2%80%93on_takata_11032015.

[38] U.S. Department of Justice, "Takata Corporation Agrees to Plead Guilty and Pay $1 Billion in Criminal Penalties for Airbag Scheme," press release, January 13, 2017, https://www.justice.gov/opa/pr/takata-corporation-agrees-plead-guilty-and-pay-1-billion-criminal-penalties-airbag-scheme.

[39] NHTSA, *NHTSA's Path Forward*, DOT HS 812 163, June 2015, p. 2, https://www.nhtsa.gov/staticfiles/ communications/pdf/nhtsa-path-forward.pdf.

[40] Ibid., pp. 16-23.

5) NHTSA did not identify and follow up on trends in its own data sources and investigations.

The report proposed various process improvements, including increasing auto industry accountability, increasing NHTSA's knowledge of emerging technologies, and improving defects investigations.

Why Have Recalls Increased?

In addition to high-profile cases involving millions of vehicles, four other factors may have changed the magnitude of motor vehicle recalls. These are described below.

Trends in Manufacturing Efficiency

Motor vehicle manufacturers are attempting to reduce the number of separate parts they use by installing a single part on multiple vehicle models, instead of designing unique parts for each model. For example, Ford is cutting its global platforms from 15 to nine.[41] Much of the auto industry's sourcing is global, and one effect of having fewer vehicle platforms may be that a defective part is installed in a very large number of vehicles sold under several brands. The defective Takata airbags, for example, were used by nearly every automaker, leading to recalls in other countries as well as the largest recall on record in the United States.

Stricter Federal Reporting Requirements and Stiffer Penalties

More thorough and earlier reporting requirements and steeper penalties are thought to have increased the number of defects reported and hence the number of recalls.[42] In 2000, after a highly publicized recall of Ford Explorer sport utility vehicles and the Firestone tires used on those vehicles, Congress passed the Transportation Recall Enhancement, Accountability, and Documentation Act (TREAD Act).[43] The law established an Early Warning Reporting System (EWRS) that requires vehicle manufacturers to report a wide range of information, including data on defects, injuries, and deaths related to use of their products, enabling NHTSA to investigate defects without waiting for complaints from vehicle owners. In addition, the law increased civil penalties for violations of safety standards from a maximum of $925,000 to $15 million and provided criminal penalties

---

[41] A motor vehicle platform is shared design, engineering, components, and production used in a number of distinct models. Jerry Hirsch, "Auto Recalls Hit Record Level in U.S.," *Los Angeles Times*, June 23, 2014.

[42] For example, NHTSA found problems in 2015 with Fiat Chrysler Automobiles (FCA) for its execution of 23 vehicle safety recalls, affecting more than 11 million defective vehicles. In July 2015 FCA acknowledged violations of the legal requirement to repair vehicles with safety defects. In settling the case, FCA agreed to special federal oversight, bought back some defective vehicles from owners, and agreed to a $105 million civil penalty, which was at the time the largest ever imposed by NHTSA.

[43] P.L. 106-414.

for misleading NHTSA about safety defects that cause death or injury. NHTSA issued final TREAD Act regulations in 2003. EWRS regulations were not followed by manufactures in some recent recalls, however, leading NHTSA to impose additional penalties.[44]

Inadequate Data, Analysis, and Training at NHTSA

Some recalls might be smaller if they were identified earlier. NHTSA's Office of Defects Investigation (ODI) is responsible for identifying and investigating potential vehicle safety issues and requiring recalls when warranted. In June 2015, the Department of Transportation Inspector General (DOT OIG) made 17 recommendations to improve NHTSA's procedures for collecting and analyzing vehicle safety data and deciding when to investigate.[45] That report states that

> weakness in ODI's training and supervision of pre-investigation staff and its processes for identifying potential safety concerns and initiating investigations, as evidenced by NHTSA's handling of the GM ignition switch defect, deter NHTSA from successfully meeting its mandate to help prevent crashes and their attendant costs, both human and financial.[46]

DOT OIG notes that "without detailed guidance, decisions regarding key aspects of early warning reporting data are left to manufacturers' discretion—resulting in inconsistent reporting and data that ODI investigative chiefs and vehicle safety advocates consider to be of little use."[47]

While the DOT OIG has found that NHTSA has made "considerable progress" in addressing these recommendations, it told the Senate Committee on Commerce, Science, and Transportation in November 2016 that five recommendations remain open: four that will improve early warning reporting data and an improvement in the consumer complaint quality control process.[48] The 2015 surface transportation bill, the Fixing America's Surface Transportation (FAST) Act, tied an increase in NHTSA's funding

---

[44] NHTSA, "U.S. Department of Transportation Fines Honda $70 Million for Failing to Comply with Laws that Safeguard the Public," press release, January 8, 2015, https://www.nhtsa.gov/press-releases/us-department-transportation-fines-honda-70-million-failing-comply-laws-safeguard; and NHTSA, "FACT SHEET: NHTSA CONSENT ORDER ISSUED TO TAKATA," press release, November 3, 2015, http://www.safercar.gov/rs/takata/ pdfs/FactSheet-NHTSA-ConsentOrder-Takata.pdf.

[45] Department of Transportation, Office of Inspector General, *Inadequate Data and Analysis Undermine NHTSA's Efforts to Identify and Investigate Vehicle Safety Concerns*, Audit Report, June 18, 2015, https://www.oig.dot.gov/sites/default/files/NHTSA%20Safety-Related%20Vehicle%20Defects%20-%20Final%20Report%5E6-18-15.pdf.

[46] Ibid., p. 26.

[47] Ibid., p. 2.

[48] Letter from Calvin L. Scoville III, DOT Inspector General, to Honorable John Thune, Chairman, Committee on Commerce, Science, and Transportation, November 9, 2016, https://www.oig.dot.gov/sites/default/files/OIG%20Letter%20to%20Chairman%20Thune_issued%20Nov%209.pdf.

authorization to DOT certification that the inspector general's 17 recommendations had been implemented.[49]

Agency Funding

The Obama Administration requested additional funding for NHTSA. In June 2015, the NHTSA Administrator testified on behalf of the agency's budget request:

> Fixing problems such as the Takata recalls and Fiat Chrysler's recall performance is a monumental task. Yet the agency must manage this enormous and necessary task with its existing people, technology, and authorities. NHTSA must accomplish this task with a defects investigation budget of $10.6 million, a figure that, when adjusted for inflation, is actually 23 percent lower than its budget 10 years ago. The President has submitted a budget request that would fund significant improvements in NHTSA's defect investigation efforts. ...[50]

In light of the DOT OIG report, however, the Commerce Committee opted to tie additional funding to the resolution of those issues. Chairman John Thune spoke about the committee's perspective when the surface transportation bill was discussed on the Senate floor:

> [T]he Obama administration claimed NHTSA's problems could be solved by simply throwing more money at the agency, but based on the expert testimony from the inspector general, it is clear money alone is not going to solve the problem. We need to ensure that the agency fixes what is broken before we provide a significant increase in funding authorization with taxpayer dollars.[51]

Recall Completion Rates Remain an Issue

It is rare that all owners of a recalled vehicle bring their vehicles to a dealer for repairs. As a result, many defective vehicles are still on the road long after a recall is initiated. A recent review of NHTSA data by J.D. Power and Associates, a market research company, found that of the more than 120 million vehicles recalled from 2013 through 2015, 45 million had not been repaired as of mid-2016. Big recalls have the lowest completion rates: recalls affecting fewer than 10,000 vehicles have a 67%

---

[49] P.L. 114-94, §24101.
[50] U.S. Congress, Senate Committee on Commerce, Science, and Transportation, *Update on the Recalls of Defective Takata Air Bags and NHTSA's Vehicle Safety Efforts*, Testimony of NHTSA Administrator Mark Rosekind, 114th Cong., 1st sess., June 23, 2016, p. 6, https://www.commerce.senate.gov/public/_cache/files/2533c066-962b-4d9a-955b-769b0ef6b052/D68A57069B0038E44BDEB5213A83D0E3.rosekind-testimony.pdf.
[51] Senator John Thune, H.R. 22, Senate debate, *Congressional Record*, daily edition, vol. 161, no. 120 (July 28, 2015), p. S6054.

completion rate,[52] while recalls affecting more than a million vehicles have a completion rate of 49%.[53] The J.D. Power report suggests that bigger recalls are more complicated: manufacturers have more difficulty locating all owners. Obtaining an adequate supply of replacement parts can delay repairs. In addition, owners of vehicles involved in smaller recalls are easier to contact through personalized communication methods, such as a phone call.

The J.D. Power report also found that vehicle age, vehicle type, and the nature of the safety issue affected recall completion rates. Newer vehicles (model years 2013-2017) were completed at a 73% rate; older vehicles (model years 2003-2007) had a 44% completion rate. This may have reflected the difficulty of identifying the owners of vehicles that were more than six years old at the start of the period J.D. Power studied. The highest completion rates were for recalls involving powertrain, hydraulic brakes, and electrical issues: 71%, 66%, and 62%, respectively. By comparison, 47% of airbag issues and 48% of suspension problems were fixed.

In a separate, earlier study, the U.S. Government Accountability Office (GAO) reviewed vehicle recalls for the period 2000 through 2008 and found that the average completion rate in those years was 65%.[54] GAO's analysis found a wide differential among automakers: some had completion rates as low as 23%, while others had rates as high as 96%. Some manufacturers had consistently higher or lower rates.[55]

GAO called for NHTSA to implement changes that could improve the defect recall process, including

- adopting additional defect notification methods;
- modifying defect notification letters;
- better publicizing existing resources, such as the NHTSA website, and including a Vehicle Identification Number (VIN) search engine on the NHTSA website;[56] and
- developing national standards that would categorize the severity of a recall and whether a vehicle should be operated.

---

[52] A completion rate is determined by dividing the total population of affected, recalled vehicles by the number of vehicles that have been fixed. To make the calculations, NHTSA relies on data submitted quarterly by manufacturers during a recall campaign.

[53] J.D. Power and Associates, "Many Recalled Vehicles Go Without Remedy," press release, July 25, 2016, http://www.jdpower.com/cars/articles/safety-and-mpg/many-recalled-vehicles-go-without-remedy.

[54] The GAO and J.D. Power reports did not review vehicle recall performance in the same years, so their findings are not comparable.

[55] U.S. Government Accountability Office, *NHTSA Has Options to Improve the Safety Defect Recall Process*, June 2011, pp. 24-25.

[56] In August 2014, NHTSA added a VIN search engine to its website, https://vinrcl.safercar.gov/vin. NHTSA, "U.S. Department of Transportation Unveils New, Free, Online Search Tool for Recalls Using Vehicle Identification Number," press release, August 20, 2014.

As discussed later in this report, the FAST Act mandated that NHTSA and manufacturers develop new approaches to reach out to owners of recalled vehicles.

NEW TECHNOLOGY AND VEHICLE SAFETY

Many new technologies, whether mandated by Congress or NHTSA or developed by automakers, have translated incrementally into safer motor vehicles. As the introduction of new vehicle technologies has accelerated in the past decade, moving toward much more vehicle automation and a long-term goal of a fully autonomous vehicle, Congress and federal regulators are grappling with how to encourage such advancements, while recognizing that the traditional regulatory process is long and could "stymie innovation and stall the introduction of these technologies."[57]

A range of new technologies are being introduced to motor vehicles, many of them bringing automation to vehicular functions once performed only by the driver. Mary Barra, chairman and CEO of General Motors, has observed that "the auto industry will change more in the next five to 10 years than it has in the last 50."[58] There are three forces driving motor vehicle innovation:

- technological advances enabled by new materials and electronics;
- consumer demand for telecommunications connectivity and new types of vehicle ownership and ridesharing; and
- regulatory mandates pertaining to emissions, fuel efficiency, and safety.

Technological Advances

Most technological advances evolve from earlier technologies. For example, cruise control, a mechanism that takes over the throttle of the car to maintain a steady speed set by the driver, was invented in 1948 and first used on vehicles 10 years later.[59] It has developed into a more automated function called adaptive cruise control, which automatically adjusts vehicle speed to maintain a safe distance from vehicles ahead.

---

[57] U.S. Congress, House Energy and Commerce, Commerce, Manufacturing and Trade, *Disrupter Series: Self-Driving Cars*, testimony of Mark Rosekind, NHTSA Administrator, 114th Cong., 2nd sess., November 15, 2016, p. 2.

[58] Mary Barra, "The Next Revolution in the Auto Industry," *World Economic Forum Annual Meeting*, January 21, 2016, https://www.weforum.org/agenda/2016/01/the-next-revolution-in-the-car-industry/.

[59] Its inventor, Robert Teetor, was blind and obtained a patent for his invention in 1950. *Great Achievements*, "Automobile Timeline: 1948," http://www.greatachievements.org.

Several such innovations are expected to improve driver and passenger safety in the coming years.[60] These include the technologies described below.

Antilock Brake Systems (ABS)

ABS were originally invented for use on aircraft, but by the 1990s had been modified for use on automobiles. Today they are a standard feature being used as a base for further technological advances, as described below. ABS prevent the wheels from locking up during hard braking or on slippery surfaces (such as an icy road). Sensors at each wheel and a computer interact to maximize braking and prevent lock-up.

Traction Control and Electronic Stability Control (ESC)

Traction control is an electronically controlled system that limits wheel spinning during acceleration. Using the antilock braking system, traction control brakes a spinning wheel and automatically shifts power to the opposite drive wheel. ESC is an advanced form of this system that brakes the wheels and keeps the vehicle on the driver's intended path.

Automatic Emergency Braking (AEB) or Brake Assist

The AEB system detects a sudden effort to stop the car and, working with ABS, applies the brakes to reach the shortest stopping distance. By 2020, some vehicles may have driver override systems with sensor technology that will apply the brakes if a crash is imminent, even if the driver is pressing the accelerator.[61]

Forward-Collision Warning (FCW)

FCW uses cameras, radars, and lasers to search for cars ahead of a vehicle and alerts drivers if they are heading for an imminent crash with another vehicle, using visual signals and sounds to alert the driver. A similar system—pedestrian detection—is available to detect a pedestrian in the vehicle's path.

Blind-Spot Warning (BSW)

Radar or cameras prompt a device on an outside mirror to light up if another vehicle is in the driver's blind spot, preventing an accident. Advanced BSW may also include devices that steer a vehicle back to the center of a lane if another vehicle is detected in a blind spot.

---

[60] "Guide to Car Safety Features: These Features Can Help Make Driving Safer," *Consumer Reports*, June 2016.
[61] Karl Brauer, "Top 10 Advanced Car Technologies by 2020," *Forbes*, January 19, 2015.

Lane Departure Warning (LDW)

The system works by using cameras or lasers to monitor lane markings and sending visual or audible signals to a driver or vibrating the steering wheel or seat if the vehicle leaves its lane, unless a turn signal is activated. Lane-keeping assist takes LDW one step further and activates a sensor that will correct the steering direction.

The Insurance Institute for Highway Safety (IIHS) has found that drivers who fall asleep, suffer a medical emergency, or black out from drug or alcohol use are most likely to veer out of their intended lane. Lane departure is one of the major reasons for highway fatalities. Single-vehicle crashes where vehicles leave the road accounted for 40% of fatal crashes in 2014; head-on collisions and sideswipes (which also can be caused at times by lane departures) account for another 12% of the fatal crash total.[62]

Active Head Restraints

In a crash, the force of a driver or passenger in a front seat activates sensors that automatically move the head restraint forward to firmly cushion the occupant's head and reduce whiplash, which is a major consequence of such crashes.

Automatic High Beams

This technology automatically switches headlights from low to high beam and back, depending on road visibility.

Biometric Vehicle Access

Most automakers are moving away from key-based vehicle access, replacing it with electronic keyless entry systems. This links vehicle access to electromagnetic frequency and communication wavelengths that may leave the vehicle subject to hacking. In the future, biometric technology may eliminate this risk by unlocking a vehicle only with biometric identification, such as a fingerprint.[63]

Telematics

Drivers or passengers can use telematics—a combination of telecommunications with information and communications technology—to communicate with a central dispatch center or 911 emergency call center using cellular telephone and Global Positioning Satellite (GPS) technologies. The vehicle location is transmitted and, if airbags deploy, emergency service can be notified. These telematics can also be used as Remote Vehicle Shutdown to immobilize stolen cars.[64]

---

[62] Insurance Institute for Highway Safety, *Drivers who drift from lane and crash often dozing or ill*, September 1, 2016, http://www.iihs.org/iihs/sr/statusreport/article/51/7/3.

[63] Iritech Inc., "Biometric vehicle access to grow 20% during 2016-2020," press release, August 9, 2016, http://www.iritech.com/blog/biometric-vehicle-security-0816/.

[64] Karl Brauer, "Top 10 Advanced Car Technologies by 2020," *Forbes*, January 19, 2015.

Automated Vehicles

Table 2. Levels of vehicle automation

SAE Automation Category	Vehicle Function
Level 0	Human driver does everything.
Level 1	An automated system in the vehicle can sometimes assist the human driver conduct some parts of driving.
Level 2	An automated system can conduct some parts of driving, while the human driver continues to monitor the driving environment and performs most of the driving.
Level 3	An automated system can conduct some of the driving and monitor the driving environment in some instances, but the human driver must be ready to take back control if necessary.
Level 4	An automated system conducts the driving and monitors the driving environment, without human interference, but this level operates only in certain environments and conditions.
Level 5	The automated system performs all driving tasks, under all conditions that a human driver could.

Source: DOT and NHTSA, *Federal Automated Vehicles Policy*, September 2016, p. 9, https://www.transportation.gov/AV/federal-automated-vehicles-policy-september-2016.
Note: SAE is the Society of Automotive Engineers International, http://www.sae.org.

Increasingly, such innovations are being combined as manufacturers produce vehicles with higher levels of automation. Some envision a day when vehicles will be fully automated, with little or no involvement of the human passengers. With each level of automation, it is forecast that crashes may be dramatically reduced. Vehicles do not fall neatly into two categories of automated and nonautomated, because all of today's motor vehicles have some element of automation. The Society of Automotive Engineers International (SAE), a 100-year-old international standards- setting organization, has developed six categories of vehicle automation, a classification that has also been adopted by NHTSA to foster standardization and clarity in discussions about growing vehicle automation and safety (Table 2).

Consumer Demand

Motor vehicles and consumer electronics are increasingly connected. A sign of this transformation is seen in the annual Consumer Electronics Show (CES), which now serves as a showcase for automakers' near-term and future vehicle models.[65] Vehicles

---

[65] Cadie Thompson, "All the most important car tech that came out of CES 2017," *Business Insider*, January 10, 2017, http://www.businessinsider.com/ces-2017-car-tech-concept-cars-2017-1/#ford-also-officially-announced-that-it-was- adding-alexa-to-its-vehicles-2.

began using more electronics in the 1990s with telematics and infotainment. As more sensors, cameras, and telecommunications features, including Internet, are added to vehicles, consumer digital technology is becoming one of the driving forces of motor vehicle innovation. These new systems provide consumers with vehicles with capabilities for *entertainment and navigation assistance*; *convenience* through easier entry, ignition, and phone mobility; *greater comfort* through suspension adjustment, brake assist, and cabin temperature control; as well as more *security* through ABS, blind-spot detection, and 911 crash notification.[66]

A survey by the Boston Consulting Group (BCG) shows that consumers seek digital innovations in vehicles: when considering purchase of a new car, U.S. consumers said that connectivity and safety are ranked in the top five of new features. The same survey showed that consumers under 30 years of age value digital-device integration in vehicles.[67] A McKinsey & Company report, which forecasts motor vehicle revenues between 2015 and 2030, shows growth of vehicle and aftermarket sales in those years. However, the largest sales increases are forecast in on-demand, shared mobility services, such as car sharing, and in vehicle-related data-connectivity, including remote services and software upgrades.[68]

Regulatory Mandates

Emission, fuel economy, and vehicle safety regulations are a third factor increasing the demand for more technologically advanced vehicles. In the past decade, hybrid and electric vehicles have established a beachhead, while internal combustion engines—which are forecast to remain dominant in passenger motor vehicles for many decades—have been retooled so that their fuel economy has increased and emissions have dropped.

Plug-in electric new vehicle sales have grown from just over 17,000 units in 2011 to nearly 160,000 units in 2016 (out of total U.S. passenger and light-truck sales in 2016 of 17.6 million vehicles).[69] Sales grew by 37% in 2016 when compared to 2015. While many electric vehicles are purchased by "early adopters" who want to experience this type of relatively new technology, state and federal emissions and fuel economy rules also play a part. More than half of the new plug-ins sold in 2016 were sold in California, influenced by the state's zero-emission vehicle (ZEV) mandate, which requires that a

---

[66] Transportation Research Board Special Report 308, *The Safety Promise and Challenge of Automotive Electronics*, National Research Council, 2012, pp. 45-46.

[67] Boston Consulting Group, *Accelerating Innovation: New Challenges for Automakers*, January 2014, p. 9, http://www.bcg.de/documents/file153102.pdf.

[68] Paul Gao, Hans-Werner Kaas, and Detlev Mohr, et al., *Disruptive trends that will transform the auto industry*, McKinsey & Company, January 2016, p. 2, http://www.mckinsey.com/industries/high-tech/our-insights/disruptive-trends-that-will-transform-the-auto-industry.

[69] Inside EVs, *Monthly Plug-in Sales Scorecard*, viewed March 4, 2017, http://insideevs.com/monthly-plug-in-sales- scorecard/.

certain percentage of an automaker's sales must be ZEVs (electric and fuel cell vehicles).[70] California has established a goal of placing 1.5 million ZEVs on its highways by 2025.[71]

The Obama Administration's greenhouse gas (GHG) emissions program—a joint regulatory initiative of NHTSA and the Environmental Protection Agency (EPA)—seeks reductions in GHG emissions and an increase of vehicle fuel economy (to 54.5 miles per gallon by model year 2025).[72] In announcing the program in 2012, the Obama White House noted the expected technology-enhancing effects of the program:

> [A]chieving the new fuel efficiency standards will encourage innovation and investment in advanced technologies that increase our economic competitiveness and support high- quality domestic jobs in the auto industry.
>
> [M]ajor auto manufacturers are already developing advanced technologies that can significantly reduce fuel use and greenhouse gas emissions beyond the existing model year 2012-2016 standards. In addition, a wide range of technologies are currently available for automakers to meet the new standards, including advanced gasoline engines and transmissions, vehicle weight reduction, lower tire rolling resistance, improvements in aerodynamics, diesel engines, more efficient accessories, and improvements in air conditioning systems.[73]

President Trump announced in Detroit in March 2017 that his Administration will review the GHG emissions program, which may lead to a change in the emissions and fuel economy standards.[74]

The convergence of a high level of motor vehicle industry innovation, consumer choice, and federal regulatory mandates are key factors in making motor vehicles safer. Technologies developed in one regulatory context may reinforce other regulatory requirements.[75] Mandates to reduce motor vehicle greenhouse gases, for example, are leading manufacturers to cut tailpipe emissions by using vehicle-to-vehicle communications that reduce unnecessary braking and acceleration, and enable more efficient driving patterns. Vehicle safety is enhanced by these changes. Similarly, the

---

[70] "US Electric Car Sales Rose by 37% in 2016," Greentech Media, February 6, 2017, pp. https://www.greentechmedia.com/articles/read/us-electric-car-sales-rose-by-37-in-2016.

[71] Office of Governor Edmund G. Brown Jr., *Governor's Interagency Working Group on Zero-emission Vehicles*, February 2013, https://www.opr.ca.gov/docs/Governor's_Office_ZEV_Action_Plan_(02-13).pdf.

[72] For more information about the NHTSA-EPA program, see CRS Report R42721, *Automobile and Truck Fuel Economy (CAFE) and Greenhouse Gas Standards*, by Brent D. Yacobucci, Bill Canis, and Richard K. Lattanzio.

[73] The White House, "Obama Administration Finalizes Historic 54.5 MPG Fuel Efficiency Standards," press release, August 28, 2012, https://obamawhitehouse.archives.gov/the-press-office/2012/08/28/obama-administration-finalizes-historic-545-mpg-fuel-efficiency-standard.

[74] Remarks by President Trump at American Center for Mobility, Detroit, MI, March 15, 2017, https://www.whitehouse.gov/the-press-office/2017/03/15/remarks-president-trump-american-center-mobility-detroit- mi.

[75] Julia Pyper, "Self-Driving Cars Could Cut Greenhouse Gas Pollution," *Scientific American*, September 15, 2014, https://www.scientificamerican.com/article/self-driving-cars-could-cut-greenhouse-gas-pollution/.

sensors and lidar[76] that are being developed for automated vehicle safety may well help improve vehicle fuel efficiency.

Reforming the Regulatory Process

The development of a new Federal Motor Vehicle Safety Standard can be lengthy, often lasting many years. Former DOT Secretary Anthony Foxx and former NHTSA Administrator Mark Rosekind broadened the agency's approach beyond the traditional rulemaking to include new means of interacting with manufacturers and other vehicle safety stakeholders. In congressional testimony in November 2016, then-NHTSA Administrator Rosekind said the agency's regulatory process was too slow, given the pace of technological development. He explained that

> a traditional approach to regulating these new technologies would be to engage solely in rulemaking process, writing new regulations that prescribe specific standards. Our view is that approach would stymie innovation and stall the introduction of these technologies....
>
> Any rule we might offer today would likely be woefully out-of-date by the time it took effect, given the pace of technological development[77]

Among the steps DOT and NHTSA took in 2016 to address these issues and establish new forms of enhancing vehicle safety are the following:

- Secretary Foxx announced a voluntary agreement in January 2016 with 18 automakers to collectively analyze and share safety data, increase the number of car owners who respond to recall notices, and develop a joint approach to automotive cybersecurity.[78] While automakers supported the agreement, former NHTSA Administrator Joan Claybrook reportedly criticized it as ineffective.[79]
- In March 2016, NHTSA and the IIHS announced a commitment of 20 vehicle manufacturers to make automatic emergency braking (AEB) a standard feature on virtually all new passenger vehicles by 2022. This voluntary agreement makes AEB standard on vehicles three years earlier than had NHTSA pursued a

---

[76] Lidar (an acronym for light detection and ranging) uses a laser beam to measure the distance to an object in its path; when used in motor vehicles, lidar creates a three-dimensional map of the vehicle's surrounding environment and, with accompaniment of sensors, would control aspects of the vehicle's direction and speed.

[77] U.S. Congress, House Committee on Energy and Commerce, Subcommittee on Commerce, Manufacturing, and Trade, *Disrupter Series: Self-driving Cars*, 114th Cong., 2nd sess., November 15, 2016.

[78] The industry-government agreement is called *Proactive Safety Principles*. U.S. Congress, House Committee on Energy and Commerce, Subcommittee on Commerce, Manufacturing, and Trade, *Oversight of the National Highway Traffic Safety Administration*, 114th Cong., 2nd sess., April 14, 2016, p. 6.

[79] Bill Vlasic, "18 Carmakers Agree to Share Safety Data," *New York Times*, January 15, 2016.

traditional rulemaking. In those three years, IIHS estimates that 28,000 crashes and 12,000 injuries will be prevented.[80]

- NHTSA's September 2016 *Federal Automated Vehicles Policy* officially adopted SAE International's levels of automation, and provides guidance to automakers and other vehicle developers with a 15-point "Safety Assessment" that discusses safety areas that manufacturers should evaluate in developing highly automated vehicles. In addition, the policy statement delineates federal and state roles in the absence of an FMVSS regulatory process for automated vehicles, and also discusses how NHTSA might use current regulatory tools—such as exemption and interpretation authorities—to expedite the development of safe highly automated vehicles.[81]

NEW VEHICLE SAFETY LAWS

Congress dealt extensively with vehicle safety issues in the FAST Act, the five-year surface transportation law enacted in December 2015. Its provisions on vehicle safety are described below.

Rental Cars[82]

Rental car companies with more than 35 vehicles must repair vehicles subject to recalls before renting, leasing, or selling them. NHTSA was given authority to investigate rental car company violations of recalls.[83]

Motor Vehicle Dealers[84]

Motor vehicle dealers are required to notify owners of open recalls when an owner brings a vehicle to the dealer for servicing. The provision does not require dealers in used motor vehicles to repair vehicles subject to a recall prior to selling them to consumers.

---

[80] U.S. Congress, House Committee on Energy and Commerce, Subcommittee on Commerce, Manufacturing, and Trade, *Oversight of the National Highway Traffic Safety Administration*, 114th Cong., 2nd sess., April 14, 2016, pp. 3-4.

[81] U.S. Congress, House Committee on Energy and Commerce, Subcommittee on Commerce, Manufacturing, and Trade, *Disrupter Series: Self-driving Cars*, 114th Cong., 2nd sess., November 15, 2016.

[82] Rental car provisions are found in 49 U.S.C. §30101 note, 49 U.S.C. §30102, 49 U.S.C. §30120, 49 U.S.C. §30122, and 49 U.S.C. §30166.

[83] NHTSA, "Effective Today: New Federal law for recalled rental cars protects consumers from vehicle safety defects," press release, June 1, 2016, https://www.nhtsa.gov/press-releases/effective-today-new-federal-law-recalled-rental-cars-protects-consumers-vehicle.

[84] 49 U.S.C. §30120(f).

Recall Notifications

Several provisions address the low recall completion rate in many vehicle recalls and seek to boost vehicle owner participation in recall campaigns. In the past, the law required notification of consumers by first-class mail; the FAST Act expands the requirement to include electronic means of notification, including use of email, social media, and targeted online campaigns. DOT is required to conduct a series of multiyear analyses of recall completion rates and report the findings to Congress, including information on recall completion rates by manufacturer, model year, components, and vehicle type. NHTSA is also required to report on how it will improve recall completion rates based on the analyses. The DOT Inspector General is required to audit NHTSA management of safety recalls.[85] The law also requires DOT to initiate a two-year pilot grant program with no more than six states to evaluate the feasibility of using each state's motor vehicle registration process to inform consumers of open recalls on their vehicles.[86]

In addition, DOT is given two years to adjust its website by using current information technology, web design trends, and other best practices to ensure that motor vehicle safety recall information is more easily accessible to the public.[87]

DOT is directed to study the feasibility of adding to each new vehicle a technical system that would tell the vehicle owner when the vehicle was subject to an open recall, and to report the findings to Congress within one year.[88] This study has not been completed.

Increase in Civil Penalties and Automotive Accountability

For each violation of the law, the statutory civil penalty cap is increased from a maximum of $35 million to $105 million.[89] It is thought that the risk of higher punitive penalties will encourage automakers to more readily disclose potential defects that could lead to a recall.

In addition, the time period during which automakers must pay to remedy defects is increased from 10 to 15 years (after a consumer is notified of the recall); the time period they must retain safety records is doubled from five to 10 years.[90] The law also includes a whistleblower provision that encourages industry employees to come forward with

---

[85] 49 U.S.C. §30119.
[86] 49 USC §30119(g).
[87] 49 U.S.C. §30119 note and 49 U.S.C. §30166 note.
[88] P.L. 114-94, §24113.
[89] 49 U.S.C. §30165.
[90] 49 U.S.C. §30120, §30117(b).

information about possible motor vehicle safety violations and allows DOT to pay awards to whistleblowers from a portion of recovered civil penalties.[91]

Driver Privacy[92]

The Driver Privacy Act of 2015 was included in the FAST Act, stipulating that data retained by an event data recorder (EDR) is the property of the vehicle owner.[93] EDR data can be accessed by someone other than the owner only in certain circumstances, such as under a court order. Most vehicles include EDRs, and owner's manuals describe their use, but there was congressional concern over how this data could be used and who owns it. NHTSA is required to

- submit a report to Congress within one year, evaluating the amount of time EDRs should capture and record vehicle data that is sufficient to investigate the cause of motor vehicle crashes; and
- promulgate within two years a regulation establishing the appropriate time period for EDR data capture.

Child Occupants

Congress has shown concern about infants left in car seats for prolonged periods of time. A 2012 law[94] recommended (but did not require) that DOT research methods to reduce these risks; the FAST Act requires DOT to initiate research into ways to reduce the risks of hyperthermia or hypothermia to children left unattended in vehicles' rear seats.[95] It also requires NHTSA to revise its crash data collection system to capture additional information on types of child restraints employed in crashes and to report its findings to Congress.[96]

---

[91] 49 U.S.C. §30172.
[92] 49 U.S.C. §30101 nt.
[93] An EDR is a device in a vehicle that records certain elements of a vehicle in the seconds before a crash, such as pre- crash speed, brake use, driver seat belt use, and airbag deployment timing.
[94] Moving Ahead for Progress in the 21st Century Act (MAP-21), P.L. 112-141, §31504(a).
[95] 49 U.S.C. §30111.
[96] 49 U.S.C. §30127.

Crash Avoidance Disclosure[97]

DOT is required to develop a rulemaking that will add crash avoidance information, such as automatic braking and lane departure prevention,[98] next to crashworthiness information on motor vehicle window stickers.

Tires[99]

The FAST Act includes several provisions related to motor vehicle tires, including requirements that NHTSA update its standards for tire pressure monitoring, develop a rule for tire fuel efficiency minimum performance standards, and establish an electronically searchable tire recall database. The time period for remedying tire defects is extended from 60 to 180 days (from the time a consumer is notified of a recall).

ISSUES BEFORE CONGRESS

Although many of the changes in federal vehicle safety policy made by the FAST Act have yet to take full effect, Members of Congress have advanced several other proposals that would extend NHTSA's authority to regulate motor vehicles. Among them are:

Obligations to Repair Recalled Vehicles

Current law does not require auto dealers to fix used cars on their lots, or taxi and ride-sharing services to repair vehicles being used to transport customers. Some Members of Congress have called for including used cars in the recall process.[100] When a House floor amendment was debated during consideration of the surface transportation bill in 2015, it was argued that auto dealers do not in practice sell cars with defects and that some recalls are "overly broad because the majority of vehicle recalls do not require the drastic step of grounding the vehicle."[101] NHTSA presently has no authority to order repairs of recalled vehicles used by taxi and ride- sharing services.[102]

---

[97] 49 U.S.C. §32302.
[98] Insurance Institute for Highway Safety, *Crash avoidance features by make and model*, viewed March 6, 2017, http://www.iihs.org/iihs/ratings/crash-avoidance-features.
[99] 49 U.S.C. §30120, §30123, §32304A, §30119(g).
[100] 114th Congress, H.R. 1181, Vehicle Safety Improvement Act of 2015, §301.
[101] National Automobile Dealers Association, *Grounding All Recalled Used Vehicles Devalues Trade-Ins*, January 23, 2017, https://www.nada.org/CustomTemplates/General Page.aspx?id=21474836504.
[102] Patrick Olsen, "Is the Cab, Uber or Lyft You're Getting Into Unsafe?," *Cars.com*, November 21, 2016, https://www.cars.com/articles/is-the-cab-uber-or-lyft-youre-getting-into-unsafe-1420692342479/.

Imminent Hazard Authority

Currently, NHTSA cannot require manufacturers to immediately stop sales of vehicles or equipment without following the substantial procedural steps needed to complete a recall investigation. The Obama Administration asked Congress to grant NHTSA "imminent hazard authority," which would allow the agency to take immediate action when it believed there was the likelihood of death or serious injury. Congress did not include such authority in the FAST Act.

Public Access to Safety Information

Some Members of Congress have called for amending the Early Warning reporting provisions to require NHTSA to make information it receives from manufacturers more publicly available in a searchable, website format, contending that consumers and safety analysts could better evaluate potential defects.[103]

Prohibition of Regional Recalls

NHTSA may allow auto manufacturers to limit a recall to a certain geographic area if there is evidence that the defect is primarily found in vehicles registered in that area. For example, the recall of Takata airbags was initially deemed a regional recall because excess humidity seemed to play a role, so only vehicles in more humid parts of the country were subject to the recall. Critics contended that a regional recall was inappropriate because vehicles registered in other areas at the time of the recall could subsequently be sold or moved to high-humidity areas, putting owners and passengers at risk.[104] The Takata recall was broadened to a national recall after airbag defects were found in vehicles in other parts of the country. Legislation proposed during the consideration of the FAST Act would have eliminated regional recalls.[105]

---

[103] S. 1743, 114th Congress, Early Warning Reporting System Improvement Act, §102.
[104] Sens. Edward Markey and Richard Blumenthal, "Senator Markey and Blumenthal Reintroduce Legislation to Improve Cybersecurity of Vehicles and Airplanes," press release, March 22, 2017, https://www.markey.senate.gov/ news/press-releases/senator-markey-and-blumenthal-reintroduce-legislation-to-improve-cybersecurity-of-vehicles-and- airplanes.
[105] Representative Jan Schakowsky, H.R. 22, House debate, *Congressional Record*, daily edition, vol. 161, part No. 164 (November 4, 2015), p. H7723.

Cybersecurity

The Security and Privacy in Your Car Act of 2017 (S. 680) would direct NHTSA and the Federal Trade Commission to establish federal standards to secure connected features and other motor vehicle data from hackers and data trackers. The legislation would also require the two agencies to develop a "cyber dashboard" rating that would show on a vehicle window sticker how well each vehicle model protects security and privacy of vehicle owners.[106]

The Security and Privacy in Your Car Study Act of 2017 (H.R. 701) would require NHTSA to report to Congress after conducting a study to determine the appropriate cybersecurity standards for motor vehicles, including how critical vehicle software systems can be separated from other software systems, and techniques necessary to prevent intrusions into motor vehicle software systems.

Civil Penalties

The Obama Administration asked Congress to increase the maximum civil penalty on a manufacturer for selling vehicles that violate Federal Motor Vehicle Safety Standards from $35 million to $300 million per violation.[107] The FAST Act increased the maximum penalty to $105 million.

---

[106] The bill also called for vehicle privacy standards, similar to those later included in the FAST Act. Sens. Edward Markey and Richard Blumenthal, "Sens. Markey, Blumenthal Introduce Legislation to Protect Drivers from Auto Security, Privacy Risks with Standards & 'Cyber Dashboard' Rating System," press release, July 21, 2015, http://www.markey.senate.gov/news/press-releases/sens-markey-blumenthal-introduce-legislation-to-protect-drivers-from-auto-security-privacy-risks-with-standards-and-cyber-dashboard-rating-system.

[107] See https://www.transportation.gov/sites/dot.gov/files/docs/GROW_AMERICA_Act_Summary_1.pdf, §4110.

In: Highway Safety
Editor: Bertha G. Baldwin

ISBN: 978-1-53617-176-1
© 2020 Nova Science Publishers, Inc.

Chapter 6

COMMERCIAL TRUCK SAFETY: OVERVIEW[*]

David Randall Peterman

SUMMARY

More than 11 million large trucks travel U.S. roads, and almost 4 million people hold commercial driver's licenses. In 2015, large trucks were involved in more than 400,000 motor vehicle crashes serious enough to be registered by police, with nearly 100,000 of those crashes causing injuries and around 3,600 resulting in fatalities. To address this situation, Congress has assigned the U.S. Department of Transportation (DOT)—primarily the Federal Motor Carrier Safety Administration (FMCSA)—responsibility for regulating the safety practices of commercial motor carriers and drivers. In addition, the National Highway Traffic Safety Administration (NHTSA) in DOT is responsible for the safety of the vehicles themselves through its role in setting vehicle safety standards.

Truck crash, injury, and fatality rates have generally been rising since 2009 after declining over many years. This increase may be due in part to marginally skilled or inexperienced drivers entering the industry, or to higher levels of work and stress among veteran drivers, or to other factors.

Two FMCSA proposals concerning driver safety have proven particularly contentious.

- In March 2017, FMCSA abandoned its attempt to require drivers to take a 34-hour rest period, including two consecutive early morning periods, at least once a week. The proposed "restart rule" encountered strong objections from drivers as well as motor carriers, and an FMCSA study could not confirm that the rule would lead to sufficient improvement in safety to satisfy Congress.
- In March 2016 FMCSA began a joint rulemaking with the Federal Railroad Administration to require that commercial drivers (or train operators) who exhibit certain risk factors be screened for obstructive sleep apnea, which

---

[*] This is an edited, reformatted and augmented version of Congressional Research Service, Publication No. R44792, dated March 21, 2017.

interferes with sound sleep and thus increases the risk of crashes. In the past, efforts to address sleep apnea among drivers met resistance from drivers who feared they might be prohibited from driving commercial vehicles, and Congress prohibited FMCSA from addressing sleep apnea among drivers except through a formal rulemaking.

FMCSA has introduced stricter training standards for new drivers, and has instituted a database intended to help prevent drivers barred from commercial driving due to convictions for driving under the influence of drugs or alcohol from bypassing the prohibition and continuing to drive. FMCSA has also barred drivers from using handheld phones or texting in order to reduce driver distraction.

Motor carriers have frequently sought to increase driver productivity and reduce costs by pushing for standards allowing longer or heavier trucks. Although efforts to permit longer trucks were rejected by Congress in 2015, Congress did approve a number of exceptions and waivers to federal weight limits. FMCSA and NHTSA have jointly proposed to require that all large trucks be equipped with speed limiters, a proposal over which the trucking industry is divided. Congress also has taken an interest in FMCSA's Compliance, Safety, and Accountability Program, which is intended to allow it to focus resources on carriers most in need of supervision from a safety standpoint. Legislation in 2015 required FMCSA to obtain external review of the system it proposes to use to measure carrier safety.

INTRODUCTION

More than 11 million large trucks (trucks weighing over 10,000 pounds) travel U.S. roads, and almost 4 million operators hold commercial driver's licenses.[1] In 2015, large trucks were involved in more than 400,000 motor vehicle crashes serious enough to be registered by police, with nearly 100,000 of those crashes causing injuries and around 3,600 resulting in fatalities.[2] To address this situation, Congress has assigned the U.S. Department of Transportation (DOT) — primarily the Federal Motor Carrier Safety Administration (FMCSA)—responsibility for regulating the safety practices of commercial motor carriers and drivers. In addition, the National Highway Traffic Safety Administration (NHTSA) in DOT is responsible for the safety of the vehicles themselves through its role in setting vehicle safety standards.[3]

This responsibility involves oversight of an industry comprising over 500,000 motor carriers, with around 35,000 new carriers beginning operation and many existing carriers exiting the industry each year. The agencies concerned with truck safety are relatively small; FMCSA has 1,175 full-time-equivalent personnel, including 600 front-line enforcement staff, and NHTSA personnel are involved in truck safety primarily at times

---

[1] Federal Motor Carrier Safety Administration (FMCSA), *FY2017 Budget Justification*, p. 5.
[2] FMCSA, *Large Truck and Bus Crash Facts 2015*, early release, November 2016, pp. 7, 13, 18.
[3] FMCSA and NHTSA exercise similar shared responsibility for commercial bus safety; this report focuses on commercial trucking (i.e., the hauling of freight) and does not deal with commercial buses (i.e., the hauling of passengers).

when vehicle safety standards are under consideration.[4] Truck safety efforts are assisted by roughly 12,000 state employees, including highway patrol officers. Federal enforcement agents and state agents enforcing federal regulations conduct over 3.5 million roadside inspections of trucks and buses annually, as well as over 16,000 on-site investigations and over 30,000 safety audits of new motor carriers. Some 10,000 motor carriers and drivers are the subject of FMCSA enforcement actions each year.[5] Freight rates and other economic matters are not subject to federal regulation.

Although crashes involving unsafe trucks or drivers often lead to public outrage, regulatory efforts to improve truck safety are often controversial. Truck safety laws and regulations directly affect the profitability of hundreds of thousands of companies, most of them small, and the livelihoods of millions of commercial drivers. Trucking regulations may also affect the cost of freight to shippers and alter the competitive balance between the trucking industry and its railroad and barge competitors.

Both government and private-sector analysts have forecast significant increases in trucking activity over the coming decades, reflecting expected growth in the U.S. economy and the role of trucks in moving freight. For example, DOT projects a 43% increase in freight ton-miles carried by truck between 2012 and 2040.[6] Greater truck mileage could result in increasing numbers of truck crashes. Some say various safety technologies now under development, culminating in "self-driving" trucks, may eventually make truck crashes less common.[7]

This report briefly reviews heavy truck safety trends, then looks at FMCSA's role in promoting safety in the heavy truck industry. It then divides heavy truck safety issues into three categories, and addresses each in turn: issues related to motor carriers (the companies that make up the industry, the majority of which have only a handful of vehicles); issues related to the vehicles themselves; and issues related to commercial drivers.

HEAVY TRUCK SAFETY TRENDS

The crash rate for large trucks, measured as the number of crashes involving fatalities, injuries, or property damage per million vehicle miles traveled, has declined over time. Crash rates typically drop significantly during recessions and then rise as economic growth resumes; this dynamic was evident during the 2010-2014 period, as

---

[4] Of these, fewer than 600 are front-line enforcement staff: investigators, auditors, and inspectors. FMCSA, *FY2017 Budget Justification*, Exhibit II-8, and p. 105.
[5] FMCSA, *FY2017 Budget Justification*, p. 37.
[6] United States Department of Transportation, *Beyond Traffic 2045: Trends and Choices* (Draft), no date but approximately 2015, p. 47, https://www.transportation.gov/sites/dot.gov/files/docs/ Draft_Beyond_ Traffic_Framework.pdf.
[7] Jeffrey Short and Dan Murray, *Identifying Autonomous Vehicle Technology Impacts on the Trucking Industry*, American Transportation Research Institute, November 2016.

truck crash rates rose from their historic lows during the 2007-2009 recession (Figure 1). Nonetheless, the crash rate in 2014, the most recent year for which data are available, was still below the pre-2007 level.[8]

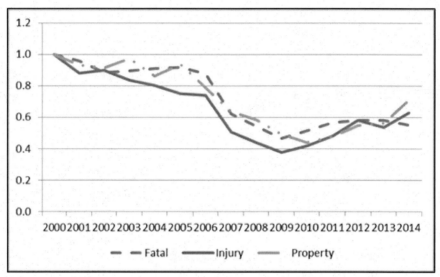

Source: CRS; data from Federal Motor Carrier Safety Administration, *Large Truck and Bus Crash Facts 2015*, November 2016, Trends Table 4.

Notes: The rates are indexed to their 2000 levels for ease of visual comparison of trends. The rates for injury and property damage crashes per million vehicle miles traveled are many times higher than the fatality rate.

Figure 1. Crash Trends Involving Large Trucks, 2000-2014.

The number of people killed in crashes involving large trucks increased by 4% from 2014 (3,908) to 2015 (4,067), although it is still unknown whether the fatality rate per million vehicle miles traveled increased. Only additional data will reveal whether the long-term decline in the truck crash rate has run its course. If so, this could indicate that the safety performance of large trucks is decreasing, raising questions about FMCSA's ability to further improve truck safety.

Historically, trends in truck crashes resulting in fatalities, in injuries, and in only property damage have been roughly similar. However, in recent years the fatal crash rate has been relatively steady while the rates of crashes involving injuries and property damages have risen. The vast majority of fatalities in crashes involving large trucks are experienced by the occupants of the other vehicle(s), typically passenger vehicles. Safety improvements to cars and light trucks, such as the increasing number of airbags, may be reducing the number of fatalities from truck-car collisions.

---

[8] FMCSA released an early version of its annual *Large Truck and Bus Crash Facts* for 2015 in November 2016, but it does not include crash rates for 2015 because the underlying vehicle miles traveled data for 2015 were not yet available. See https://www.fmcsa.dot.gov/sites/fmcsa.dot.gov/files/docs/LTCF2015%20Early%20Release.pdf.

According to an FMCSA study, two-thirds of commercial truck crashes are caused by the other driver, not the commercial driver.[9] This finding implies that additional attention to truck driver behavior would be relatively ineffective in reducing the number of crashes involving large trucks. However, some critics question the validity of the proportion of crashes caused by commercial drivers, noting that crashes between commercial and noncommercial vehicles kill noncommercial drivers more frequently than the commercial drivers, often leaving investigators with only the commercial driver's account of the crash. Thus, these critics assert, the proportion of crashes attributed to noncommercial drivers may be overstated.

FMCSA'S ROLE

Congress established FMCSA as a separate administration within DOT through the Motor Carrier Safety Improvement Act of 1999 (P.L. 106-159), transferring responsibilities that had previously been handled by an office within the Federal Highway Administration. FMCSA's responsibilities can be divided into two parts: creating and enforcing safety rules and regulations, and implementing programs and procedures to promote the safety of motor carriers, commercial vehicles, and drivers.

The constitutional provision granting Congress the power to regulate interstate commerce[10] has been construed to give the federal government much greater authority over commercial vehicles and drivers engaged in interstate commerce than over commercial vehicles not engaged in interstate commerce. Commercial vehicles that typically operate within a single state, such as waste haulers and cement mixers, are generally not subject to federal safety regulations.[11]

Regulation of intrastate commercial transportation is generally a state matter. So, for example, Congress has long required that commercial drivers in interstate commerce must be at least 21 years of age, but most states allow a person to get a commercial driver's license (CDL) starting at age 18. This has resulted in a population of 18- to 20-year-olds who have CDLs but may operate commercial vehicles only within the state that issued their license. Congress can affect the operations of intrastate carriers indirectly, by encouraging states to adopt laws that govern them.

In addition to licensing truck drivers, FMCSA reviews trucking companies to check their compliance with federal requirements and audits the safety practices of companies entering the industry. Although FMCSA has authority to conduct roadside safety inspections of trucks, it usually relies on state law enforcement personnel for that

---

[9] FMCSA's *Large Truck Crash Causation Study* is available at https://ai.fmcsa.dot.gov/LTCCS/default.asp.
[10] Article I, §8.
[11] In practice, the line between interstate and intrastate commerce is not always clear. In some cases carriers that operate entirely within a state, but which are carrying goods that originated outside the state, are considered to be engaged in interstate commerce.

purpose. State officials also conduct many compliance reviews and new entrant safety audits.

In creating FMCSA, Congress specified that its intent was the furtherance of the highest degree of safety in motor carrier transportation, and that FMCSA should consider safety as the highest priority.[12] Congress required FMCSA to develop a long-term strategy for improving commercial motor vehicle, operator, and carrier safety, including a schedule and an annual plan for achieving certain goals set by Congress.[13] FMCSA publishes an updated strategic plan periodically;[14] the annual implementation plan is submitted to Congress as part of the annual budget process.

CARRIER SAFETY ISSUES

In 1999, Congress established a two-pronged approach to improving the safety of new entrants to the motor carrier industry. It required FMCSA to conduct a safety audit of each new entrant within 18 months of starting operations, and it directed FMCSA to establish minimum requirements for firms wishing to enter the industry to ensure that they know the federal safety standards before they are granted registration.[15] The latter directive included a requirement that DOT consider establishing an examination that would test officers of new applicants on their knowledge of federal safety standards. FMCSA has not yet determined that new entrants should have to pass such an exam.

In 2015, Congress tightened these requirements, directing FMCSA to audit new entrants within 12 months of their entry into the industry.[16] The focus on new entrants is due to studies finding that new entrants to the motor carrier industry have lower rates of compliance with basic safety management requirements than do experienced carriers. FMCSA observed that the shortened time frame will increase its audit workload. An average of more than 35,000 firms enter the industry each year, but a certain percentage of carriers typically go out of business between months 12 and 18. The 12-month deadline requires FMCSA to audit many carriers that will go out of business soon after the audit.

Under current practice, a new trucking firm may engage in interstate commerce before FMCSA conducts a safety assessment. In August 2009, in response to a petition from Advocates for Highway and Auto Safety, FMCSA issued an Advanced Notice of Proposed Rulemaking in which it requested information on the costs and benefits of

---

[12] Codified at 49 U.S.C. §113(b).
[13] The goals are reducing crash and fatality numbers, improving enforcement and compliance programs, targeting enforcement to high-risk operators, and improving research on safety and performance.
[14] The current Strategic Plan covers FY2015-FY2018; see https://www.fmcsa.dot.gov/sites/fmcsa.dot.gov/files/docs/FMCSA_FY2015_FY2018_Strategic_Plan_082618.pdf.
[15] P.L. 106-159, §210(a) & (b).
[16] Fixing America's Surface Transportation (FAST) Act (P.L. 114-94), §5304. The deadline is four months for passenger carriers.

requiring new entrants to pass an examination of their knowledge of federal safety requirements, and of alternatives to a proficiency exam that would also improve the safety performance of new entrants.[17] In September 2009 FMCSA's Motor Carrier Safety Advisory Committee, made up of industry representatives, recommended that FMCSA take a number of steps to ensure that new entrant motor carriers are knowledgeable about safety requirements, including testing.[18] The Advanced Notice of Proposed Rulemaking continues to be listed in DOT's monthly report on the status of significant rulemakings, but FMCSA has taken no further action.

The Commercial Vehicle Safety Alliance (CVSA), an association of federal, state, and local commercial motor vehicle safety officials and industry representatives, has recommended that Congress request a study of the costs and benefits of expanding the new entrant safety assurance program to include intrastate carriers.[19] The CVSA notes that only motor carriers that operate in interstate commerce, and thus are subject to federal regulation, are required to undergo a safety audit. While no official figure is available, CVSA cites estimates that half of all motor carriers operate solely with a single state and hence are not subject to federal safety audits. Congress may lack the authority to require states to conduct such audits for intrastate carriers, although it could provide incentives for states to do so.

VEHICLE SAFETY ISSUES

Congress set limits for the size and weight of motor vehicles on certain portions of the nation's road network in 1956, as part of legislation providing federal funding for the creation of the Interstate Highway System.[20] These limits affect the costs of highway transportation of freight, and so are perennially contested.[21] At the time Congress established nationwide limits, some states had already established limits that allowed larger or heavier trucks than the federal limit; Congress allowed these preexisting state

---

[17] FMCSA, "New Entrant Safety Assurance Process: Advance Notice of Proposed Rulemaking," 74 *Federal Register* 42883, August 25, 2009.

[18] Motor Carrier Safety Advisory Committee, letter and report to FMCSA regarding Docket No. FMCSA-2001-11061, September 2, 2009, https://www.regulations.gov/document?D=FMCSA-2001-11061-0065.

[19] Commercial Vehicle Safety Alliance, "Recommendations related to reauthorization of federal surface transportation legislation," p. 10, no date (but approximately 2014), at http://cvsa.org/policypage/policy/reauthorization/.

[20] The weight standards apply to the Interstate Highway System, which is approximately 44,000 miles; the size standards apply to the National Network, which is approximately 200,000 miles and includes the Interstate Highway System. Due to requirements that vehicles have reasonable access to and from these networks, there can be some impact on adjacent roads if the federal limits exceed the limits a state has imposed on other roads. See http://ops.fhwa.dot.gov/freight/sw/faqs/qa.cfm?category=10 for information on reasonable access requirements.

[21] For example, Congress requested that the Transportation Research Board examine truck size and weight limits in 1988 and again in 1998; DOT issued its own studies of truck size and weight limits in 2000 and again in 2016.

limits to continue (i.e., "grandfathered" them). States determine the size and weight limits for vehicles using roads not subject to the federal limits.[22]

Calls to loosen these limits typically come from industry, and are typically motivated by the desire to increase productivity by enabling a driver to haul larger or heavier loads. These efforts are typically opposed by highway safety groups, which assert that larger or heavier vehicles will pose a greater danger to other motorists.[23] Calls for heavier vehicles are also often opposed by highway agencies concerned about the costs of increased wear and tear on highways and bridges. In some cases, they have been opposed by elements of the trucking industry, who say that if larger or heavier trucks are allowed, companies using them will have a cost advantage over companies using smaller vehicles, forcing competitors to invest in new equipment.

Weight Limits

The federal weight limits—20,000 pounds on a single axle, 34,000 pounds on a tandem axle, and 80,000 pounds overall gross vehicle weight—have been unchanged since 1974.[24] But in recent years Congress has approved a number of waivers, generally on a state-by-state basis. For example, in 2015 Congress exempted emergency vehicles and certain heavy-duty tow and recovery vehicles from weight limits, waived weight limits on certain highways in Texas and Arkansas, and provided waivers for logging trucks in Wisconsin and Minnesota.[25]

Length Limits

Federal truck length regulations apply on the roughly 200,000 miles of road known as the National Network (although due to a requirement for "reasonable access," there is some impact on adjacent roads). Thus, states are generally prohibited from allowing twin 33-foot trailers on the National Network, but there are some exceptions. Outside of this network, states do not have to comply with federal truck size regulations.

In 2015, proponents of allowing longer trucks sought to enact a provision to increase the maximum allowable length of trailers hauled in tandem—two trailers attached together and pulled by a tractor unit—on the National Network from 28 feet each to 33

---

[22] States also are allowed to issue permits for movement of oversized or overweight loads under certain conditions.
[23] For example, http://www.cabt.org/about-us/. The railroad industry, which competes with the trucking industry for hauling many types of freight, also typically opposes efforts to increase truck size or weight limits.
[24] The weight limits are subject to a separate calculation to protect bridges.
[25] P.L. 114-94, §1410.

feet each. The provision was inserted into an appropriations bill,[26] so it was subject to little debate. As is often the case, industry representatives cited the benefit of the longer trucks in reducing freight transportation costs, while opponents cited safety concerns. Technical appendices to a DOT study on truck size and weight that was under way in 2015 noted the lack of data on the safety impact of 33-foot double trailers, as none were in use; an analysis of their potential impact on pavement performance found that they could cause additional damage to the road surface and thus an increase in life-cycle costs for road construction and maintenance. The provision was dropped from the final version of the appropriations bill.

Truck Underride Guards

In 2015, 17% of fatal crashes involving large trucks involved a passenger vehicle rear-ending a large truck. The reason these crashes are fatal is often because the front of the car travels under the rear of the truck so that the passenger compartment of the passenger vehicle strikes the rear of the truck, resulting in head injuries to the occupants of the passenger vehicles. NHTSA regulations require large trucks to have underride guards, which are intended to stop a car from being able to travel under the rear of the truck. However, these bars have typically not been strong enough to stop vehicles.

In 2011 the Insurance Institute for Highway Safety studied 115 crashes in which a passenger vehicle ran into the back of a heavy truck or semitrailer; it found that roughly 80% of those crashes involved the passenger vehicle going under the rear of the truck. Nearly half of the passenger vehicles had severe or catastrophic underride damage, and those vehicles accounted for 80% of the fatal crashes in the study.[27] However, in 2015 the Insurance Institute found that several trailer manufacturers were producing underride guards that exceed NHTSA regulations and prevented passenger vehicle underride even in extreme circumstances. One possible reason for the improvement in underride guards, in the absence of tighter federal regulations, is that Canada enacted stricter underride guard performance standards in 2007.

Electronic Stability Control

Electronic stability control is a vehicle technology that uses engine torque control and computer braking to assist a driver in maintaining control under certain challenging

---

[26] The provision was in Section 125 of H.R. 2577 (114th Congress) as passed by the House and in Section 137 of H.R. 2577 as reported in the Senate.

[27] Insurance Institute for Highway Safety, "NEW CRASH TESTS: Underride guards on most big rigs leave passenger vehicle occupants at risk in certain crashes," news release, March 14, 2013.

conditions, reducing the risk of a crash. Citing compelling evidence of the technology's safety impact, NHTSA required that trucks over 26,000 pounds manufactured after August 2017 be equipped with electronic stability control. Roughly one-quarter of trucks manufactured in 2012 were already so equipped; this rule was expected to accelerate the penetration of electronic safety control into the heavy truck fleet. It is expected to prevent roughly 1,400 to 1,700 crashes, 40 to 49 fatalities, and 500 to 650 injuries per year.[28]

Speed Limiters

NHTSA (which has authority over standards for most motor vehicles sold in the United States) and FMCSA have jointly proposed that all trucks (and buses and multipurpose passenger vehicles) over 26,000 pounds be equipped with a speed limiting device. According to NHTSA estimates, limiting the speed of heavy trucks (and buses) would save between 27 and 498 lives annually, depending upon the maximum speed allowed (Table 1).

Table 1. Estimated Costs and Benefits of Limiting Heavy Vehicle Speeds

Speed Limit	Lives Saved Annually	Serious Injuries Prevented Annually	Value of Greenhouse Gas Emission Reduction (millions of 2013 dollars)	Social Cost (millions of 2013 dollars)
60 mph	162 to 498	179 to 551	—	$1,561
65 mph	63 to 214	70 to 236	—	$523
68 mph	27 to 96	30 to 106	$376	$209

Source: NHTSA/FMCSA, Notice of Proposed Rulemaking, 81 *Federal Register* 61942, September 7, 2016.
Note: Estimates assume limits apply to buses as well as heavy trucks.

The proposal to require heavy vehicles to be equipped with speed limiters is supported by the American Trucking Associations, which generally represents the views of motor carriers with large fleets of vehicles, as well as by highway safety advocates. It is opposed by the Owner-Operator Independent Drivers Association, which contends that the safety benefits of speed limiters are unproven and that limiting the speed of heavy trucks would increase the risk of highway crashes by increasing the difference between the speeds of heavy trucks and passenger vehicles on highways.

Virtually all heavy trucks sold in the past decade have technology that allows a limit to be placed on their speed by controlling the revolutions per minute of the engine, so a

---

[28] The 2017 deadline applies to three-axle trucks; manufacturers of two-axle trucks have until 2019 to meet the requirement. NHTSA, "Final Rule: Federal Motor Vehicle Safety Standards; Electronic Stability Control Systems for Heavy Vehicles," 80 *Federal Register* 36049, June 23, 2015.

requirement that speed limiters be installed on all trucks would have the greatest financial impact on owners of older trucks. These are more likely to be independent operators.

DRIVER SAFETY ISSUES

Truck drivers are typically paid by the mile, and face several constraints on how many miles they can drive: speed limits provide a limit on how quickly drivers can cover a mile; hours-of-service rules limit how much time drivers can spend driving in a day; and delays in loading and unloading cargo and highway congestion limit the ability of drivers to maximize their income within the limited hours they are legally allowed to drive. Drivers may have financial incentives to exceed the speed limit or the number of hours they are allowed to drive in order to drive more miles, and thus earn more income, in a day. Federal and state efforts to regulate vehicle speeds and commercial drivers' time behind the wheel are thus in conflict with the basic incentive drivers face.

One way to address this issue is to change the driver's incentive. DOT, in its 2015 surface transportation reauthorization proposal, proposed allowing the Secretary of Transportation to require that drivers who do not receive an hourly wage be paid for time spent on duty but not driving.[29] This change might reduce the financial incentive drivers feel to make up for on-duty time not spent driving. This provision was not included in the reauthorization legislation passed by Congress that year.

New Driver Training Standards

In December 2016, FMCSA issued a final rule regarding the training requirements for entry-level commercial drivers—those applying for a commercial driver's license (CDL) for the first time; or for an upgrade of their CDL; or for a hazardous materials, passenger, or school bus endorsement for the first time.[30] The rule requires applicants to complete a prescribed course covering both knowledge and behind-the-wheel performance that is provided by an entity approved by FMCSA. FMCSA will certify to state driver licensing agencies that an applicant has completed the required instruction, after which the state agencies can conduct CDL skills tests (or the knowledge test required for an endorsement to allow the driver to haul hazardous materials). The rule is to take effect in February 2020.

FMCSA's final rule omitted a provision in its earlier proposed rule that would have required new drivers to complete at least 30 hours of behind-the-wheel training in order

---

[29] §5507 of the GROW America Act, introduced in the 114th Congress as H.R. 2410 and H.R. 3064.
[30] Military drivers, farmers, and firefighters, who are generally exempted from CDL requirements, are also exempted from this rule.

to be eligible for a commercial driver's license. Instead, the skill of a new driver will be judged by an instructor during a skills proficiency test (as well as by the state official who administers the skills test for CDL applicants). The explanation FMCSA gave for dropping the 30-hour requirement was that there is no evidence that a certain amount of behind-the-wheel training has an impact on the safety performance of new drivers. It cited executive orders directing agencies to design regulations based on performance objectives rather than specifying the manner of compliance.[31]

Hours-of-Service Limits

Improvements in vehicles and in highway design have contributed to reductions in truck crashes over time. Improvements in driver safety are more difficult to produce. One of the limiting human factors for large truck safety is the driver's experience of fatigue. Fatigued drivers are more likely to be involved in a crash. For this reason, Congress has authorized FMCSA to limit the amount of time a commercial driver may drive;[32] FMCSA has implemented that limitation through the Hours of Service Rule.[33]

Currently, commercial drivers who are subject to the Hours of Service (HOS) rule[34] are limited to driving no more than 11 hours in a 24-hour period, and may not be on duty (working but not driving) for more than 14 hours in a 24-hour period. Over the course of a week, a driver may not drive for more than 60 hours (or more than 70 hours over eight consecutive days), unless the driver takes a 34-hour break from work during the seven- or eight-day period, in which case they can "restart" the work cycle (this is referred to as the "34-hour restart" provision).

The "34-Hour Restart" Rule

The most active regulatory issue related to commercial driver hours of service in recent years has been the "34-hour restart" requirement. In June 2013, new FMCSA regulations enacted in 2011 took effect, restricting use of the 34-hour restart period by (1) requiring that the 34-hour off-duty period cover two consecutive 1 a.m.-5 a.m. periods

---

[31] "... Executive Order 12866, as supplemented by Executive Order 13563, requires that Federal Agencies propose or adopt regulations that 'to the extent feasible, specify performance objective, rather than specifying the behavior or manner of compliance that regulated entities must adopt.' In light of this Executive Order, and bearing in mind the Agency's obligation to identify and use 'the least burdensome tools for achieving regulatory ends,' FMCSA has determined not to impose a mandatory minimum behind the wheel hours requirement ..." Federal Motor Carrier Safety Administration, "Minimum Training Requirements for Entry-Level Commercial Motor Vehicles Operators: Final Rule," 81 *Federal Register* 88732, December 7, 2016.

[32] 49 U.S.C. §31502.

[33] The Hours of Service regulation (which is also commonly referred to as the Hours of Service Rule) is found at 49 C.F.R. Part 395.

[34] As of 2014, FMCSA reported that 2.84 million commercial drivers were subject to the HOS rule. "Agency Information collection activities: HOS of drivers," 79 *Federal Register* 54776, September 12, 2014.

and (2) allowing drivers to take this 34-hour "restart" only once in a 168-hour (seven-day) span.[35]

The purpose of the amended rule was to promote highway safety by reducing the risk of driver fatigue. Under the previous rule, drivers could start their 34-hour rest period at any time of the day, and could take more than one such rest period per seven-day period. Thus a driver could work the maximum permitted time per day (14 hours) and take the 34-hour restart after five days, and then, after a rest period of as little as one night and two daytime periods, work 14 hours a day for another five consecutive days. FMCSA asserted that this schedule allowed a driver to work up to 82 hours over a seven-day period, which it judged did not allow sufficient rest to prevent driver fatigue.

By requiring that the 34-hour restart period cover two 1 a.m.-5 a.m. periods, the new requirement was intended to allow drivers to get more sleep during the night hours, when studies indicate that sleep is most restorative (compared to sleeping during other times of the day). FMCSA published a cost-benefit analysis in the final rule that implemented the 2013 changes. The analysis found that the changes were cost-beneficial, but critics of the changes said that when the change went into effect the costs were greater than FMCSA had estimated, including increased congestion during daytime traffic hours (since drivers who previously might have driven during the night were required to rest during nighttime hours).[36]

Congress suspended enforcement of the 2013 restart rule change in the FY2015 DOT appropriations act, the FY2016 DOT appropriations act, and the FY2017 Continuing Resolution adopted in December 2016, pending the results of a study of the costs and benefits of the change.[37] This effectively reestablished the restart requirement that had been in effect prior to June 2013, and the left the rollback in place unless the study required by the FY2015 act found that commercial drivers operating under the new restart provisions showed "statistically significant improvement in all outcomes related to safety, operator fatigue, driver health and longevity, and work schedules."

The cost-benefit study mandated in the FY2015 DOT appropriations act was transmitted to Congress on March 2, 2017.[38] The study did not find a net benefit from the

---

[35] If drivers work no more than 60 hours in a week, they do not have to take the 34-hour restart; for example, if a driver works eight hours every day, for a total of 56 hours in any seven-day period, that driver could continue to work the same schedule indefinitely.

[36] Office of the Inspector General, U.S. Department of Transportation, Letter to the House and Senate Committees on Appropriations and the Secretary Regarding OIG's Audit of FMCSA's Hours of Service Restart Study, March 2, 2017, p. 3, https://www.oig.dot.gov/sites/default/files/OIG%20 Correspondence%20on%20HOS%20Restart%20Study%5E3- 2-17.pdf.

[37] This suspension was included in the FY2015 DOT appropriations act (§133, Division K of P.L. 113-235), repeated in a slightly different form in the FY2016 DOT appropriations act (§133 of Division L of P.L. 114-113), and in the FY2017 continuing resolution (P.L. 114-254, §180).

[38] Federal Motor Carrier Safety Administration, U.S. Department of Transportation, *Commercial Motor Vehicle Driver Restart Study Report to Congress*, https://www.fmcsa.dot.gov/sites/fmcsa.dot.gov/ files/docs/CMV%20DRS%20Report%20to%20Congress%20FINAL%20March%202017.pdf; Office of the Inspector General, Department of Transportation, Letter to the House and Senate Committees on Appropriations and the Secretary Regarding OIG's Audit of FMCSA's Hours of Service Restart Study, March 2, 2017, p. 3,

two suspended provisions—the one restart per week and the two consecutive 1 a.m. to 5 a.m. rest periods—on driver operations, safety, fatigue, and health.

Hours-of-Service Rule Enforcement—Electronic Logging Device Requirement

To enforce the rule limiting drivers' hours of service, FMCSA requires drivers to keep records of how many hours they have driven each day and each week. These records are subject to inspection. The paper-based records require time and attention to maintain, and are subject to falsification.

In order to better enforce the hours-of-service rules and thus deter drivers from driving while fatigued, Congress mandated that commercial drivers subject to hours-of-service recordkeeping requirements should have vehicles equipped with electronic logging devices (ELDs), which will track how long they have been driving. To address concerns that carriers might use that information to harass drivers who have taken a break, Congress also directed FMCSA to prevent companies from using the ELD information to harass drivers.

FMCSA issued a final rule on ELDs in 2015. The rule provided for a two-year phase-in period, and is to take effect in December 2017.[39]

Sleep Apnea

Obstructive sleep apnea is a respiratory condition that can interfere with sound sleep. This condition interferes with a person's breathing while asleep, causing repeated awakening. As a result, a person with sleep apnea can be fatigued even after getting what might seem to be a reasonable amount of sleep. Studies suggest that for people with sleep apnea, eight hours of sleep can be less refreshing than four hours of uninterrupted sleep.

Sleep apnea is associated with a higher risk of being involved in a highway crash. The National Transportation Safety Board has determined that sleep apnea played a role in several truck crashes.[40] Sleep apnea has also been linked to health problems, including high blood pressure, heart disease, and stroke. People with sleep apnea are often unaware they have it. Risk factors for developing sleep apnea include obesity, male gender, advancing age, large neck size, small throat, and family history of sleep apnea.

FMCSA has the authority to set minimum qualifications, including medical and physical qualifications, for commercial drivers operating in interstate commerce. It has determined that obstructive sleep apnea can be a physically disqualifying condition for a commercial driver.

---

https://www.oig.dot.gov/sites/default/files/OIG%20Correspondence%20on%20HOS%20Restart%20Study%5E3-2-17.pdf.

[39] See FMCSA, "Final Rule: Electronic Logging Devices and Hours of Service Supporting Documents," 80 *Federal Register* 78292, December 16, 2015.

[40] 81 *Federal Register* 12643, March 10, 2016.

FMCSA regulations require every commercial driver to undergo an annual examination by an authorized physician to determine whether the individual is medically fit to drive. FMCSA's guidance to medical examiners has included a reference to sleep apnea since the guidance was first issued in 2000.[41] The current guidance simply lists sleep apnea as one of several respiratory conditions that may interfere with a driver's ability to drive safely, and FMCSA's medical advisory committee has expressed concern that the guidance is not helpful in cases where a medical examiner does not have sufficient experience or information to suspect that a driver has sleep apnea.

FMCSA therefore has sought to strengthen the guidance by providing criteria for medical examiners to be alert for sleep apnea in drivers. The simplest criterion is obesity; studies indicate that around 80% of people with a body mass index (BMI) of 35 or greater have sleep apnea. In December 2011, the FMCSA's Motor Carrier Safety Advisory Committee and Medical Review Board recommended that medical examiners should routinely test drivers whose BMI is 35 or greater for sleep apnea. In April 2012 FMCSA published the recommendation in the *Federal Register*, seeking public comment. A week later FMCSA announced it was withdrawing the proposed guidance, and would reissue proposed guidance later in the year. No further guidance proposals were published. In October 2013 Congress legislated that DOT can require that commercial vehicle operators be screened for sleep disorders, including sleep apnea, only through a formal rulemaking procedure, a more rigorous process than that required for proposals for regulatory guidance.[42]

In March 2016 FMCSA began a joint rulemaking with the Federal Railroad Administration to consider requiring that any commercial driver (or train operator) who exhibits certain risk factors must be screened for obstructive sleep apnea. If adopted, such a rule would eliminate the discretion of a medical fitness examiner to determine whether such screening is necessary.[43]

Drug and Alcohol Enforcement

Alcohol or drug impairment appears to be a minor factor in large truck crashes resulting in fatalities, with around 1% of large truck drivers in such incidents found to be impaired by alcohol, drugs, or medicine.[44] However, the consequences of a commercial

---

[41] Regulations for the medical examination are at 49 C.F.R. §391.43; see http://www.fmcsa.dot.gov/rules-regulations/administration/fmcsr/fmcsrruletext.aspx?reg=391.43. FMCSA's guidance for medical examiners is available at http://nrcme.fmcsa.dot.gov/mehandbook/MEhandbook.aspx.

[42] P.L. 113-145, §1. Note that this does not apply to requirements that were in place prior to September 1, 2013.

[43] The Advance Notice of Proposed Rulemaking is at https://www.gpo.gov/fdsys/pkg/FR-2016-03-10/pdf/2016-05396.pdf.

[44] U.S. Department of Transportation, *Federal Motor Carrier Safety Administration, Large Truck and Bus Crash Facts 2014*, "People," Table 31: Drivers of Large Trucks in Fatal Crashes by Distraction-Related and Impairment-Related Factors, 2012-2014.

driver driving while impaired can be significant due to the size and weight of their vehicles.

Commercial drivers are subject to more stringent impairment standards than other drivers. A commercial driver with a blood alcohol concentration of 0.04 is considered impaired,[45] whereas all states now set the impairment threshold for noncommercial drivers at 0.08. A driver is to be disqualified from driving a commercial vehicle for one year upon first conviction for driving under the influence of alcohol or a controlled substance, or upon refusal to be tested for drug and alcohol use when driving any vehicle. Upon a second conviction or refusal to be tested, the driver is to be disqualified for life.[46]

Motor carriers are required to review the drug and alcohol test status of their prospective employees at the time of hiring, but must rely on the drivers to provide this information. Some drivers have failed to disclose their test results. Motor carriers are also required to test drivers for drug use prior to employment and for both drug and alcohol use after a crash, when the employer has a reasonable suspicion that a driver is impaired, and randomly.[47]

In 1999, the National Transportation Safety Board recommended that FMCSA develop a database to track drug and alcohol test results and test refusals and that it require prospective employers and certifying authorities to check the system before making decisions on job applicants.[48] This recommendation was echoed by the Government Accountability Office (GAO) in reports about commercial drivers who changed employers to evade the impact of failed tests.[49] In 2012, Congress directed FMCSA to establish such a national database with alcohol and controlled substances test results for all CDL holders.[50] FMCSA issued the final rule establishing this database in December 2016. The database is to become operational in 2020.

Driver Distraction

Federal regulations bar commercial drivers from texting or using handheld phones while driving. Regarding the ban on handheld phones, researchers contend that the

---

[45] This applies to all commercial drivers, not just those in interstate commerce.
[46] 49 C.F.R. §383.51; if the driver is transporting hazardous materials, the penalty for a first conviction or refusal to be tested is a three-year disqualification.
[47] FMCSA requires that employers conduct random tests at certain rates, based on the reported random test violation rates for the entire industry. In 2016 the required random test rates were 25% for drug testing and 10% for alcohol testing; this meant that an employer who had 100 drivers had to conduct at least 25 drug tests and 10 alcohol tests of randomly selected employees during the year.
[48] National Transportation Safety Board, *Highway Accident Report: Motorcoach Run-Off-The-Road, New Orleans, Louisiana, May 9, 1999*, NTSB Report Number HAR-01-01.
[49] GAO–08–600, *Improvements to Drug Testing Programs Could Better Identify Illegal Drug Users and Keep Them Off the Road*, May 15, 2008; and GAO–08–829R, *Examples of Job Hopping by Commercial Drivers After Failing Drug Tests*, June 30, 2008.
[50] Moving Ahead for Progress in the 21st Century Act (MAP-21), P.L. 112-141, §32402.

primary risk to drivers using phones is not from the physical distraction of holding them but from the cognitive distraction of carrying on a conversation while driving.

It is difficult to enforce driver distraction laws in general, and perhaps even more difficult to enforce them against drivers who sit high above the level of highway patrol cars. Drivers who have been in crashes may be reluctant to incriminate themselves by admitting to having been in violation of such laws at the time of the crash.

Compliance, Safety, and Accountability (CSA) Program

Since 2010, FMCSA has used information from roadside inspections and crashes to rank each carrier's safety performance relative to other carriers in seven categories in an effort to identify high-risk carriers. These carriers can then be targeted to enforcement actions.

The program has three parts:

1. the Safety Measurement System (SMS), which uses roadside inspection and crash data to identify high-risk carriers;
2. a variety of compliance and enforcement interventions, ranging from warning letters to putting a carrier out of operation, which are intended to address safety problems; and
3. the Safety Fitness Determination, a rating of a carrier's safety performance based on a review of its compliance with federal rules or other investigations tied to a requirement that a carrier receiving a rating of "unsatisfactory" must cease operations within 45 days.

Safety Measurement System Issues

There are three major issues for the SMS: (1) the availability of data used in the system, (2) the quality of this data, and (3) the effectiveness of the SMS in predicting crashes given the current limitations on data availability and quality.

Data Availability

Most carriers have few trucks and are not often inspected. GAO found that there is not enough information for these carriers to produce reliable scores, so that most carriers either receive no percentile ranking or receive a ranking that has a large margin of error because it is based on a small number of data points. Because the percentile rankings of carriers are based on comparison with other carriers rather than a fixed standard, unrepresentative results for some carriers can affect the rankings of other carriers. As a result, GAO found that FMCSA had unjustifiably identified many carriers as high risk. GAO found that by limiting the carriers for which scores were generated to those that had more information available, FMCSA could better identify high-risk carriers and thus make better use of its limited resources to prevent crashes.[51]

Data Quality

The data in the SMS come from both FMCSA inspectors and state safety personnel who conduct roadside inspections, investigate crashes, and ticket moving violations. The stringency and thoroughness of the activities of these personnel vary from state to state, as well as from person to person, and may be affected by other random factors (e.g., inspections and investigations may be less thorough in harsh weather conditions or dangerous traffic conditions).

Predictive Value

In an analysis published in 2014, GAO found that most of the regulations that are used to calculate SMS scores are not violated often enough to determine whether they are strongly associated with the risk that individual carriers will be involved in crashes.

Compliance and Enforcement Intervention Issues

Fewer Interventions

GAO found that FMCSA has been applying fewer interventions over time since implementing CSA, with about 26% fewer investigation interventions in FY2015 compared to FY2012 (from over 18,000 to under 14,000).[52] FMCSA responded that this was due to its investigators spending more time reviewing motor carriers' safety management practices to identify the underlying causes of safety problems. FMCSA said it made this change in response to a recommendation from an independent review team and as part of continuous improvement efforts instituted in FY2013.

Evaluating the Effectiveness of Interventions

FMCSA has declared that improving the effectiveness and efficiency of its safety interventions is a goal. It has evaluated its interventions and found them to be effective, but GAO reported that limitations in the design and methodology of FMCSA's effectiveness model limited the usefulness of the results. For example, the model does not assess the individual types of interventions, so that FMCSA is limited in assessing the effectiveness of intervention types. Also, FMCSA lacks current cost estimates of the

---

[51] U.S. Government Accountability Office, Federal Motor Carrier Safety: Modifying the Compliance, Safety, Accountability Program Would Improve the Ability to Identify High Risk Carriers, GAO-14-114, February 2014.

[52] U.S. Government Accountability Office. Motor Carriers: Better Information Needed to Assess Effectiveness and Efficiency of Safety Interventions, GAO-17-49, October 2016.

various interventions, and so is limited in its ability to evaluate the efficiency (that is, the cost-effectiveness) of the various interventions.

Safety Fitness Determination Issues

FMCSA's current Safety Fitness Determination (SFD) process is resource-intensive (since it relies on compliance reviews or other investigations), reaches only a small portion of the industry each year,[53] allows carriers to receive a rating that is less than "safe" ("conditional") and yet continue to operate indefinitely, and does not make use of all the information FMCSA has about carriers' safety performance. The National Transportation Safety Board has recommended changes to the SFD process, including using SMS rating scores to help determine the safety fitness rating, and allowing FMCSA to rate a carrier as "unsatisfactory" based only on driver and vehicle performance-based data.

FMCSA proposed to amend the SFD process to address these issues in January 2016.[54] No schedule for the next stage of the rulemaking has been determined.[55]

Recent Congressional Actions Related to the CSA Program

Congress passed a surface transportation reauthorization act in December 2015[56] that contained several provisions affecting the CSA program. The act

- directed the National Research Council to study the CSA program, particularly its Safety Measurement System (SMS);
- directed FMCSA to give some credit or an improved SMS percentile to a motor carrier that implements certain safety measures;
- directed FMCSA to remove the percentile rankings of carriers from public view until the National Research Council study is completed;
- directed FMCSA to develop specifications to ensure consistent and accurate input of data into systems and databases relating to the CSA program; and

---

[53] In 2012, FMCSA and its state partners completed roughly 17,000 ratable reviews (reviews that could have resulted in an unsatisfactory SFD) out of roughly 525,000 active carriers, or 3% of the industry population. FMCSA, "Notice of Proposed Rulemaking: Carrier Safety Fitness Determination," 81 *Federal Register* 3569, January 21, 2016.

[54] Ibid.

[55] As of the DOT's December 2016 *Status of Significant Rulemakings Report*, the most current one available as of March 2017.

[56] P.L. 114-94.

- directed FMCSA's Motor Carrier Safety Advisory Committee to review the treatment of preventable crashes in the SMS.[57]

FMCSA'S REGULATORY BACKLOG

Much of FMCSA's regulatory agenda is set by congressional action through new laws that need new regulations for implementation. Other sources of rulemakings include court decisions that call for revisions to existing rules. As of December 2016, FMCSA had 13 rulemakings in progress, some of which had been under way for more than a decade.[58]

Some Members of Congress and others have expressed concern that FMCSA is moving too slowly to complete its regulatory workload. In the Fixing America's Surface Transportation (FAST) Act, Congress directed that FMCSA complete outstanding rulemakings that were required by statute before beginning any new rulemakings. The same law directed FMCSA to initiate 20 new rulemakings. These include changes to FMCSA's major grant program to states to support truck safety; allowing testing of hair as an alternative to urine tests for certain drug tests; enabling certain veterans to more easily obtain commercial driver's licenses; and a variety of exemptions from commercial motor vehicle regulation for specialized vehicles.[59]

---

[57] Preventable is defined by reference to 49 C.F.R. 385, Appendix B: "Preventability will be determined according to the following standard: 'If a driver, who exercises normal judgment and foresight could have foreseen the possibility of the accident that in fact occurred, and avoided it by taking steps within his/her control which would not have risked causing another kind of mishap, the accident was preventable.'"
[58] U.S. Department of Transportation, *Report on Significant Rulemakings*, December 2016.
[59] Federal Motor Carrier Safety Administration, *FAST Act: Overview*, February 24, 2016, https://www.fmcsa.dot.gov/ fastact/overview.

In: Highway Safety
Editor: Bertha G. Baldwin

ISBN: 978-1-53617-176-1
© 2020 Nova Science Publishers, Inc.

Chapter 7

SMART CARS AND TRUCKS: SPECTRUM USE FOR VEHICLE SAFETY[*]

Bill Canis and Jill C. Gallagher

BACKGROUND

Increasing the autonomy of cars and trucks is seen as an effective way to reduce the 94% of vehicle-related accidents that are caused by human error. While some semiautonomous safety technologies, such as automatic braking and adaptive cruise control, are in use today, autonomous safety technologies under development would require cars and trucks to communicate with each other (vehicle-to-vehicle, or V2V) and with their surroundings (vehicle-to-infrastructure, or V2I). V2V communication is expected to reduce the number of accidents by improving detection of oncoming vehicles and providing driver warnings. V2I communication is expected to help highway operators monitor and manage traffic and provide drivers with information such as weather and traffic conditions.

These technologies are part of a congressional mandate to invest in and advance a broader set of intelligent transportation systems to improve traffic flow and safety.

For vehicles to communicate wirelessly, they need access to radio waves, or radio frequencies. In the United States, the Federal Communications Commission (FCC) manages commercial use of the radio frequency spectrum, and allocates spectrum for specific uses. In 1999, the FCC allocated the 5.9 gigahertz (GHz) band to Dedicated

---

[*] This is an edited, reformatted and augmented version of Congressional Research Service Publication No. IF11260, dated June 28, 2019.

Short- Range Communications (DSRC) uses. DSRC technologies, installed in cars and trucks and on roadways, enable V2V and V2I communications.

Integrating DSRC technologies in vehicles and on roadways is in its early stages. Meanwhile, the proliferation of cell phones and other devices has increased demand for spectrum, and a competing technology, Cellular Vehicle-to- Everything (C-V2X), has emerged as an alternative to DSRC for vehicular communications.

In May 2019, the FCC announced it would consider whether the 5.9 GHz band should (1) remain dedicated to DSRC technologies, (2) be allocated to C-V2X, (3) be allocated to automotive communications technologies generally, or (4) be shared with wireless devices. The FCC's decision has important competitive implications for the automotive, electronics, and telecommunications industries, and may affect the availability of safety technologies and the path toward vehicle automation.

DSRC

In 1998, the Transportation Equity Act for the 21st Century (TEA-21; P.L. 105-178) directed the FCC, in consultation with the U.S. Department of Transportation (DOT), to consider spectrum needs for transportation, including the DSRC wireless standard. The goal of the initiative was to leverage technologies to improve traffic flow and safety.

From FY2003 through FY2014, DOT provided about $570 million for research, development, and testing of DSRC technologies. In 2015, it awarded $43 million to three pilot sites (with an additional $9 million in local matches):

- *Safety in a large metropolitan area.* The New York City Department of Transportation is outfitting 8,000 taxis, buses, and sanitation vehicles with DSRC safety devices to demonstrate connected-vehicle capabilities focused on alerting drivers to potential crashes and reducing accidents with pedestrians.
- *Interstate routes and commercial vehicles.* During severe winter weather along I-80 in Wyoming, DSRC technologies are used to notify cars and trucks of disabled vehicles. Vehicles rebroadcast the warning. The goal is to prevent weather-related crashes.
- *Mid-sized urban area.* Cars, buses, and pedestrians are part of a DSRC pilot in downtown Tampa, FL, that alerts drivers to reduce speeds when approaching heavy traffic, when forward collisions may be imminent, and where intersections are unsafe.

In addition to these pilot projects, several manufacturers in the United States and Europe have begun integrating DSRC technologies into cars and trucks; truck platooning (the linking of multiple trucks into a convoy through V2V communications) has been demonstrated on U.S. highways; and additional DSRC deployments are under way in more than two dozen states (see *Figure 1*.)

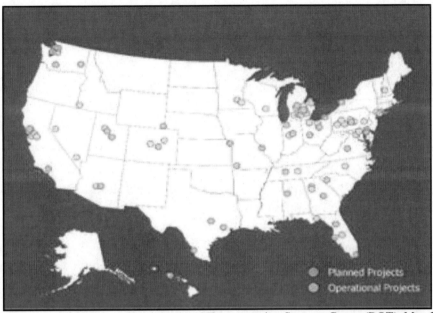

Source: CRS, based on data from Volpe National Transportation Systems Center (DOT), May 2019.
Notes: DOT has 52 operational projects and 35 more planned, including more than 26,000 devices deployed on vehicles in urban, rural, and suburban settings.

Figure 1. DSRC Deployments.

C-V2X

In addition to research on DSRC, some automakers and telecommunications and technology companies continue to explore other vehicle connectivity options. The 3rd Generation Partnership Project, a standards organization for global wireless networking, created the C-V2X standard in 2017. Like DSRC, C-V2X can operate independently from the cellular network for V2V and V2I communications. C- V2X can also connect to cellular networks and is expected to be able to use future 5G networks. 5G, when fully deployed, is expected to provide high-speed, low latency (i.e., reduced lag time) services needed for autonomous vehicles, allowing information between vehicles and infrastructure to be shared almost instantaneously.

The 5G Automotive Association (5GAA), a consortium of automakers, technology companies, telecommunication providers, standards bodies, and others, supports C-V2X. The 5GAA asserts that C-V2X performs better than DSRC in testing and is emerging as the global standard. In November 2018, 5GAA asked the FCC for a portion of the 5.9GHz band to develop and deploy C-V2X.

Testing of C-V2X has so far been limited. DOT plans to begin tests in three states in summer 2019.

PROPOSED DOT STANDARD

At the end of the Obama Administration in January 2017, the National Highway Traffic Safety Administration (NHTSA) proposed a new federal safety standard that would require all new light vehicles—passenger cars, sport- utility vehicles, and pickup trucks—to be equipped with DSRC technology by 2023. Proponents say that this mandate is necessary to ensure compatibility and connectivity across all vehicles and systems; DOT projected that implementing it could prevent more than 1,000 fatalities annually. The Trump Administration has taken no further action on this proposal; it has stated that DOT should remain technology-neutral rather than mandate a specific technology. It encourages the development of multiple technologies that utilize the 5.9 GHz band for transportation safety.

Policy Considerations

In 2012, Congress directed the FCC to determine whether the 5.9 GHz band could be shared to support unlicensed devices such as cordless phones, wireless speakers, and Wi-Fi devices (P.L. 112-96, Title VI). The FCC is conducting extensive testing to determine whether these devices would cause interference with DSRC technologies.

In May 2019, FCC Chairman Ajit Pai called for reexamination of the 5.9 GHz band. Several FCC commissioners have supported this move, noting that the pace of deployment of DSRC technologies left spectrum underutilized while consumer demands for spectrum are increasing, and that new technologies surpassing DSRC's capabilities need access to spectrum to develop.

Motor vehicle, telecommunications, and technology firms have both competing and overlapping interests in the outcome. Some automakers have invested in DSRC and have plans to include it in their fleets: Cadillac markets a model now that includes it. Ford, Volkswagen, and Toyota planned to follow suit, but have paused deployment due to the lack of a federal standard and spectrum uncertainties, and also see benefits in C-V2X. Telecommunications providers stand to benefit from C-V2X, as it relies in part on cellular networks and has the potential to increase their customer base and revenues. Telecommunications technology companies, such as Qualcomm, which makes both DSRC and C-V2X chips, stand to benefit from an expanded connected car market.

DSRC advocates, such as the Safety Spectrum Coalition, which includes the Association of Global Automakers and the American Trucking Associations as well as many state departments of transportation, argue that millions of dollars have been invested in DSRC and that the technology has been thoroughly tested and is currently being deployed.

They argue that 5G deployment is years away in many areas, so the benefits of C-V2X will take years to arrive.

Both DSRC advocates and 5GAA agree that the 5.9 GHz band should remain dedicated to vehicle safety and other intelligent transportation uses and should not be made available for other purposes.

While the issue may be framed as a choice between DSRC and C-V2X, these two technologies could coexist. The Colorado Department of Transportation states that its intelligent transportation system, RoadX, can accept and transmit V2V and V2I information on both DSRC and cellular platforms; in time, vehicles and roadside infrastructure may be able to communicate under both standards.

The Coalition for Safety Sooner—comprising 15 state DOTs and other state highway authorities—says it is not in the public interest to delay the deployment of currently available safety technologies while waiting for other technologies to emerge. On the other hand, the Wi-Fi Alliance, whose members include major electronics companies such as Apple, Cisco, and others, along with consumer groups and wireless internet service providers, is urging the FCC to complete the interference testing before adding new users to the band. These groups argue that sharing the band with unlicensed devices, including Wi-Fi devices, will expand public access to broadband.

The challenge for policymakers is balancing the interests of multiple stakeholders: investors in DSRC who committed funding to develop car and truck safety technologies and other intelligent transportation systems; consumer safety advocates and others who want currently available technologies to be diffused quickly; potential users of expanded Wi-Fi services; C-V2X advocates who are eager to deploy the next generation of vehicle safety technologies; and the nation at large, which could benefit from expanded deployment of technologies that would improve vehicle safety, make roadways more efficient, and provide the economic gains that often accompany the development of new technologies.

INDEX

A

accidents, vii, xi, 1, 2, 3, 4, 5, 7, 9, 11, 12, 13, 17, 18, 26, 42, 43, 56, 72, 79, 98, 101, 105, 107, 110, 117, 118, 120, 128, 130, 131, 132, 133, 145, 158, 167, 223, 237, 260, 265, 305, 306
adaptive cruise control, xi, 25, 91, 214, 241, 272, 305
airbags, ix, 15, 17, 105, 214, 240, 241, 259, 262, 263, 264, 266, 274, 288
automatic braking, ix, xi, 132, 222, 241, 282, 305
automatic emergency braking, x, 16, 25, 29, 42, 91, 107, 121, 138, 214, 260, 273, 278
automobile design, viii, 221, 223
automotive communications technologies, xii, 306

B

behavioral factors, vii, 179, 182
buses, vii, 2, 17, 23, 24, 30, 37, 38, 39, 40, 42, 120, 132, 136, 138, 142, 143, 151, 167, 286, 287, 294, 306

C

Cellular Vehicle-to- Everything (C-V2X), xii, 306, 307, 308, 309
civil penalties, x, 133, 260, 268, 280, 281, 284
commercial driver's licenses, x, 285, 286, 304
commercial drivers, xi, 43, 103, 212, 216, 217, 233, 234, 285, 287, 289, 295, 296, 297, 298, 300
commercial vehicles, xi, 24, 26, 41, 103, 107, 216, 233, 242, 286, 289, 306
congestion, viii, 44, 45, 48, 50, 51, 67, 74, 103, 130, 136, 158, 159, 161, 166, 185, 210, 221, 222, 295, 297
crash-prevention technologies, ix, 222

D

Dedicated Short- Range Communications (DSRC), xii, 306, 307, 308, 309
Department of Transportation (DOT), vii, viii, x, 2, 9, 10, 11, 13, 16, 23, 25, 26, 27, 28, 44, 45, 48, 49, 50, 52, 53, 54, 64, 69, 80, 92, 96, 98, 101, 104, 128, 129, 130, 134, 136, 137, 138, 139, 141, 146, 148, 149, 150, 152, 154, 156, 158, 159, 166, 168, 173, 177, 178, 179, 180, 182, 183, 185, 186, 197, 202, 203, 207, 209, 210, 211, 212, 213, 214, 215, 216, 221, 222, 223, 224, 225, 226, 228, 229, 230, 231, 232, 234, 235, 237, 238, 240, 241, 243, 247, 248, 249, 250, 252, 253, 254, 256, 258, 260, 263, 264, 265, 266, 267, 269, 270, 271, 275, 278, 280, 281, 282, 285, 286, 287, 289, 290, 291, 293, 295, 297, 299, 303, 304, 306, 307, 308, 309
driver behavior, viii, 2, 15, 64, 68, 69, 78, 154, 160, 185, 211, 213, 218, 221, 222, 223, 239, 242, 247, 251, 263, 289
driver error, viii, 25, 221, 223
driver productivity, xi, 286
driver warnings, xi, 305
driving too fast, viii, 18, 90, 221, 223, 242
driving under the influence of drugs, xi, 58, 286

driving while drunk, viii, 221, 223

E

electronic motor vehicle data, x, 260
emergency services, viii, 150, 153, 156, 210

F

fatalities, vii, ix, x, 1, 2, 4, 5, 9, 10, 11, 12, 13, 16, 19, 20, 21, 22, 23, 24, 26, 27, 28, 29, 35, 36, 47, 49, 50, 56, 57, 64, 65, 66, 68, 69, 71, 72, 73, 75, 76, 77, 79, 80, 81, 82, 83, 84, 85, 86, 87, 88, 89, 90, 92, 93, 96, 97, 98, 102, 103, 104, 107, 114, 118, 134, 137, 138, 139, 141, 142, 144, 145, 149, 152, 153, 154, 156, 157, 158, 160, 161, 163, 164, 167, 168, 172, 173, 181, 182, 183, 185, 186, 187, 188, 189, 190, 191, 192, 193, 197, 198, 199, 201, 202, 210, 211, 212, 222, 223, 224, 227, 235, 236, 237, 238, 240, 241, 249, 251, 253, 257, 259, 260, 261, 264, 274, 285, 286, 287, 288, 294, 299, 308
Federal Motor Carrier Safety Administration (FMCSA), x, xi, 2, 39, 101, 117, 118, 129, 185, 211, 216, 217, 218, 223, 231, 233, 242, 285, 286, 287, 288, 289, 290, 291, 294, 295, 296, 297, 298, 299, 300, 301, 302, 303, 304
Federal Railroad Administration, xi, 117, 154, 285, 299
Fixing America's Surface Transportation (FAST) Act, vii, 2, 3, 4, 5, 6, 7, 10, 11, 12, 13, 55, 65, 67, 70, 81, 82, 83, 85, 94, 99, 125, 134, 147, 152, 153, 154, 182, 213, 218, 219, 234, 246, 253, 257, 272, 279, 280, 281, 282, 283, 284, 304

G

General Motors, x, 259, 266, 267, 272

H

hackers, x, 260, 284
highway capital improvement programs, ix, 222, 223
highway fatality rates, ix, 222
highway infrastructure, vii, ix, 147, 179, 222, 223, 239
highway safety, vii, viii, 2, 3, 4, 10, 11, 13, 15, 17, 18, 20, 21, 22, 27, 30, 31, 33, 34, 35, 36, 65, 67, 71, 77, 80, 81, 84, 90, 94, 98, 101, 110, 128, 131, 132, 138, 144, 147, 149, 150, 152, 153, 154, 168, 175, 179, 181, 182, 183, 184, 185, 186, 187, 188, 189, 191, 192, 193, 194, 198, 199, 200, 201, 203, 204, 205, 206, 212, 213, 214, 215, 216, 217, 218, 221, 222, 223, 225, 229, 230, 231, 234, 235, 236, 239, 242, 243, 244, 246, 247, 250, 251, 252, 253, 255, 257, 258, 260, 262, 274, 282, 292, 293, 294, 297

I

ignition switch, x, 259, 266, 267, 269
inexperienced drivers, x, 285
injuries, vii, viii, ix, x, 1, 2, 4, 5, 12, 15, 16, 17, 18, 19, 20, 21, 23, 24, 25, 26, 27, 28, 29, 30, 35, 36, 45, 50, 56, 78, 81, 86, 100, 102, 107, 133, 137, 138, 139, 141, 143, 144, 145, 152, 161, 164, 165, 167, 174, 182, 185, 186, 188, 194, 196, 209, 211, 218, 222, 223, 224, 226, 237, 238, 241, 251, 253, 257, 258, 259, 262, 263, 265, 266, 267, 268, 279, 285, 286, 287, 288, 293, 294
injury rates, ix, 45, 53, 154, 222, 238, 255
insurance, viii, 22, 90, 137, 138, 210, 214, 229, 251, 274, 282, 293
International Transport Forum's Road Safety Annual Report, ix, 222

J

J.D. Power, x, 260, 270, 271

L

lane departure warning, ix, x, 25, 91, 138, 214, 216, 222, 260, 274
lane departure warnings, ix, 222
legal costs, viii, 221, 222
legal services, viii, 210
life expectancy, viii, 146, 209

M

medical costs, viii, 210, 221, 222
misbehavior, viii, 215, 221, 223
motor carriers, x, xi, 35, 43, 66, 216, 285, 286, 287, 289, 291, 294, 300, 302

Index 313

motor vehicle crashes, vii, viii, x, 1, 4, 15, 18, 23, 26, 66, 84, 86, 87, 88, 131, 134, 137, 138, 146, 161, 164, 209, 210, 211, 212, 221, 222, 224, 252, 257, 263, 281, 285, 286
motor vehicle fatalities, ix, 87, 125, 237, 259
motor vehicle safety regulation, ix, 259

N

National Highway Traffic Safety Administration (NHTSA), vii, ix, x, xi, 1, 2, 4, 5, 6, 7, 10, 11, 15, 18, 20, 21, 22, 23, 24, 25, 26, 27, 28, 29, 30, 32, 33, 34, 36, 39, 41, 55, 57, 58, 66, 77, 78, 88, 90, 99, 101, 104, 107, 109, 115, 128, 129, 130, 131, 134, 135, 137, 140, 141, 142, 160, 161, 164, 167, 168, 169, 176, 179, 180, 181, 182, 183, 184, 185, 186, 187, 188, 189, 190, 191, 192, 193, 194, 195, 196, 197, 198, 199, 200, 202, 203, 204, 205, 209, 210, 211, 212, 213, 214, 215, 218, 219, 222, 223, 224, 225, 226, 228, 229, 230, 231, 232, 234, 235, 237, 238, 240, 241, 242, 246, 247, 248, 249, 250, 252, 253, 254, 255, 256, 259, 260, 261, 262, 263, 264, 265, 266, 267, 268, 269, 270, 271, 272, 275, 277, 278, 279, 280, 281, 282, 283, 284, 285, 286, 293, 294, 308
National Traffic and Motor Vehicle Safety Act, ix, 259, 262

O

obstructive sleep apnea, xi, 18, 43, 117, 285, 298, 299

P

parts recalls, x, 259
preventable deaths, viii, 86, 178, 209
productivity, viii, 5, 158, 210, 221, 222, 292
property damage, viii, 4, 5, 17, 18, 56, 210, 221, 222, 224, 287, 288

Q

quality of life, viii, 46, 57, 62, 63, 173, 174, 210

R

radio frequencies, xii, 305
radio waves, xii, 305
replacement parts, x, 260, 271
restart rule, xi, 285, 297
road design, viii, 78, 91, 112, 127, 150, 166, 167, 169, 215, 221, 222, 223, 239, 240, 241
roadway infrastructure, vii, 2, 8, 65, 144, 147, 148, 158

S

safety defects, x, 141, 214, 259, 263, 268, 269, 279
safety improvements, ix, 4, 8, 15, 17, 18, 30, 50, 78, 96, 147, 154, 182, 213, 215, 216, 222, 223, 240, 241, 255, 288
safety measures, vii, 2, 132, 172, 218, 234, 240, 257, 303
seat belts, ix, 24, 37, 38, 39, 88, 132, 212, 213, 222, 240, 241, 247, 256, 259, 261, 262, 263, 264
semiautonomous safety technologies, xi, 305
serious injuries, vii, viii, 3, 4, 50, 64, 65, 66, 68, 71, 142, 143, 149, 152, 153, 154, 156, 158, 180, 181, 182, 185, 186, 187, 188, 194, 195, 196, 197, 209, 223, 294
sleep apnea, xi, 101, 117, 118, 129, 217, 286, 298, 299
speed limiters, xi, 15, 21, 30, 97, 119, 286, 294, 295

T

Takata airbags, x, 259, 268, 283
traffic conditions, xi, 302, 305
traffic crashes, vii, viii, 27, 63, 138, 140, 169, 179, 182, 184, 188, 209, 213, 215, 221, 222, 235, 237, 247, 248, 257
traffic deaths, ix, 29, 79, 169, 174, 211, 215, 222, 225, 237, 258
traffic fatalities, vii, 3, 5, 19, 28, 47, 57, 76, 80, 81, 83, 105, 134, 140, 149, 169, 174, 180, 183, 185, 187, 188, 189, 190, 201, 210, 211, 212, 238, 240, 247, 251, 260, 261
traffic management, viii, 57, 221, 223
traffic safety, v, vii, viii, 1, 2, 5, 6, 7, 8, 9, 14, 19, 20, 21, 23, 26, 27, 28, 31, 34, 54, 55, 56, 57, 59, 60, 61, 62, 63, 65, 76, 83, 99, 113, 130, 133, 153, 167, 168, 169, 174, 175, 176, 179, 180, 182, 183,

184, 185, 186, 189, 190, 192, 197, 198, 199, 200, 202, 203, 209, 210, 211, 212, 213, 214, 215, 218, 221, 222, 223, 224, 225, 226, 228, 229, 230, 231, 232, 234, 235, 237, 238, 239, 240, 241, 242, 245, 247, 248, 249, 250, 252, 253, 254, 255, 256, 257, 262, 263, 264
train operators, xi, 285
truck crash, x, 137, 141, 231, 232, 233, 285, 287, 288, 289, 296, 298, 299
trucks, v, vii, x, xi, 2, 9, 25, 30, 66, 102, 103, 106, 107, 118, 119, 136, 137, 138, 142, 145, 163, 164, 167, 227, 228, 230, 231, 232, 233, 263, 264, 285, 286, 287, 288, 289, 291, 292, 293, 294, 299, 301, 305, 306, 308

U

U.S. roadways, vii, 1, 85, 91, 101, 107, 131, 160

V

V2I, xi, 101, 134, 135, 305, 306, 307, 309
V2V, xi, 134, 135, 305, 306, 307, 309

vehicle automation, xii, 272, 275, 306
vehicle injuries, x, 5, 24, 260
vehicle occupants, ix, 24, 25, 26, 58, 88, 212, 214, 222, 223, 241, 256, 293
vehicle safety laws, ix, 259, 279
vehicle safety technologies, ix, 222, 241, 256, 260, 263, 264, 309
vehicle-related accidents, xi, 305
vehicle-to-infrastructure, xi, 3, 305
vehicle-to-vehicle, ix, xi, 222, 277, 305
vehicle-to-vehicle communication, ix, 222, 277
veteran drivers, xi, 285

W

weather, xi, 30, 135, 166, 188, 233, 264, 302, 305, 306
windshield wipers, ix, 259, 261, 262
wireless devices, xii, 306
workplace costs, viii, 210